Pakistan – The Political Economy of Growth, Stagnation and the State, 1951–2009

This book provides a comprehensive reassessment of the development of the economy of Pakistan since independence to the present. It employs a rigorous statistical methodology, which has applicability to other developing economies, to define and measure episodes of growth and stagnation, and to examine how the state has contributed to each. Contesting the orthodox view that liberalisation has been an important driver of growth in Pakistan, the book places the state at the centre of economic development, rather than the market. It examines the state in relation to its economic roles in mobilising resources and promoting a productive allocation of those resources, and its political roles in managing the conflict inherent in economic development. The big conclusions for economic growth in Pakistan are that liberalisation, the market and the external world economy in fact have less influence than that of the state and conflict. Overall, the book offers analyses of the different successive approaches to promoting economic growth and development in Pakistan, relates these to medium-term economic outcomes – periods of growth and stagnation – and thereby explains the mechanisms by which the state can better promote growth and development.

Matthew McCartney is Lecturer in the Economics of South Asia, School of Oriental and African Studies, University of London, UK. His previous publications with Routledge include *India – The Political Economy of Growth, Stagnation and the State, 1951–2007* and *Political Economy, Growth and Liberalisation in India, 1991–2008*.

Routledge Studies in the Growth Economies of Asia

1 The Changing Capital Markets of East Asia
Edited by Ky Cao

2 Financial Reform in China
Edited by On Kit Tam

3 Women and Industrialization in Asia
Edited by Susan Horton

4 Japan's Trade Policy
Action or reaction?
Yumiko Mikanagi

5 The Japanese Election System
Three analytical perspectives
Junichiro Wada

6 The Economics of the Latecomers
Catching-up, technology transfer and institutions in Germany, Japan and South Korea
Jang-Sup Shin

7 Industrialization in Malaysia
Import substitution and infant industry performance
Rokiah Alavi

8 Economic Development in Twentieth Century East Asia
The international context
Edited by Aiko Ikeo

9 The Politics of Economic Development in Indonesia
Contending perspectives
Edited by Ian Chalmers and Vedi R. Hadiz

10 Studies in the Economic History of the Pacific Rim
Edited by Sally M. Miller, A.J.H. Latham and Dennis O. Flynn

11 Workers and the State in New Order Indonesia
Vedi R. Hadiz

12 The Japanese Foreign Exchange Market
Beate Reszat

13 Exchange Rate Policies in Emerging Asian Countries
Edited by Stefan Collignon, Jean Pisani-Ferry and Yung Chul Park

14 Chinese Firms and Technology in the Reform Era
Yizheng Shi

15 Japanese Views on Economic Development
Diverse paths to the market
Kenichi Ohno and Izumi Ohno

16 Technological Capabilities and Export Success in Asia
Edited by Dieter Ernst, Tom Ganiatsos and Lynn Mytelka

17 Trade and Investment in China
The European experience
Edited by Roger Strange, Jim Slater and Limin Wang

18 **Technology and Innovation in Japan**
Policy and management for the 21st century
Edited by Martin Hemmert and Christian Oberländer

19 **Trade Policy Issues in Asian Development**
Prema-chandra Athukorala

20 **Economic Integration in the Asia Pacific Region**
Ippei Yamazawa

21 **Japan's War Economy**
Edited by Erich Pauer

22 **Industrial Technology Development in Malaysia**
Industry and firm studies
Edited by Jomo K.S., Greg Felker and Rajah Rasiah

23 **Technology, Competitiveness and the State**
Malaysia's industrial technology policies
Edited by Jomo K.S. and Greg Felker

24 **Corporatism and Korean Capitalism**
Edited by Dennis L. McNamara

25 **Japanese Science**
Samuel Coleman

26 **Capital and Labour in Japan**
The functions of two factor markets
Toshiaki Tachibanaki and Atsuhiro Taki

27 **Asia Pacific Dynamism 1550–2000**
Edited by A.J.H. Latham and Heita Kawakatsu

28 **The Political Economy of Development and Environment in Korea**
Jae-Yong Chung and Richard J Kirkby

29 **Japanese Economics and Economists since 1945**
Edited by Aiko Ikeo

30 **China's Entry into the World Trade Organisation**
Edited by Peter Drysdale and Ligang Song

31 **Hong Kong as an International Financial Centre**
Emergence and Development 1945–65
Catherine R. Schenk

32 **Impediments to Trade in Services: Measurement and Policy Implication**
Edited by Christoper Findlay and Tony Warren

33 **The Japanese Industrial Economy**
Late development and cultural causation
Ian Inkster

34 **China and the Long March to Global Trade**
The accession of China to the World Trade Organization
Edited by Alan S. Alexandroff, Sylvia Ostry and Rafael Gomez

35 **Capitalist Development and Economism in East Asia**
The rise of Hong Kong, Singapore, Taiwan, and South Korea
Kui-Wai Li

36 **Women and Work in Globalizing Asia**
Edited by Dong-Sook S. Gills and Nicola Piper

37 **Financial Markets and Policies in East Asia**
Gordon de Brouwer

38 **Developmentalism and Dependency in Southeast Asia**
The case of the automotive industry
Jason P. Abbott

39 **Law and Labour Market Regulation in East Asia**
Edited by Sean Cooney, Tim Lindsey, Richard Mitchell and Ying Zhu

40 **The Economy of the Philippines**
Elites, inequalities and economic restructuring
Peter Krinks

41 **China's Third Economic Transformation**
The rise of the private economy
Edited by Ross Garnaut and Ligang Song

42 **The Vietnamese Economy**
Awakening the dormant dragon
Edited by Binh Tran-Nam and Chi Do Pham

43 **Restructuring Korea Inc.**
Jang-Sup Shin and Ha-Joon Chang

44 **Development and Structural Change in the Asia-Pacific**
Globalising miracles or end of a model?
Edited by Martin Andersson and Christer Gunnarsson

45 **State Collaboration and Development Strategies in China**
The case of the China–Singapore Suzhou Industrial Park (1992–2002)
Alexius Pereira

46 **Capital and Knowledge in Asia**
Changing power relations
Edited by Heidi Dahles and Otto van den Muijzenberg

47 **Southeast Asian Paper Tigers?**
From miracle to debacle and beyond
Edited by Jomo K.S.

48 **Manufacturing Competitiveness in Asia**
How internationally competitive national firms and industries developed in East Asia
Edited by Jomo K.S.

49 **The Korean Economy at the Crossroads**
Edited by MoonJoong Tcha and Chung-Sok Suh

50 **Ethnic Business**
Chinese capitalism in Southeast Asia
Edited by Jomo K.S. and Brian C. Folk

51 **Exchange Rate Regimes in East Asia**
Edited by Gordon de Brouwer and Masahiro Kawai

52 **Financial Governance in East Asia**
Policy dialogue, surveillance and cooperation
Edited by Gordon de Brouwer and Yunjong Wang

53 **Designing Financial Systems in East Asia and Japan**
Edited by Joseph P.H. Fan, Masaharu Hanazaki and Juro Teranishi

54 **State Competence and Economic Growth in Japan**
Yoshiro Miwa

55 **Understanding Japanese Saving**
Does population aging matter?
Robert Dekle

56 **The Rise and Fall of the East Asian Growth System, 1951–2000**
International competitiveness and rapid economic growth
Xiaoming Huang

57 **Service Industries and Asia-Pacific Cities**
New development trajectories
Edited by P.W. Daniels, K.C. Ho and T.A. Hutton

58 **Unemployment in Asia**
Edited by John Benson and Ying Zhu

59 **Risk Management and Innovation in Japan, Britain and the USA**
Edited by Ruth Taplin

60 **Japan's Development Aid to China**
The long-running foreign policy of engagement
Tsukasa Takamine

61 **Chinese Capitalism and the Modernist Vision**
Satyananda J. Gabriel

62 **Japanese Telecommunications**
Edited by Ruth Taplin and Masako Wakui

63 **East Asia, Globalization and the New Economy**
F. Gerard Adams

64 **China as a World Factory**
Edited by Kevin Honglin Zhang

65 **China's State Owned Enterprise Reforms**
An industrial and CEO approach
Juan Antonio Fernandez and Leila Fernandez-Stembridge

66 **China and India**
A tale of two economies
Dilip K. Das

67 **Innovation and Business Partnering in Japan, Europe and the United States**
Edited by Ruth Taplin

68 **Asian Informal Workers**
Global risks local protection
Santosh Mehrotra and Mario Biggeri

69 **The Rise of the Corporate Economy in Southeast Asia**
Rajeswary Ampalavanar Brown

70 **The Singapore Economy**
An econometric perspective
Tilak Abeyshinge and Keen Meng Choy

71 **A Basket Currency for Asia**
Edited by Takatoshi Ito

72 **Private Enterprises and China's Economic Development**
Edited by Shuanglin Lin and Xiaodong Zhu

73 **The Korean Developmental State**
From dirigisme to neo-liberalism
Iain Pirie

74 **Accelerating Japan's Economic Growth**
Resolving Japan's growth controversy
Edited by F. Gerard Adams, Lawrence R. Klein, Yuzo Kumasaka and Akihiko Shinozaki

75 **China's Emergent Political Economy**
Capitalism in the dragon's lair
Edited by Christopher A. McNally

76 **The Political Economy of the SARS Epidemic**
The impact on human resources in East Asia
Grace O.M. Lee and Malcolm Warner

77 **India's Emerging Financial Market**
A flow of funds model
Tomoe Moore

78 **Outsourcing and Human Resource Management**
An international survey
Edited by Ruth Taplin

79 **Globalization, Labor Markets and Inequality in India**
Dipak Mazumdar and Sandip Sarkar

80 **Globalization and the Indian Economy**
Roadmap to a convertible rupee
Satyendra S. Nayak

81 **Economic Cooperation between Singapore and India**
An alliance in the making
Faizal Yahya

82 **The United States and the Malaysian Economy**
Shakila Yacob

83 **Banking Reform in Southeast Asia**
The region's decisive decade
Malcolm Cook

84 **Trade Unions in Asia**
An economic and sociological analysis
Edited by John Benson and Ying Zhu

85 **Trade Liberalisation and Regional Disparity in Pakistan**
Muhammad Shoaib Butt and Jayatilleke S. Bandara

86 **Financial Development and Economic Growth in Malaysia**
James Ang

87 **Intellectual Property and the New Japanese Global Economy**
Ruth Taplin

88 **Laggards and Leaders in Labour Market Reform**
Comparing Japan and Australia
Edited by Jenny Corbett, Anne Daly, Hisakazu Matsushige and Dehne Taylor

89 **Institutions for Economic Reform in Asia**
Edited by Philippa Dee

90 **Southeast Asia's Credit Revolution**
From moneylenders to microfinance
Aditya Goenka and David Henley

91 **Economic Reform and Employment Relations in Vietnam**
Ngan Thuy Collins

92 **The Future of Asian Trade and Growth**
Economic development with the emergence of China
Linda Yueh

93 **Business Practices in Southeast Asia**
An interdisciplinary analysis of Theravada Buddhist countries
Scott A. Hipsher

94 **Responsible Development**
Vulnerable democracies, hunger and inequality
Omar Noman

95 **The Everyday Impact of Economic Reform in China**
Management change, enterprise performance and daily life
Ying Zhu, Michael Webber and John Benson

96 **The Rise of Asia**
Trade and investment in global perspective
Prema-chandra Athukorala

97 **Intellectual Property, Innovation and Management in Emerging Economies**
Edited by Ruth Taplin and Alojzy Z. Nowak

98 **Special Economic Zones in Asian Market Economies**
Edited by Connie Carter and Andrew Harding

99 **The Migration of Indian Human Capital**
The ebb and flow of Indian professionals in Southeast Asia
Faizal bin Yahya and Arunajeet Kaur

100 **Economic Development and Inequality in China**
The case of Guangdong
Hong Yu

101 **The Japanese Pharmaceutical Industry**
Its evolution and current challenges
Maki Umemura

102 **The Dynamics of Asian Labour Markets**
Balancing control and flexibility
Edited by John Benson and Ying Zhu

103 **Pakistan – The Political Economy of Growth, Stagnation and the State, 1951–2009**
Matthew McCartney

104 **Korean Women Managers and Corporate Culture**
Challenging tradition, choosing empowerment, creating change
Jean R. Renshaw

Pakistan – The Political Economy of Growth, Stagnation and the State, 1951–2009

Matthew McCartney

LONDON AND NEW YORK

This first edition published 2011
by Routledge
2 Park Square, Milton Park, Abingdon, Oxon, OX14 4RN

Simultaneously published in the USA and Canada
by Routledge
711 Third Avenue, New York, NY 10017

Routledge is an imprint of the Taylor & Francis Group, an informa business

First issued in paperback 2013

© 2011 Matthew McCartney
The right of the Author to be identified as author of this work has been asserted by him/her in accordance with sections 77 and 78 of the Copyright, Designs and Patents Act 1988.

All rights reserved. No part of this book may be reprinted or reproduced or utilised in any form or by any electronic, mechanical, or other means, now known or hereafter invented, including photocopying and recording, or in any information storage or retrieval system, without permission in writing from the publishers.

British Library Cataloguing in Publication Data
A catalogue record for this book is available from the British Library

Library of Congress Cataloging in Publication Data
McCartney, Matthew, 1974-
　Pakistan: the political economy of growth, stagnation and the state, 1951–2009/
　Matthew McCartney.
　　p. cm. – (Routledge studies in the growth economies of Asia; 103)
　Includes bibliographical references and index.
　1. Pakistan – Economic policy. 2. Pakistan – Economic conditions. I. Title.
　HC440.5.M38 2011
　330.95491'05 – dc22　　　2010049349

ISBN13: 978-0-415-57747-2 (hbk)
ISBN13: 978-0-415-72824-9 (pbk)
ISBN13: 978-0-203-81476-5 (ebk)

Typeset in Perpetua by Taylor & Francis Books

For Ranjana, the book was 5% inspiration, 5% perspiration and the rest was fuelled by your chai, thank you.

Contents

List of illustrations	xv
Acknowledgements	xvii
Preface	xviii
Abbreviations	xx

1 Introduction   1
 Key theoretical and empirical ideas in this book   1
 Structure of the book   6

2 A methodological critique and framework   11
 Introduction   11
 Episodes of growth and stagnation in developing countries   11
 Public policy, endogenous growth models and empirical problems   14
 And theoretical problems ...   21
 The proposed methodology: case studies of growth   25
 The proposed model   28

3 Episodes of growth and stagnation in Pakistan, 1951–2008   33
 Introduction   33
 Methods of measuring episodes of growth and stagnation   33
 Episodes of growth and stagnation in Pakistan   36
 An episode of growth, 1951/52 to 1958/59   41
 An episode of growth, 1960/61 to 1969/70   43
 An episode of stagnation, 1970/71 to 1991/92   45
 An episode of stagnation, 1992/93 to 2002/03   47
 An episode of growth, 2003/04 to 2008/09   47

4 Theoretical framework   49
 Introduction   49
 The economic and political schools of the developmental state   49
 An integration of the economic and political schools   53
 The (economic) role of the state: finance   56
 The (economic) role of the state: production   65
 The (political) role of the state: institutions   67

xiv Contents

5 An episode of growth, 1951/52–1958/59 77
   Summary of chapter findings 77
   Recap from Chapter 3 78
   Limitations of alternative explanations 78
   The (economic) role of the state, 1951/52 to 1958/59: finance 79
   The (economic) role of the state, 1951/52 to 1958/59: production 88
   The (political) role of the state, 1951/52 to 1958/59: institutions 92

6 An episode of growth, 1960/61–1969/70 100
   Summary of chapter findings 100
   Recap from Chapter 3 101
   Limitations of alternative explanations 101
   The (economic) role of the state, 1960/61 to 1969/70: finance 103
   The (economic) role of the state, 1960/61 to 1969/70: production 115
   The (political) role of the state, 1960/61 to 1969/70: institutions 126

7 An episode of stagnation, 1970/71–1991/92 136
   Summary of chapter findings 136
   Recap from Chapter 3 137
   Limitations of alternative explanations 137
   The (economic) role of the state, 1970/71 to 1991/92: finance 139
   The (economic) role of the state, 1970/71 to 1991/92: production 154
   The (political) role of the state, 1970/71 to 1991/92: institutions 162

8 An episode of stagnation, 1992/93–2002/03 173
   Summary of chapter findings 173
   Recap from Chapter 3 173
   Limitations of alternative explanations 174
   The (economic) role of the state, 1992/93 to 2002/03: finance 175
   The (economic) role of the state, 1992/93 to 2002/03: production 183
   The (political) role of the state, 1992/93 to 2002/03: institutions 187

9 An episode of growth, 2003/04–2008/09 192
   Summary of chapter findings 192
   Recap from Chapter 3 192
   Limitations of alternative explanations 193
   The (economic) role of the state, 2003/04 to 2008/09: finance 193
   The (economic) role of the state, 2003/04 to 2008/09: production 199
   Institutions to manage conflict 203

10 Conclusion 207
   Implications for economic principles and policy 207

   Notes 212
   Bibliography 217
   Index 237

Illustrations

Figures

3.1	Raw and trend real GDP growth for Pakistan 1951–52 to 2008–9	37
3.2	Comparison of mean GDP growth in different subsets	38

Tables

3.1	Significance of controls for the Quandt-Andrews test equation for GDP	39
3.2	Quandt-Andrews test for real GDP growth	40
3.3	Average growth rates in the periods between breakpoints	40
5.1	The terms of trade for agriculture, three-year moving average: 1951–54 to 1958–61	86
5.2	Comparative cost ratios	90
5.3	Output of yarn per cotton spindle	91
6.1	Effective exchange rates of imports and exports	102
6.2	Selected indicators for evaluating the performance of state-owned electric power industry in Pakistan, 1961–71	124
6.3	Growth rate of total factor productivity, 1960–70	125
6.4	Yield per hectare performance for main crops in main producing countries, 1961–65	125
7.1	Tax to GDP ratio overall and for individual taxes of the central government	140
7.2	Indicators of financial deepening	144
7.3	External debt indicators	147
7.4	Workers' remittances, 1970/71–1979/80	148
7.5	Components of balance of payments, 1980–2002	148
7.6	Various concepts of net profit margin on sale of state-owned electric power industry in Pakistan, 1960–95	151
7.7	Impact of trade reform on effective protection and profitability, 1988–93	152

7.8 Yield level of major crops and imports inputs, 1977–1995   160
7.9 Selected indicators for evaluating the performance of state-owned electric power industry in Pakistan, 1972–1995   161
9.1 Composition of GDP growth (point contribution)   200
9.2 Sectoral contribution to GDP growth   201

Acknowledgements

I would like to thank first of all Professor Aditya Mukherjee at the Jawaharlal Institute of Advanced Studies in Delhi, whose generous hospitality and wonderful facilities provided the space to undertake much of the reading and research for this book during the first six months of 2009. Mr Jain the administrative officer with friendly efficiency ensured all those little disruptions disappeared quickly.

For their hospitality and warm welcome at a later stage, when reading had turned to writing, I would like first to thank Professor Naved Hamed and Professor Shahid Amjad Chaudhry at the Lahore School of Economics (LSE). The LSE gave me the chance to test a few ideas on unsuspecting students. At the LSE, Azam and Theresa Chaudhry added a dash of humour, Anum Bukhari an excellent meal and Zenab Haseen found missing taxi drivers at all hours. At the Pakistan Institute of Development Economics (PIDE) in Islamabad, I would like to thank in particular Professor Rashid Amjad for his welcome and pleasures in reminiscing about balmy undergraduate days by the Cam. Many thanks to Grace Kite for the econometric work in Chapter 3.

There are also the usual suspects to thank. Marko, Ashwin and Daryl contributed nothing directly again but revived spirits after long days of writing with refreshing glasses of lemonade. And of course Professor Barbara Harriss-White, ever an inspiration, mentor and dear friend.

Preface

This book begins with a critique of orthodox regression-based investigations of economic growth in developing countries. There are severe empirical and theoretical problems with using cross-country growth regressions to identify the important link between economic policy and growth. This book develops an empirical framework based on this critique of orthodox methodology and uses the case study of Pakistan since independence. Using a rigorous statistical measure of an episode of growth or stagnation this book finds five episodes in Pakistan since independence. These are three episodes of growth, 1951/52 to 1958/59, 1960/61 to 1969/70 and 2003/04 to 2008/09, and two episodes of stagnation, 1970/71 to 1991/92 and 1992/93 to 2002/03.

From the statistical the book then turns to the theoretical and develops a model to explain and evaluate the role of the state in economic development. The financial role of the state is in allocating the economic surplus to those able to invest productively. The production role of the state is to ensure financial resources so allocated are used productively, to either raise productivity in an existing market niche (learning) or upgrade to a higher technology market niche. The final crucial role is how the state can utilise institutions to mediate the relationship between conflict and economic growth.

The key empirical chapters of the book (5-9) each examine one of the episodes of growth or stagnation, they are divided into three parts, with each focusing on one particular role that the state has in promoting economic growth (finance, production and institutions). The final chapter concludes by drawing out some big themes from the book. This book shows that the other policies of the Washington Consensus and later Good Governance agenda are not of first-order importance in Pakistan in determining patterns of growth and stagnation over the medium-term. Episodes of growth between 1951/52 and 1958/59 (Chapter 5), between 1960/61 to 1969/70 (Chapter 6) and 2003/04 to 2008/09 (Chapter 9) were not associated with liberalisation. Liberalising efforts under President Zia (especially after 1983) were more half-hearted than many realise and were not associated with any increase in economic growth (Chapter 7). The very substantial liberalisation efforts at the end of the 1980s and early 1990s were associated with an episode of stagnation between 1992/93 and 2002/03 (Chapter 8). Instead this book finds that state-business relations, especially those moments when the state was able to act developmentally were of prime important in explaining episodes of growth and stagnation in Pakistan since independence. A very common unifying hypothesis to explain Pakistan's growth and development since independence has been its dependence on foreign aid inflows. This book finds that not only is there no good evidence to link episodes of growth with favourable and episodes of stagnation with unfavourable circumstances emanating from the world economy, the entire hypothesis of 'dependent Pakistan' is simply not supported by the evidence.

Abbreviations

ABL	Allied Bank Limited
ADCs	Agricultural Development Corporations
ADB	Asian Development Bank
ANP	Awami National Party
APCOL	All Pakistan Confederation of Labour
AWT	Army Welfare Trust
BJP	Bharatiya Janata Party
CCI&E	Chief Controller of Imports and Exports
CENTO	Central Treaty Organisation
CGE	Computable General Equilibrium
C.i.f.	Cost, insurance and freight
CIRC	Corporate and Industrial Restructuring Corporation
CML	Council Muslim League
COAS	Chief of Army Staff
CPP	Communist Party of Pakistan
CRR	Cash Reserve Ratio
CSP	Civil Service of Pakistan
DFI	Development Finance Institutions
DHA	Defence Housing Authority
EBS	Export Bonus System
EPZ	Export Processing Zone
ERP	Effective Rate of Protection
FAO	Food and Agricultural Organization of the United Nations
FCA	Foreign Currency Account
FDI	Foreign Direct Investment
FF	Fauji Foundation
F.o.b.	Free on board
FSF	Federal Security Force
G-8	Group of Eight Governments
GDP	Gross Domestic Product
GNP	Gross National Product
HBL	Habib Bank Limited
HP	Hodrick-Prescott

HYVs	High-Yield Varieties
ICS	Indian Civil Service
IDA	International Development Agency
IDBP	Industrial Development Bank of Pakistan
IEPR	Implicit Effective Protection Rate
IJI	Islami Jamhoori Ittihad
IMF	International Monetary Fund
INTUC	All-India Trade Union Congress
ISI	Inter-Services Intelligence
JI	Jamaat-i-Islami
JCSC	Joint Chiefs of Staff Committee
JUI	Jamait-Ulema-e-Islami
JUP	Jamiat Ulema-e-Pakistan
KESC	Karachi Electricity Supply Company
KSE	Karachi Stock Exchange
LDC	Less Developed Country
M2	Broad Measure of Money Supply
MAF	Million Acre Feet
MCB	Muslim Commercial Bank
MMA	Muttahida Majlis-e-Amal
MQM	Muttahida Quami Movement
MNC	Multinational Company
MRD	Movement for the Restoration of Democracy
MW	Mega Watt
NAP	National Awami Party (in NWFP).
NASSCOM	The National Association of Software and Services Companies
NBFI	Non-Bank Financial Institution
NBP	National Bank of Pakistan
NDFC	National Development Finance Corporation
NIC	Newly Industrialising Country
NPL	Non-Performing Loan
NSS	National Saving Scheme
NWFP	North-West Frontier Province
OGL	Open General Licence
PC	Planning Commission
PFC	Provincial Finance Commission
PIA	Pakistan International Airlines
PICIC	Pakistan Industrial Credit and Investment Corporation
PIDC	Pakistan Industrial Development Corporation
PIDE	Pakistan Institute of Development Economists
PIFCO	Pakistan Industrial Finance Corporation
PML	Pakistan Muslim League
POL	Pakistan Oilfields Limited
PPP	Pakistan People's Party
PRI	National Revolutionary Party

PTUF	Pakistan Trade Union Federation
Q-A	Quandt-Andrews
QMP	Qayyum Muslim League
R	Rupees
R&D	Research and Development
RCA	Revealed Comparative Advantage
SBP	State Bank of Pakistan
SDP	State Domestic Product
SEATO	Southeast Asia Treaty Organization
SECP	Security and Exchange Commission of Pakistan
SLR	Statutory Liquidity Ratio
TFP	Total Factor Productivity
TVE	Township and Village Enterprise
UBL	United Bank Limited
UF	United Front
UN	United Nations
UNIDO	United Nations Industrial Development Organization
US(A)	United States (of America)
WAPDA	Water and Power Development Authority
WTO	World Trade Organization

1 Introduction

The introduction first reviews some of the key theoretical and empirical ideas in this book, and then outlines the structure of the book.

Key theoretical and empirical ideas in this book

This section briefly reviews some of the key theoretical and empirical ideas in this book. These are the role of the state, political economy, development and conflict, and the book's focus on the medium term and methodological problems with cross-country growth regressions.

The role of the state

As I write this Introduction, the Republican Party has re-taken control of the House of Representatives in the USA.[1] The result, argued many Republican candidates and voters, was driven by a desire to reclaim America from an intrusive and debt-laden government, its reach having been destructively extended during two years of Obama as President. This book argues instead that government has a crucial role in promoting economic development, particularly in the world's poorest countries. Pakistan has had a lot of government since 1947. If in many cases, to paraphrase Ronald Reagan, government in Pakistan has clearly been one of Pakistan's many problems, it has at other times and in other ways been instrumental in solving the profound problems of development. And if not entirely fulfilling the most optimistic aspirations at independence, it has proved those idealists who strove to create Pakistan not irredeemably impractical and misguided.

Chapter 4 provides a coherent statist political economy framework that is used as the basis of the empirical chapters, 5–9. The schools elucidating the capability of the state (the political school) and what the state could do to promote growth and development (the economic school) are too often considered separately. This book is part of a recent and welcome trend that attempts to unify the political and economic roles of the state. The state has two economic roles, to mobilise and allocate an economic surplus to those able and willing to utilise it productively, and a political role to build and maintain institutions to manage the conflicts associated with growth and development. First, the state, argues chapter 4, has a crucial role in mobilising and allocating an economic surplus. Neo-classical economics conjures up a world of developing countries beginning the transition to modern economic growth, where savers miraculously appear bearing their deposits to a pristine banking system. Profit-maximising firms compete for the privilege to acquire those deposits by scouring the economy for an optimal portfolio of investment projects. The tribe of savers and investors emerges as an act of creation much as a 'Big Bang'. In reality, the state will play a crucial role in mobilising an economic surplus and transferring it to those willing and able to utilise it to promote economic growth. Much of the economic surplus in a developing country will be in existence, but squandered by luxuriating landlords, recycled in repressive relations of rural money-lending or finding its way overseas, as the profits perhaps of plantations are returned to shareholders in developed countries. The allocation of a surplus is a profoundly political question in a developing country. Those who can use it productively will accumulate and become the large-scale capitalists of the future. Those who hold political power at the outset of growth may be traditional landlords, with neither the capacity nor vision to utilise the economic surplus beyond dominating local politics. A strong developmental state may be required to enforce the re-allocation of property rights, and more generally the surplus from the latter to the former.

There is no sense in trying to measure the relative merits of big government versus small government. Government intervention is all but impossible to measure. Cross-country growth regressions have often used crude proxy measures for government intervention with predictably poor results. To mobilise an economic surplus, the state could utilise subsidies (which indicate an enlarged fiscal role for the state), tax incentives (which imply a reduced fiscal role for the state) and/or policies such as labour repression that raise the profitability of private sector firms (which implies no fiscal role for the state). Such policies are complementary ways of achieving the same fiscal outcome, and hence there is no reason to assume why, for example, the 'share of government expenditure in GDP' should have any particular sign or significance in a cross-country growth regression.

Even once those willing and able to utilise the economic surplus for productive investment have hold of that surplus, they will be faced by severe market failures in learning. Neo-classical economics assumes that innovation takes place in advanced countries and that learning in LDCs is no more difficult than selecting the most appropriate among innovations. Neo-classical analysis of technology transfer assumes that all firms operate with full knowledge of all possible technologies, to which they have equal access through imports based on a known market price. There are assumed to be no tacit elements in the transfer, no learning costs or need to make adaptations. This book assumes that much technology is tacit and, to effectively master it, extensive experience in using it is necessary. The process of learning to reach the efficiency frontier is slow, risky, and costly. Learning by doing may imply a lengthy and unpredictable period of losses, as firms learn and adapt technology to make it more appropriate to developing country conditions. In theory, private capital markets could fund firms through the period of learning. In practice uncertainty, risk and illiquidity mean that private capital will be reluctant. This is especially relevant when economies are industrialising and undergoing profound structural changes, where past history is a poor guide to the future. The state has a vital role in both inducing and facilitating learning by the private sector. Without such state prompting, firms in developing countries may simply compete on the basis of sweated, unskilled labour, and producing simple products more cheaply. Such a low road of development may be an ideal path for a single firm, but there are likely to be collective and dynamic benefits from following a high road of competition based on learning and upgrading.

Chapter 4 provides a theoretical critique of the orthodox analysis of the role of institutions in economic development. This book takes as a starting point that economic growth is a process naturally laden with conflict, involving unprecedented changes in the pattern of property rights and income distribution. Although there is a good deal of existing literature looking at the relation between institutions (often property rights) and economic growth, this book looks at a related but as yet less-researched issue. How can institutions overcome the (negative) relationship between conflict and economic growth? This book argues that there are three generic types of institution that serve this role and enhance the autonomy of the state to pursue growth and development. The first are 'repressive institutions', to exclude and/or crush groups that oppose growth and industrialisation. The second are 'integrating institutions'. An important means of securing legitimacy for a given (re-)allocation of rights may be in compensating the (potential) losers, rather than repressing them. Identifying those requiring compensation, minimising the transaction costs associated with such transfers, and minimising rent-seeking by other entities requires a state that is more 'embedded' than 'autonomous'. A dominant political party may provide just such an inclusive and embedded institution. A third institution to overcome the conflict associated with economic development is ideology. Even groups excluded from development or suffering from rising levels of inequality may acquiesce in their own exclusion for ideological reasons or a belief in the development project being pursued. The empirical chapters (5–9) flesh out this theoretical perspective with the practice in Pakistan since independence.

One may reasonably wonder how the theoretical foundations of a book concerned with the role of the state have fared during the convulsions affecting the world economy and discipline of economics over the last few years. That the state should have an important role in regulating or otherwise influencing the financial sector is a key theme of this book. A successful financial system, as assessed here, is not one that maximises profits, but one that is able to direct the economic surplus to investors able and willing to invest it productively. The banking system is different: it requires deposit insurance from the state and in return needs some element of push to divert its resources to productive investment, rather than potentially more lucrative speculation and gambling. This book, though, takes a much broader perspective and argues that the state can also utilise its own budget (taxes and subsidies), influence the profitability of the private sector (labour repression), or manage inflows of foreign capital as other means to mobilise and allocate the economic surplus. To this end, the current concern with just the financial sector is too narrow.

Political economy

The phrase 'political economy' shares with 'the state' a prominent place in the title of this book for good reason. An 'efficient' allocation of the economic surplus by the state is unlikely once we consider political economy factors. The state may tax individuals and use the money to subsidise emerging capitalists, but there can be no credible contracts or enforceable commitments on which the state will then be able to raise tax from those capitalists to the benefit of the original taxpayers. Whether the state can overcome this time-inconsistency problem will ultimately be a question of political economy. Existing powerful interest groups may block the introduction of 'efficient' transfers because it may simultaneously affect the distribution of political power. The prospect of the state being able to tax a newly created capitalist class may even be reduced once that class has accumulated and gained added political leverage over the state and other classes in society. Efforts to overcome the market failures associated with learning may generate a need for intervention in both factor and product markets. In factor markets, deliberate government efforts to direct resources to particular activities create rents that may both induce and facilitate learning by private actors. There is no guarantee that such rents will promote learning. Rents must be allocated in a contingent manner, and be withdrawn from those firms failing to learn, or perhaps more objectively to export or reduce costs. The bureaucracy must be competent enough to allocate rents ex-ante to potentially dynamic capitalists or, ex-post, strong enough to withdraw them from failing capitalists. The relation of the state to various classes is important: in the case of capitalists to enforce discipline, and ensure that rents are contingent on desired performance. The relation of the state to other, non-capitalist classes must be such that they do not mobilise and dissipate efficient rents towards non-productive areas.

Development and conflict

The analysis of conflict is extremely limited in orthodox economics. Economists have tried to quantify the economic impact of 'armed conflict'. More generally, orthodox economics sees conflict as a consequence of state intervention. State intervention, it is argued, creates rents, and agents then engage in often-destructive rent-seeking activities to gain access to those rents. Liberalisation, according to this view, will remove politics from the economy and replace extra-economic conflict over resources with the impersonal competition of the market. The contrast is the atomistic capitalism of neo-classical economics, where labour and firms are small relative to aggregate supply and demand and act independently in response to changing market signals. This book takes as a basic assumption that economic development is a conflictual process. Economic development is concerned with shifting resources from low- to high-productivity areas. The mobility of some assets will be limited; owners will then face problems of obsolescence and unemployment. Those having sunk investments into physical capital, skills, contractual relationships, and political patronage are likely to resist change (Chang 1999). There may also be a natural political tendency to conflict in developing countries. The social and economic change associated with economic growth, such as urbanisation, increased literacy, industrialisation, and expansion of the mass media will extend political consciousness and political participation. The new elite of civil servants and teachers employed by the central government can fragment and challenge traditional sources of political authority, the secular and religious leaders of the villages, and traditional social networks based around family, class and caste. Economic development also creates newly wealthy groups that are not assimilated into the existing social order. There is no guarantee that political institutions will emerge to ensure political stability. Economic development and political stability are two independent and possibly contradictory goals.

The ability of the state to manage conflict is crucial in allowing the state to allocate rents to their most productive uses, rather than expending them in the form of political transfers to try and buy political stability. Institutions to control conflict studied in this book are ideological, repressive or inclusive. There is a general possibility that pursuing a policy of liberalisation and rolling back the state will weaken those institutions that control conflict. Reductions in subsidies, for instance, may violate a social contract that had previously kept a lid on conflict. A smaller state may be less able to support inclusive or repressive institutions. There should be no surprise, for example, that measures of corruption did not decline in India following liberalisation in the 1990s (Harriss-White and White 1996). There are other dramatic and relevant examples. In the early-1990s Russia and other transition countries were encouraged to break up their communist parties and move rapidly towards democracy in the belief that this would permit a faster pace of liberalisation (Nolan 1995). Such reforms did lead to rapid reform, but not to rapid economic growth. Subsequent scholarship focused on the perceived neglect to create in parallel those institutions argued to be necessary for the successful functioning of a market economy. The institutions included in this debate were primarily property rights and a stable, enforceable legal framework. The dramatic disintegration of those political institutions (Communist Parties) that had previously managed conflict and allocated rents according to clear and (for insiders) transparent rules has been neglected as a causal variable in the economic failure of the transition economies. The problem in Russia was not so much an increase in corruption, as the collapse of the Communist Party and the resulting fragmentation of the organisational structure of rent-seeking and subsequent rise of destructive roving 'mafia-type' bandits (Shleifer and Vishny 1996; Olson 2000). An even more recent example was the rapid break-up of the Baathist party's military and security apparatus of the Iraqi state following the 2003 invasion. Iraq has mobilised massive quantities of resources via the USA, and had democratic elections. Unsurprisingly, there has been a massive increase in conflict and a complete failure to allocate those resources productively.

Focus on the medium-term and methodological problems with cross-country growth regressions

This book focuses on growth over the medium term, something neglected by much economic analysis of growth. The medium term is a longer period than either Keynesian models of stabilisation or Solow growth models imply and a shorter period than embraced, for example, by current work on the fundamental sources of economic growth over the very long term – colonialism, institutions, integration and geography. Chapter 2 makes a critique of orthodox investigations of economic growth in developing countries. First, it shows that the use of averages hides an important empirical reality of the growth process. These are the structural breaks and periods of expansion and stagnation that actually characterise growth, particularly in developing countries. The chapter notes that policy provides the most straightforward explanation for episodes of growth and stagnation and, were this true, we would expect to see that changes in growth were causally correlated with changes in policy. In practice, there are severe empirical and theoretical problems with uncovering any link from policy to growth through cross-country regressions. These include complementarity among policy variables, the relation between different theories of growth, the question of growth itself as an endogenous process, hysteresis effects, growth regressions and dynamics, and the assumption of universalism. The final section outlines an alternative model, using the case study approach to explain episodes of growth and stagnation, emphasising the role of the state, and relating it to these theoretical and empirical problems. Chapter 3 introduces the case of Pakistan since independence as the case study of economic growth for this book. The chapter uses a rigorous statistical measure of an episode of growth (or stagnation) that will be used in the rest of the book. This chapter finds that there are three episodes of growth, 1951/52 to 1958/59, 1960/61 to 1969/70 and 2003/04 to 2008/09, and two episodes of stagnation, 1970/71 to 1991/92 and 1992/93 to 2002/03.

Structure of the book

Chapter 2: A methodological critique and framework

This chapter makes a critique of orthodox investigations of economic growth in developing countries. First, it shows that the use of averages hides an important empirical reality of the growth process. These are the structural breaks and periods of expansion and stagnation that actually characterise growth. The second section notes that policy provides the most straightforward explanation for episodes of growth and stagnation and, were this true, we would expect to see that these episodes were causally correlated with changes in policy. In practice, there are severe empirical and theoretical problems with uncovering any link from policy to growth through cross-country regressions. These include complementarity among policy variables, the relation between different theories of growth, the question of growth itself as an endogenous process, hysteresis effects, growth regressions and dynamics, and the assumption of universalism. The final section outlines an alternative model, using the case study approach to explain episodes of growth and stagnation, emphasising the role of the state, and relating it to these theoretical and empirical problems.

Chapter 3: Episodes of growth and stagnation in Pakistan, 1951–2008

This chapter develops an empirical framework based on the methodological critique in Chapter 2. We use the case study of Pakistan since independence. This chapter begins by outlining the definition and rigorous statistical measure of an episode of growth or stagnation as will be used in this book. The book focuses on the very aggregate level of growth, GDP. Future work will extend this perspective to consider episodes of growth and stagnation by sector, agriculture, industry and type of service. This chapter finds there are three episodes of growth, 1951/52 to 1958/59, 1960/61 to 1969/70 and 2003/04 to 2008/09, and two episodes of stagnation, 1970/71 to 1991/92 and 1992/93 to 2002/03.

Chapter 4: Theoretical framework

This chapter critically reviews the literature on the role of the state in economic development. This falls into two schools, the economic and political. The limitations of the economic school include the limited scope of analysis, the lack of a political economy, and the importance of complementarity. Weaknesses of the political school include the limited analysis of the state's role, the relation between different theories, and lack of dynamics. A number of efforts have emerged to integrate these two schools, which are reviewed here. The following theoretical section attempts an integration that is relevant for the empirical context outlined in Chapter 3, focusing specifically on the role of the state. The financial role of the state is in allocating the economic surplus to those able to invest productively. The production role of the state is to ensure that financial resources so allocated are used productively, either to raise productivity in an existing market niche (learning) or to upgrade to a higher-technology market niche. The final section looks at how institutions can mediate the relationship between conflict and economic growth. The existing literature looking at this relationship is very limited. In this book, a broader institutional perspective is considered. A repressive state, an inclusive state or an ideological state can help reduce the negative implications of conflict on development. Chapter 4 here draws heavily on Chapter 4 in McCartney (2009a), which looked at the role of the state and the political economy of India since independence. The chapter in this book has been revised, in particular with insights from the work of Samuel Huntingdon and Mancur Olson, and utilises statistical results from the case of Pakistan (rather than India) since independence.

Chapters 5–9 are each divided into three parts, with each focusing on one particular role that the state has in promoting economic growth. These relate to finance, production and institutions. The underlying hypothesis here is that the state needs to be successful in all three to initiate and sustain an episode of growth.

Chapter 5: An episode of growth, 1951/52–1958/59

The first section shows that the surplus mobilised by the state between 1950/51 and 1958/59 was small. Slow growth of savings and tax revenue forced a reliance on capital inflows from abroad. The principal means to finance investment was via the very high rates of profit earned by private industry. Profits were mainly explained by the economic dislocations of Partition in 1947, though these were complemented by government trade and exchange rate policy. The state made some limited direct contribution to investment.

The second section examines the role of the state in achieving a productive use of the surplus in both the public and private sectors. The principal source of growth over this period was import substitution. There were signs of inefficiency in production, but also of declining costs and rising productivity in industry and, to a lesser extent, agriculture.

The third section focuses on institutions that may or may not allow the state to overcome the inherent conflicts associated with economic growth. The institutions of autonomy and repression (the civil service and the military) were reconstructed quickly after independence. There is no consistent evidence that this relative autonomy allowed the government to implement policies over the 1950s in general and systematic accordance with long-term goals. The state failed in its efforts to promote inclusionary institutions. There was no successful attempt to project any unifying ideology. The episode of growth was not sustainable. The exhaustion of opportunities for import substitution was limiting further growth solely to expansion of (slow-growing) domestic demand. Without sufficient autonomy or the development of inclusive institutions to absorb groups, it was unlikely that the state would have been able to sustain growth through either an aggressive export-orientated strategy, or through deepening the pattern of import substitution to more capital-intensive and technologically demanding segments of industry, or by pushing the growth of agriculture.

Chapter 6: An episode of growth, 1960/61–1969/70

The first section shows that the government of Pakistan aimed to mobilise an increased surplus, but that such aims met with limited success, as savings and tax revenue increased from low to not-quite-so-low levels. As in the 1950s, the bulk of the increase in the surplus came from foreign capital inflows. The state proved well able to sustain high profit rates in the private sector, complementing traditional trade and exchange rate policies with reforms to corporate taxation and anti-union policies.

The second section examines the role of the state in achieving a productive use of the surplus in both the public and private sectors. The principal sources of growth were domestic demand and a green revolution in agriculture, while export growth also contributed. There is evidence of high levels of inefficiency and low productivity in both industry and agriculture at the outset of this period. Production was very capital-intensive and there were few signs of labour-intensive growth. There were indications of learning during the 1960s; relative costs of production were declining, while labour, capital and overall (TFP) productivity increased.

The third section focuses on institutions that may or may not allow the state to overcome the inherent conflicts associated with economic growth. In the early years the autonomy of state policy making was enhanced by a more repressive stance with regard to groups such as newspapers, students and unions. The 1962 Constitution also strengthened the power of the central Presidency. This autonomy was reflected in more-coherent planning and agricultural policy making. The episode of growth had its successes. A more autonomous state was able to intensify the more *ad hoc* process of import substitution of the 1950s through policies that sustained profitability in the private sector. The state was also able to push industry both into upgrading the structure of production through high levels of investment and successful learning and into high-value-added niches in world export markets. The episode of growth was ultimately sustainable. By the late 1960s this autonomy gradually declined, and policy became increasingly determined by political criteria. The state failed in its efforts to promote inclusionary institutions. Social change unleashed by the green revolution, urbanisation and industrialisation was not accommodated by President Ayub's system of 'Basic Democrats' or, later, the return to party-based politics. The attempt to project a modernist ideology had no substantial effect.

Chapter 7: An episode of stagnation, 1970/71–1991/92

The first section shows that the domestic surplus mobilised by the state after 1970/71 was stagnant, but compensated for by international capital inflows. Total savings stagnated; this was true for both public and private sector savings, the former being linked to stagnant tax revenues and the latter to a slowdown in the growth of the domestic financial sector. Savings remained below the level of investment; the gap was filled by international capital inflows. A poor record of corporate profitability was not explained by the relative growth of the state. There was substantial expansion in public investment under Prime Minister Z.A. Bhutto, which supported growth throughout this period.

The second section examines the role of the state in achieving a productive use of the surplus in both the public and private sectors. This section shows that Pakistan did not follow a growth pattern based on its (labour-intensive) comparative advantage. There are indications of dynamic learning/upgrading: both capital and labour productivity improved significantly, and the capital-intensive path of growth in agriculture alleviated some key constraints in the sector and supported rapid growth. The performance of state-owned enterprises contributed to productivity growth. Broader measures of productivity, TFP, showed improvement, particularly in the 1980s.

The third section focuses on institutions that may or may not allow the state to overcome the inherent conflicts associated with economic growth. The elections of 1970 and rise of the PPP gave Pakistan a chance to re-assert the supremacy of the democratic (integrative) over the repressive (autonomous) institutions of the state. Early efforts to reduce the role of the military and civil service were short lived, and Bhutto came to depend on both; the coup of 1977 was a continuation of such trends. The PPP failed in its possible role as an inclusionary institution – it was gradually taken over by more conservative groups and failed to incorporate the groups emerging in a changing society. The 1973 constitution, despite its federal and formal decentralised structure, was undermined by the centralising and anti-democratic instincts of Bhutto. The rule of President Zia further strengthened the power of the central political leadership. The emergence of a two-party democratic system in the 1990s failed to promote institutionalisation of social groups and exacerbated conflict. Zia tried to implement a more ideological approach (Islamisation) to the management of Pakistan, but succeeded only in worsening conflict. After a hiatus in the early 1970s the repressive institutions of the state re-emerged under Bhutto and were formally re-established in power with the military coup of 1977. By domestic criteria, this episode of stagnation (though quite successful when judged in terms of average growth rates) probably was sustainable. The government lacked the developmental autonomy or inclusionary institutions or ideology to promote a real development drive. The government in the 1980s was secure enough in power to rule, and able to mobilise sufficient resources and utilise them productively enough, to keep GDP at a reasonable rate. The end of the episode we can trace to exogenous factors, the death of Zia in that ever-mysterious plane crash, the rise of neo-liberalisation, and the worldwide democratic upsurge that gave Pakistan no option other than to return to competitive party politics and adopt a neo-liberal programme of reforms. This combination pushed Pakistan into a further episode of stagnation, as we will see in Chapter 7.

Chapter 8: An episode of stagnation, 1992/93–2002/03

The first section shows that the state found it increasingly hard to mobilise a domestic surplus after 1992/93. Total savings were stagnant, and the state failed to increase its own contribution. Foreign capital inflows increased, but at high cost. The stock market played no role in mobilising savings, there is little evidence to suggest any increase in corporate profitability, FDI remained very low, and public investment showed signs of becoming less productive over this period. The second section examines the role of the state in achieving a productive use of the surplus in both the public and private sectors. There are indications that the episode of stagnation is linked to deflationary macro-economic policy after the late 1980s. There is mixed evidence from indicators of efficiency in Pakistan, in industry, banking, and public investment. Exports remained stuck at the low end of the market; there were few indications of learning or upgrading. Broader measures of productivity (TFP) declined in the 1990s relative to the 1980s. The third section focuses on institutions that may or may not allow the state to overcome the inherent conflicts associated with economic growth. The relative autonomy of the state declined drastically over the 1990s, and party politics led to an upsurge in uncontrolled and chaotic factionalism that undermined the clarity and coherence of policy making. The main political parties frequently turned to the military to find allies in politics; this undermined the institutionalisation of democracy. Inclusionary or ideological institutions to manage conflict were non-existent. Pakistan over the 1990s was locked into a destructive episode of stagnation with no internal means to exit.

Chapter 9: An episode of growth, 2003/04–2008/09

The first section shows that the state was relatively successful in mobilising a surplus after 2003/04. The government was successful in raising savings, reducing current expenditure and imports, managing domestic and external debt, raising public and private corporate profitability, and boosting public investment. These efforts faded noticeably as this period wore on. The second section examines the role of the state in achieving a productive use of the surplus in both the public and private sectors. There were signs of efficiency and productivity improving from the very low levels achieved in the 1990s, but this improvement at most represented a better performance in the low-value-added end of traditional export markets, rather than upgrading to higher-value-added niches. The third section focuses on institutions that may or may not allow the state to overcome the inherent conflicts associated with economic growth. After 1999 the government passed power to a team of technocrats with the capacity and commitment to implement reforms. The best evidence of the new-found autonomy of policy makers was that for the first time in its history Pakistan was able to complete the 2000 standby arrangement with the IMF without delays or interruptions. This section shows that the military coup temporarily strengthened institutions of autonomy and repression, but that this effect declined over time and there was no corresponding creation of inclusive institutions. Hence, the episode of growth was ultimately unsustainable and would likely have faded even without the global financial crisis of 2008–10.

2 A methodological critique and framework

Introduction

This chapter makes a critique of orthodox investigations of economic growth in developing countries. First, it shows that the use of averages hides an important empirical reality of the growth process: the structural breaks and periods of expansion and stagnation that actually characterise growth. The second section notes that policy provides the most straightforward explanation for episodes of growth and stagnation and, were this true, we would expect to see that these episodes were causally correlated with changes in policy. In practice, there are severe empirical and theoretical problems with uncovering any link from policy to growth through cross-country regressions. These include complementarity among policy variables, the relation between different theories of growth, the question of growth itself as an endogenous process, hysteresis effects, growth regressions and dynamics, and the assumption of universalism. The final section outlines an alternative model, using the case study approach to explain episodes of growth and stagnation, emphasising the role of the state, and relating it to these theoretical and empirical problems.

Episodes of growth and stagnation in developing countries

The analysis of growth in developing countries suffers from a theoretical and empirical problem. Theoretical perspectives on growth tend to look either at the long or the short term. Long-term growth frameworks include (among many) the nature of the colonial state (Acemoglu *et al.* 2001), factor endowments (Sokoloff and Engerman 2000), malaria (Gallup and Sachs 2000), geography (Gallup and Sachs 1999), the organisation of distributional coalitions (Olson 1982), and ethnic divisions (Easterly and Levine 1997). Short-term frameworks include (among many) volatility in the terms of trade (Lutz 1994), international capital flows (Wade 1998) and fiscal policy (Easterly and Rebelo 1993). This section shows that, using the averages typical of cross-country growth regressions since Barro (1991), hides an important empirical reality of the growth process in contemporary developing countries. Growth averages over 25–30 years conceal the structural breaks, and episodes of growth and stagnation, that actually characterise growth experiences in developing countries.

The historical (long-run) experience of developed countries

Long-run averages of growth are a reasonable approximation of historical patterns of growth in the now developed countries. The steady state assumptions of Solow (1957), for example, are a good guide to the historical experience of the USA. The USA experienced steady growth (the Great Depression aside) after 1870, despite large shifts in policy (Kenny and Williams 2001). A simple linear trend to the natural log of per capita US GDP between 1880 and 1929 gives a forecast for 1987 that is off by only 5%. Output is captured well by a growth process with a constant mean (Jones 1995a). The idea of convergence to steady state growth also makes sense when looking at the small set of now developed countries whose historical growth performance showed strong (club) convergence (Maddison 2001). Despite large differences in policy within the OECD between 1870 and 1989, two-thirds of the present high-income countries had GDP growth rates within 0.2% of that of the USA.

The 'take-off' into modern economic growth: an insufficient theoretical concession

Within traditional theorising about growth in developing countries, the only concession to the universal applicability of growth theory has been ideas such as the 'Big Push' or 'take-off' into self-sustained modern growth. A relevant example is the heterodox versus orthodox debate over how the Korean government launched its economic miracle in the early-1960s.[1] There has been a great deal of research on the political, economic and social conditions of what generated the economic take-off, but very little on what then sustained growth. One strand of the debate revolves around why the Korean state became developmental in the early-1960s, and the literature assumes that this same state was able to launch later initiatives such as the Heavy and Chemical Industrialisation programme that sustained growth in the 1980s. Another strand of the debate argues that the Korean state made a decisive shift towards outward-orientation in the early-1960s and that this then sustained subsequent growth. The implicit assumption in this literature is that growth is something that has to be started and then is automatically sustainable. In practice, growth must also be sustained (potentially a different question) and can come to a grinding halt.

The historical experience of developing countries

Since Barro (1991), theoretical and empirical research on growth has focused on averages over 25–30 years. A decade of 10% growth followed by another of 0% drops into Barro-type regressions with the same average as two decades of 5% growth. Such averages conceal the periods of stagnation, growth spurts, structural breaks, volatility and instability[2] that actually characterise growth experiences in developing countries. Pritchett (2000) finds that GDP growth is not well characterised by a single exponential trend. For 40% of LDCs the R^2 on such a trend is less than 0.5, suggesting that shifts and fluctuations are the dominant feature of the evolution of per capita GDP. Pritchett (2000) finds six distinct patterns of growth, before and after statistically chosen structural breaks, which he calls steep hills, hills, plateaus, mountains, plains and accelerations. The correlation of per capita growth between 1977 and 1992 with that for 1960 to 1976 across 135 countries is only 0.08 (Easterly and Levine 2001: 195). A regression of growth between 1975 and 1989 against growth between 1960 and 1975 produces an R^2 of only 0.12 (Easterly et al. 1993). Temple (1999: 116) finds a similar pattern for developing countries between 1960 and 1975 and in 1975 to 1990.

Rodrik (1999a) finds that some LDCs were hardly affected by the volatility of the world economy in the second half of the 1970s and others suffered negative impacts out of all proportion to the direct economic consequences of those shocks. Between 1960 and 1973 the growth performance in Latin America and the Middle East was equal to and superior in some respects to that in East Asia. Latin America, for example, surpassed East Asia in terms of Total Factor Productivity (TFP) growth. The East Asian miracle therefore rests on the collapse in productivity and output growth in the Middle East and Latin America after 1973, while growth in East Asia was sustained.

There are very striking instances of growth accelerations and growth collapses among developing countries. Rodrik (2003b) finds 64 cases of growth accelerations since the 1950s. These he defines as an increase in per capita growth of 2.5% relative to the previous five years, sustained over at least ten years. Such accelerations include well-known cases – Taiwan 1961, South Korea 1962, Botswana 1966, Brazil 1966, Singapore 1968, Mauritius 1969, China 1978, and Chile 1985 – and also less well-known cases, such as Egypt 1976. Berthelemy and Soderling (2001) find 14 examples of episodes of growth in Africa between 1960 and 1996, defined as a period of more than ten years in which the five-year moving average of annual GDP growth exceeds 3.5%. Examples include South Africa between 1960 and 1974 (5.1%), Cote D'Ivoire 1960 to 1978 (9.5%), Gabon 1965 to 1976 (13.1%), and Namibia 1961 to 1979 (6.4%). Mkandawire (2001) finds that between 1967 and 1980 ten countries in Africa experienced average growth of more than 6% p.a. These included Gabon, Botswana, Congo, and Nigeria, and those without mineral resources such as Kenya and Cote D'Ivoire. These fast growers were outperforming both Malaysia and Indonesia.

Hausmann et al. (2004) conducted a very broad empirical test to locate episodes of growth. They located an episode of growth by finding the year that maximises the F-statistic of a spline regression with a break at the relevant year. For countries with a number of consecutive years for which these criteria of growth are met, they chose the best fit for a single starting date. Countries can have more than one instance of growth acceleration as long as the dates are more than five years apart. This filter yielded 83 growth accelerations. They found that this method captured the most well known episodes,[3] such as China 1978, Argentina 1990, Mauritius 1971, Korea 1962, Indonesia 1967, Brazil 1967, Chile 1986, and Uganda 1989. They found the magnitude of accelerations to be striking. Their definition was conditional on a growth acceleration of at least 2% p.a.; the average acceleration though was 4.7% p.a. There were many episodes with growth of 7% or more, such as Ghana 1965 (8.4%), Pakistan 1962 (7.1%), and Argentina 1990 (9.2%). The occurrence of an episode was quite common; of 110 countries in their sample between 1957 and 1992, 54.5% had at least one episode of growth and 20.9% two. The occurrence was also common across space: 21

14 *Methodological critique and framework*

episodes occurred in Asia, 18 in Africa, 17 in Latin America, 12 in Europe and 10 in the Middle East and North Africa.

Public policy, endogenous growth models and empirical problems

This section shows that theory offers strong reasons to expect a clear link between policy change and episodes of growth and stagnation. The empirical evidence for the link is, however, very weak. This holds in a general sense and also for four specific examples: fiscal policy and the role of the state, investment, education, and R&D. If the policy-growth hypothesis were true, we would expect to see first, that episodes of growth and stagnation should be strongly correlated with changes in policy and second, that the result should be causal. A typical example is from the World Bank (1994), which purports to show that 'strong adjusters' (policy) in sub-Saharan Africa during the 1980s were followed by increased rates of economic growth (an episode of growth). Relevant empirical work from the case of Pakistan is reviewed where appropriate.

The supposed empirical link between policy and growth has been enhanced by theoretical developments, in particular endogenous growth models. The older vintage Solow growth model predicted that policy (investment) would impact on the level of, but not the long-run rate of, growth, so would have at most only a transitional effect.[4] Endogenous growth models, by contrast, were motivated by the lack of convergence to steady state among developing countries and the inability of traditional models to account for differences in income and growth rates across countries (Romer 1986: 1008–13; Pritchett 1997). 'A theory of economic development needs mechanics that are consistent with sustained growth and with sustained diversity in income levels' (Lucas 1988: 41).

Arrow (1962) modelled the productivity of a given firm as an increasing function of cumulative output in the industry. Romer developed an equilibrium model of technological change, in which optimising agents drove long-run growth through the accumulation of knowledge. In his model the creation of knowledge by one firm has a positive external effect on the production possibilities of other firms (1986: 1003). Adding to capital and labour a third input[5] generates externalities, allows constant returns to scale at the level of the individual firm, and rewards factors with their marginal productivity (i.e. preserves the competitive solution). Due to the externality these models yield a sub-optimal equilibrium/market solution. This in turn generates a potential role for the state. Policy has been shown to affect growth through its impact on the incentives to accumulate capital and knowledge and so generate technological change.

General statistical work lends little support to the policy-growth hypothesis. Growth rates in developing countries are highly volatile, whereas many of the causal factors (policies and institutional factors) change only slowly. The correlation across 1960 to 1976 and 1977 to 1992 for investment is 0.85, for primary enrolment 0.82, and for secondary enrolment 0.91. The variance of per capita GDP growth within country is 0.73, and only 0.22 for investment rates, 0.07 for level of education and 0.02 for population size (Easterly and Levine 2001). Other growth determinants, such as measures of democracy and civil liberties (Barro 1999: 166; Przworski et al. 2000) and inequality (Deininger and Squire 1996), have strong persistence.

The robustness of empirical results

While the link between episodes of growth and stagnation and changes in policy seems intuitively reasonable and is supported by recent economic theorising, there is very little empirical evidence for this proposition. Levine and Renelt (1992) took a number of variables commonly used in econometric growth analyses and ran them in thousands of regressions with different conditioning sets of other variables – judging them robust if they remained significantly related to growth. Their tests excluded variables that are only correlated with another factor that has a causal relationship with growth, i.e. those factors with an indirect impact on growth. They found only investment was robustly related to economic growth. This analysis is perhaps unnecessarily pessimistic. There will be a natural tendency for the sign of a coefficient to not be robust across a set of regressions representing different combinations of other variables if the coefficient is collinear with variables suggested by other growth theories.[6] Allowing for this problem, Sala-i-Martin (1997) ran two million regressions and found 21 robust variables. Among variables surviving are region (Africa), primary goods orientation (including agriculture and mineral exporting), latitude (near equator), political and civil rights, the rule of law, war, revolutions and coups, investment, foreign exchange variables, country's degree of capitalism, and number of years the economy can be classified as open. There is limited relevance of this finding for the growth-policy hypothesis, as many of these variables can be considered structural rather than policy-related. This reduces the potential role of economic policy and implies that the growth process will be something of a random walk around a mean, with the mean set by those structural factors.[7]

Even those factors that many would accept as self-evidently related to economic growth, fiscal policy and the role of the state, investment, education and R&D have an ambiguous empirical relation to economic growth within cross-country regression analysis. The relevant theory and empirical results concerning these four policy variables are analysed in turn.

Fiscal policy and the role of the state

Theory linking fiscal policy to economic growth is very clear. King and Rebelo (1990) developed a model where modest variations in tax rates are associated with large variations in long-run growth rates, with both stagnation and growth miracles. Barro (1990) extended a simple production function to include productive government expenditure. Production here involves decreasing returns to private inputs if complementary government inputs (such as enforcement of property rights) do not expand in a parallel manner. There is an optimal level of government expenditure that maximises the growth rate. Rebelo (1991) developed a model where an increase in the tax rate lowers the return to private investment and hence permanently lowers the rate of investment and economic growth.

Barro (1991) measured government intervention as the ratio of real government consumption, less spending on education and defence, to real GDP. He found a significant negative association between this variable averaged between 1970 and 1985 and real growth between 1960 and 1985. Using standard Barro-type regressions for Pakistan, Tahir (1995) found government defence expenditure had a positive relation with GDP growth, Iqbal and Zahid (1998) found the government budget deficit had a negative relation, and Ghani and ud Din (2006) found government consumption had a positive relation. Kazmi (1993) found a negative relationship between defence spending and national savings rates. Malik *et al.* (2006) use various measures to gauge at what level of government public expenditures occur in Pakistan and find a mixed relation between fiscal decentralisation and economic growth. More generally, as estimated by Levine and Renelt (1992), there is no robust relation between growth and the ratio of total government expenditure to GDP, government consumption expenditure, capital formation, or educational expenditure. The coefficient in the Barro (1991) measure becomes insignificant when Levine and Renelt (1992: 951) include the ratio of exports to GDP in the conditioning set.[8] There is good theoretical reason for the relation between government expenditure and growth to become more complex once trade openness is considered. Openness may increase the cost of government intervention by promoting the overseas migration of taxed factors (Slemrod 1995: 405). Rodrik (1998) finds a positive correlation between a country's exposure to international trade and the size of its government. A possible explanation, he suggests, is that the government plays a risk-reducing role in economies exposed to increased external risk.

There are severe empirical problems with any attempt to quantify the role of the state. Cross-country growth regressions typically regress the rate of economic growth on the level of government expenditure. Any government using Keynesian-style demand management policies will likely be raising government spending when GDP growth slows. This will generate a spurious negative relation between the 'size' of government and economic growth. Tax exemptions and fiscal transfers may have similar policy effects, but have opposite implications for the measured size of government. Knowles and Garces-Ozanne (2003) examine these concerns and indeed find that measures of government spending are a very poor statistical proxy for the actual influence of the government on the economy. Finally, the demand elasticity for government services is typically greater than one (Wagner's Law); the level of government expenditure would then be determined endogenously by GDP growth (Slemrod 1995).

Investment and economic growth

Investment was the one factor that Levine and Renelt (1992) found robustly related to economic growth. The average investment rate is frequently used as an independent variable in growth regressions, though there remain severe empirical problems in identifying causality.

De Long and Summers (1991, 1992, 1993) and Jones (1994) found a positive correlation between investment, specifically in machinery and equipment, and productivity. They argue that studies using aggregate measures of investment (including structures) underestimate the contribution of investment to growth. They argue that the result is causal, robust, strong and statistically significant. While transport investment reflects differences in need caused by urbanisation, geography and population density, the equipment aggregate (comprising electrical and non-electrical machinery), they argue, is more directly correlated with the manufacturing sector. Lee (1995) finds a positive and significant relation between the ratios of imported to domestically produced capital goods for a large cross-country regression between 1960 and 1985.

Evidence for Pakistan based on simple regression analysis supports this general finding, though there is not yet any work looking specifically at equipment investment. Khan et al. (2005) find a positive relation between investment and growth in Pakistan between 1971 and 2004, and Khan (2005) finds a positive relation between investment and GDP growth between 1980 and 2002. Iqbal and Zahid (1998) find a positive relation between investment and growth between 1959/60 and 1996/97. Evidence more generally fails to support these findings. Between 1950 and 1988 the composition of investment in the OECD shifted sharply. The increase in the share of investment in producer durables is especially marked, from 3% or 4% to more than 7% of GDP in France, Germany, the USA and the UK, and in Japan from 3.5% to 9%. Growth in OECD countries, however, shows no equivalent upward trend over this period. Blomstrom et al. (1996) find an inverse causal relation between growth and investment that is robust to the inclusion of other determinants of growth. Growth, they find, induces subsequent capital formation for a sample of 101 countries between 1965 and 1985. There are severe empirical problems with using instruments to test the issue of causality between investment and growth. 'In general there is a shortage of good instruments. So many variables could be used to explain growth that it is difficult to find variables that are not only highly correlated with the endogenous variable but can also be plausibly excluded from the regression' (Temple 1999: 128).

A particular theoretical development relevant for empirical studies of the investment-growth relation is that of 'credibility'. Rodrik (1989) argues that it is not policy changes, so much as 'credible' policy changes, that will be likely to promote growth in the private sector. Credibility, though, is a very difficult concept to test using cross-country regression techniques. Disaggregated components of what influences credibility, particularly uncertainty, have received more attention. Uncertainty has been widely theorised as having an influence on the growth rate through its effect on investment (Rodrik 1991; Dixit and Pindyck 1994). Measuring uncertainty remains a problem; various proxies have been used by scholars, all of which remain unsatisfactory: coups and revolution (Barro 1991); the standard deviation of inflation (Easterly and Rebelo 1993); the mean and variance of inflation and exchange rates (Ojo and Oshikoya 1995); the standard deviation of output and the rental cost of capital (Athukorala and Sen 2002); and measures of poor macroeconomic management (Bleaney 1996).

All these studies are testing proxies that are at best weakly correlated with uncertainty. There is no particular reason why, for example, exchange rate or interest rate instability should be associated with uncertainty if agents can hedge foreign currency dealings, insure themselves or pool risk. These measures may capture at most contemporaneous uncertainty, but uncertainty is more properly considered a forward-looking concept. Studies using proxies for the security of property rights or corruption focus on a very narrow aspect of uncertainty. Such proxies may reflect the more narrow concerns of (foreign) experts, but not give an overall indication of uncertainty relevant for (local) entrepreneurs. Unpredictable changes in laws may be irrelevant if such laws are not implemented. Discretionary and easily corrupt bureaucracies may reduce instability if they enable entrepreneurs to bribe their way around inconvenient changes in laws: to grease the wheels of the administration, (Leys 1965).

Empirical work for the case of Pakistan has paid passing reference to the issue of uncertainty and credibility, but has not engaged with any of the more fundamental concerns. In growth regressions, uncertainty has been measured using the standard deviation of the exchange rate over three years (Naqvi 2002), the lagged measure of the inflation rate (Nasir and Khalid 2004), and the standard deviation of the inflation rate (Ahmed and Qayyam 2007).

Education and economic growth

Intuitively, education has an evident link with economic growth; again, there is no clear empirical link. Pritchett finds a robust and *negative* correlation between higher school enrolment and educational attainment and TFP growth in developing countries. Between 1960 and 1985 educational capital grew faster in sub-Saharan Africa and South Asia than in East Asia, even though the latter region grew more rapidly (1999: 3). The failure of micro and macro evidence to show a positive return is, he argues, due to an institutional environment that ensured new skills were devoted to privately remunerative but socially wasteful activities (1999: 38), and to policies that retarded the demand for skilled labour (such as protectionism, which slowed down technological diffusion from abroad). Bils and Klenow (2000) find only a *weak* relation between initial schooling and subsequent economic growth, even allowing for the indirect effects of schooling in permitting greater technology absorption. They find that the relation is either largely spurious, in that the expected return and incentive to acquire education increases in an expanding economy when the skilled wage is growing rapidly, or reflects omitted variables related both to initial schooling rates and subsequent economic growth rates.

A particular problem for regression analysis is finding a satisfactory measurement of human capital (Mankiw *et al*. 1992: 418–19). A large part of investment in education takes the form of forgone earnings by students (which vary positively with the student's initial level of human capital). In addition, explicit spending on education takes place by the individual, family and state. Another problem is that not all expenditure on education is intended to generate productive human capital (for example, the teaching of philosophy versus literacy). The typical proxy used in many cross-country regression equations is the share of the working-age population in secondary school. This fails to measure the quality of education, and the learning-on-the-job that takes place in the workforce.[9] Education could be treated as being relevant to facilitate technological transfer and learning, which would suggest that the stock, rather than growth rate, of 'education' is the important variable driving economic growth.

Studies looking at the education-growth link are mixed for Pakistan. Khan (2005) finds positive and significant results linking literacy rates, average years of schooling, gross secondary school enrolment, life expectancy and GDP growth. Iqbal and Zahid

(1998) find various measures of education, including primary, secondary and high school enrolment, are either insignificantly or negatively related to GDP growth. Khan (2005) finds that education expenditures have no clear link with TFP growth. Easterly (2001b) finds that social measures including education have increased more slowly in Pakistan than in other LDCs with comparable growth rates. There is a growing cross-state regression literature looking at the growth of state-level GDP for the case of India; the results for education are empirically chaotic (Rao *et al.* 1999; Subrahmanyam 1999; Shand and Bhide 2000; Ahluwalia 2001).

R&D and economic growth

Theoretical work, such as Romer (1986), and intuition suggest that there is a clear link between R&D and economic growth. Again, this link has not been uncovered by orthodox empirical analysis. Between 1950 and 1988 the total number of scientists engaged in R&D in the USA increased from 200,000 to over 1,000,000. A similar pattern was evident in Germany, France and Japan. Measured by R&D expenditure, the results are similar (Jones 1995b: 13). Despite this extra R&D, there has been no permanent increase in growth. Between 1900 and 1987 US growth rates fluctuated around a constant mean for the entire period; in Japan growth fluctuated around a constant mean until post-1945, after which it jumped upwards, then slowly declined. In other OECD countries growth showed little or no persistent increase between 1950 and 1988; for some countries there was even a downward trend.

Strong policy conclusions despite poor results

Despite these poor empirical results, there are strong policy conclusions throughout this literature. These recommendations are typically implementing the neo-liberal and good governance agenda and exhortations to improve education and infrastructure. Studies do not address the issue that regression analysis at best reveals a causal statistical relationship, not the mechanism by which one variable 'causes' another. Iqbal and Zahid (1998) argue that primary education is 'an important pre-condition for promoting economic growth', and argue in favour of more investment, more openness and more domestic resource mobilisation. Khan (2005) goes to extremes in his precision, using his regression results to identify policy priorities and noting, for example, that increasing the investment rate by 5%–6% p.a. would increase GDP growth by 1%, or raising average years of schooling by 1.5–2 years would raise the permanent growth rate by 0.5% p.a. The IMF (2004: 16), using regression results for 1980–2002, argues that contributors to per capita real GDP growth of 2.2% were investment (2.5%), initial income (-8.6%), inflation (-0.02%), institutional quality (3.2%), average years of schooling (0.08%) and a residual (0.6%); hence, Pakistan should focus on improving its institutions.

Responses to the empirical problems

Researchers have generally acknowledged these empirical issues and have sought various remedies, but have remained within the confines of conventional regression analysis.

Such remedies have included attention to outliers, model uncertainty and measurement error (Temple 1999), robustness checks (Hall and Jones 1999; Acemoglu et al. 2001), least trimmed squares (Temple 1998), the system of generalised methods of moments (Hoeffler 2002), and panel data (Temple 1998: 131). This general approach has filtered through to the literature on Pakistan, and the statistical methodology in the growth literature has correspondingly gradually become more sophisticated: Naqvi (2002) uses vector autoregression to capture the forward-looking nature of investment spending; Din et al. (2003) use Granger causality to test the link between openness and growth; Khan et al. (2005) use an autoregressive distributed lag to test for unit roots in their study of finance and growth; Khan and Qayyum (2007) use an error-correction model to examine long-run relationships between GDP, liberalisation, financial development and the interest rate; and so on. Easterly (2001a) by contrast argues in favour of retreating from such complexity and emphasising simple correlations, chosen from the 'greatest hits' of the cross-country growth literature to restrict the range of possible causal statements. An example of the latter idea of simplicity in the Indian context is Ahluwalia (2001), who compiles a host of simple, single variable regressions to analyse state-level growth.

Some argue that empirical problems are due to a failure to separate the proximate (accumulation, technological change) from deeper causes (institutions, geography, integration) of growth (Rodrik et al. 2002). Typically, reduced form regressions are estimated in which all variables appear simultaneously on the right-hand side of the regression. This insight has inspired a new wave of general regression analysis, making explicit the distinction between proximate and deeper determinants of growth. The geography hypothesis, for example, argues that differences in economic performance reflect differences in transport costs, human health, agricultural productivity and proximity to natural resources (Gallup and Sachs 1999; Easterly and Levine 2003: 3). Others concur with the general thrust of focusing on the deeper determinants of growth, but differ in their emphasis and argue that institutions are the ultimate deep determinant of growth (Acemoglu 2003). There is an ongoing problem in finding reliable proxy measures for institutional quality (Hall and Jones 1999). The more general growth literature has used many measures, such as the enforceability of property rights, quality and independence of the judiciary, bureaucratic capacity, and political stability (Mauro 1995). There are a few indications that this literature is being absorbed by the India-related literature, in terms of measures such as geography (Kurian 2000; Sachs et al. 2002), or adding tenuous proxies for institutional quality (Kochhar et al. 2006; Baddeley et al. 2006). There are no indications that such discussion is influencing work on Pakistan.

A common effort in the wider cross-country growth literature has been to improve relevant proxy measures of theoretically important variables. In the wider literature, researchers have constructed indices of government intervention, rather than use crude measures of government spending (Hausman and Rodrik 2003b). Gallup and Sachs (1999: 31) have written extensively on the economic implications of geography and, to this end, advocate building data sets on, for example, the economic costs of malaria and its quantitative extent. Other researchers have sought improved and longer data sets, such as that on inequality (Deininger and Squire 1996). There is a debate about the appropriate measure of human capital (Mankiw *et al.* 1992: 418–19; Pio 1994). There are efforts in the Indian growth literature to experiment with different proxies, such as using life expectancy (Shand and Bhide 2000), or enrolment for 11–13-year-olds (Baddeley *et al.* 2006) as proxies for 'human capital'. The Pakistan literature lacks even these basic experiments. One gets the impression from the Pakistan literature that the choice of variables is purely passive, whatever is available will have to do. For both India and Pakistan, systematic empirical efforts to improve data in accordance with developments in theory, and in particular the distinction between proximate and deeper/fundamental determinants of growth, is almost entirely absent.

And theoretical problems …

Recent theorising on endogenous growth models is clear: there should be a strong link between policy and growth. This section shows that any empirical link between changes in policy and changes in growth rates will be intrinsically difficult to isolate using traditional cross-country regression analysis. There are severe theoretical problems. These include complementarity among policy variables, the relation between different theories of growth, the question of growth itself as an endogenous process, hysteresis effects, growth regressions and dynamics, and the assumption of universalism.

Complementarity among policies

There is very little empirical work on the relation between variables in the same regression. Cross-country regressions have become theoretical melting pots, containing level (e.g. infrastructure proxies) and growth (e.g. investment) indicators. The same regressions are crowded with both the deeper causes of economic growth (institutions and geography) and the proximate causes (accumulation and productivity), without any clear indicator of how the former affects growth through the latter. Policy variables typically enter the right-hand side of regressions separately, without diagnostic tests allowing for any but very limited interaction among them. Theory does, however, suggest that complementarity is important. For example, investment may be only causally related to growth in the presence of strong property rights, or reforms to growth, if considered credible or when correctly sequenced. There is some limited empirical support for the importance of complementarity between policies. Mosley (2000) finds little evidence of complementary effects on growth of inflation, openness and the government share, but when corrected for sequencing, the coefficient increases and becomes significant.[10] Such concerns motivated Easterly (2001a) to argue for a renewed emphasis on aid conditionality, dispensing aid only to those countries implementing a complementary and concurrent cluster of 'good policies'. Studies of state-level growth in India have coped with this problem in an *ad hoc* manner, splitting states into subgroup samples according to their reform orientation (Bajpai and Sachs 1999) or income level (Lall 1999; Kurian 2000) to look for changes in the strength and direction of causal relations. Occasionally *ad hoc* interaction effects between two variables have been included in regressions. Aghion *et al.* (2005) find that the removal of industrial licensing has a greater positive impact on SDP growth in states with pro-employer labour regulations. Purfield (2006) causes the initial income variable to interact with a post-1991 dummy to assess whether divergence/convergence has accelerated post-1991 (and finds that policy has a stronger relation with growth in the liberalised environment). There is no equivalent work for the Pakistan case.

It would in theory be feasible to add all possible interaction effects by adding multiplicative relations in a regression between all combinations of variables and adding a welter of dummy variables for all possible structural breaks and geographical regions. The resulting loss of degrees of freedom would then render the regression all but meaningless.

The relation between different theories of growth

There are numerous cross-country econometric studies finding some policy variable to be linked with economic growth. These variables include investment (positive), education (positive) and government consumption (negative) (Barro 1991), openness to international trade (Frankel and Romer 1999), fiscal policy (Easterly and Rebelo 1993), financial development (King and Levine 1993), macroeconomic policies (Fischer 1993), and human capital (Pio 1994). There is no consensus on which of these policy variables to include in cross-country regression analysis. Over 90 variables have been proposed as potential growth determinants (Brock and Durlauf 2001: 234).[11] Economic theory rarely generates a complete listing of variables to be held constant when trying to gauge the impact on the relation between the dependent and the independent variable.

Khan and Qayyum (2007) for example add an index of financial development, and Khan (2005) measures of human capital, to standard Barro-type regressions. There is no means to compare the merits of these two approaches, and the relationship between these and other theories remains confusing. A causal relation between two variables (e.g. finance and growth) does not imply the falsity of another (e.g. human capital and growth). Levine and Renelt find that 'statistical relationships between long-run average growth rates and almost every particular policy indicator considered by the profession are fragile: small alterations in the "other" explanatory variables overturn past results' (1992: 943).

Growth as an endogenous process

When policies are not random but are used systematically by governments to achieve certain ends, they can be described as being endogenous. Governments may intervene in response to market failures. Intervention may also be motivated by political economy arguments to favour certain social groups. In both these cases there is likely to be a negative relationship between the extent of government intervention and economic performance. The one would suggest a negative effect of government policy, the other a potentially optimal government policy response to market failure. Which is the most important driver cannot be observed by the econometrician; hence, the problem cannot be treated as one of omitted variables (adding new regressors), or parameter heterogeneity (addressed by splitting the sample). There is a common belief that growth regressions can help us restrict the range of possible causal statements that can be made, but this argument will be invalid in the case of policy endogeneity (Rodrik 2005). There are other endogenous determinants of government policy besides market failure. Earlier, this chapter discussed Keynesian economic policy and poor GDP growth outcomes. Alesina and Rodrik (1994) and Alesina *et al.* (1999) find government policy to be determined endogenously by levels of income inequality. Temple (1998) finds policy outcomes such as black market premium, schooling, financial depth and infrastructure proxies to be correlated with various measures of initial conditions: income inequality, social development and ethnic fragmentation. Easterly and Levine (1997) find that ethnic fragmentation explains poor policy choice.[12]

Growth and hysteresis effects

A growth-hysteresis effect occurs when a short-term shock leads to a long-term/permanent effect on growth. We should then see long-run impacts on growth from short-term shocks (Dixit, 1992: 122).

Growth rates in developing countries are highly volatile (Easterly *et al.* 1993) and more volatile than many of the supposed causal policy factors such as investment, education and population (Easterly and Levine 2001). There is evidence that short-term shocks could be responsible for such sharp changes in growth. Rodrik (1999) conducts an empirical study of growth instability in LDCs over the last few decades. Some countries, he finds, were hardly affected by volatility in their external environment during the second half of the 1970s (oil, other commodity prices, interest rates). Others suffered permanent losses to income out of all proportion to the direct economic consequences of those shocks. There is good reason to think hysteresis effects may be present in the Indian economy. There have been sharp and sustained shifts in growth rates at the state level in India (Dholakia 1994). The earlier section in this chapter showed that evidence linking changes in growth to changes in policy is weak. This pattern is echoed at the aggregate level in Pakistan. There were structural breaks in growth in 1951/52, 1960/61, 1970/71, 1992/93 and 2003/04. The implication of the hysteresis effect is that growth is not a linear process, and regression analysis will have trouble capturing this effect. Hysteresis effects show that variables have a large and robust effect on certain countries at certain times and are insignificant/negatively related at other times. Neat econometric models with fixed coefficients will, by definition, then be impossible to find.

Cross-country growth regressions and dynamics

Theories of cyclical and adjustment dynamics of output are not well developed within growth theories. Reliable data sets in Pakistan for many of the traditional growth determinants (inflation, government expenditure, tariffs, inequality, etc.) run for 25 years or more. Averages over this sample length are too short for history and too long to model macroeconomic policy changes and short-run dynamics. In cross-sectional regression analysis it is not clear whether variables affect long-term growth, the steady state, or both. Some growth effects are contemporaneous (macroeconomic and cyclical factors), some take several years (transitional dynamics due to changed investment incentives), and others even decades (incentives affecting the rate of technical change). Some right-hand-side variables may have output/growth effects at all three horizons – cyclical, transitional and steady state. There is no reason to assume that these are of the same magnitude or even the same sign (Temple 1999: 124). What little *ad hoc* empirical work for India that has been carried out finds regression parameters commonly to be unstable over time, and there is little effort ever to explain this. Rao *et al.* (1999), for example, find literacy has a negative and significant correlation with state-level growth over certain periods and no impact at others. Shand and Bhide (2000) find that railway infrastructure has a positive correlation with state-level growth in the 1980s and a negative correlation in the 1990s. There are no equivalent statistical efforts for the case of Pakistan. To make assertions about time varying relationships between growth determinants and outcomes requires theory to specify not only what these relationships are, but also how they shift over time.

Universalism in cross-country growth regressions

In order to run large cross-country regressions, researchers are making the assumption of universalism. Such analysis assumes that parameters describing growth are identical across countries – each individual country provides evidence that can be used to elucidate one underlying universal economic relation. An increase in openness, for example, is hypothesised to have the same effect on growth in all countries. There are a small number of exceptions. Islam (1995) and Gordon and Gupta (2004) allow the constant term to differ across countries (controls for fixed effects), using panel data. More commonly, an occasional dummy variable is added for regions and notable events such as the 1973 oil crisis or 1982 debt crisis. In practice there is evidence to suggest that the processes and components of growth do work differently over time and space.

Many studies account for Africa's slower growth as a function of different levels of explanatory variables (Easterly and Levine 1997; Sachs and Warner 1997; Bloom and Sachs 1998). They seek to explain growth as the result of a *common* growth process that begins from different *levels* of the same explanatory variables. However, significant regional dummies remain common in much of the empirical literature, particularly for sub-Saharan Africa. The usual assumption is that significant dummy variables are capturing the influence of missing variables, which must then be unearthed. This has led researchers to propose ever more variables in the hope that the dummy variable will be rendered insignificant and that growth in sub-Saharan Africa will finally be 'explained'. The alternative methodology is to drop the assumption that only the levels of explanatory variables are different and explore the idea that the growth process in sub-Saharan Africa works differently. There are a limited number of studies that suggest this latter idea may be true.

Block (2001) conducts a flexible analysis and allows for the slope coefficients to differ. Block finds that openness[13] in sub-Saharan Africa has a much stronger effect and fiscal policy a weaker effect on growth than his sample average. Block uses a further series of auxiliary regressions to test why Africa differs in the operation of its growth determinants. The determinants of institutional quality (ethnic divisions, education and raw material abundance) and population growth, he finds, operate differently in Africa.

Block concludes that homogenous adjustment policies are unlikely to work where the growth process is heterogeneous, when the mechanisms of growth differ in Africa from elsewhere. Brock and Durlauf find that 'the operation of ethnic heterogeneity on growth is different in Africa, not just the levels of ethnic heterogeneity. ... a comparison of the other regressor coefficients for Africa with those of the rest of the world makes clear the growth observations for African countries should not be treated as partially exchangeable with the growth rates of the rest of the world' (2001: 264). Asiedu (2002) finds that, for a given level of trade openness, infrastructure and return on capital, sub-Saharan Africa receives less FDI. Mosley (2000) finds that financial repression is a significant influence on growth in Asia, and inequality only has a negative impact on growth in regions other than sub-Saharan Africa.

Econometrics relies on the population from which data is drawn being homogenous. When the population is heterogeneous, additional cases are expensive, each extra element needs to be separately modelled and each modelling adjustment requires a separate assumption (Gerring 2007). Splitting country samples by region or income level to look for changes in the strength and direction of causal relations is ultimately at best only an *ad hoc* methodology. There are too many potential fixed effects to be easily dealt with. The broader implication of this discussion is that growth is not a universal process, cross-country growth regressions are an intrinsically poor mechanism to analyse growth, and each growth experience should be treated as potentially unique, i.e. as a case study.

The proposed methodology: case studies of growth

The analysis of economic growth is as Cramer (1998) argues, 'obsessed with an a-historical functionalism of connected variables'. Any empirical problems with cross-country regressions are met with predictable methodological responses – to improve proxy variables in regressions, add more explanatory variables, use more complex regression techniques, and look at longer data series. An earlier section in this chapter has argued that this approach is fundamentally flawed and the theoretical problems of cross-country/state growth regressions will not be addressed by empirical 'solutions'. This section presents a positive case for the greater use of case studies to solve some of these problems.[14]

Advantages of case studies in the study of economic growth

The use of case study research in economics has long been considered inferior to statistical methods. The proportion of published work in the social sciences using the case study approach declined sharply in the 1960s and 1970s (George and Bennett 2005: 4). Case studies were increasingly regarded as subjective, non-rigorous and non-replicable (Gerring 2007: 5–6). More recently, though, there has been a formalisation of the case study approach (George and Bennett 2005: 8). Numerous books and papers devoted to the methodology have started to appear (Sambanis 2003; Yin 2003; George and Bennett 2005; Gerring 2007).

Econometrics measures the magnitude of a causal effect – the expected effect on Y given a change in X – and provides details on the precision/uncertainty of that point estimate. Case studies focus on the causal mechanism and the reasons for correlations between X and Y. While econometrics typically focuses on linear causality, case studies can examine any form of causal process. Other more complex causal relations can be considered when using case studies, such as the convergence of several conditions, interacting causal variables, path dependency, complex interaction effects, qualitative variables, hysteresis effects, tipping points and feedback loops. While econometric analysis typically places a lot of emphasis on statistical robustness checks in regressions, there is only ever minimum attention paid to the mechanisms that link the variables being examined (Wacziarg 2002). The collection of growth case studies edited by Rodrik, for example, allowed a 'thick description' of interactions between geography, trade and institutions (Rodrik 2003b: 9).

Econometrics focuses on outcome, case studies on the process (Gerring 2007). The use of case studies to examine the causal mechanism is known as 'process tracing' (George and Bennett 2005: 205). In its simplest form it provides a detailed narrative specific to a given situation and without the use of theory that suggests possible causal/historical processes. Process tracing can go much further and become a theoretically orientated narrative. All intervening steps between cause and effect can be taken into account, and all such steps be preceded by a hypothesis (Gerring 2007: 181). A focus on the causal mechanism allows case studies to pay attention to the relation between different theories of growth, growth and policy as an endogenous process, hysteresis effects, and dynamics, all of which were identified as a particular problem for cross-country regressions in this chapter. Comparative case study analysis was useful, for example, in distinguishing the paradox between deep reform and stagnation in post-Soviet Russia and moderate/heterodox/gradual reform and rapid growth in post-Mao China (Nolan 1995). Case studies can produce theories on how different combinations of independent variables interact to influence the dependent variable. Case studies can focus on the mechanisms through which the independent variables influence the dependent variable and explore interaction effects among the independent variables to illuminate the logic of the argument, rather than just the statistical significance of coefficients. Such a method often throws up important contingent generalisations, which can often be the most useful kind of theoretical conclusions from case studies (George and Bennett 2005: 110). Rodrik highlighted a number of contingent hypotheses in his collection of case studies. It was argued, 'transitional institutions', such as dual-track pricing and Township and Village Enterprises (TVEs), succeeded in China because there was a high rate of economic benefit to cost and they improved incentives without large redistribution or the need for large-scale institutional change (2003b: 13).

Case studies can deal with endogeneity by establishing the sequence of events. A strength of comparative historical research (more than one case study) is its particular ability to deal with multiple causal paths leading to the same outcome and different results arising from the same factor/factor combination. This situation is known as 'equifinality' (George and Bennett 2005: 161). A classic example is that of Moore (1967), who in six case studies of long-term growth found three paths to political modernity. Large N cross-country growth regressions ignore the equifinality and settle for a probalistic finding regarding only one causal path at work (Gerring 2007).

Econometrics lacks any procedure to generate new hypotheses. Case studies can be used for theory testing and are also valuable in theory development (George and Bennett 2005: 209; Gerring 2007: 39). Sambanis (2003) extends a formal-theoretical model of conflict by drawing causal inferences from a set of comparative case studies to examine variables that might be significant determinants of conflict, but are omitted from the formal model.

A frequent problem with cross-country growth regressions is that many variables that theory argues to be important are very hard to quantify; common examples in the growth literature are 'democracy', 'trade liberalisation' and 'government intervention'. Case studies make it easier to gauge the extent to which empirical proxies from the cross-country model actually measure the theoretically significant variable. The analysis of historical sequences allows historians to 'bring to bear a much deeper conception of the social, political, institutional and technological sources of growth than theoretical and empirical economists are usually able to incorporate in formal models' (Temple 1999: 120).

There are two strands of existing work on economic growth in Pakistan. The first is a large and steadily growing growth literature based on Barro (1991), either using time series data for Pakistan or else running large cross-country regressions and focusing on the implications of the findings for Pakistan. As described earlier in this chapter, the usual suspects make their appearance as independent variables, initial income, education, investment, government spending, etc. This literature is gradually absorbing theoretical progress into its methodology and procedures, such as testing for stationarity and causation/endogeneity (Iqbal 1994; Iqbal and Zahid 1998; Din *et al.* 2003; Ahmad *et al.* 2003; Atique *et al.* 2004; Khan 2005; Ghani and ud Din 2006; Khan and Qayyum 2007, etc.). The second and perhaps most widely used methodology is to differentiate the period in Pakistan since independence into political regimes and to analyse patterns and averages of economic growth in each. Almost always these include, the period of chaotic democracy 1947–58, the military dictatorship of Ayub Khan 1958–68, the rise and fall of Bhutto 1971–77, the military dictatorship of Zia 1977–88, the return of democracy 1988–99, and the military dictatorship of Musharraf 1999–2008. Such works include numerous of *the* key cited references on the Pakistani economy (Ahmed and Amjad 1984; Noman 1988; Talbot 1998; Hasen 1998; Burki 1999; Ansari 1999; Husain 1999; Zaidi 2005; Ali 2008).[15] This chapter has offered a critique of the first methodology and in this section accepted the idea of the second methodology that growth can be usefully analysed with a case study approach. This book, though, offers a more rigorous method of selecting those case studies.

A common criticism of the case study methodology is that it has no formal method of case study selection (George and Bennett 2005). While some form of randomisation is possible in large-N studies, there is a frequent suspicion that the results of a case study analysis will be pre-determined by the choice of the case study. Recognising that growth and stagnation occur in distinct episodes, as discussed earlier in this chapter, is the key to solving this problem; such episodes represent easily identifiable case studies. Pritchett (2000) suggests that the economic, political, institutional and policy conditions that accompany these break points can then be examined as a case study. Rodrik (2003b), as was discussed earlier in this section, selects case studies based on 'growth

28 *Methodological critique and framework*

puzzles'. These are only two examples of a much broader and rigorous array of possible methodologies. Even single case studies can be useful. A single case study may be enough to falsify a necessary or sufficient hypothesis. Such single case studies can be chosen because they are *typical*, or feature *extreme* or *deviant* values for important variables, or because they have *influential* or *diverse* configurations of the independent variables; comparative case studies can be *similar* or *different* in the range of variations in independent and dependent variables (Gerring 2007: 86–150). Each of these various methodologies has clear 'general principles that might guide the process of case selection' (Gerring 2007: 91). Chapter 3 will describe the statistical methodology used to identify the case studies of growth and stagnation in this book.

The proposed model

The first parts of this chapter outlined the various empirical and theoretical reasons why cross-country growth regressions are unlikely to yield good empirical results. This section outlines the alternative model that shall be used in this book and in particular shows how it relates to these theoretical and empirical problems.

Complementarity is important

Chapter 4 will show that there are three variables that must be in place to initiate and sustain an episode of growth. If any one of them is missing, the economy will be stuck in an episode of stagnation. The first two variables relate to crucial roles for the state in finance (mobilising and allocating the economic surplus to those wishing to invest productively), and in production (ensuring the surplus is invested productively). The third variable relates to institutions that are necessary to overcome the conflict inherently associated with economic development. None of these variables alone is likely to have a consistently significant causal impact on economic growth. The various complementary roles of the financial role of the state cannot be measured or analysed using cross-country regression analysis. To allocate resources, the state could utilise subsidies (which indicate an enlarged fiscal role for the state), tax incentives (which imply a reduced fiscal role for the state), or policies that raise the profitability of private sector firms, such as repression of labour mobilisation (which implies no fiscal role for the state). Such polices are complementary ways of achieving the same outcome. There is no reason to assume why, for example, the 'share of government expenditure in GDP' used by Barro (1991) should have any particular sign or significance in a cross-country growth regression.

Hysteresis is (potentially) important

The importance of complementarity between these three variables means that hysteresis effects can have a very significant impact. If any of these variables fails, an episode of growth can quickly turn into an episode of stagnation. In Chapter 5 we will see how economic growth increased after the late 1950s, as the 1958 military coup led to a temporary cessation in conflict and strengthened the autonomy of the state. As the

1960s wore on, the government of Ayub Khan proved unable to manage the conflicts associated with economic growth. New socio-economic groups emerged, and institutional reforms such as the Basic Democrats and a return to party political systems failed in their intended role as 'inclusive institutions'. In response to escalating conflict, the government re-allocated resources away from productive investment to try and buy political peace; the effort proved unsuccessful and economic growth correspondingly fell away.

The state is important (finance)

The previous empirical section showed that there is little empirical evidence to support the view that the state has an important role to play in economic growth. In practice, the state is crucial to economic development, but not in a way that can be captured by one crude regression variable. The various roles of the state are complementary (see above). A crucial (financial) role of the state is in allocating the economic surplus to those wishing to invest productively. In a developing economy, there is no particular reason why the surplus should naturally find its way into the hands of those wishing to invest. This idea is distinct from neo-classical economics, which holds that the surplus will be automatically transferred from those wishing to save (households) to those (firms) able to offer the highest-return investment projects. In developing countries the state is likely to play the most important role in facilitating the transfer of the surplus – through promoting the banking system, through taxation/subsidies, by influencing the rate of profit and hence retained earnings, and by influencing patterns and levels of the flow of international capital. Together, these imply that the role of the state in allocating the surplus must be analysed as a question of political economy. Chapter 4 will explore these issues in more detail.

The state is important (production)

Investment has a robust presence in cross-country growth regressions. Investment is not sufficient; important as well is the productivity of that investment. The second complementary role for the state is with regard to production, to ensure that investment resources allocated to the private sector or utilised directly by the state either raise productivity in an existing market niche (intensive growth, or learning) or upgrade to a higher-technology market niche (extensive growth).

The state has a crucial role in promoting learning because of the prevalence of market failures. Neo-classical economics assumes that innovation takes place in advanced countries and that learning in LDCs is no more difficult than selecting the most appropriate among innovations (Lall 1995, 1999). In practice, there is less difference between innovation in developed countries and industrialisation based on learning how to use already-commercialised technology. Much technology is tacit, and to effectively master it requires extensive experience and experimentation. The process of learning to reach the efficiency frontier is slow, risky, and costly. Learning by doing may imply a lengthy and unpredictable period of losses, as firms learn and adapt technology to make it more appropriate to developing country conditions. In theory, private capital markets could fund firms through the period of learning. In practice, uncertainty, risk and illiquidity mean that private capital will be reluctant to do so.

It is important that rents created by the state to induce learning be conditional. There is a good chance that learning rents will fail to generate growth. Numerous infant industries protected from international competition have not become dynamic and have instead rested in pleasant lethargy on guaranteed profits. There are important pre-conditions for rents to be used to promote learning. Rents must be allocated in a contingent manner, and withdrawn from those firms failing to learn, export or reduce costs. The bureaucracy must be competent enough to allocate rents ex-ante to potentially dynamic capitalists or strong enough to withdraw them, ex-post, from failing capitalists. The relation of the state to these various classes can only be explored as a political economy question. Chapter 4 will explore these issues in more detail.

Institutions are important for episodes of growth and stagnation

This chapter has shown that the typical growth experience of a developing country is characterised by episodes of stagnation, growth spurts, structural breaks, and instability. A research agenda on geography and institutions has stepped back from this problem in seeking to explain differences in average growth rates over the long term, over 50 or 100 years. Such explanations include the nature of the colonial state (Acemoglu *et al.* 2001), factor endowments (Sokoloff and Engerman 2000), malaria (Gallup and Sachs 2000), and geography (Gallup and Sachs 1999). This book seeks to explain the distinct episodes of growth and stagnation existing over the medium term, more like a decade than a century. It would be difficult, for example, to envisage how the nature of the colonial state or geography could explain the sudden lurch to stagnation in Cote D'Ivoire after 1978 following several decades of rapid growth, or how factor endowments or income inequality could account for rapid economic growth in China after 1978. This book does argue that institutions are important in explaining episodes of growth and stagnation. While there is a good deal of literature looking at the effect of institutions in promoting economic growth, this book looks at the under-researched topic of how institutions can mediate the (negative) relationship between conflict and economic growth.

Economic development is concerned with shifting resources from low- to high-productivity areas, which is an inherently conflictual process. The mobility of some assets will be limited; owners will then face problems of obsolescence, unemployment and inequality. Those having sunk investments into physical capital, skills, contractual relationships, and political patronage are likely to resist change (Chang 1999). Conflict may also arise from political mobilisation outpacing the growth of representative political organisations (Huntingdon 1968). The financial role of the state in allocating resources to those wishing to invest productively and the production role of the state in ensuring that those resources are used productively are not sufficient. Such an allocation and use of resources could be undone, for example, by groups mobilising and seeking those resources by reallocation to satisfy immediate consumption wants.

Those institutions that have been widely tested in regressions are mainly those theorised as being important in neo-classical economic theory. In particular, analysis in work such as Easterly (2001c) and Rodrik (1999a) has focused on democratic political institutions. Chapter 4 will provide a critique of the view that these are the only institutions able to mediate the conflict inherent in economic growth. There are other institutions that may reduce the impact of conflict on economic growth: those discussed here are (i) a repressive state, (ii) inclusive institutions, and (iii) ideological institutions.

Leftwich (1995, 2000) focused on the autonomy of the state as being important in allowing the state to implement distributionally non-neutral policies. This view is too narrow; a more inclusive institution-building strategy is also possible. An important part of securing legitimacy for a given (re-)allocation of rights may be in compensating the (potential) losers rather than repressing them. Identifying those requiring compensation, minimising the transaction costs associated with such transfers, and minimising rent-seeking by other entities requires a state that is more 'embedded' than 'autonomous'. The Pakistan People's Party (PPP) in the 1970s looked as though it could have become an inclusive institution and performed this. As chapter 6 shows, the PPP failed to develop an elaborate system of factions to provide a system of co-ordination between the various levels of government or a well-defined network for the distribution of the spoils of office. The PPP also failed to manage to absorb dissent by systematically co-opting leaders of subordinate classes.

Even groups excluded from development or suffering from rising levels of inequality may acquiesce in their own exclusion for ideological reasons. A political party that can subordinate members' individual aspirations to a collective ideology, and exclude opponents, can be an important institution to manage conflict and facilitate economic reform. In Pakistan there is a general failure of any leader or party to successfully promote such an ideology; efforts included 'Pakistan nationalism' in the 1950s (Chapter 4), 'modernisation' (Chapter 5), 'Islamic Socialism' and 'Islamisation' (Chapter 6). There is some limited evidence for Pakistan that tightly organised ideological parties have been better able to provide stable government. An example is the MQM in the 1990s in Karachi. The MQM is a cadre-based, ideological political party relying on a network of activists. The MQM functioned after its formation in 1984 as a highly successful and disciplined political party, characterised by high levels of ideological commitment, and a tightly knit party structure that dominated the politics of Karachi from the late 1980s onwards.

The relation between different theories

It was noted in the discussion of cross-country growth regressions earlier in this chapter that there is an ambiguous relation between different theories of growth. Numerous cross-country growth regressions find various indicators of policy to be positively related to economic growth. There is no clear way to reconcile these findings. Using the framework here, this is no longer a dilemma. There are complementary/alternative means by which the state can mobilise and allocate resources and ensure learning and complementary/alternative institutions that can mitigate the problems of conflict. These means can and do shift over time. For example, the role of capital inflows being funnelled through public sector development banks and raising productive investment was crucial in promoting economic growth in Pakistan between 1960/61 and 1969/70 (Chapter 5). Large-scale remittance inflows and foreign aid between 1970/71 and 1992/93 (Chapter 6) and foreign borrowing between 1993 and 2003 (Chapter 7) had little impact on productive investment, and so were associated with episodes of economic stagnation. After 1970/71 increases in public investment (Chapter 6) and after 1992/93 reductions in public investment (Chapter 7) were associated with episodes of stagnation. This apparently contradictory finding would spoil any long-run cross-country growth regression, but can be easily explained in this framework. The state after 1970/71 and 1992/93 lacked the institutions to manage the conflicts associated with growth and development, and so was unable to ensure public investment was used productively.

The case-study approach: growth as a historical process

Cross-country growth regressions assume that economic growth operates according to universal laws and statistical regularities that operate across all economies across time and space. There are only a few exceptions, and the occasional dummy variable for regions and notable events. Discussion in this chapter demonstrated that there is evidence that the growth process differs significantly between different regions and countries and over time. This book uses a specific historical case study, that of Pakistan in the post-independence period. The case study approach is justified in this book in part on the assumption that growth processes are not universal. The comparison of episodes of growth and stagnation in the post-independence Pakistan economy allows us to focus on the factors that influence growth and how their impact has altered over time. The case studies are periods across time in the same country, rather than different countries at a single moment in time. Chapter 3 will establish that there were three episodes of growth (1952/52 to 1958/59, 1960/61 to 1969/70 and 2003/04 to 2008/09) and two episodes of stagnation (1970/71 to 1991/92 and 1992/93 to 2002/03).

3 Episodes of growth and stagnation in Pakistan, 1951–2008

Introduction

This chapter[1] develops an empirical framework based on the methodological critique in Chapter 2. We use the case study of Pakistan since independence. This chapter begins by outlining the definition and rigorous statistical measure of an episode of growth or stagnation as will be used in this book. The book restricts itself to the very aggregate level of growth, looking at GDP. Future work will extend this perspective to consider episodes of growth and stagnation by sector, agriculture, industry and services. This chapter finds that there are three episodes of growth, 1951/52 to 1958/59, 1960/61 to 1969/70 and 2003/04 to 2008/09, and two episodes of stagnation, 1970/71 to 1991/92 and 1992/93 to 2002/03.

Methods of measuring episodes of growth and stagnation

This section reviews some of the methods that have been used by other scholars to define and measure episodes of growth and stagnation in India, a source of much richer literature than is the case for Pakistan.

Episodes of growth and stagnation in India

McCartney (2009a) uses both quantitative and qualitative criteria to define episodes of growth and stagnation and finds that there are four episodes of growth and stagnation in independent India. These are the break from colonial stagnation after 1951, industrial stagnation from 1965 to 1980, an increase in economic growth after the late 1970s/early 1980s, and a continued episode of growth after reforms in 1991.

The existing analytical attention devoted to the various episodes of growth and stagnation in post-independence India is inconsistent. The post-1965 slowdown in industrial growth, while being hotly debated in the 1970s is now largely forgotten. The episode of growth after 1979 is as yet mainly a statistical exercise, although there are some signs of scholars attempting to explain and draw wider conclusions. There is a huge literature on the reforms of 1991; much of this simply assumes reforms to have had a significant impact on growth, so it amounts to little more than descriptive before-and-after studies. There is a growing recognition that aggregate GDP growth did not change after 1991, and productivity growth actually slowed in the 1990s, relative to the 1980s. There remain few attempts to integrate the aforementioned assumption and the actual outcome. Agriculture has been frequently exposed to a spotlight trying to find trends, turning points and structural breaks. Notable debates include the green revolution after 1965 and the reasons for rapid agricultural output growth in West Bengal during the 1980s, after several decades of stagnation. There is a small literature looking at episodes of growth and stagnation and their likely sustainability at state level, the break from stagnation in Kerala during the 1990s being the most prominent example (Harilal and Joseph 2003; Jeromi 2005).

Phases of growth and stagnation in India

Virmani (2004) constructs a Hodrick-Prescott (HP) filtered GDP series and a moving average for India after 1947. Virmani finds that there are two clear 'phases', revealed by the growth rate trends of the HP-filtered series and the ten-year moving average. As measured by the HP series, the growth trend recorded a downswing after independence and reached a low point of 3.3% p.a. between 1971/72 and 1973/74. Growth then recovered during a second (upswing) phase to a highpoint of 6.1% between 1994/95 and 1995/96. The ten-year moving average fluctuated mainly between 3%–4% during the first 30 years. Starting from 1978/79 there is a clear trend upwards, after which the average never fell below 4%, and on occasion exceeded 5%.

Comparative episodes of growth and stagnation

Some scholars have unearthed episodes of growth and stagnation in India through international comparisons. Here, an episode of growth is defined as one in which India is either growing relatively rapidly compared to other developing countries, or is converging (however slowly) on the leader. Clark and Wolcott (2001) have shown that there is a very long episode of (relative) stagnation lasting from the mid-nineteenth century to the mid-1980s, when India's income stagnated relative to that of the UK and USA. The second was an episode of growth after 1980. Per capita income rose 10% relative to the USA between 1987 and 1991, and by another 14% between 1991 and 1998. The pattern changes when we compare India to other LDC's. Virmani (2004: 56) shows that between 1950 and 1964 India's growth performance was similar to the mean of all developing countries, and that between 1965 and 1979 India's growth performance declined dramatically, to 69th from a set of 79 countries for which comparable data is available. After 1980 India's growth accelerated, whilst growth elsewhere declined. This led to an improvement in India's relative performance: between 1980 and 2000 India's growth ranking improved to 9th from 86 countries. Rodrik (1999a) notes that developing countries fall into two groups, those that sustained growth after the 1979/80 global crisis and those that collapsed into stagnation. India fell into the former category. An international comparison reveals in starker clarity the success of countries like South Korea, Taiwan and India, which managed to sustain (or even increase) their growth rates – this fact would be missed by focusing only on the domestic economy.

Comparative episodes of sectoral growth and stagnation

In recent years India has been characterised as having service-led economic growth. A comparative analysis reveals a more nuanced picture. Virmani (2004) measured the share of services in India's GDP and compared it to the 'norm' for other countries. Between 1980 and 1991 India had a slightly lower, and between 1992 and 2000 a normal, share of services in GDP. Faster service sector growth in the 1990s has thus corrected an imbalance that emerged earlier. This suggests that the notion of 'service-led' growth in India being a distinct developmental pattern is something of a mirage. The oddity is, rather, the unusually low growth of manufacturing. Service sector growth in India increased from less than 7% in the 1980s to 7.5% p.a. in the 1990s. Manufacturing growth remained below 7%. By comparison, manufacturing growth in China between 1979 and 1990 exceeded 10% (Nolan 1995).

Episodes of growth and stagnation at state level

Episodes of growth and stagnation in India have also been analysed at the state level (cross-section) as opposed to time series analysis. Growth in some states (Orissa, Rajasthan, Gujarat, etc.) shows large year-to-year fluctuations, and in others (Kerala, Punjab, West Bengal) growth is relatively stable. The average also varies considerably between states (Dasgupta *et al.* 2000: 2416). There are some interesting cases of episodes of growth (acceleration) at state level, such as Rajasthan and Tamil Nadu in the 1980s. Such disaggregated analysis allows us to shine a spotlight on the regional contributions to shifts in all-India growth averages. The national shift in growth rates in the early 1980s, for example, was actually a regionally concentrated phenomenon shared by only a few states (Dholakia 1994).

Existing studies of Pakistan

The most widely used methodology is to divide the post-independence history of Pakistan into political regimes and to analyse simple patterns and averages of economic growth in each. The dramatic nature of regime change and the personalities associated with each provide obvious motivations for such a choice. Almost always these include, the period of chaotic democracy 1947–58, the military dictatorship of Ayub Khan 1958–68, the rise and fall of Bhutto 1971–77, the military dictatorship of Zia 1977–88, the return of democracy 1988–99, and the military dictatorship of Musharraf 1999–2008. Such works include most of *the* key cited references on the Pakistani economy (Ahmed and Amjad 1984; Noman 1988; Talbot 1998; Hasen 1998; Burki 1999; Husain 1999; Zaidi 2005; Ali 2008). A recent, prominent and very detailed statistical treatment of the Pakistani economy simply divided the period since independence into calendar decades (Kemal *et al.* 2006).

There is almost no statistical work looking at episodes of growth and stagnation in Pakistan in a historical sense. A couple of works have tested for structural breaks in growth for British India/post-independence India using GDP data across the entire twentieth century (Hatekar and Dongre 2005, Nayyar 2006). This has not been done specifically for Pakistan. A limited exception is a study of agriculture, which finds (for Pakistan) that there was a break (though not tested for statistical significance) in growth averages of total output, output per capita and land productivity after 1950 (Kurosaki 1999: 163).

There is very little comparative analysis of growth in Pakistan. What work does exist tends to confine itself to comparison of simple statistical averages. For example Ul Haque finds that between 1970 and 1979 real GDP growth in Pakistan was slower than for developing countries in general and for both Africa and Asia. And between 1980 and 1989 real GDP growth in Pakistan increased to rates above those of LDCs in general and in Africa, though remaining below those of Asia. In the 1990s Pakistan was again doing badly relative to other LDCs (1999: 30).

Episodes of growth and stagnation in Pakistan

This section presents the results of an original statistical analysis of GDP growth in Pakistan since independence. The analysis seeks to identify episodes of growth and stagnation as significant step changes in the rate of GDP growth (referred to here as breakpoints). The data reveal 5 episodes of growth and stagnation in Pakistan since independence. The strongest of these are the episodes of growth between 1950 and 1960/61 and 1960/61 to 1992/93 and the episode of stagnation between 1992/93 and 2008. There is slightly weaker evidence of an episode of stagnation from 1970/71 to 1991/92 and episode of growth between 2003/04 and 2008/09.

These episodes have been obtained by applying techniques from the Indian literature on growth breakpoints in India to the Pakistan case. Methods in this literature fall into one of two major groups. The first includes analyses that start with a hypothesised breakpoint year and then use statistical methods to verify or disprove their theory (Bhargava and Joshi 1990, Nagaraj 1990, Sinha and Tejani 2004, Kaur 2007). The second group takes a more agnostic approach, in that candidate breakpoint years are both identified and tested using the data (Wallack 2003, Hateker and Dongre 2005, Virmani 2005 and Balakrishnan and Parameswaran 2007). The first group has been criticised both because there is a possibility of overlooking breakpoints that were not included in the original hypothesising (Wallack 2003: 4312) and because they run a much higher risk of accepting a false breakpoint date, particularly where the hypothesised year was identified with some a-priori assumption about the data (Hansen 1992). For these reasons, the analysis in this chapter follows the majority of the more recent literature on India by confining attention to the agnostic approaches of the second group.

The following section offers some simple descriptive and preliminary analysis of the data on GDP similar in spirit to that on India in Virmani (2005). Figure 3.1 presents real GDP growth in Pakistan over the period 1950/51 to 2008/09 as reported in Kemal et al. (2006).[2]

Figure 3.1 includes two filters of the raw GDP growth series: a 10-year centred moving average of the data and the Hodrick-Prescott filter. Both of these filters are designed to extract underlying trends from noisy data. The filters differ in the weights that they apply to growth rate observations that are nearer or further away from the year concerned, but they are largely agreed on several stylised facts. First, there is a

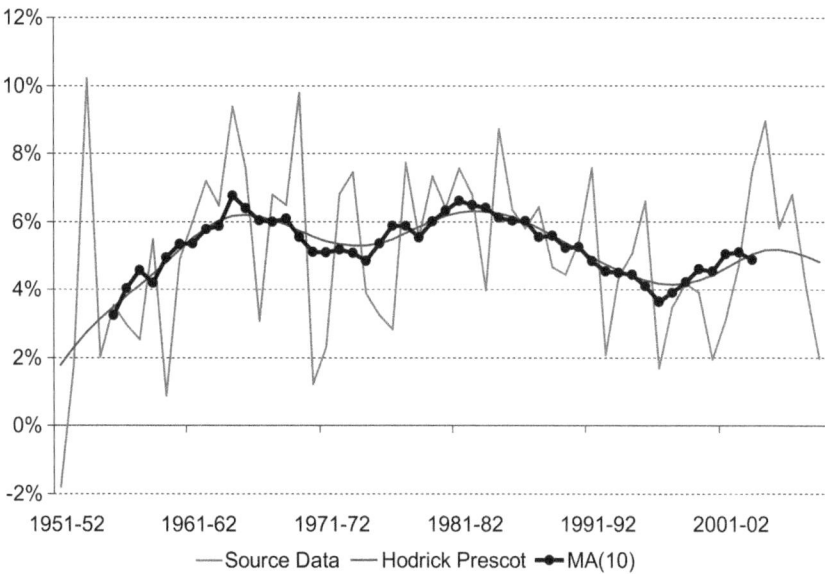

Figure 3.1 Raw and trend real GDP growth for Pakistan 1951–52 to 2008–09.
Source: Kemal *et al.* (2006) and Kite and McCartney (forthcoming)

clear acceleration in output from 1950/51 to the early-1960s. After that the (smoothed) growth rates fluctuate between about 5% and 7% until the 1980s, when there is a marked deceleration lasting until the mid-1990s. At its trough in the 1990s, (smoothed) GDP growth slows to the lowest level since 1950/51, at about 4%. Growth then recovers, though next peaking at a rate lower than in the high-growth years. This method is suggestive of a very different pattern of episodes of growth and stagnation than one corresponding with the political regimes of Pakistan since independence (see earlier discussion). This method smoothes and filters away any breakpoints in GDP growth. It is therefore not possible to use this methodology to identify any specific breakpoint years.

The simplest methodology in the literature that can begin to identify breakpoints proceeds by splitting the data into two subsets for before and after each year in the data and then examining the mean growth rate in each subset (Virmani 2005: 9). For the Pakistan data there are 58 annual observations on GDP growth in the dataset, so the procedure involves 57 possible ways of splitting the observations into two groups.[3] To find a candidate breakpoint year, the ratio of mean growth rates in the two periods can be calculated.[4] If this ratio is 'close' to one, then the date at which we split the sample is unlikely to be a break point, because the two means are very close to one another. On the other hand, if the ratio is 'very far' away from one, it reveals that there may be a breakpoint in that particular year. If the ratio is greater than one, it indicates a step-up in GDP growth, or output acceleration, whilst if the ratio is less that one, it indicates deceleration. Figure 3.2 plots the results of this comparison of means for Pakistan (with the outlier in 1953/54 excluded from the analysis).

38 *Episodes of growth and stagnation*

The classical method for assessing the significance of structural change in the context of an econometric model is the Chow test (Chow 1960). Application of the Chow test to the problem at hand would involve splitting the data into two sub-samples and then regressing the real GDP growth rates on a constant and any relevant controls. A dummy variable that takes the value 1 for one of the sub samples and 0 for the other would also be included, and the significance of this dummy variable assessed using an F-test. If its coefficient is significantly different from zero, the test would demonstrate the existence of a breakpoint in the year that split the data. Here, the analysis proceeds by applying the Chow procedure iteratively to all possible splits of the Pakistan data into two sub-samples. It is a procedure that was suggested by Quandt (1960) for application to situations where there is no candidate breakpoint hypothesised in advance, and hence where it is desirable to identify breakpoints from the data. Quandt's method involves estimating T-1 equations, where T is the sample size, and assessing the significance of T-1 dummy variables by calculating T-1 F-statistics. The largest of these, $supF$, can then be the subject of a test whose null hypothesis is no breakpoint, versus the alternative, that there is a break in the year where the maximum F-statistic was found. Clearly, this procedure involves estimating substantially more parameters than a one-equation version of the Chow test. Quandt recognised that this would leave the critical values for a one-equation Chow test inappropriately small. Andrews (1993) took his work forward by deriving the correct critical values for the procedure. Vogelsang (1997) and Hansen (1997) extended the theme further by modifying the critical values for models with serial correlation, and deriving asymptotic p-values.

Applying Quandt's methodology to Pakistan's GDP data begins by assessing which control variables should be included in the test equations, and which of Andrews' or

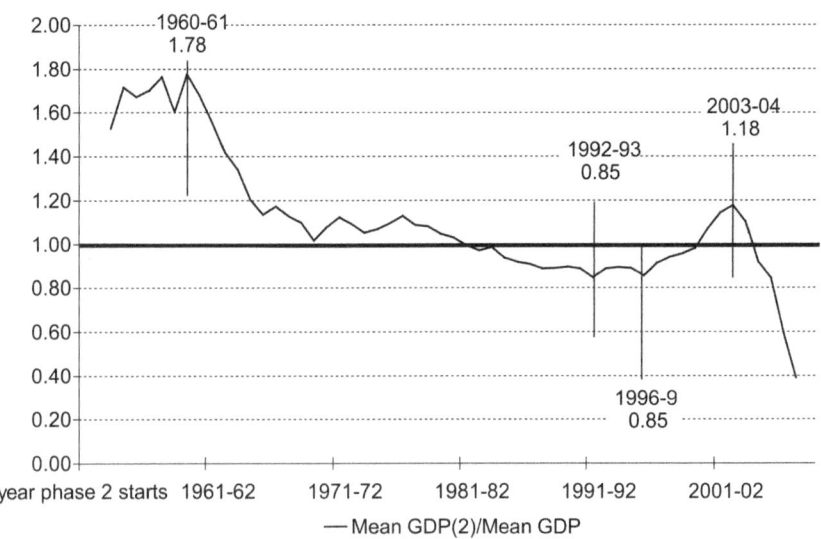

Figure 3.2 Comparison of mean GDP growth in different subsets (dividing year on the x-axis).
Source: Kemal *et al.* (2006) and Kite and McCartney (forthcoming).

Volgelsang's critical values are appropriate. Table 3.1 shows the results of estimating equations for real GDP growth to test which controls should be included. Column 1 includes the baseline equation with just a constant term. Controls suggested in the literature on growth breakpoints in India are lagged values of GDP growth (Wallack 2003, Hateker and Dongre 2005) and a time trend (Hateker and Dongre 2005). These are included separately in columns 3 and 4 and together in column 5. All these control variables are shown to be insignificant, and so column 1 is the chosen test equation. The bottom half of Table 3.1 reports the results of Breusch-Godfrey serial correlation tests for up to four periods of auto-correlated errors. The p-values are all well over 10%, and it is therefore reasonable to conclude that there is no serial correlation problem and Andrews' critical values are appropriate for the Quandt-Andrews (Q-A) test.

The next step is to carry out the Q-A test using the chosen test equation over the whole of the sample period, and testing for the significance of a breakpoint in the year with the maximum F-test. It is a significance test that takes into account problems with small samples. It is generally suggested that the ends of the sample period not be included in the testing procedure. A standard level for this 'trimming', followed below, is 15%, with the first and last 7.5% of the observations in the test equation ruled out as potential breakpoint years. The procedure identifies the first breakpoint and then repeats the Q-A test using a test equation that only includes the period after that year. This process is repeated until there are no more significant *supF* statistics (Wallack 2003: 4312).

Table 3.2 presents the results of following this procedure on Pakistan's GDP data. When the test equation includes the whole sample period, the first breakpoint identified is 1960/61 and is significant at the 10% level. If this break is accepted and the procedure continues to look at the period after 1960/61, the number of observations in the test equation starts to get rather small. Looking for breaks in small sections of

Table 3.1 Significance of controls for the Quandt-Andrews test equation for GDP

	(1)	(3)	(4)	(5)
Constant	5.07	3.70	4.77	3.96
	(15.5***)	(2.91***)	(7.14***)	(2.87***)
Outlier for 1953–54				
GDP Growth (–1)	0.22	(1.55)	0.22	(1.56)
GDP Growth (–2)	-0.02	(-0.15)	-0.02	(-0.15)
GDP Growth (–3)	-0.05	(-0.36)	-0.05	(-0.35)
GDP Growth (–4)	0.15	(1.21)	0.15	(1.25)
Time Trend	0.01	(0.52)	-0.01	(-0.51)
Sample size	58	54	58	58
Breusch-Godfrey Serial Correlation LM Test, p-values				
AR(1)	0.28	0.79	0.29	0.70
AR(2)	0.46	0.95	0.45	0.93
AR(3)	0.59	0.92	0.60	0.83
AR(4)	0.58	0.81	0.58	0.84

Notes: T-stats in parentheses *** Denotes statistical significance at 1% level
Source: Kemal *et al.* (2006) and Kite and McCartney (forthcoming).

the data runs into problems, because the Q-A test has low power to reject a false null (of no breakpoint) in small samples (Andrews 1993: 821). With this concern in mind, Table 3.2 includes the years where the maximum F-tests were identified in the between-breaks sample and at the end of the period, even though (as the p-values in the last three rows of the table show) these are not significant. These years are 1970/71, 1992/93 and 2003/04, respectively.

Table 3.3 below indicates the direction of the growth rate shifts in the years identified by the Q-A test by presenting simple mean growth rates for each of the possible splits of the sample. The first column splits the sample only at the significant breakpoint in 1960/61, whilst the second column also accepts a breakpoint in 1992/93. The final case where there are 5 different episodes of growth and stagnation in the post independence period is in the last column.

It seems clear from these results that the 1960/61 breakpoint can be accepted; however all the other three breakpoints need to be treated with some caution. The period 1992/93 emerges as the most likely of the other three, not just because it has the highest maximum F-stat and the lowest p-value in Table 3.2, but also because the smoothed GDP series in Table 3.1 clearly shows that the cycle after 1992/93 had both a lower peak and a deeper trough than the two cycles that came before that year. Evidence for potential breakpoints in 1970/71 and/or 2003/04 is weaker, but cannot be discounted. As the example given earlier showed, 1970/71 could well be a breakpoint that the methodologies used here are ill-suited to identify. Its position between two more significant breakpoints leaves us with only a small-sample test with much less

Table 3.2 Quandt-Andrews test for real GDP growth

Sample	Trim	#Breaks Compared	Year of Max F-test	Maximum F-stat	Hansen's p-value
1951–52 to 2008–09	15%	40	1960–61	7.73	0.07*
1960–61 to 2008–09	15%	33	1992–93	5.51	0.19
1992–93 to 2009–09	15%	11	1903–04	4.9	0.25
1960–61 to 1992–93	15%	23	1970–71	3.02	0.55

* Denotes statistical significance at 10% level
Source: Kemal *et al.* (2006) and Kite and McCartney (forthcoming).

Table 3.3 Average growth rates in the periods between breakpoints

	1 breakpoint	2 breakpoints	5 breakpoints
1951–52 to 1958–59	3.1%	3.1%	3.1%
1960–61 to 1969–70		5.9%	6.8%
1970–71 to 1991–92	5.4%		5.6%
1992–93 to 2002–03		4.5%	3.7%
2003–04 to 2008–09			5.9%

Source: Kemal *et al.* (2006), Kite and McCartney (forthcoming).

power to find a significant breakpoint. As for the truth of a breakpoint in 2003/04, more time and data will be the best solution to the existing 'small-sample problem'.

An episode of growth, 1951/52 to 1958/59

Economic growth, 1951/52 to 1958/59

The statistical analysis in this chapter showed that GDP growth averaged 3.1% p.a. between 1951/52 and 1958/59. Population growth was steady over the 1950s, averaging 2%–2.5% p.a., which translated into per capita GDP growth of no more than 1% p.a. Growth in GDP was showing signs of slowing after the mid-1950s (though not statistically significant). This was due to a slowdown in manufacturing growth.

Growth in agricultural value added (1.7%) fell short of population growth in the 1950s, though it showed an increase to over 2.0% p.a. after the mid-1950s. Within agriculture, growth came mainly from 'major crops' (cereals, gram, cotton, sugar cane, tobacco, rapeseed, mustard and sesamum), rather than the 'minor crops' (pulses, vegetables and fruits) (Lewis 1969: 3, 1970: 8; Griffin and Khan 1972: 6; Khan 1999: 100–1; Kemal et al. 2006: 194). Rates of growth of livestock production were consistently faster than those of crops, the difference being particularly pronounced in the early 1950s (Chaudhry et al. 1996: 528). Agricultural growth was notably unstable, with a big increase in 1953/54 and absolute declines in 1951/52 and 1954/55 (Kemal et al. 2006: 294). Statistical tests do show that the variability of foodgrain growth increased in the 1950s relative to the 1930s and 1940s (Kurosaki 1999: 163). Growth of the manufacturing sector was around 7.7% in the 1950s; this was led by rapid growth of the large-scale sector (just below 16%), rather than the small-scale sector (around 2.3%) (Griffin and Khan 1972: 6; Afridi 1985: 160; Kemal 1999: 160; Kemal et al. 2006: 273). Growth of manufacturing slowed considerably in the second half of the 1950s, from over 10% p.a. between 1950 and 1955 to slightly more than 5% between 1955 and 1960 (Zaidi 2005: 130). The growth rates of GNP, agriculture, industry, and exports were all significantly below those targeted in the First Five-year Plan (1955–60) (Griffin 1965: 601).

The industries with notably rapid growth were where import substitution progressed earliest and most rapidly; this was in industries primarily producing consumption goods. Another characteristic of these industries was their dependence on domestically produced agricultural raw materials. Between 1951/52 and 1954/55 growth of gross value added in tea manufacturing was 42% (27% from 1954/55 to 1959/60), in tobacco manufacturing 19.8% (17.5%), in cotton and other textiles 55% (15.2%), in sugar manufacturing 7.2% (13.8%), in rubber and rubber products 24% (18.3%), and in edible oils 28% (19.1%). Lacking data for the first period, but growing rapidly in the second period were wood and furniture manufacturing 41%, silks and artificial silk textiles 16.1%, footwear 9.9%, soaps and cosmetics 31%, jute textiles 35%, fertiliser 50%, machines except electrical 34% and electrical machinery and equipment 40% (Lewis and Soligo 1965: 109; Lewis 1969: 114–15; Lewis 1970: 106).

Growth tended to be more rapid in West than East Pakistan. Between 1949/50 and 1959/60 gross value added in agriculture grew 2.0% and 0.5% respectively, gross provincial product 1.4% and 3.5%, gross provincial product per capita 1.1% and -1.0%. Interestingly, growth in large-scale manufacturing was slightly faster in East (19.4%) than West Pakistan (18.8%) (Papanek 1967: 20; Lewis 1970: 139).

Structural change, 1951/52 to 1958/59

At independence, Pakistan's GDP and employment was dominated by agriculture. Over the 1950s the share of agriculture fell from 53% to 45% of GDP, from 80% to 70% of total exports, and from 68% to 59% of the labour force employed (Lewis 1969: 4, 1970: 9; Khan 1999: 99; Kemal et al. 2006: 295). The share of manufacturing in GDP increased from around 6.4% in 1949/50 to just below 10% in 1959/60. This was led by the large-scale manufacturing sector (from below 2% to nearly 6%) rather than the small-scale sector (around 4.5% to just above 4.2%) (Griffin and Khan 1972: 8; Afridi 1985: 464; Kemal 1999: 161; Kemal et al. 2006: 271).

The dominant industrial sector over the 1950s was textiles, its share of value added in the manufacturing sector declining marginally from 45.52% in 1955 to 42.61% in 1959/60. Sectors gaining over this period included chemical and chemical products (6.65% to 8.68%), other non-metallic industries (2.80% to 4.55%), fabricated metal products except machinery and transport equipment (2.50% to 3.89%), electrical machinery (0.82% to 1.85%), tobacco (4.18% to 5.29%), machinery except electrical (1.22% to 2.11%) and transport equipment (1.10% to 2.94%). Sectors losing shares included footwear and other apparel (2.57% to 2.06%), and other industries (15.81% to 8.80%) (Kemal et al. 2006: 275–6). Structural change was more rapid in West than East Pakistan. In West Pakistan between 1949/50 and 1959/6 the share of agriculture dropped from 54.5% to 49.1% of GDP and the share of industry increased from 14.7% to 20.7%. In East Pakistan the changes were from 65.2% to 63.5% and 9.4% to 13.7% respectively (Lewis 1970: 140; Griffin and Khan 1972: 4).

Sources of growth, 1951/52 to 1958/59

Growth in manufacturing over the first five years of the decade (1950/51 to 1954/55) was met almost entirely by import substitution (96.6% of total growth); domestic demand (2.4%) and export expansion (1.85%) made only very marginal contributions. This pattern changed dramatically in 1954/55 to 1959/60, when the growth of domestic demand (53.1%) became the leading source of manufacturing growth, exceeding both export expansion (24%) and import substitution (22.9%) (Kemal et al. 2006: 273).

The impact of import substitution is evident in production statistics. The share of domestic production in total supply increased from 22.8% in 1951/52 to 99.9% in 1959/60 for sugar manufacturing, from 63.6 to 96.6% in edible oils, 14.5 to 97.3% in cotton and other textiles, 10.9% to 100% in matches, 5.3% to 99.9% in jute textiles and 22.5% to 91.7% in consumption goods. By the mid-1950s sectors hitherto engaged in import substitution turned to exports. By the end of the 1950s more than 75% of production in jute textiles and leather manufacturing was exported, as was around

50% of production in fertiliser and miscellaneous manufacturing industries and around 20% of production in food manufacturing and footwear. In general, import substitution and export growth were significantly less in investment and related goods than in consumption goods (Lewis 1969: 116–17). There was some shift away from exports of raw jute and raw cotton to jute and cotton textiles, this being more pronounced in the case of cotton than jute (Lewis 1970: 12). There was little change in the volume of imports in 1959/60 relative to 1951/52, but the composition shifted away from consumption goods, such as cotton yarn and cloth, towards machinery, transport and electrical equipment (Lewis 1970: 11).

An episode of growth, 1960/61 to 1969/70

Economic growth, 1960/61 to 1969/70

The statistical analysis in this chapter showed that GDP growth averaged 6.8% p.a. between 1960/61 and 1969/70.

Growth in agricultural value added of 5.1% exceeded population growth of 2.7% in the 1960s, and showed an increase after the mid-1960s, from 3.8% p.a. between 1960 and 1965 to 6.4% between 1965 and 1970 (Lewis 1969: 3, 1970: 8; Griffin and Khan 1972: 6; Amjad 1982: 16; Khan 1999: 100; Naseem 2002: 248). Agriculture growth again came mainly from 'major crops' (cereals, gram, cotton, sugar cane, tobacco, rapeseed, mustard and sesamum), rather than the 'minor crops' (pulses, vegetables and fruits) (Khan 1999: 101). In contrast to the 1950s, the growth of crop production vastly outpaced that of livestock production, reflecting the impact of green revolution technology (Chaudhry et al. 1996: 528).

Growth in manufacturing was almost 10% p.a. in the 1960s, with growth in the large-scale sector of over 13% p.a. and in the small-scale sector of under 3% (Amjad 1982: 16; Kemal 1999: 160; IMF 2002: 10; Kemal et al. 2006: 273). Growth in large-scale manufacturing was more rapid in the first half of the decade, at 16.0% between 1960 and 1965; this included sugar manufacturing: 28% p.a.; edible oils: 24%; tobacco manufacturing: 32%; silks and silk art textiles: 32%; printing and publishing: 17.7%. In all these sectors there was a notable acceleration of growth relative to the 1950s. In other sectors there was rapid growth, though a slowdown relative to the previous five years: tea manufacturing: 12.1%; wood and furniture manufacturing: 20%; paper manufacturing: 19.9%; fertiliser: 36%; chemicals and pharmaceuticals: 18.2%; non-metallic mineral products: 17.2%; non-electrical machinery: 26%; electrical machinery and equipment: 36%; and transport equipment: 26%. There was no particular pattern by user-group (consumption, intermediate and investment goods) in terms of rapid/ slow growth or acceleration/deceleration (Lewis 1970: 106).

There was a notable slowdown in manufacturing growth after the mid-1960s. Growth in total manufacturing declined to 10.0% between 1965 and 1970. By sector, there was little change in the growth of consumer goods manufacturing (10.6 to 9.0%), a sharp slowdown in investment goods (20.0% to 8.0%), and a less dramatic slowdown in intermediate goods (12.0% to 8.0%).[5] The slowdown in investment goods was across the board and included sectors such as non-metals, basic metals, metal products, machinery, electrical machinery and transport equipment. The textiles sector saw increased growth (5.9% to 8.7%) (Zaidi 2005: 101).[6] Service sector growth was 6.4% p.a. between 1961 and 1971 (IMF 2002: 10).

Some sources argue that there was very little difference in growth of provincial GDP per capita between 1959/60 and 1964/65, around 2.6%–7% p.a. in both years. In general, faster growth of agriculture in West Pakistan was matched by faster growth of large-scale manufacturing in East Pakistan. After falling in the 1950s, the relative GDP of East Pakistan stabilised at a level of around 75% of that in West Pakistan (Lewis 1970: 139–40). Over the same period, other sources show that GDP growth per capita in West Pakistan (4.4%) was significantly faster than in East Pakistan (2.6%), and by contrast agricultural growth in West Pakistan was slower than in East Pakistan (3.9% and 4.3%, respectively), and growth in manufacturing faster (16.3 and 9.9%) (Papanek 1967: 20).

Structural change, 1960/61 to 1969/70

Over the 1960s the share of agriculture fell from 45% to 38% of GDP, 70% to 63% of total exports, and 59% to 57% of the labour force employed (Khan 1999: 99).

Manufacturing increased its share of GDP from 9.91% in 1959/60 to 13.44% in 1969/70. This was almost entirely accounted for by large-scale manufacturing (the contribution of which rose from 5.66% to 10.46%) rather than small-scale manufacturing (the contribution of which fell from 4.23% to 2.98%) (Kemal et al. 2006: 101). The pattern of change is borne out, though the exact numbers differ in other studies (Lewis 1970: 9; Kemal 1999: 161; Afridi 1985: 464). The relatively capital-intensive nature of large-scale manufacturing meant that, even by the end of the 1960s, it accounted for only 2.4% of total employment in Pakistan, up from 2% at the end of the 1950s (Sayeed 2002: 205).

The dominant industrial sector over the 1960s was textiles, though its share of manufacturing declined sharply, from 42.61% in 1959/60 to 30.31% in 1970/71. Sectors gaining over this period included food manufacturing (its share rising from 8.56% to 16.24%), beverage industries (0.36% to 0.75%), tobacco (5.29% to 10.88%), chemical and chemical products (8.68% to 10.99%), rubber (0.35% to 1.32%), and electrical machinery (1.85% to 3.61%). Sectors losing out over this period included footwear and other apparel (its share falling from 2.06% to 0.44%), paper and paper products (2.20% to 1.63%), printing and publishing (2.39% to 1.66%), fabricated metal products (3.89% to 1.75%), non-electrical machinery (2.11% to 0.96%), and transport equipment (2.94% to 2.59%) (Kemal et al. 2006: 275–6). At a more aggregate level, there was little structural change within industry. As a proportion of total industrial value added between 1960 and 1970, the share of consumer goods remained virtually unchanged (rising from 60.5% to 60.9%), capital goods declined slightly (from 8.8% to 6.6%) and intermediate goods showed a small increase (from 30.7% to 32.5%) (Sayeed 2002: 208).

Structural change was quite similar in West and East Pakistan, in both about 8% of GDP shifted from agriculture to industry. The higher initial share of agriculture in East Pakistan meant that it had a higher share in 1969/70 (55.7%) than West Pakistan (41.6%). Between 1959/60 and 1969/70 similar patterns of employment change were observed in both, though the change was more rapid in East Pakistan (Griffin and Khan 1972: 4). Other data show a less sharp fall in the share of agriculture in GDP over the 1960s (Lewis 1969: 4; Griffin and Khan 1972: 4; Kemal et al. 2006: 302). The increase in large-scale manufacturing as a share of GDP was relatively faster in East Pakistan, (from 2.7% to 5.4%), but was dwarfed in absolute terms by the increase in West Pakistan (from 7.0% to 12%) (Griffin and Khan 1972: 8).

Sources of growth, 1960/61 to 1969/70

Growth in manufacturing over the first five years of the decade (1959/60 to 1963/64) was met almost entirely by domestic demand (95.7% of total growth), while export expansion (4.6%) and import substitution (-0.3%) made little contribution. This pattern changed over the remainder of the decade (1963/64 to 1970/71): the growth of domestic demand (60.0%) continued to be the leading source of manufacturing growth, but both export expansion (15.0%) and import substitution (25.0%) increased their relative share (Lewis and Soligo 1965: 106; Kemal et al. 2006: 273).

A sectoral decomposition of growth for the periods 1960 to 1965 and 1965 to 1970 shows that agriculture accounted, respectively, for 23.95% and 36.72% of total GDP growth, manufacturing for 22.92% and 18.63% (the bulk of which was large scale), electricity and gas 1.26% and 4.94%, wholesale and retail trade 16.22% and 14.47%, banking and insurance 2.58% and 2.97%, public administration 6.36% and 6.90%, and services 4.92% and 4.89% (Burney 1986: 584–5).

An episode of stagnation, 1970/71 to 1991/92

Economic growth, 1970/71 to 1991/92

The statistical analysis in this chapter showed that GDP growth averaged 5.6% p.a. between 1970/71 and 1991/92.[7] During the 1970s GDP averaged 4.66%, this growth being led by manufacturing (5.5%), and services (5.94%), while agriculture lagged (2.32%) (Kemal et al. 2006: 310). During the 1980s GDP growth increased to 6.12% p.a. (though this increase was not significant). This was founded on a broad-based acceleration relative to the 1970s; agriculture grew by 4.1%, manufacturing by 8.21% and services by 6.6% p.a. (Kemal et al. 2006: 318). Within agriculture, growth had been led by the crop sector in the 1960s, but after 1969/70 this gave way to more balanced growth. The growth of livestock production steadily accelerated and caught up with (fluctuating) crop production. By the early-1990s the livestock sector was growing (at around 6%) almost twice as fast as crop production and had shown more growth over the previous 20 years (Nawab et al. 1984: 22; Chaudhry et al. 1996: 528).

The growth rate of the manufacturing sector increased from 5.5% in the 1970s to 8.21% in the 1980s; in the large-scale sector this increase was more noticeable (from 4.84% to 8.16%) than in the small-scale sector (from 7.63% to 8.4%) (Kemal et al. 2006: 273), while the consistently rapid growth of the small-scale sector marked a big difference with the 1960s (Nawab et al. 1984: 12; Afridi 1985: 466; Kemal 1999: 160; Naseem 2002: 248; Zaidi 2005: 101). Sectors in large-scale manufacturing experiencing rapid growth over the 1980s included food (13.5% p.a.), textiles (20.1%), leather and leather products (19.9%), printing and publishing (21%), industrial chemicals (19.9%), plastic products (24.3%), iron and steel basic industries (20.8%), non-electrical goods (19.9%), and sports and athletic goods (32.5%) (Wizarat 2002: 37).

Structural change, 1970/71 to 1991/92

Between 1970/71 and 1991/92 the share of agriculture's contribution to GDP continued its decline (from 38.02% to 25.83%), that of manufacturing increased slightly (from 14.16% to 17.59%) and of services increased (from 41.8% to 48.62%) (Kemal et al. 2006: 311, 319). The rising share of manufacturing was accounted for by some increase in the share of large-scale manufacturing (from 10.46% to 12.70%) and of small-scale manufacturing (from 2.98% to 4.89%) (Kemal et al. 2006: 271). The pattern of change is borne out, though the exact numbers differ, in other studies (Lewis 1970: 9; Nawab et al. 1984: 14; Kemal 1999: 161; Afridi 1985: 464). There was a gradual decline in the share of total employment accounted for by large-scale manufacturing, from 2.4% in 1969/70 to 1.8% in 1989/90 (Sayeed 2002: 205).

Between 1970/71 and 1990/91 the industrial sector remained highly concentrated, and the output share of (traditional) industries (dependent on indigenous raw materials) accounted for over 60% of value added, though this share was declining over time. Some industries increased their share of industrial output over this time: beverage industries from 0.75% to 1.59%; footwear and other apparel from 0.44% to 1.87%; printing and publishing from 1.66% to 2.01%; chemical and chemical products from 10.99% to 16.26%; basic metals from 2.41% to 4.18%; other non-metallic industries from 3.39% to 7.15%; non-electrical machinery from 0.96% to 1.96%; electrical machinery from 3.61% to 7.67%; and transport equipment from 2.59% to 3.50%. Other industries lost share: food manufacturing from 16.24% to 15.19%; tobacco from 10.88% to 6.18%; textiles from 30.31% to 22.31%; leather and leather products from 1.18% to 0.78%; and rubber from 1.32% to 0.88% (Kemal et al. 2006: 275–6). These patterns are broadly similar in other studies (Kemal 1999: 163; Wizarat 2002: 37). Between 1970 and 1990, at a more aggregate level, the share of consumer goods in total industrial value added declined from 60.9% to 54.2%, that of intermediate goods increased from 32.5% to 35.6%, and that of capital goods increased from 6.6% to 10.2% (Sayeed 2002: 208). Over the 1970s and 1980s Pakistan did not manage to emulate the high-growth Asian economies, where there were spectacular increases in the relative size and growth rates of metal products and machinery (Husain 1999).

Sources of growth, 1970/71 to 1991/92

Data about the sources of growth in manufacturing between 1970/71 and 1991/92 are not fully available. Between 1980/81 and 1988/89 domestic demand was responsible for almost 80% of manufacturing growth, while export expansion (10.1%) and import substitution (10.1%) were a long way behind. Between 1988/89 and 1991/92, the share of domestic demand fell (to 60.4%), while that of export expansion increased quite sharply (to 37.9%) and that of import substitution declined (to 1.7%) (Kemal 1997: 935).

A sectoral decomposition of growth until the mid-1980s shows how each sector contributed to aggregate GDP growth. Agriculture contributed 23.09% of total GDP growth between 1975 and 1980 (a rise from only 6.6% between 1970 and 1975). The contribution of manufacturing showed a gradual increase, from 17.21% of the total between 1970 and 1975 to 26.88% between 1980 and 1985 – most of this increase was accounted for by large-scale manufacturing. Public administration and defence contributed an unusually large proportion (24.79%) of total GDP growth between 1970 and 1975, and never as much before or since. The other major contributors were wholesale and retail trade, whose contribution peaked at 17.63% between 1970 and 1975, and transport and communication, whose contribution remained below 9%, but showed a rising trend. The contribution of services declined over time, from 8.34% between 1970 and 1975 to 6.11% between 1980 and 1985 (Burney 1986: 584–5).

An episode of stagnation, 1992/93 to 2002/03

Economic growth, 1992/93 to 2002/03

The statistical analysis in this chapter showed that GDP growth averaged 3.7% p.a. between 1992/93 and 2002/03. Some have argued, though without rigorous statistical evidence, that growth was gradually slowing (Wizarat 2002: 18). Growth of agriculture (4.54%) and services (4.5%) showed little change in the 1990s relative to the 1980s (Kemal et al. 2006: 328). The growth rate of manufacturing slowed sharply in the 1990s (3.88%) relative to earlier decades, the small-scale sector (5.06%) showing more resilience than the large-scale sector (3.54%) (Kemal et al. 2006: 273).

Structural change, 1992/93 to 2002/03

The share of agriculture and services in GDP increased marginally over the 1990s, from 25.68% to 25.93% and 48.45% to 49.06%, respectively (Kemal et al. 2006: 329). There was little change in the share of manufacturing in GDP, which increased (with some fluctuations) marginally from 17.59% in 1989/90 to 17.65% in 2001/02, the large-scale contribution declining from 12.7% to 12.39% and the small-scale contribution rising from 4.89% to 5.26% (Kemal et al. 2006: 271).

An episode of growth, 2003/04 to 2008/09

Economic growth, 2003/04 to 2008/09

The statistical analysis in this chapter showed that GDP growth averaged 5.9% p.a. between 2003/04 and 2008/09. There was a gradual acceleration in the growth rate; starting in 2002/03 the rate of GDP increased and it eventually reached 9.0% in 2004/05. The government maintained that 2004/05 marked a significant break with the past and had set the economy on a new trajectory of growth (Burki 2007: 20).

Growth of agriculture remained positive through this episode, peaking at 6.5% in 2004/05 and 6.3% in 2005/06 and reaching a low of 1.1% in 2007/08. Manufacturing growth rates had averaged under 5% p.a. in the 1990s, reached 6.9% in 2002/03, 14.0% in 2003/04 and 15.5% in 2004/05, and then declined to 5.4% in 2007/08 and -3.3% in 2008/09. Construction growth had averaged 2.6% p.a. in the 1990s. Its growth was rapid but unstable during this episode, reaching 24.3% in 2006/07, but declining by more than 10% in both 2003/04 and 2008/09. Service growth was steady, at 6%–8.5%, before falling to 3.6% in 2008/09. Whether this marks the end of the episode of growth, only time and more data will tell fully. There were initial indications of a sharp improvement in growth rates in 2009/10, with agriculture growing 2.0%, manufacturing 5.2%, services 4.6% and GDP 4.1% (Government of Pakistan 2009: 7, 2010: 3).

Structural change, 2003/04 to 2008/09

Between 2003/03 and 2008/09 the share of agriculture in GDP declined from 24.0% to 21.8%, while that of manufacturing increased from 16.3% to 18.2% and of services from 52.4% to 53.4% (Government of Pakistan 2008: 10, 2009: 13).

4 Theoretical framework

Introduction

This chapter critically reviews the literature on the role of state in economic development. This falls into two schools, the economic and political. The limitations of the economic school include the restricted scope of analysis, the lack of a political economy, and the importance of complementarity. Weaknesses of the political school include the limited analysis of the state's role, the relation between different theories, and lack of dynamics. A number of efforts have emerged to integrate these two schools, which are reviewed here. The following theoretical section attempts an integration relevant for the empirical context outlined in Chapter 3, focusing specifically on the role of the state. The financial role of the state is to allocate the economic surplus to those able to invest productively. The production role of the state is to ensure that financial resources so allocated are used productively, either to raise productivity in an existing market niche (learning) or to upgrade to a higher-technology market niche. The final section reviews how institutions can mediate the relationship between conflict and economic growth. The existing literature looking at this relationship is very limited. In this book a broader institutional perspective is considered. A repressive state, an inclusive state, or an ideological state can help reduce the negative implications of conflict on development.[1]

The economic and political schools of the developmental state

The literature on the role of the state in economic development falls into two schools. The first identifies market failures and corrective economic policies, with examples often being drawn from the East Asian experience. The second focuses on the capacity of the state to identify and implement such policies. These are the 'economic' and the 'political' schools (Fine and Stoneman 1996). This section makes a critical review of these two schools. A number of efforts have emerged since the mid-1990s to integrate them; the next section makes a critical review of some of these efforts. An important drawback of such efforts is their very often stylised and mathematical approach.

The economic school

There is an enormous literature on the economic rationale for state intervention. This section critically reviews some of the limitations of this literature: the limited scope of analysis, the lack of a political economy, and the importance of complementarity.

Limited scope of analysis

Much of the analysis from the economic school is limited in its wider relevance. An example is the high-debt model. Unlike in Western developed countries, in Japan and Korea companies' debt-equity ratios have typically exceeded one (Wade and Veneroso 1998). This made such companies very vulnerable to any shock that reduced the supply of bank capital, which pushed the two governments into close relations with banks, hence implying a protective role for the state. Such collaboration is not simply 'crony capitalism', but an important and necessary response to market failure by the state. The state was then in a position to influence the pattern of bank lending, which, according to Wade and Veneroso, was the developmental state. Amsden (1989) places the subsidy as the defining role of the developmental state. A subsidy conditional on a firm's performance, she argues, will both allow and compel manufacturers to become competitive in LDCs where there is an existing comparative advantage in agriculture or simple processing. These two models are of limited relevance. Developmental states have included countries without such high-debt models, including Mauritius and Botswana (Leftwich 2000), Austria and Finland (Vartiainen 1999), and France (Loriaux 1999). The developmental role of the state is potentially wider than mediating bank-based borrowing or subsidies. The mobilisation of resources through the state's own budget was crucial in achieving developmental outcomes in Brazil between 1968 and 1980 (Krieckhaus 2002). In Singapore the government used its monopoly in utilities to turn the internal terms of trade against workers and boost the profitability of public enterprises and so also government savings (Huff 1999). In Taiwan production was often carried out in state enterprises (Wade 1990). The Pakistani state achieved developmental-type outcomes in the 1960s through high levels of private investment (funded by foreign aid) directed through state development banks (Chapter 5).

Lack of a political economy

The economic school can sound like a wish list of desirable policies, with little attention being paid to the practicalities of implementation. Late industrialisation is a case of pure learning-by-doing, utilising technological innovations already commercialised in developed countries. A subsidy represents one method of getting prices wrong, to make manufacturing activity profitable enough to compensate for the uncertainty, expense and effort of learning-by-doing (Amsden 1989). Proponents of such policies tend to have no political economy of learning (Amsden 1989, 1997; Lall 1992, 1995, 1999). Producing is a necessary, but not sufficient, condition to learn. Firms may simply follow a low road of growth, relying on low wages, long hours and cheap costs to remain competitive, or simply remain as high-cost, inefficient producers. There are important political economy pre-conditions for rents to be used to promote learning. Rents must be allocated in a contingent manner, and withdrawn from those firms failing to learn, export or reduce costs. The bureaucracy must be competent enough to allocate rents ex-ante to potentially dynamic capitalists or, ex-post, strong enough to withdraw them from failing capitalists. The political economy relation of the state with the capitalist class is crucial (Khan 2000a).

Another example is New Growth Theory. This seeks to model the sources of productivity growth, focusing on technological spillovers or learning-by-doing (Romer 1986, 1990; Lucas 1988). An important implication of the theory is that government policies can have a permanent impact on the growth rate, to boost human capital (Lucas 1988), to provide goods complementary to private production such as infrastructure (Barro 1990), to promote R&D (Romer 1990). It is difficult, when desirable policy is theoretically so obvious, to explain why governments continue for example to fail to attain 100% literacy. Only by going beyond the narrow confines of the economic school to a broader political economy perspective can we answer such questions. Easterly (2001b) examines the 'political economy of growth without development' that he argues has characterised Pakistan since independence. Social indicators in Pakistan have improved more slowly than in countries with similar GDP growth/levels of per capita income. Hasnain (2008) finds that the distinction in Pakistan is between targeted and general public goods and is a consequence of politicians building personal support bases in the context of weak and fragmented political party systems. School buildings and teacher salaries have identifiable (grateful) beneficiaries who are useful to cultivate in political patron–client networks. More general public goods such as the 'quality' of education are hard to verify and claim credit for by political patrons. Easterly (2001b) argues that the oligarchy[2] that rules Pakistan may prefer a low-growth low-education outcome in preference to the risk of a more educated population demanding political power.

There is a large literature on the role of public investment in creating profitable investment opportunities for the private sector. Crowding in occurs when private sector investment is conditional or contingent on public investment. This may be for many reasons: the long gestation of investments such as power-supply; the limited size of domestic capital markets; the risk of large investments without precedent in an LDC; and the fact that much of the benefit from such projects is external to the original investment. Investment in energy supply, for example, may not in itself be profitable, but the social benefits of creating investment opportunities in private sector industry may be enormous (Hirschman 1958). There has been some work on crowding in of private investment in the Pakistan context. The general finding is that public investment has a positive impact on private investment (Khan 1988; Hyder 2001; Naqvi 2002; Ahmed and Qayyam 2007), though some argue the opposite (Ghani and ud Din 2006). We need to venture into the realms of political economy for an explanation. An influential effort in the Indian context is that of Bardhan (1984). He argued that India has a fragmented social structure and, in order to appease everyone, the state was forced to expand unproductive subsidies at the expense of productive public investment. Burki (1999) echoes this argument for Pakistan in the 1990s, when the politicisation of public investment allocation reduced its economic productivity.

Complementarity is important (but not enough)

There has been some limited discussion of complementarity in the economic school. An important lesson from early development economists such as Scitovsky and Rosenstein-Rodan is that system-wide change, such as industrialisation, requires co-ordination. A stylised example is that of a steel mill and a shipbuilding industry, the former supplying

52 *Theoretical framework*

inputs to the latter, and neither being profitable without the other. Contracts between individual private agents to guarantee and, if necessary, enforce complementary investment may be too costly to draw up and monitor. The state has potentially a number of roles to co-ordinate investment, open both sectors as state-owned enterprises, or subsidise private production (Chang 1999). This debate is useful but limited; it focuses entirely on production and neglects the related and necessary complementary roles of finance (mobilising and allocating the economic surplus to those wishing to invest) and institutions (necessary to overcome the inherent conflicts associated with development).

The political school

The political school focuses on the capacity of the state to identify and implement policies that can correct for the various market failures outlined by the economic school. Criticisms reviewed here are the limited analysis of what the state should do, the relation between different theories, and lack of dynamics.

What should the state do?

Quite frequently, the political school gives a very clear story about the constraints facing the state, but no clear idea of what exactly the state is constrained from doing. Jaffrelot (2002) notes the heterogeneity of Pakistan, its division by caste, biraderi, tribe and language. Harriss-White (2003) argues that the local state in India is constrained by various similar 'social structures of accumulation'. With a social structure of patriarchy, for example, gender influences access to the state, and males are better able to secure loans, subsidies, and production licences. Social structures help explain why state intervention is distorted, and the most efficient potential producers are unable to secure access to resources. For India, Bardhans' (1984) political economy featured three dominant proprietary classes, the industrial bourgeoisie, rich farmers and professionals. There is wide agreement that such classes were similarly influential in Pakistan (Amjad 1982; Rashid and Gardezi 1983; Alavi 1983; Easterly 2001b), and for the case of Pakistan we may want to add the military (Jalal 1990) and foreign sectors (Ali 2008) as other dominant proprietary classes. Bardhan argues that this class structure compelled the state to reduce productive investment and expand subsidies to placate the various dominant proprietary classes. In these few examples the detailed discussion of the constraints facing the state is juxtaposed with a very simple discussion of what the state should be doing. The only desirable state policy analysed by Bardhan is public investment. How exactly his political economy influences all those other factors relevant for growth – mobilisation of tax revenues, learning, technology policies, provision of education and health, complementarity between investment projects and so on is not discussed.

The relation between different theories

Chapter 2 showed that numerous variables have been proposed and tested as potential determinants of growth, but that there is no way to reconcile these findings. There is the same problem with the political economy school. Each political economy seeks to answer its own question within its own terms of reference; it is not clear how any of these relate to each other. Ali (2008), for example, argues that Pakistan has since independence been a dependent economy, and subservient to the interests of the USA. Burki (1974) argues that the rise of small-town-based industrialists and workers was a crucial socio-political change that undermined Ayub's attempts to de-politicise Pakistan in the 1960s. Jalal (1990) argues that Pakistan is dominated by the military. Zaidi (2005) argues that the rise of the middle classes in Pakistan, particularly from the 1990s, has led to a decline of ideology and a more narrow-minded and self-interested politics. There is very little effort to explore the ways in which these different political economy explanations relate to each other, or whether they are all true, contradictory or complementary.

The lack of dynamics

The political school has catalogued the various ways in which the state is constrained from implementing 'ideal' growth-promoting policies. Rarely is it explored how these constraints change over time. Without dynamics, such analysis is wooden, deterministic and a-historical, as events overtake theorising. Alavi (1983) argues that the benefits of the green revolution in the 1960s were enjoyed by the existing class of large and influential farmers. This is difficult to reconcile with the agricultural bias and pro-industry strategy of the 1950s (Chapter 4). Alternatively, Amjad (1983) argues that the strength of merchant capital dictated the shift to an industrialisation strategy in the 1950s; this is difficult to reconcile with the very successful efforts to promote the green revolution in the 1960s (Chapter 5). Burki (1999) argues that the advent of democratisation in the 1990s politicised investment and reduced its productivity (Chapter 7). It is difficult to reconcile this argument with the huge increases in public investment that occurred during the democratic period under Bhutto in the 1970s and that are widely argued to have been still sustaining growth into the 1980s (Chapter 6). The strong autonomous and military government of Zia in the 1980s made only slow progress at liberalisation, while the weak governments of Benazir and Nawaz in the 1990s made much more progress (Chapter 7). This problem echoes a key idea of this book. When analysing economic growth, all too often long-run averages are taken and a long-run explanation sought. This fails to acknowledge that, in Pakistan, as in other LDCs, growth is a process characterised by episodes of growth and stagnation. We need to begin with a political economy that lends itself to dynamic analysis and can model sharp changes in economic growth. To take Bardhan (1984) as an example, how did the three dominant proprietary classes emerge and change over time? How then did public investment increase after 1951, decline after 1965 and rise again in the early 1980s?

An integration of the economic and political schools

Fine and Stoneman (1996) argued that, as of 1996, attempts to integrate these two schools were limited. After 1996 a number of new efforts have emerged, this section reviews some of these.

Grabowski (1994) analysed the process by which the developmental state emerges and the constraints that exist on its capacity to successfully intervene to promote learning. Export-led development, argues Grabowski, requires prior learning in the use of new technology in production for the domestic market (import-substitution). The success of government policy in promoting learning depends on the state's ability to make rents (subsidies and protection) conditional on learning. The credibility of the threat to withdraw protection is directly linked to the size of the domestic market. With a large domestic market, the state can withdraw protection and promote another sector or firm, making the threat to withdraw rents more credible. In a small market, it is more likely that only one firm can be established in an industry, so the threat to withdraw protection is less credible. Huff et al. (2001) extend Grabowski's model. They developed a multi-period model to capture the interaction of the state with the private sector. The model examines more closely the features of the developmental state highlighted by Leftwich (2000). The first three (a developmental elite, relative autonomy of the developmental state and a powerful, competent and insulated economic bureaucracy), they argue, are important initial conditions. The next three (the capacity for effective management of private economic interests, and a mix of repression, poor human rights, legitimacy and performance), they argue, are likely only to emerge over time. In their model, the state undertakes investment complementary to private sector investment (infrastructure, training, social overhead capital, etc.), at the cost of forgone consumption. The private sector responds with more directly productive investment that generates economic growth. A soft state is unlikely to overcome the opportunity cost of forgoing current consumption. If the private sector believes the state to be soft, it is unlikely to invest. The state requires credibility, followed by reputation building, and reinforced by success, to mature into a developmental state. Huff et al. (2001) model the process as a repeated prisoner's dilemma game, with simultaneous investment by each player. The developmental state is one that manages to convince the private sector by building up a reputation that it won't renege[3] and reduce investment for higher current consumption.

Khan (2000 a, b, c) takes three criteria and uses them to model the emergence of *political* constraints on and the *economics* of state intervention in general and developmental states in particular. These are the nature of patron-client regimes, primitive accumulation[4] and learning. For example, the emergence of both economic dynamism and corruption in East Asia (South Korea under President Park and the Kuomintang in Taiwan) he attributes to a distribution of social power, which sustained patrimonial networks. The state was able to enforce rights and re-allocate/change them at low cost. The state was able to channel primitive accumulation towards creating a dynamic capitalist class. In a clientelist regime, such as India, state officials, he argues, can be challenged by other officials and private agents in competing clientelist coalitions. Rights are then likely to be allocated, not to those able to use them most efficiently, but to those with superior organisational power. Competition resulted in the creation of excessive new rights, excessive entry into industries and white-collar employment, and transfers to retain political allegiance, rather than promote learning.

Pingle (1999) lacks a clear statement of the *economic* role of a developmental state. His analysis revolves around bureaucrats acting as entrepreneurs by promoting exports, allocating credit and using trade protection to create national and competitive industries. His analysis is interesting in that it focuses on how the Indian state was differentially developmental in relation to different economic sectors. He argues, for example, that the state successfully promoted the dynamic growth of the computer software sector and restricted the growth of the steel sector. Pingle's *political* analysis of the state focuses on whether the state has a cohesive organisational structure – in particular, whether the bureaucracy is autonomous from special interests, has informal channels of communication with industry that permit the successful two-way flow of information, and whether politicians give the bureaucracy space for innovative policy making. One relevant example in his comparative discussion is that of the software sector. Software was dominated by small firms that were unable to develop clientelist ties with the bureaucracy (Department of Electronics). Software entrepreneurs were largely demanding public goods, such as satellite facilities, that could not be provided by private individuals. Software had a focus on international markets, which necessitated policies to nurture growth, not protect markets. Finally, the sector had a successful and strong industry association (NASSCOM) that demonstrated a remarkable capacity for collective action.

Chibber (2003) has a clear conception of the *economic* role of the state. His developmental state is one that subsidises learning and extracts performance from private firms through setting standards, monitoring performance and influencing the direction of investment. Chibber argues that *political* constraints on the ability of the state to make subsidies conditional on learning were severely compromised at the outset of independence. He argues that the choice of development strategy acted as a constraint on the developmental aspirations of the state. The Quit India movement in 1942 motivated large-scale withdrawal of British capital, which provided ample market niches for domestic capital to reap profits without requiring state intervention. The subsequent choice of import substitution as a development strategy furthered this dynamic. Without the threat of being exposed to world class competition, the connection between profitability and performance was severed, and local business had even less reason to accept a disciplinary state. The Planning Commission (PC) and resulting industrial policy legislation were both severely compromised by the inability of the state to override these incentives faced by domestic capital. The PC after independence was mainly an advisory body, its punitive and disciplinary components were drastically watered down, and real power was left with the ministries (Chibber 2003: 146). The PC had no power to demand compliance by the other ministries in transmitting information, abiding by plan targets, or monitoring firms. From these unpromising initial conditions, planning and state capacity were eroded further by a dynamic that delegitimised state intervention. The PC was associated with failure, domestic capital managed to work the system, and other Ministries increasingly ignored the requisites of planning. The death of Nehru in 1964 deprived planning of its most influential supporter. Nehru's replacement, Lal Bahadur Shastri, undermined the PC by forming the alternative Prime Minister's Secretariat. Indira Gandhi after 1966 marginalised the institution further, treating it as simply an advisory body (Chibber 2003: 207).

This book is a follow up to McCartney (2009a), which looked at the case of India, and a contribution to these other efforts to integrate the political and economic roles of the state. These two books see that the state has two *economic* roles, first, the financial role, to allocate the economic surplus to those able to invest productively and second, the production role, to ensure that financial resources so allocated are used productively, to either raise productivity in an existing market niche (learning) or to upgrade to a higher-technology market niche. The *political* role of the state focuses on the institutions necessary to mediate the relationship between the inherent conflicts associated with economic growth. In this work a broad institutional perspective is considered. A repressive state, an inclusive state or an ideological state can help reduce the negative implications of conflict on development.

The (economic) role of the state: finance

This section explores the financial role of the state in allocating the economic surplus to those able to invest productively. This section also explores the four complementary means of doing so, mobilising resources through the domestic financial system or through the state budget, influencing the profitability of the private sector (accumulation through retained earnings), and utilising international capital.

This book is rooted in classical theory, which places at the centre of its analysis the mobilisation and allocation of the economic surplus. Smith, Ricardo and Marx all argued that the pursuit of profit was the principle motive for investment and hence economic growth (Hunt 1989; Caporaso and Levine 1992; Clarke 1994; Eltis 2000). From Ricardo, this book agrees that agriculture is important. Agriculture produces the principal wage-good, food, which influences the labour costs of production and hence the profitability of the corporate sector. The transfer of resources from agriculture to industry is also often an important source of the available economic surplus. Chapter 4 shows that influencing the agricultural terms of trade was an important source of industrial profits in 1950s Pakistan. From Marx, this book draws the view that, in the case of production with a surplus, the price is no longer determined solely by the structure of production. The distribution of income becomes a matter of political struggle, for example, as emphasised by Marx, the conflict between labour (wages) and capital (profits). Chapter 5 in this book shows how the Pakistani state in the 1960s was crucial in mediating this conflict to the benefit of profits. From the neo-Marxists including Baran, this book notes that much of the surplus in an LDC is likely to be latent, and wasted on luxury consumption, speculation, land and real estate trade. And even if mobilised, the surplus can be wasted on unproductive investments or drained from the domestic economy through various forms of unequal exchange with developed economies. Chapter 5 of this book shows that the economic surplus raised productive investment in the 1960s, while Chapter 7 demonstrates that much of the surplus in the 1990s was wasted on political patronage. Ricardo noted that rich landlords had a high propensity to consume from rental income, while Lewis argued that capitalists tended to save and invest profit income. Chapter 4 here shows that much of government development policy in Pakistan after the 1950s was based on very similar assumptions.

The allocation of the surplus

Neo-classical economics does not acknowledge the problems inherent in allocating the surplus. Rational individuals will make rational decisions about their optimal time path of consumption, as modelled by theories such as the Life-Cycle and Permanent Income Hypotheses. Where income exceeds consumption, the resulting savings will provide a pool of savings for profit-maximising firms to compete for. Product market competition will compel firms to invest those savings in the most efficient manner possible.

The role of the state in allocating the surplus must be analysed as a question of political economy; an 'efficient' allocation is unlikely to occur simply through the market. Groups may block the allocation of the surplus to an emerging capitalist class even if, as in neo-classical theory, they are maximising their interest income and capitalists are maximising growth/profits. Groups may resist taxation, the revenues from which are intended for productive subsidies, even if they may receive higher incomes in the future from growth of GDP or increased employment. Groups may block such potentially Pareto optimal allocations for two reasons, one connected with commitment and the other with political power. In the case of commitment, we have what Acemoglu (2002) called a 'Political Coase Theorem'. When property rights are well defined and there are no transaction costs, economic agents will contract to achieve efficient (output- or surplus-maximising) outcomes, irrespective of who has the property right. Extending this to the political sphere would imply that economic and political transactions would create a strong tendency towards policies and institutions that achieve the best economic outcome regardless of which social group has political power. The surplus, in other words, would be allocated by the state to those best able to invest it productively, and those from whom the surplus was mobilised would receive a credible promise of dividends, higher employment or some other tangible future reward. In reality, groups may block such transfers, because there can be no credible or enforceable commitment that they will be compensated once economic change has occurred. The state may tax individuals and use the money to subsidise capitalists, but there can be no credible commitment that the state will then be able to tax those capitalists to the benefit of the original taxpayers. The second related reason is that existing powerful interest groups may block the introduction of 'efficient' transfers because it may simultaneously affect the distribution of political power. The prospect of the state being able to tax a newly created capitalist class may be reduced once they have accumulated and gained added political leverage over the state and other classes in society.

A further critique of the neo-classical model is the black box at the centre of its analysis. The model assumes that financial intermediaries automatically emerge to facilitate the transfer of the surplus. The next sections of the chapter show that, in developing countries, the state is likely to play an important role, through promoting the banking system, taxation/subsidies, influencing the rate of profit (hence retained earnings) and influencing patterns and levels of the flow of international capital.

Domestic capital: the financial system and economic development

The economic role of a financial system

Financial markets have five basic functions, to mobilise savings, to allocate resources, to facilitate risk management, to monitor managers and exert corporate control, and to facilitate the exchange of goods and services (Levine 1997). Mobilisation is assisted by the creation of small-denomination financial instruments that provide opportunities for households to hold diversified portfolios and still invest in large firms. Financial markets and institutions may arise to ease the trading, hedging and pooling of risk. Individual savers may not have the time or capacity to evaluate firms, managers and market conditions. Pooled groups of individuals under the auspices of a financial intermediary can share the fixed costs of acquiring and processing information about investments. The financial sector also provides liquidity and debt instruments that can facilitate the exchange of goods and services.

The role of the state in a financial system

The state has six potential roles in a financial system in an LDC: (i) to protect deposits in a fractional reserve system; (ii) to mobilise domestic savings; (iii) to allocate resources to projects essential for development; iv) to create institutions to mobilise private sector savings; (v) to correct market failures that may exist in the allocation of credit to small firms; and (vi) to protect high-debt financial systems.[5]

To protect deposits

In any fractional reserve banking system there is a possibility of a run on deposits leading to a collapse of the financial system. This creates the need for prudential regulation and deposit insurance. The banking system differentiates between good and bad borrowers, builds up expertise in evaluating borrowers, and establishes long-term relationships with customers. Bernanke (1983) blames the severity of the 1930s economic depression on the interruption of these relationships. The (temporary) shocks between 1930 and 1933 and the resulting disruption to long-term relationships, he argues, undermined the effectiveness of the financial system in performing these roles.

To mobilise domestic savings through the state budget

Wade (1990) focuses on the state's role in allocating resources for investment, Amsden (1989) in accelerating learning, Evans (1995) in promoting certain industrial sectors, and Khan (various dates) the creation of rents. The role of subsidies and state expenditure presupposes the mobilisation of resources, but little attention is paid to how this is achieved by the state. Krieckhaus (2002) notes that the state played an important role in resource mobilisation in East Asia. Weyland (1998) charts the rise and fall of the developmental state in Brazil in terms of its ability to raise public savings.[6] Sindzigre (2007) blames the absence of developmental-state-type efforts in sub-Saharan Africa on the inability of states to raise tax revenue. In general, the literature goes no further than an implicit discussion of the state's role, hinting that individuals have a 'psychology of impatience' and place an excessive premium on current consumption. More detailed discussion has been taken up by the extreme left, and the discussion of collectivisation as a means to mobilise a surplus from an 'irrational' peasantry class. 'In a socialist planned economy, both the structure of the social product and the disposal of it are subject to conscious, rational determination on the part of the socialist society. ... the vital need for the mobilization of the economic surplus generated in agriculture' (Baran 1957: 424).

Allocating resources to projects essential for development

The state has an important role in allocating the surplus towards projects essential for economic development, which are otherwise not likely to be undertaken by the private sector. This may be for many reasons: the long-gestation of certain investments such as power-supply; the limited size of domestic capital markets; the risk of large investments without precedent in a country undergoing the initial uncertainties of industrialisation; and the fact that much of the benefit from such projects is external to the original investment. For example, investment in energy supply may not in itself be profitable, but the social benefits of creating profitable investment opportunities in private sector industry may be enormous (Hirschman 1958).

In Taiwan state enterprises took over production in sectors where the efficient scale of production was very capital-intensive and large relative to both factor and product markets, and where linkages to downstream enterprises were high. These included petroleum refining, petrochemicals, steel and other basic metals, shipbuilding, heavy machinery, transport equipment, and fertiliser (Wade 1990: 179). The output share of public enterprises consistently exceeded 12% of GDP between 1951 and 1980, over 30% of total national investment,[7] and by the 1990s over 50% of total investment (Amsden 2001). In Korea by comparison, the state facilitated, guaranteed and co-ordinated foreign borrowing by privately owned firms (Amsden 1989: 128–9). The impact need not be deliberate. Tahir (1995) for example found that there is a positive relationship between defence spending and economic growth in Pakistan. This, he explains, was due to defence expenditure providing skills, modern attitudes and infrastructure, boosting aggregate demand, and perhaps reducing domestic conflict.

Government influence over the price and allocation of bank lending to the private sector was central to economic development in Japan, Continental Europe, East and Southeast Asia and Brazil. Priority lending targets and supporting tax incentives were established by sector. The state also assisted in the provision of stable long-term finance by creating specialised development banks.[8] The need to socialise risk applies in the case of those sectors exposed to correlated risk, such as interest rate changes or recession. This applies particularly in sectors with high minimum efficient scale and large volumes of sunk capital. This necessitates a further role for the state, to reduce the risk of financial instability, through deposit insurance, lender-of-last-resort facilities, subsidies to firms in financial difficulties, banks' shareholdings in companies, and government ownership of banks (Wade 1990: 366). Financial systems have proved most successful in promoting development when the state has effectively subordinated them to the goal of economic development (Chang and Grabel 2004: Ch10). The principal criterion for evaluating the performance of the financial system in this book will be consideration of its functional efficiency, whether it promotes rapid economic growth, rather than criteria such as liquidity and international integration.

Creating institutions to mobilise private sector savings

The state can also play an important role in mobilising resources indirectly, by creating institutions to mobilise private sector savings. Risk-averse households are more likely to be responsive to deposit security and intermediation efficiency than to interest rates. Household savings depend crucially on the extent of the bank branching network, which the state has a crucial role in spreading. The state can intervene by regulating the spread between loan (higher) and deposit rates (lower). This creates an economic rent for banks, relative to the situation prevailing in a fully liberalised financial sector. With higher returns to intermediation, banks will have a stronger incentive to increase their own deposit base, by for example opening new branches in rural areas. The state needs to restrict competition in the banking sector that could eliminate these rents. Under this model of financial restraint, the dominant mode of competition will be non-price competition, such as locality and quality of service (Kok-Fay and Jomo 2000).

Correcting market failures in the allocation of credit to small firms

The state has an important role in ensuring finance is available on reasonable terms for small firms. Much economic theory and empirical work assumes that capital markets are perfect, with a representative firm facing an infinitely elastic supply of capital. Investment then depends on the demand for and cost of capital, and state-directed credit will be ineffective. In practice, there are transaction costs and/or information asymmetries that mean the supply of credit will be imperfectly inelastic. External equity is subject to agency costs associated with the verification of firms' performance. Legal and accounting systems in LDCs may make verification more difficult. There are likely to be scale economies in verification, leading to a situation in which only large firms can access private sector capital markets. With asymmetric information, firms may find that credit is rationed at a fixed rate of interest on the basis of criteria that differ between large and small firms. Small firms may be constrained in investment by internal financing. Directed credit can then be effective in overcoming credit rationing faced by small firms. Eastwood and Kohli (1999) found that large firms were better able to obtain external finance in India than small firms.

Tax, transfers and subsidy

The economic role of transfers and subsidies

In the standard Heckscher-Ohlin trade model, the assumption of perfect knowledge (technology) is the key assumption that renders all countries in the same industry equally productive. The only policy choice for an uncompetitive country is to adjust prices (reduce wages), not to develop know-how (subsidise learning). Amsden (2001) questions these assumptions, arguing that there are three generic knowledge capabilities that nurture knowledge-based assets. These, she notes, are production capabilities (the ability to transform inputs into outputs), project execution skills (the skills necessary to expand capacity), and innovation capabilities (the skills necessary to design entirely new products and processes). Given differences in knowledge capabilities, productivity will tend to vary sharply among firms in the same industry.[9] Endowments, and hence the price of land, labour and capital, no longer uniquely determine competitiveness. Low wages (labour abundance) may be no compensation for high productivity (knowledge abundance). 'In late industrialising countries, the state intervenes with subsidies deliberately to distort relative prices to stimulate (manufacturing) economic activity' (Amsden 1989: 8). Late industrialisation is a case of pure learning-by-doing, utilising technological innovations that have been already commercialised in developed countries.[10] 'The subsidy serves as a symbol of late industrialisation, not just in Korea and Taiwan, but also in Japan, the Latin American countries, and so on. The First Industrial Revolution was built on laissez-faire, the Second on infant industry protection. In late industrialisation, the foundation is the subsidy – which includes both protection and financial incentives. The allocation of subsidies has rendered the government not merely as a banker, as Gerschenkron (1962) conceived it, but an entrepreneur, using the subsidy to decide what, when, and how much to produce. The subsidy has also changed the process whereby relative prices are determined' (Amsden 1989: 143–4).

Role of the state in transfers and subsidies

The most obvious prerequisite for subsidies is that the state has raised sufficient resources. Rapidly growing Asian NICs did not have small states as was suggested by Kuznets (1988) and others. They were successful in mobilising the resources necessary to subsidise the industrial sector extensively (Wade 1990: 173).

Retained earnings and profitability

The economic role of retained earnings and profitability

The state can influence private sector profitability and hence the private sector's capacity to finance investment from internal resources.

The role of the state in boosting retained earnings and profitability

In contrast to neo-classical economic theory, the state may influence the distribution of income by shifting income from wages to profits. The neo-classical view that all factors of production will be paid their marginal products and so income distribution will be market-determined is mistaken. When production takes place with a surplus, all prices are potentially political (Chang 1999). This role of the state draws attention to the idea, discussed later in this chapter, that development is an inherently conflictual process.

Potential mechanisms to ensure high profit rates are many and varied. Kuznets (1988) emphasises the roles of 'flexible' labour markets and union repression that allow rapid growth in labour demand, and ensure that productivity growth consistently exceeds wage growth. Many late industrialising countries retained strict controls on entry into industries to prevent over-expansion and declining profitability. Such

62 *Theoretical framework*

controls were used frequently (in Taiwan) in sectors where the minimum efficient scale of production was large (Wade 1990: 185). In many sectors, controls on commodity markets prevented firms from competing with one another on the basis of price and undermining profitability, for example, in Korean chaebols (Amsden 1989: 152) or in Malaysian banks (Koy-Fay and Jomo 2000). In Singapore the government used its monopoly in utilities to turn the internal terms of trade against workers and boost the profitability of public enterprises (Huff 1999).

International capital

The Economic Role of International Capital

International capital in its various forms can supplement domestic capital (portfolio investment and lending) and also add directly to production (foreign direct investment). These are examined in turn.

The role of the state vis-à-vis international capital

The state has five principal roles with respect to international capital: (i) co-ordinating foreign borrowing; (ii) influencing the end use of foreign debt; (iii) controlling the disruptive potential of short-term capital flows; (iv) influencing the composition of capital inflows; and (v) segmenting domestic and international capital markets.

Co-ordination of private foreign borrowing

The state needs to co-ordinate private foreign borrowing. International capital now comprises 70 times the volume of world trade, and 80% of net global foreign exchange transactions have a maturity of seven days or less. It is important for the government to maintain information on government holdings of currency reserves relative to private and public foreign currency debt. Unco-ordinated financial liberalisation in Korea in the early 1990s was a disaster. The domestic banking sector drove explosive growth in Korea's foreign debt, from $44bn in 1993 to $120bn in 1997; much of this was private, and 65% was short term (Wade 1999). Almost one-third of total foreign debt moved outside the scope of financial regulation and supervision, though it constituted foreign exchange liabilities for the government.

Influencing the end use of foreign debt

The state needs to influence the end use of foreign debt to ensure that it is used for productive developmental purposes. Prior to financial liberalisation in the 1990s, East and Southeast Asia had tightly co-ordinated allocation and access to foreign loans. After liberalisation in the 1990s, capital inflow into five Asian NICs[11] increased from $47bn in 1993 to $93bn in 1996. Much of the inflow took the form of borrowing in dollars and yen by banks, investment houses and insurers and was invested in short-term debt (Wade 1998).

Controlling the disruptive potential of short-term capital flows

The state has an important role in controlling the disruptive potential of short-term capital flows. Foreign loans are often associated with the problems of maturity mismatch, where long-term investment is financed by short-term loans. Capital outflow can then force asset sales to realise debt repayments and lead to a downward spiral in asset prices. Accompanying devaluation will increase the cost of imported industrial inputs. High debt/equity ratios worsen the problem by generating a bigger multiplier effect to a given reduction in demand and cash flow. Such a situation can become a crisis even without poor underlying economic fundamentals – or a self-fulfilling crisis: 'the expectations, even the prejudices of investors become economic fundamentals' (Krugman 1999: 110). A self-fulfilling withdrawal of short-term loans can be fuelled by the recognition by each investor that others are withdrawing; since the debt is short term, it is rational for each investor to join in the panic. There is a large literature exploring the inherent instability of a private financial system (Keen 2001: Ch10). There were some very sharp reversals in capital flows during the 1990s. Examples include Mexico between 1993 and 1996: a net shift of $55bn (or 12% of GDP); South Korea in 1996/97: $40bn (9% of GDP); and Thailand 1996/97: $23bn (15%).

Influencing the composition of capital inflows

The state has an important role in influencing the composition of capital inflows. In general FDI has greater potential benefits than short-term portfolio investment. FDI was far more stable during the Mexican crisis in 1994/95 and the Asian crisis in 1997/98. Policy can distinguish between short-term capital and FDI that is accompanied by technology transfer, capital equipment and management expertise.

Segmenting domestic and international capital markets

To implement a sectoral industrial policy, the state needs to segment domestic and international capital markets. With firms free to borrow on international markets and foreign banks free to lend, the government's influence over lending will be weakened. 'Foreign exchange controls are needed to intensify the cycle of investment and reinvestment within the national territory' (Wade 1990: 367). There is evidence that capital controls in Malaysia in 1998 were effective in segmenting Malaysia's financial markets from international capital markets. Such controls were implemented transparently, efficiently and with no increase in petty corruption. As a result, economic recovery was faster, employment and wages did not suffer as much, the stock market did better, interest rates fell more and inflation was lower than in other countries suffering from the 1997 Asian crisis (Kaplan and Rodrik 2001).

The role of the state and foreign direct investment (FDI)

The literature highlights both positive and negative effects of FDI, and empirical evidence is mixed. The role of the state is to maximise the net benefits of FDI.

64 *Theoretical framework*

Theoretical costs of FDI

There is a long tradition analysing the potential problems of FDI. The traditional critique of FDI centres on ideas that MNCs tend to transfer inappropriate technology, could exercise power over political and economic conditions in the host nation,[12] and have been able to evade taxes through transfer pricing. There is a long history of thinking among followers of the dependency school that foreign investment will perpetuate underdevelopment and increase internal polarisation within the periphery (Hunt 1989: Ch7). In the long run 'foreign investment must be looked upon as a method of pumping surplus out of under-developed areas, not as a channel through which surplus is directed into them' (Baran and Sweezy 1966: 110). There is a long history of such thinking being influential in the Indian nationalist movement Nehru, (1946: 544) and beyond (Bagchi 1976).

Theoretical benefits of FDI

MNCs that develop forward and backward linkages in the host economy are more likely to be beneficial than those that operate as highly integrated units. Competition in one sector may be beneficial to firms in others through price reductions and forward linkages to customer firms. FDI may also create demand for local output, and these 'backward linkages' may strengthen supply industries, in turn via forward linkages benefiting other local firms. MNCs in East Asia were successful in creating backward linkage effects to local suppliers (Hobday 1995). The most important linkage effects are through technological externalities. Local firms may adopt MNC technology through imitation or reverse engineering (the demonstration effect). This effect represents a potential positive externality. Workers trained by an MNC may transfer knowledge to a local firm (knowledge-spillover effect), or start their own firms (labour-turnover effect). Rhee (1990) studied the importance of this effect for the textile sector in Bangladesh. Initial investment and training by the Korean firm Daewoo led to massive transfer of skills and learning to other textile firms by the movement of workers from the pioneer firm. Rhee calls this 'the catalyst model of economic development'. MNCs may transfer technology to firms that are potential suppliers of intermediate goods or buyers of their own products (a vertical linkages effect). There are quite a few empirical studies confirming evidence of positive spillovers (Kokko and Blomstrom 1995; Chuang and Lin 1999; Aitken and Harrison 1999; Saggi 2002).

The role of the state in promoting benefits from FDI

The state has an important indirect role, to maximise the net benefits from FDI. The magnitude of positive spillovers has been found to depend on local endowments of skills and technology, the capability of local educational and research institutions, technological capability of local firms, and infrastructure (Lall 1992; Pantibala and Petersen 2002; Gorg and Greenaway 2004). The state also has a potentially more strategic role. An industrial policy that targets particular types of technology can be important. Higher-end technologies such as R&D investment generate more spillovers than low-end operations of MNCs such as data-feeding and coding operations (Pantibala and Petersen 2002). Enforcing an export obligation on FDI is also important. FDI attracted by high domestic tariffs to produce for the domestic market in an LDC can lead to negative spillovers (Brecher and Diaz-Alejandro 1977). Within a protective regime, MNCs may not be motivated to transfer new technologies, as initial technology advantages continue to provide them with an edge over local firms. Balasubramanyam *et al.* (1996) find that FDI in export-promoting countries has a positive effect on economic growth and no significant effect on growth in import-substitution countries. Delderbos *et al.* (2001) note that if the main motivation of FDI is to avoid trade barriers, limiting production to simple assembly operations may be the most cost-effective activity by MNCs. Granting foreign firms unnecessarily large subsidies, reducing restrictions on profit repatriation, liberalisation of regulations on technology transfer, and exemptions on national labour and environmental regulations can lead to a race to the bottom. Japan, South Korea and Taiwan mandated local content requirements (the proportion of local inputs used in the production process), with these requirements set at low, but increasing, levels and limited royalties on technology licences paid by partners of MNCs.

The (economic) role of the state: production

The crucial role of the state with regard to production is to ensure that financial resources allocated to private sector firms are used productively, to either raise productivity in an existing market niche (learning) or to upgrade to a higher-technology market niche.

Neo-classical economics and production

In the neo-classical paradigm there is no role for the state to promote growth, save for removing state-created restrictions on the operation of the free market. An important and explicit theoretical rationale of liberalisation according to neo-classical economics is to achieve an efficient (static) allocation of resources (the theory of comparative advantage). The link to economic growth is implicit: rational individuals will save according to criteria such as the life-cycle hypothesis, and profit-maximising firms will utilise these available resources to invest efficiently.

Need for learning

The theory of comparative advantage assumes that technology is freely available to all countries and firms, which then operate on the same production function. Countries will settle on the appropriate capital/labour ratio in accordance with their factor price ratios (determined by relative endowments of labour and capital) and will shift effortlessly along the production function as these ratios change. International technology markets are assumed to be efficient, thus firms in LDCs can find, select, buy and transfer the technologies they need without additional cost or effort. There is assumed to be no problem in assimilating technology from developed countries, no adaptations are required, and alternatives are available for all factor price combinations. Such models assume that innovation (movements of the production frontier rather than along it) is a completely distinct activity from mastering technology or adapting it to different conditions (the only admissible country differences are capital/labour ratios). In practice, with imperfect knowledge, productivity may differ among firms in the same industry. Technological knowledge is not easily transferred between firms, and much technology is tacit, so requires learning. Firms will not be operating on the same production function. Simply 'getting prices right' may be insufficient for countries to compete internationally.[13] Neo-classical economics assumes that innovation takes place in advanced countries and that learning in LDCs is no more difficult than selecting the most appropriate innovation. There is actually less difference between innovation in developed countries and industrialisation based on learning already-commercialised technology (Lall 1992, 2000; Amsden 1997).

State policy

A typical LDC is most competitive in price-sensitive, low-value, low-priced items. An LDC could compete over time by trying to enhance its price competitiveness by extending hours, reducing overheads (subcontracting), and intensifying work conditions (a low road of competition). A high road of competition would consist of remaining in an existing production niche and raising productivity (learning), or upgrading to a less (price) competitive market niche to capture rents. State intervention is needed to push an economy up the high road of competition.

Specialising in the production and export of labour-intensive, simple, manufactured goods or primary products will leave a country vulnerable. Where barriers to entry are low, global competition will drive prices and profits down. These market conditions can apply both to product markets (primary products) or factor markets (unskilled labour). Rents arise from innovation, and the ability to appropriate rents is crucial for sustained income growth (Kaplinsky 1999). Countries have to raise productivity and product innovation faster than the decline in margins due to competitive pressures. These considerations, rather than market or information failures, are what creates the potential for successful industrial policy by the government.[14]

Neo-classical theory argues that export structures are simply a product of comparative advantage and factor prices, and that the composition of exports does not matter. In practice, while many allocations may be (neo-classically) efficient, some are more (dynamically) efficient than others. Growth in world trade, and spillover benefits for the whole economy, are positively related, and ease of market entry of competitors negatively related, to the technological complexity of a product (Lall 1999: 1775, 2000: 344).

Market failures in learning

Much technology is tacit and, to effectively master it, extensive experience in use is necessary. Learning-by-doing may imply a costly, lengthy and unpredictable period of losses as firms learn and adapt technology to make it more appropriate to LDC conditions. Some learning involves serious externalities and co-ordination problems. In theory, private capital markets could fund firms through the period of learning. In practice, uncertainty, risk and illiquidity mean that private capital will be reluctant. This is especially relevant when an LDC is industrialising and where past history is a poor guide to evaluating future investment and lending decisions. Investment in learning by one entrepreneur who discovers a commercial niche that can be profitably exploited is likely to lead to rapid imitation. Rhee (1990) notes that the number of export-orientated textile factories in Bangladesh exploded after the single firm, Desh, proved that it was a profitable proposition at the end of the 1970s, and by 1985 there were 700 such firms. Learning is an investment, the returns to which cannot be fully appropriated. Entrepreneurs in LDCs face similar problems to innovators in developed countries. Learning is likely then to be under-supplied, so profits/rents that reward and motivate learning may lead to a more dynamically efficient economy, even if they are a sign of resource misallocation according to considerations of static/allocative efficiency (Lall 1992, 2000). While neo-classical economics subscribes to the need for patent protection to generate an incentive for innovation, it advocates complete freedom of market entry in all other scenarios.

These various market failures may generate a need for intervention in both factor and product markets to direct resources to particular activities. By creating rents to motivate the re-allocation of resources, the state will induce and facilitate learning by private actors. Policy needs to increase the expected payoff to learning, hence it is important to distinguish those firms that are engaged in costly learning and those that simply imitate the learning of others. Temporary trade protection, for example, may increase profits from producing and learning, but only for firms producing for the domestic market (Hausmann and Rodrik 2003). Trade protection or export subsidies do not discriminate between innovators and imitators. Export subsidies, or government credit contingent on exporting, can allow policy makers to discriminate between firms.

There is a good chance that learning rents will fail to generate growth. The widespread failures of many infant industries protected from international competition to become dynamic, and their instead stagnating on guaranteed profits, are oft cited examples. There are important pre-conditions for rents to promote learning. Rents must be allocated in a contingent manner, and be withdrawn from those firms failing to learn, export or reduce costs. The bureaucracy must be competent enough to allocate rents ex-ante to potentially dynamic capitalists or strong enough, ex-post, to withdraw them from failing capitalists. The relation of the state to various classes is important: to the capitalist class in order to enforce discipline, and ensure that rents are contingent on the state's desired performance criteria. The relation of the state to other non-capitalist classes must be such that they do not mobilise and compel the creation of rents for political, rather than economic, reasons (Khan 2000a).

The (political) role of the state: institutions

There is a large literature looking at the effect of institutions in promoting economic growth (North 1990; Sokoloff and Engerman 2000; Rodrik *et al.* 2002). This section looks at the related but under-researched topic of how institutions can mediate the (negative) relationship between conflict and economic growth. The first part defines development as a conflictual process; the second shows that conflict is bad for economic growth; the third demonstrates how conflict and states' capacities to manage it will be measured here; and the fourth shows that institutions can reduce conflict. Existing analysis of institutions and conflict mainly considers those institutions compatible with neo-liberal economic theory. This book has a broader institutional perspective. A repressive state, an inclusive state, or an ideological state may help reduce the negative implications of conflict on development.

Development and conflict

Economic development is concerned with shifting resources from low- to high-productivity areas. The mobility of some assets will be limited; owners will then face problems of obsolescence and unemployment. Those having sunk investments into physical capital, skills, contractual relationships, and political patronage are likely to resist change (Chang 1999). Elsewhere, this chapter has demonstrated how the process of surplus allocation is inevitably a conflictual process. The dangers to development of ignoring conflict are profound. Many have argued that the failure to incorporate Bengalis during the 1960s led to civil war in 1970/71 and the secession of Bangladesh.

For many LDCs, political evolution after 1945 was characterised by increasing ethnic and class conflict, rioting, mob violence, frequent coups, the alienation of urban political groups, loss of authority by legislatures and courts, and complete disintegration of broadly-based political parties. There was a decline in political order, implying the undermining of the effectiveness, authority and legitimacy of government. Huntingdon argues that 'in large part it was due to rapid social change and mobilisation of new groups into politics and slow development of political institutions' (1968: 4). Social and economic change, such as urbanisation, increased literacy, industrialisation, and expansion of the mass media, had extended political consciousness, multiplied political demands, and increased political participation. The new elite of civil servants and teachers employed by the central government undermined traditional sources of political authority, the secular and religious leaders of the villages, and traditional social networks based around family, class and caste. Economic development also created newly wealthy groups not assimilated into the existing social order. The primary problem of politics was the slower development of political institutions, relative to social and economic change, 'economic development and political stability are two independent goals and progress toward one has no necessary connection with progress toward the other' (Huntingdon 1968: 6).

In the case of India, Kohli described a growing 'crisis of governance' after the mid-1960s, which he defined as a situation of a failure of political coalitions to endure, policy ineffectiveness, and the incapacity to accommodate political conflict without violence (1990). His work is a specific example of Huntingdon's more general thesis. Kohli argued that competitive politics of distribution had politicised existing divisions in society, such as class, ethnicity, language, religion, region and caste. The spread of democratic values had hastened the decline of traditional sources of authority, the 'big men' often of high caste, who had previously controlled vote banks. This was exacerbated by the decline of party organisation and the rise of low-quality leaders with demagogic rather than programmatic appeal. This mobilisation had been focused on the state, which by the mid-1960s was highly interventionist and a key source of livelihoods in a poor developing country.

Conflict is bad for economic growth

Most studies examine a proxy for conflict in the form of 'social divisions' and examine their link with conflict. Persson and Tabellini (1991) find that inequality is bad for economic growth. Mauro (1995) and LaPorta *et al.* (1998) find that ethnic diversity predicts poor quality of government services in developing countries. Goldin and Katz (1997) find lower school graduation rates, and Goldin and Katz (1999) find lower public support for higher education, in US states with more religious and ethnic heterogeneity. Alesina *et al.* (1999) find that ethnically diverse cities in the USA spend less on public goods. Miguel (2000) finds lower primary school funding in more ethnically diverse districts in Kenya. Mauro (1995) and Annett (1999) find that linguistic or religious diversity leads to greater political instability. Easterly and Levine (1997) find an adverse impact of ethno-liguistic fragmentation on income, growth and economic policies in sub-Saharan Africa. Sachs and Warner (1997) find that ethnically diverse countries in sub-Saharan African were more likely to be closed to trade and had lower levels of institutional quality. Rodrik (1999a, 2000b) finds that ethnically polarised nations react more adversely to external terms of trade shocks.

There are various studies that try to capture the specific link between measured conflict and poor economic outcomes. Collier (2007) finds that the risk of war is linked to low incomes. Arunatilake *et al.* (2001) measures the cost of conflict in Sri Lanka. Fosu (1992) finds that political instability (using coups as a proxy) is bad for economic growth. Englebert (2000) finds that government legitimacy is positively associated with economic growth.

Measures/descriptions of state capacities

There are several works that seek to measure the conflict resolution capacities of the state. Rowthorn (1977) agreed that conflict over the distribution of income was endemic in capitalism. Conflict, he argued, occurred between prices relevant to capitalists (profits) and labour (wages) and generated inflation if the combined demands of both classes exceeded total national income. The problem with using inflation as a proxy for conflict is that numerous other factors, such as drought, that are not initially related to conflict, cause inflation. Rudolph and Rudolph (1987) measure conflict that spills outside the normal political system. They record the activities of 'demand groups', such as labour, students, and agricultural interest groups. Their measures of conflict are indices such as strike activity, demonstrations and student indiscipline. The problem with such a measure is that it does not consider latent conflict. A powerful adversarial union need never strike; management or the government will concede quickly for fear of the consequences. The Rudolphs are actually considering a special case of conflict, where contending parties are more equally matched and conflict results in struggle. Kohli (1990) measures conflict occurring through the political system. He argues that electoral competition and the struggle by political entrepreneurs for office has mobilised poorer and lower-caste groups and politicised pre-existing social cleavages. Conflict he measures as the absence of enduring coalitions, policy ineffectiveness, and an inability to accommodate political disagreement without violence. Again, this is too narrow: conflict need not necessarily only occur through the formal political system.

This book draws on this range of sources: from Rowthorn the idea that conflict between labour and capital and the role of profits/income distribution is important; from the Rudolphs that conflict can be society-centred and can be manifest through demand groups; from Kohli that the capacity of the state to govern is an important determinant and result of the effects of conflict. We need, however, a more objective and encompassing measure of the conflict resolution capacity of the state. Budgetary allocations in which investment, tax revenue and national savings are rising are an indication that conflict is being successfully managed. Earlier in this chapter it was argued that discipline is necessary to induce learning; hence, diversification and productivity growth are also signs that conflict is being successfully managed. It is a key idea of this book that conflict is endemic in development, but that the state can overcome conflict through a variety of institutions, inclusive, repressive or ideological.

Institutions can reduce conflict

Easterly (2001c) finds that the ethnic conflict effect on growth in the original Easterly and Levine (1997) growth regressions disappears if institutions are of sufficiently high quality. Good institutions, he finds, also reduce the risk of wars and genocide. Rodrik (1999a, 2000b) explores how institutions may reduce the negative implications of external shocks. He finds that, when social divisions are deep and (his measures of) institutions of conflict management are weak, the economic cost of exogenous shocks such as a decline in the terms of trade are magnified by the resulting distributional conflicts.[15] Once latent social conflict and the quality of conflict management institutions are controlled for, Rodrik finds that various measures of government policy (trade policies, debt-export ratios, government consumption, etc.) contribute almost nothing to explaining growth differentials before and after economic shocks. Mulligan *et al.* (2004) finds that dictatorships tend to spend more of their GDP on the military and are more likely to utilise the death penalty, indicating perhaps a greater reliance on 'repressive institutions' to manage conflict.

Which institutions?

Those institutions tested in the existing literature are mainly those theorised as being important in neo-classical economic theory, in particular, property rights and democratic political institutions. Easterly tests proxies for property rights: 'Institutions that give protection to legal minorities, guarantee freedom from expropriation, grant freedom from repudiation of contracts, and facilitate co-operation for public services would constrain the amount of damage that one ethnic group could do to another. Such pro-business rules of the game may prevent ethnic groups from expropriating business owners of a different ethnic group' (2001c: 6–7). Rodrik (1999a, 2000b) examines institutions that 'adjudicate distributional contests within a framework of rules and accepted procedures without open conflict and hostilities'. These, he argues, include democracy, an independent and effective judiciary, an honest and un-corrupt bureaucracy, and institutionalised modes of social insurance. As proxies, Rodrik uses measures of civil liberties and political rights, quality of governmental institutions, rule of law, competitiveness of political participation, and public expenditure on social insurance.

Democracy and conflict: a critique of Rodrik

Democracies are now commonly argued to be conducive to market-orientated economic reforms. The mechanism is not often made clear, but seems to revolve around the argument that open flows of information, guided by public opinion, can coalesce around optimal (market) solutions. Sen (1999) makes one of the clearest expositions of this general thesis, arguing that economic and political freedoms will reinforce each other. Famously, Sen (1982) pointed out that no substantial famine has ever occurred in an independent country with a democratic form of government and a free-press. Rodrik (1999a) argues that democracy also generates more predictable long-run growth rates, greater economic stability, handles adverse shocks better and has superior distributional outcomes.

A case study of India shows that there is no reason to suppose that democracy will reduce conflict. Democracy can serve to sharpen existing social cleavages through continual pressures for competitive political mobilisation (Kohli 1990). A good example is the impact of the 1969 split of the Congress Party on the politics of the state of Gujarat. Indira Gandhi's branch of the Congress won political power in the state through appealing to backward groups, the Kshatriyas, Harijans, Adivasis and Muslims. The rump of the old Congress retained the support of the high-caste Patidars, who owned the land and dairy co-operatives and were well represented in educational institutions. The numerically dominant Khastriyas came to political power in the 1970s. This generated a separation of socio-economic power (in the hands of the Patidars) and control over local political institutions (wielded by the Kshatriyas), which was resented by the Patidars, who began to resist their political expulsion by force. In 1981 riots and violence spread throughout central Gujarat. Urban riots were centred among medical students in Ahmedabad, where reservation policies for lower-caste students were impacting on the chances of higher-caste students. This pattern has been common across India. Bardhan argues, 'the political arithmetic of group equity and democratic mobilisation, apart from bankrupting the state treasuries and debilitating the government's capacity to invest in necessary social economic infrastructure, has been eating away at the institutional insulation of administrative and economic decision making' (2001: 239).

There is no reason to suppose that democracy will lead to greater protection of property rights. Democracy equalises the right to influence the allocation of resources and so may exacerbate the threat to property from landless peasants and organised labour in particular. The contrary assumption is so widespread that economists regularly use dictatorship as a proxy for weak property rights. Przworski *et al.* (2000: 211) find, to the contrary, that average tax rates are no higher in dictatorships and that dictatorships are less likely to nationalise private firms. Mulligan *et al.* (2004) find that democracy has no effect on corporate tax rates, but does have a slight (negative) effect on rates of personal income tax.

There is widespread empirical evidence to show that democracy is an outcome of development. The typical franchise during industrialisation in today's developed countries was tiny: in France between 1830 and 1848, only 0.6% of the population, while the 1832 Reform Act in England extended voting rights from 14% to 18% of men. Economic development promotes the prerequisites for democracy. (Lipset 1959; Rueschemeyer *et al.* 1992; Huber *et al.* 1993; Barro 1999). Przeworski *et al.* (2000) examined whether democracies are more likely to emerge as countries develop under dictatorships, or, having emerged for reasons other than economic development, are only more likely to survive in countries that are already developed. They conclude that democracy is only likely to emerge/consolidate at high levels of development. Rodrik (1999a) in his analysis of conflict and institutions is actually unearthing the result that countries at high levels of development have lower levels of conflict.

Other institutions

There are other institutions that may reduce the impact of conflict on economic growth. Those analysed in this book are: (i) a repressive state; (ii) inclusive institutions; and (iii) ideological institutions.

A repressive state

The strengthening of repressive institutions is most typical of a traditional society in the early stages of development. Typically, the first challenge of modernisation in a dispersed and weakly articulated traditional feudal system is to concentrate the power necessary to produce changes in the traditional society and economy (Huntingdon 1968). In his characterisation of the developmental state, Leftwich (1995, 2000) argued that institutions may allow the state to implement growth, promoting distributionally non-neutral policies. Among his seven components of a developmental state, Leftwich listed 'relative state autonomy', 'bureaucratic power' and 'a weak or flattened civil society'. These three components focus on the ability of the state to exclude or crush groups that do not benefit from or would oppose growth and industrialisation. Authors have discussed this idea in a variety of contexts. Of India, Bardhan said 'In the context of economic growth it is rather the capacity of the system to insulate economic management from political processes of distributive demands, rent-seeking and patronage disbursement that makes the crucial difference' (1984: 72). Harriss wrote in the late 1980s that 'a real attempt to liberalise the economy probably would require the establishment of a much more authoritarian regime, able to ride over the powerful interests represented in the dominant coalition' (1987: 38). Kohli (1994) argued that the impact of Japanese colonialism in South Korea was to transform the Korean state from a relatively corrupt and ineffective social institution into a highly authoritarian institution capable of both transforming and controlling Korean society. The colonial state established new production alliances with dominant classes and brutally suppressed and systematically controlled the lower classes. The colonial state broke the hold of the landowning classes, pensioned off the old rural elite, and replaced them with Japanese career civil servants.

It is not the case that all repressive institutional structures must inevitably degenerate into predation. The first important distinction is the time frame and competition faced by the leadership. An autocrat with a monopoly of power and a reasonable expectation of surviving in office for an indefinite period (a 'stationary bandit'), will have an incentive to use their power to promote production, trade and social cooperation. A stationary bandit will have an encompassing interest in their domain and will bear a substantial portion of losses, excessive taxation or violation of property rights. A secure stationary bandit will conduct 'theft' through predictable taxes, leaving producers with an incentive to generate incomes. The stationary bandit also has an incentive to provide necessary public goods[16] (Olson 1993, 2000).

Inclusive institutions

A more inclusive institution-building strategy is possible. An important part of securing legitimacy for a given (re-)allocation of rights may be in compensating the (potential) losers rather than repressing them. Acemoglu and Robinson (1999) argue that the House of Lords in Britain gave the landed classes a guaranteed stake in political power during the nineteenth century, which served to compensate them as their relative economic power declined with the onset of industrialisation. Without such compensation, in Austria-Hungary and Russia landed groups opposed industrialisation for longer. Jomo and Gomez (2000) argue that the New Economic Policy instituted in Malaysia after the 1969 ethnic riots managed to ensure a stable redistribution of rents from the ethnic Chinese to the indigenous Bumiputra. As well as raising the share of the latter in total corporate capital, it has reduced contestation costs and allowed the more successful ethnic Chinese to accumulate.

Compared to repressive institutions, a more inclusive strategy is typical of the stage after the old feudal society has undergone substantial change and the economy and society are already developing at pace. To expand the power of the state, it is necessary to assimilate newly emerging social groups, such as entrepreneurs and urban workers. Strategies that then continue to rely on repressive institutions at this stage are those that can be labelled praetorian political systems. Such systems are incapable of either the sustained concentration of power necessary for reform or the sustained expansion of power involved in the identification of new groups with the system (Huntingdon 1968: 146).

Bardhan said 'In the context of economic growth it is rather the capacity of the system to insulate economic management from political processes of distributive demands, rent-seeking and patronage disbursement that makes the crucial difference' (1984: 72). Bardhan's argument is too narrow. An important part of securing legitimacy for the (re-)allocation of rights and income streams that resulted from rapid industrialisation was in compensating the losers. Identifying those requiring compensation, minimising the transaction costs associated with such transfers, and minimising rent-seeking by other entities requires a state that is not 'autonomous' but 'embedded in a concrete set of social ties that binds the state to society and provides institutionalised channels for the continual negotiation and re-negotiation of goals and policies' (Evans 1995: 12). A state that is only autonomous lacks the intelligence to resolve collective action problems. Where this book departs from Evans (1995) is in that, he argued, the concept of embedded autonomy implies dense links between the state and industrial capital and an exclusionary arrangement with other groups. This is insufficient: there are many other potentially powerful groups in society whose opposition may at least have to be neutralised to permit a policy of sustained industrialisation.

The level of institutionalisation of any political system can be defined by the adaptability, complexity, autonomy and coherence of its organisations and procedures. In every society affected by social change new groups arise to participate in politics. Where the system lacks autonomy, these groups gain entry into politics without being identified with established political organisations or political procedures. In a more institutionalised political system there are mechanisms that either slow down the entry of new groups into politics or that, through a process of political socialisation, impel changes in the attitudes and behaviour of the politically most active of the new group. In such a system the most important positions of leadership can normally only be achieved by those who have served an apprenticeship in less important positions. The institutions impose political socialisation as the price of political participation. In a praetorian society groups become mobilised into politics without becoming socialised by politics (Huntingdon 1968). While bureaucracies, assemblies, parliaments, elections, and constitutions are long established, the distinctive institution in the modern polity is the political party (Huntingdon 1968: 89).

The Congress party in India between independence and the mid-1960s provided an embedded institution that was able to dominate civil society, provide compensation and ideological incorporation. The chief mechanism of the Indian system was the elaborate system of factions at every level of political and governmental activity through which Congress functioned (Menon 2003: 24, 48). The party provided a system of co-ordination between the various levels, through vertical faction chains that 'provided a subtle and resilient mechanism for conflict management and transactional negotiations among the proprietary classes' (Bardhan 1984: 77). It provided a well-defined network for the distribution of the spoils of office, institutionalised procedures of transaction, and absorbed dissent by co-opting leaders of subordinate classes. In power, Congress monopolised patronage resources right down to the village panchayats, sugar co-operatives, banking corporations, and state allocated resources such as licences, fertilisers, seeds and road construction. Even those losing out had the incentive to remain within the party and resume the argument at a later stage. The central leadership provided a system of mediation, arbitration and inter-level co-ordination in the party. Congress acted to neutralise some of the more important cleavages within society, incorporating, for example, the labour movement, promoting the linguistic re-organisation of states, and absorbing the movement's leadership.

A second example is the National Revolutionary Party (PRI) in Mexico. Between 1880 and 1919 Mexico experienced rapid industrial growth and rising inequality. Political power was concentrated in the hands of an oligarchy and dictator. New, literate middle-class groups in the cities were denied opportunities to participate in politics. After the revolution, at the end of the 1920s various military leaders created the PRI and in effect institutionalised the revolution. The PRI was an autonomous, coherent, and flexible political system with an existence of its own, separate from social forces. It demonstrated the capacity to combine the reasonably high centralisation of power with the expansion of power and, by the 1940s, organised social forces such as the military, labour and farmers had been successfully incorporated into the party. Once inside, they were subject to the institutionalised bargaining and compromise of the party structure. A limit to six-year Presidential terms gave candidates an incentive to remain in the party and attain office at a later attempt. After repeated military interventions in politics before the 1930s, Mexico subsequently acquired striking political stability (Huntingdon 1968).

A single-party system in a modernising country can help promote both concentration of power and also expansion/group assimilation; such examples in the 1950s and 1960s would have included Mexico, Tunisia, North Korea, and North Vietnam. Similar capabilities are likely to exist in dominant-party systems, where there is a single major party and numerous small parties (parochial, ethnic and ideological). More-competitive two-party or multi-party systems may have considerable capacity for expansion and the assimilation of groups, but less capability for the concentration of power and the promotion of reform. Political competition in a two-party system, for instance, may serve to mobilise new groups into politics and in this sense to expand the power of the system; however, at the same time, this mobilisation also tends to divide power and fracture the existing consensus on modernisation. A good example of this is the 1956 election in Ceylon/Sri Lanka, in which the modernising urban groups were defeated by a rural electorate. The standard critique against multi-party systems is that they split society and promote conflict. Such an argument was used by President Ayub Khan after the military coup in Pakistan in 1958. Such arguments are less against parties than against weak parties. Uncontrolled corruption, division, instability, and susceptibility to outside influence all characterise weak party systems and are features of weak political systems generally. As political parties become stronger, they can bind various social forces and create a basis for loyalty and identity, transcending more parochial groupings. By regularising the procedures for leadership succession and for assimilation of new groups into the political system, parties provide the basis for stability and orderly change rather than instability (Huntingdon 1968).

Ideology

Huntingdon (1968) argues that a complex society requires some definition in terms of general principle or ethical obligation of the bond that holds the group together. The obligation is to some principle, myth, purpose, or code of behaviour that the persons/ groups have in common. Woo-Cumings (1999) argues that the authoritarian states of East Asia did not obtain their legitimacy through a mandate from civil society, or by following rules to gain office, rather by the project they were carrying out. Legitimacy was obtained by successfully achieving rapid economic development in an uncertain and dangerous Cold War world. A political party that can subordinate its members' individual aspirations to a collective ideology, and exclude opponents, can reduce conflict and facilitate economic reform. Kohli (1987) argues that tightly organised ideological parties were better able to penetrate rural society in India without being co-opted by propertied groups and were able to implement modest reforms. Again, for the case of India Harriss (2000) argues that a regime with a coherent leadership, an ideological and organisational commitment to exclude propertied interests, and an organisation that is both centralised and decentralised (embedded-autonomy) will facilitate a degree of regime autonomy from the propertied classes.

The BJP is clearly a different political construct from the 1950s-vintage Congress.[17] Congress built its support through vertical mobilisation: obtaining the support of local notables heading vote banks. The BJP mobilised on the basis of a strong organisation. The BJP is a cadre-based, ideological political party relying on a network of activists owing allegiance to the BJP and the wider Hindu nationalist organisation (the Sangh Parivar). Activists are used to majoritarian discipline, and factionalisation has been relatively less of an issue. The BJP has functioned (since its formation in 1980) as a highly successful, disciplined political party, characterised by mass membership, high levels of ideological commitment, and a tightly knit party structure that has endured without splits since its formation (Basu 2001). The BJP provided a clear ideological message to which people could owe allegiance and subordinate their particular interests. The BJP has an organic view of society, that all castes are harmonious components of society. They emphasised integrating the low castes through fear of the 'Muslim other', efforts to provide welfare, and an intense effort to propagate particular ideological moral and cultural ideals (sanskritisation).[18]

West Bengal provides a good case study of a political-economic environment before and after the impact of an ideological party. West Bengal between 1967 and 1977 was characterised by political chaos. The Left United Front (UF) government in 1967 sponsored a land-grab movement; this was taken to further extremes by the revolutionary violence of the Naxalbari movement. The central government responded by dismissing the state government and, between 1971 and 1977, a more compliant Congress party in (local) power cracked down on extremist political opposition. There were large numbers of politically motivated 'encounter killings' by the police and widespread arrests of UF members. The Communist Party (the largest constituent of the UF government) reformed itself, stressing a commitment to democracy, and making itself more social democratic and less communist, whilst retaining the democratic centralism of internal party organisation. It was an ideological party. This removed the worst elements of factional conflict and made the party subservient to larger organisational goals, enabling the party, once returned to power (1977), to implement modest, but genuine, redistributive goals. Government was decentralised, and competitive elections held for the village panchayats. Many central government programmes (Food for Work, Employment Guarantee) were better implemented in West Bengal (Swaminathan 1990). Operation Bagra in the early 1980s provided tenurial rights and improved incomes for 25% of rural households (Kohli 1990: Ch10). This ideological party provided for a cohesive and effective government that has remained in power since 1977.

5 An episode of growth, 1951/52–1958/59

Summary of chapter findings

The chapter is divided into three parts, each focusing on one particular role that the state has in promoting economic growth. These relate to finance, production and institutions. The underlying hypothesis here is that the state needs to be successful in all three to initiate and sustain an episode of growth.

The first section shows that the surplus mobilised by the state between 1951/52 and 1958/59 was small. Slow growth of savings and tax revenue forced a reliance on capital inflows from abroad. The principal means to finance investment was via the very high rates of profit earned by private industry. Profits were mainly explained by the dislocations of partitions, though these were complemented by government trade and exchange rate policy. The state made some limited direct contribution to investment. The second section examines the role of the state in achieving a productive use of the surplus in both the public and private sectors. The principal source of growth over this period was import substitution. There were signs of inefficiency in production, but also of declining costs and rising productivity in industry and, to a lesser extent, agriculture. The third section focuses on institutions that may or may not allow the state to overcome the inherent conflicts associated with economic growth. The institutions of autonomy and repression (the civil service and the military) were reconstructed quickly after independence. There is no consistent evidence that this relative autonomy allowed the government to implement policies over the 1950s in general and systematic accordance with long-term goals. The state failed in its efforts to promote inclusionary institutions. There was no successful attempt to project any unifying ideology. The episode of growth was not sustainable. The exhaustion of opportunities for import substitution was limiting further growth solely to expansion of (slow-growing) domestic demand. Without sufficient autonomy or the development of inclusive institutions to absorb groups, it was unlikely that the state would have been able to sustain growth through either an aggressive export-orientated strategy, or through deepening the pattern of import substitution to more capital-intensive and technologically demanding segments of industry, or by pushing the growth of agriculture.

Recap from Chapter 3

GDP growth averaged 3.1% p.a. between 1951/52 and 1958/59, and population growth no more than 1% p.a. Growth in GDP was showing signs of slowing after the mid-1950s. Growth in agricultural value added fell short of population growth in the 1950s, though it showed an increase after the mid-1950s. Growth of the manufacturing sector was around 7.7% in the 1950s; this was led by rapid growth of the large-scale sector, rather than the small-scale sector. The industries with notably rapid growth were where import substitution progressed earliest and most rapidly; this was in industries primarily producing consumption goods, in particular textiles. Another characteristic of these industries was their dependence on domestically produced, primarily agricultural raw materials. Growth in manufacturing over the first five years of the decade was met almost entirely by import substitution, and over the second five years by the growth of domestic demand. By 1959/60 domestic consumption in sugar manufacturing, edible oils, cotton and other textiles, matches, and jute textiles was met almost entirely by domestic production.

Limitations of alternative explanations

The world economy

There is no evidence that favourable impacts from the world economy initiated or sustained the episode of growth during the 1950s. The episode of growth did accompany a sharp improvement in the external terms of trade. Between 1948/49 and 1950/51 the price index for exports increased by 6%, and that for imports declined by 15% (Islam 1961: 59–60; Papanek 1967: 15). Rising prices and demand for exports such as jute, cotton, leather and wool were driven by the Korean War. In the year to 1950/51 total exports from Pakistan reached $135m., an increase of 2.5 times over the previous year (Burki 1999: 112). The effect was neither long lived enough nor large enough in its aggregate impact to explain the decade-long episode of growth. As the Korean War came to an end, there was a collapse in the ratio of export to import prices, from 125 in 1950/51, to 84 in 1952/53, and finally to a low of 52 in 1959/60. The price of exports declined by one-third between 1950/51 and 1952/53, and by the mid-1950s the price of imports was rising sharply (Islam 1961: 59–60; Papanek 1967: 15; Lewis 1970: 126). Over the early 1950s foreign trade shrank in terms of its aggregate importance to Pakistan's economy. Between 1950 and 1955 exports declined from 10.4% to 3.4% of GDP, and imports from 9.0% to 5.4%; there was some recovery in the second half of the 1950s (Lewis 1969: 47; Husain 1999: 324).

Liberalisation

There is no evidence that Pakistan's economy was substantially liberalised over the 1950s, such that liberalisation could be viewed as an explanation for the episode of growth. After the Korean War-driven commodity price boom in 1952, foreign exchange earnings (export prices of jute and cotton) fell sharply. The government responded by controlling imports through the use of detailed physical and exchange controls (the currency was not devalued). The share of private imports subject to licences fluctuated considerably, but remained above 60% after 1954/55 and reached a peak of 94% in 1958/59 (Naqvi 1966). While the aggregate level of imports was little different in 1959 compared to 1955, the share of import licences issued for consumer goods fell sharply (from 31.9% to 15.3%), while those for raw materials and capital goods increased (respectively, from 53.8% to 65.8% and from 14.3% to 18.9%) (Naqvi 1966: 474; Lewis 1970: 71–2). Licensing was supported by high tariffs (Lewis 1969: 72, 1970: 68). Tariff rates on luxury goods, such as alcohol, jewellery, cigarettes, musical instruments, silk cloth, perfumes and cosmetics, ranged from 100% to 300% (Radhu 1964). Taxes were systematically higher on imports than on domestic production. In many cases this difference was substantial, examples in 1954/55 being: sugar manufacturing (97% on imports and 12% on domestic production); tea manufacturing (184% and 6%); beverages (511% and 19%); cotton and other textiles (74% and 14%); chemicals and pharmaceuticals (81% and 7%); and matches (294% and 25%) (Lewis 1970: 59).

Such illiberal interventions had a clear impact on incentives facing private sector producers. The impact of these policies was to reduce imports of manufactures and to create an overvalued currency. These helped turn the terms of trade sharply against agriculture (the export sector) and in favour of manufacturing (the import-competing sector). These price movements provided abnormally high incentives for manufacturing production and transferred resources from farmers to manufacturers. Quantitatively, taxation was less important than direct controls in influencing the price structure (Lewis and Hussain 1966; Lewis 1970). Within manufacturing, the incentive structure encouraged the production of consumer, rather than producer, goods (such goods were relatively freely imported at very low duties) (Thomas 1966).

The (economic) role of the state, 1951/52 to 1958/59: finance

This section shows that the surplus mobilised by the state between 1951/52 and 1958/59 was small. There was slow growth in savings, though some success in promoting the growth of the banking system and increasing the portion of savings mediated through the formal financial system. Slow growth of government tax revenue and spending permitted public saving to make only a negligible contribution to the total. The gap between the domestic surplus and domestic investment rate was met by capital inflows from abroad. The principal means to finance investment was via the very high rates of profit earned by private industry. Most of this can be explained as a 'natural' consequence of the dislocations of partition, though it was complemented by government trade and exchange rate policy. The state made some limited direct contribution to investment.

The mobilisation of savings, 1951/52 to 1958/59

Estimates of the savings rate in Pakistan over the 1950s vary considerably.[1] These include an increase from 2.3% of GDP in 1949/50 to 6.7% in the late 1950s (Hasen

1998), or from 4.4% of GNP in 1949/50 to 6.6% in 1959/60 (Lewis 1970: 50), or from 6.9% of GNP in 1955 to 7.88% in 1961 (Ahmed and Amjad 1984: 291). Given the very slow growth in per capita incomes over the 1950s, these estimates actually represent very high marginal rates of saving, of over 20% (Lewis 1970: 50). Other, earlier estimates using less reliable data show declining savings over the 1950s, for example from 7.9% of GNP in 1955/56 to 4.3% in 1959/60 (Power 1963: 130), or between 7.9% and 10.8% of GDP in 1955/56 to between 5.5% and 6.3% in 1960/61 (Lewis and Khan 1964: 21).

The role of the state in mobilising domestic savings

Most estimates of tax revenue show it to have increased slowly over the 1950s. Estimates include a rise from 4.7% of GNP in 1949/50 to 7.0% in 1960/61 (Ahmed and Amjad 1984: 261), or from 5.9% of GDP in 1954/55 to 6.2% in 1959/60 (Lewis 1965: 409), or from 3.1% of GDP in 1949/50 to 4.2% in 1959/60 (for central government only) (Pasha and Fatima 1999: 204). Over the 1950s income and wealth tax increased from 0.6% to 1.0% of GDP, excise duty from 0.3% to 0.9%, customs duty declined from 2.0% to 1.8% and sales tax remained little changed after the mid-1950s at 0.5% (Pasha and Fatima 1999: 204). Customs duty was the main source of revenue (declining from 71% to 43% of total central tax revenue over the 1950s) and was collected on both imports and exports, especially of raw jute and cotton. The vast bulk of excise revenue was raised from very basic goods, such as tobacco, vegetable products, sugar and cement (Pasha and Fatima 1999: 207). There was quite strong growth of government non-tax revenue (state trading profits and earnings of commercial departments such as the post office and telephones), from 1.6% of GNP in 1949/50 to 2.9% in 1960/61 (Ahmed and Amjad 1984: 261).

Agricultural incomes had been exempt from income tax since the mid-1880s. The recommendation of the 1959 Taxation Enquiry Committee to tax income irrespective of source was ignored, and the introduction of a wealth tax in 1959 made little difference. There was little increase in land revenue; the ratio of land revenue to crop income fell almost continuously, from only 3% in the 1950s, which was then equivalent to only around 2% of farmers' incomes (Khan 1999: 131).

Corporations were faced with a nominal tax rate that varied between 50% and 60%. The system contained a wide range of exemptions, such as tax holidays for certain types of businesses and geographic areas of the country and accelerated depreciation allowances. Tax holidays alone accounted for approximately 50% of corporate income tax receipts (Lewis 1970: 135). The resulting pattern of incentives implied that economic growth acted to undermine the growth of tax revenue. Products with high import duties were replaced by domestic production first, so that the average duty rate on imports fell as the composition of imports shifted towards lower-taxed imports. For example, the export tax on raw jute and on raw cotton encouraged the domestic use of those commodities, and reduced tax revenue (Lewis 1970: 133).

Government current expenditure declined, from 11% to 8.6% of GNP between 1949/50 and 1959/60 (Lewis 1970: 50). The early 1950s were the years that Jalal argued marked the origins of Pakistan's 'Political Economy of Defence' (Jalal 1990).

Defence expenditure indeed rose, from $32.4m. in 1947/48 to $234.2m. in 1961, representing at times 60%–70% of tax revenues. It is easy, though, to exaggerate this trend. The growth of defence spending matched that of GDP growth, at 3.2% of GDP in 1949/50 and 3.3% in 1959/60 (Pasha and Fatima 1999: 209–10). The increase was largely covered by US military assistance, which was estimated at $522m. by late 1959 (Hashmi 1983: 159–61). Overall government expenditure was irrelevant to the wider economy. Other than defence expenditure, government spending was used for high-cost public housing (two-thirds of which for civil servants), higher education and urban health facilities (Griffin and Khan 1972). There was no recourse to deficit financing, which declined from 3.1% of GDP in 1949/50 to 0.6% in 1960/61 (Ahmed and Amjad 1984: 261). The net impact of taxing and spending was a very low level of government saving. By the late 1950s public saving had reached 0.1% (Lewis 1965: 408) or 0.2% of GDP (Papanek 1967: 187).

The role of the state in creating institutions to mobilise private sector savings

Prior to 1947, of 99 scheduled banks listed by the Reserve Bank of British India, only one had a head office in Pakistan. Many commercial banks ceased to function as Hindus left for India. United India Bank, for example, had 3,496 branches, 631 of which were in the future Pakistan, and only 231 of which were functioning at independence. Almost 75% of deposits were held by foreign-owned banks (Zaidi 2005). After 1947 the government intervened in various ways. The State Bank of Pakistan (SBP) was established and given responsibility to conduct monetary management and also, importantly, to support the development of the capital market. The government made low-cost financing available to newly established commercial banks. The banking sector frequently requested extra credit from the SBP to support the growth of their lending (Khan 1999). In the first eighteen months after independence 51 new branches opened in East and West Pakistan, 28 of which were Pakistani banks. Between 1952 and 1955 advances by Pakistani banks increased from 38% to 59% of the total. Between 1948 and 1954 bank deposits grew by 61% (Zaidi 2005).

The most striking trend was not an increase in aggregate saving, but a shift in the composition of savings by the private sector, from the holding of currency towards time and demand deposits in the banking system (Lewis and Khan 1964). The growth of the banking system led to a sharp monetisation of saving (and investment), from 2.0% to 7.6% of GDP between 1949/50 and 1959/60 (Papanek 1967: 280).

The role of the state in mobilising foreign savings

Pakistan ran a consistent balance of payments deficit over the 1950s. An early surge in raw material exports from $287m. in 1949/50 to $716m. in 1951/52 quickly faded, and exports fell to $339m. in 1954/55. This temporary boom was not managed well, imports of consumer goods and raw materials for consumer goods increased in tandem, and the balance of payments remained in deficit. Manufactured exports rose from zero in 1949/50 to $110m. in 1959/60, not enough to make a significant difference. After the mid-1950s consumer goods imports were curtailed, declining to only $84m. by

1959/60. The composition of imports by 1959/60 was a deliberate policy tool, the bulk of which (capital goods $199m. and raw materials for capital goods $90m.) were intended to support industrial growth. Pakistan never, though, escaped its balance of payments deficit; exports (6.0% of GNP) were marginally less than imports (6.5%) in 1949/50, and significantly so by 1959/60 (6.4% and 9.5%) (Papanek 1967: 187; Lewis 1970: 50). It was growing foreign savings that filled this gap.

As well as a deficit, Pakistan had to make efforts to significantly diversify its trading patterns. In 1948/49 over one-half of West Pakistan's foreign trade and 80% of East Pakistan's was with India, but by 1951 the share for all-Pakistan had fallen to 3% (Lewis 1969: 50). The fall was initiated by Pakistan's decision in 1949 not to devalue its currency, which precipitated trade sanctions by India. In the very early years after independence Pakistan established diplomatic and trading relations with the USSR and socialist regimes in Eastern Europe. Pakistan signed a trade agreement with Czechoslovakia in October 1948, Yugoslavia in April 1949, Poland in July 1949, and Hungary in November 1950 (Noman 1975). These early efforts were quite successful, and Pakistan exported significant quantities of raw cotton and some raw jute to the USSR, Czechoslovakia and China between 1947/48 and 1949/50.

These early efforts quickly faded, and Pakistan became more dependent on the USA. The principal leader of Pakistan (after the death of Jinnah), Liaquat Ali Khan, toured the USA in May–June 1950 in preference to an invitation from the USSR. During the trip Pakistan expressed support for the USA in Korea, and the invitation from the USSR was withdrawn. In July 1950 Pakistan joined the IMF and in February 1951 signed its first technical assistance agreement with the USA (Rashid and Gardezi 1983). In 1952 the World Bank gave its first project loan of $27.2m. to Pakistan. In May 1954 the first defence pact was signed with the USA. Pakistan was given $250m. of military equipment, and Pakistani military officers were sent to the USA for military training (Rashid 1983). The rise in US economic and military assistance led to a sharp decline in trade with the socialist countries (Noman 1975: 319). Throughout the 1950s there were occasional thaws in relations. A large delegation from the USSR visited Pakistan in 1956, and a return visit was made later that same year. The USSR offered to build a steel mill, similar to that constructed at Bhilai in India. A barter agreement was signed between the two, but had no effect on trade patterns until the mid-1960s. In 1959 negotiations between Pakistan and the USSR about assistance for oil and gas exploration were initiated and on the point of completion, when the U-2 spy plane incident soured relations and led to the suspension of talks. Again, it was not until the 1960s that the negotiations bore fruit in the form of aid and technical assistance. In 1956 Chou En Lai made a successful visit to Pakistan, and the Pakistani Prime Minister made a return trip to China, but the visits had no real impact on trade and aid during the late-1950s (Noman 1975; Alavi 1983).

The narrowing of Pakistan's foreign policy and its continuing dependence on foreign aid to fill its foreign financing gap gave Pakistan little negotiating leeway. In 1954 the CENTO treaty and in 1955 the SEATO treaty were signed, which bound Pakistan into a US-led anti-communist alliance. Domestic policy was also heavily influenced by the USA. The Ford Foundation, for example, supported the establishment of the Development Advisory Service at Harvard in 1952. Though still few in number in the 1950s, foreign advisors played a lead role in preparing the First Five-year Plan. The Ford Foundation also supported the launch of the Institute of Development Economists, which became the premier think tank of Pakistan. A glance at its journal, *The Pakistan Development Review*, reveals the extent to which foreign economists were engaged in domestic academic debate by the 1960s.

The majority of aid and loans came from the USA in the 1950s; there was as yet no aid or loans from the Socialist or Islamic countries. Total assistance increased from $337m. between 1950 and 1955, to $1,073m. between 1955 and 1960, or from 1.1% of GNP in 1955, to 2.75% in 1961 (Ahmed and Amjad 1984: 291). This capital inflow was crucial, but much of it was contracted on relatively unfavourable terms. The share of grants in total assistance declined from 64% to 54% during the 1950s (Rashid 1983: 180). Franco-Rodriguez *et al*. (1998) found that, from 1956 onwards, foreign aid had a small positive effect on investment.

The role of the state in influencing private sector profitability

Some argue that there was a 'natural' pattern of profitability in 1947 that drove growth independently of government policy. Partition, goes this argument, left Pakistan as a surplus producer of food and agricultural raw materials and a deficit producer of manufactures. There were only a handful of sizeable industrial undertakings in Pakistan at independence. These included the Dalmia Cement Factory in Karachi, Sri Rams cotton mills in Lyallpur (Faisalabad), and Premier Sugar mills in Mardan (which were all Hindu owned). The largest enterprise at the time was the Moghalpura Railway workshop in Lahore, which was in the public sector (Alavi 1983). Supply and demand implied high prices and potential profits for manufacturers. Even with a neutral economic policy, it is likely that industrial growth would have been relatively fast and would have occurred more rapidly than suggested by growth of per capita income alone (Lewis 1969: 13).

Evidence for this proposition lies in statistical work that finds that the principal determinant of domestic production in the late 1950s was the importance of domestically produced raw materials in the productive structure of the industry (Lewis 1970). Tariffs or effective rates of protection were not statistically important in the determination of productive structure (Lewis 1970). Further evidence comes from the comparisons between Pakistan and figures for a 'normal country'[2] of the proportion of domestic production in total supply of manufactures made by Lewis (1970). In 1951/52 the proportions in Pakistan were unusually low. By 1959/60 the share of domestic production in total supply was closing in on 'normal' levels in numerous sectors, including food, beverages and tobacco, textiles, footwear and clothing, electrical machinery, and transport equipment. For other sectors such as chemicals, petroleum and coal products, basic metals and metal products there was convergence, but the process was a long way from completion by the late-1950s. In only a few sectors, printing and publishing, rubber manufacturing and non-metallic mineral products, were there signs of divergence, (Lewis 1969: 124). A more immediate comparison is that with India. In 1951/52 Pakistan and India had very different industrial structures. India was domestically self-sufficient, and Pakistan wholly import dependent, on many basic consumer goods, such as refined sugar, footwear, soap, matches, jute textiles, and rubber products. By the end of the 1950s Pakistan was nearing domestic self-sufficiency in these same sectors (Lewis 1969: 126).

Even this work of Lewis argues that partition disequilibrium can explain at most two-thirds of subsequent economic growth. Government policy had a complementary role in influencing private sector profitability and consequent patterns of industrial growth. Pakistan in the 1950s did not have the administrative capacity to tax the peasantry directly and so did so indirectly, through manipulating relative prices.

Islam estimated the extent of exchange rate overvaluation by surveying the domestic market price of imports; this he labelled the 'mark up of scarcity price of foreign exchange on its official price'. The measure, he found, increased with fluctuations from 1.17 in 1948/49 to 2.16 in 1952/53, then declined with fluctuations to 0.80 in 1960/61 (Islam 1970: 58). Luxury goods typically had extremely high rates of import duties, with rates on items such as alcohol, jewellery, cigarettes, musical instruments, silk cloth, perfumes and cosmetics ranging from 100% to 300%. Very low or zero rates were charged on capital goods and raw materials used by industry. Export duties were used at various times during the 1950s and were charged on raw wool and cotton, cement, rice, fish, bamboo, hides and skin, jute, and tea (Radhu 1964). Since most agricultural exports were sold in highly competitive international markets, the effect of export duties was to lower producer prices. The prices of foodgrains were also depressed by government-imposed compulsory purchase, price controls, and rationing. Until 1960 wheat surplus areas could sell their surplus production only to the government at a lower price than the free market price (Papanek 1967: 149). By 1954/55 there were extremely high effective rates of protection (ERP) to many sectors in Pakistan. On average, ERP was highest among consumption goods (76%), including sugar manufacturing (170%), edible oils (106%), beverages (88%), tobacco manufacturing (94%), cotton and textiles (97%), matches (91%), and wood and furniture (174%). ERPs on intermediate goods (71%) were a little lower; these included jute goods (63%), paper manufacturing (61%), leather manufacturing (156%), chemical and pharmaceuticals (57%), fertiliser (43%), and petroleum and coal products (46%). ERP on investment and related goods (49%) were the lowest; these included transport equipment (115%), electrical machinery (28%), metal products (83%), non-electrical machinery (-5%), and basic metals (20%) (Lewis 1969: 134). An alternative method of measuring the impact of government policy is to estimate implicit exchange rates.[3] Any distortion, such as import or export duties, indirect taxes and subsidies, or quantitative restrictions, will cause the implicit exchange rate to vary among goods. Such studies show that, by the mid-1950s, agriculture was receiving only 50% of the value that its sales would have brought with free trade,[4] and the manufacturing sector was receiving about 75% more for its output than it paid for purchases of equivalent value in world trade in the mid-1950s (Lewis 1968, 1969). It was import quotas, rather than tariffs, that were the crucial influence on ERPs/implicit exchange rates in the 1950s (Pal 1964, 1965; Naqvi 1966; Lewis 1969, 1970). For example, in 1954/55 averages of nominal tariffs were, respectively, 80%, 50% and 30% on industries producing consumption, intermediate and investment goods. Domestic prices were, respectively, 194%, 185% and 167% above c.i.f. prices for these three groups of industries (Lewis 1969).

The net result of government policy was to help turn the terms of trade sharply against agriculture (export sector) and in favour of manufacturing (import-competing sector), and so transfer resources from farmers to manufacturers through the market (Lewis and Hussain 1966). Exact figures vary, but there is widespread evidence that demonstrates the magnitude of this shift. For the agricultural sector, the domestic gross barter terms[5] of trade (1959/60 = 100) declined from 97.39 in 1951–54 to 87.36 in 1953–56 for West Pakistan and from 77.09 to 62.83 for East Pakistan (Lewis and Hussain 1966: 412; Kazi 1987: 87). Agriculture's terms of trade, relative to world price standards, increased from 39.8% in 1951/52 to 1953/54, to 59.1% between 1959/60 and 1961/62 (Lewis 1970: 65). This general pattern of, first declining, then rising, terms of trade for agriculture is confirmed in Table 5.1, which includes a variety of estimates.

Over the 1950s East Pakistan ran a substantial surplus with the rest of the world and, until 1959/60, a growing deficit with West Pakistan (Lewis 1970: 142–3). This led to a substantial transfer of resources from East to West Pakistan over the 1950s (Power 1963). West Pakistan also received around 80% of foreign aid to Pakistan throughout the 1950s (Hasen 1998). This led to many arguing that East Pakistan was being squeezed for the benefit of industrial growth in West Pakistan, and that it was inter-wing trade that was providing the 'easy' profits for businessmen in West Pakistan and financing its investment by forcing East Pakistan to pay more for its manufactures than in free trade with the rest of the world. Lewis (1968), however, shows that the dominant pattern of resource transfer was from agriculture to industry, rather than between East and West Pakistan.

As a result of these various policies, there existed a large domestic price differential with world prices, and this was not absorbed by the government through licence fees or profit taxation, but rather provided a source of potential monopoly profits for those who were granted import licences (Thomas 1966). Redistribution to the manufacturing sector was not sufficient to increase its profitability. Higher prices could have been dissipated in the form of higher wages. There is reasonable evidence to show that, even as manufacturing benefited from higher prices, real wages in the sector declined. An index of real wages (all industries) declined from 100 in 1954 to 92.8 and 96.9 in 1959/60 in East and West Pakistan respectively; in textiles, the drop was to 94.6 and 92.8 (Khan 1967: 326). Estimates of the real cost of labour to employees for the textiles sectors in both East and West Pakistan (estimated by dividing money wages by the indices of respective wholesale prices of textiles) show a similar rate of decline between 1954 and 1959/60 (Khan 1967: 336). Evidence on the more-encompassing measure of labour's factor share (which also accounts for the impact of labour productivity, the prices of other inputs and output prices) shows a more mixed picture. Labour's factor share (all industries between 1954 and 1959/60) declined from 46.3% to 37.6% in East Pakistan, and increased from 30.3% to 34.1% in West Pakistan (Khan 1967: 336). Specifically in the large-scale manufacturing sector, the wage share declined from 37.3% to 34.9% between 1955/56 and 1959/60 (Wizarat 2002: 165). Direct measures of profit show that, by the middle of the 1950s, profit rates of 50%–100% were not uncommon, and by the end of the 1950s they were still in the range 20%–50% (Papanek 1967).

Table 5.1 The terms of trade for agriculture, three-year moving average: 1951–54 to 1958–61

Years	Net Barter Terms of Trade		Income Terms of Trade	Single Factor Terms of Trade	Ratio of Prices Received Relative to Paid by the Agriculture Sector for		
	Alternative 1	Alternative 2			Consumption Goods	Intermediate Goods	Investment Goods
1951–54	99.34	96.64	83.60	109.21	100.30	99.75	90.85
1952–55	91.60	91.59	81.86	102.07	90.78	95.62	92.93
1953–56	90.12	87.97	79.42	96.55	89.70	92.73	94.65
1954–57	94.16	91.17	82.78	95.83	96.08	92.12	92.74
1955–58	98.56	95.14	87.34	96.83	101.75	93.83	93.90
1956–59	100.64	98.16	92.25	97.18	104.63	97.29	95.45
1957–60	100.88	99.37	94.74	98.56	103.29	99.46	98.61
1958–61	103.44	103.11	102.44	99.39	105.23	102.21	104.06

Source: Qureshi 1985: 367–369.

Profits may of course be taxed. Total taxes on corporate profits increased from 56.25% between 1950/51 and 1956/57, to 65.00% in 1959/60. The basic rates, though, were lower for companies not declaring dividends or for public limited companies. There were widespread exemptions from corporate taxes – tax holidays, for example, accounted for the waiving of 50% of all corporate profits (Lewis 1970: 61, 135).

Some voiced pessimism about the development strategy in another way and argued that the policies used to reduce costs of production/raise the profitability of the private manufacturing sector would not raise growth and investment. With profit rates (as estimated) of 50%–100%, it would be possible for businessmen to consume almost half of borrowed capital and still meet yearly repayment obligations (Griffin and Khan 1972: 16). Some studies have suggested that a very large proportion of resources transferred from agriculture to industry were used to supplement consumption, rather than investment, and one estimate puts this figure at between 63% and 85% (Griffin 1965). There is more general support for the alternative view, that the profits earned by exporters during the Korean War were increasingly mediated through the expanding banking sector as financial savings. This chapter earlier showed how the banking system was expanding and the economy was becoming increasingly monetised. Other estimates show that approximately half of industrial profits were being reinvested in industry or non-industrial sectors (Papanek 1967: 195–6; Lewis 1970: 51). This is consistent with the fact that the total investment rate rose from 2.7% of GDP in 1949/50, to 10.8% in 1959/60 (Papanek 1967: 280), or from 4.6% of GNP in 1949/50, to 11.8% in 1959/60 (Lewis 1969: 5), or from 4.4% of GNP in 1949/50 to 11.7% in 1959/60 (Lewis 1970: 50).

Government policy complemented the post-independence economic structure to generate strong incentives (profits) for individuals to become industrial entrepreneurs. By 1959 two-thirds of private industrial investment was controlled by Muslims who had previously been traders (Papanek 1967: 41). At the end of the 1960s, the 12 largest business families were relative newcomers to large-scale industrial activity (Papanek 1972: 22).

The role of the state in allocating resources to projects essential for development

This section shows how the public sector directly contributed to raising investment.

Public sector investment increased from perhaps less than 2% to about 5%–6% of GDP over the 1950s. In 1949/50 the state accounted for less than 35% of total investment; this increased to 63% in 1959/60. State development expenditure on infrastructure (water, power, transport and communications) constituted just 60% of the total. In 1947 there were only two small hydroelectric power stations in Pakistan, with a total installed capacity of 57MW. By 1958 only an extra 46MW capacity had been added. There was fairly rapid railway track-building in Pakistan over the 1950s, and by 1960 the total length of track had reached 8,574 km (Husain 1999).

State-created credit institutions played an increasing role in allocating finance to private sector industry. The Pakistan Industrial Credit and Investment Corporation (PICIC) and Pakistan Industrial Finance Corporation (PIFCO) provided funds to more established firms with adequate security and a track record in generating profits.

More than half of total lending by PICIC went to a tiny group of large industrialists (Zaidi 2005).

The Pakistan Industrial Development Corporation (PIDC) was a semi-autonomous government agency that pioneered investment in some industries where the necessary start-up capital exceeded that available to any private firm. PIDC was also able to bypass the constraints of family businesses and hire a complete management staff from abroad for some projects. The long gestation between investment and profitable operation (for many PIDC projects, 4–5 years or more) was in striking contrast to private investment in sectors such as textiles, which often produced substantial profits within 2–3 years of the initial investment. By 1953/54 cumulative expenditures by PIDC had reached about 7% of total industrial assets; they had reached about 15% by 1959 (Papanek 1967: 97). A 1958 study analysing 14 PIDC projects showed that, for many projects, the actual completion dates were one to three years later than the estimated completion date, actual investment costs about two-thirds higher, and production averaged 50% of rated capacity (Papanek 1967: 98). By 1959 the rate of return on investment for PIDC was substantially less than half the rate reported by private firms (Papanek 1967: 98), although of course the rationale of PIDC was to invest in sectors that the private sector was avoiding.

The (economic) role of the state, 1951/52 to 1958/59: production

This section examines the role of the state in achieving a productive use of the surplus in both the public and private sectors. This section finds that the principal source of growth was import substitution. This section continues by evaluating growth over this period. There are signs of inefficiency, which many have blamed on policy-induced distortions. This section argues that, instead, there were indications of declining costs and rising productivity in industry and, to a lesser extent, in agriculture.

Sources of growth: import substitution

The earliest outline of official policy was the Statement of Industrial Policy of 2nd April 1948. The statement noted that the most striking feature of Pakistan was the marked contrast between its vast natural resources and its extreme industrial backwardness. Pakistan produced 75% of the world's jute, but had no jute mill; it produced annually 1.5m.bales of cotton, but had very few cotton mills. Pakistan also had an abundant production of hides and skins, wool, sugar cane, and tobacco. It seemed evident to policy makers that Pakistan should promote manufacturing based on processing domestic raw materials.

Earlier, this chapter argued that the main source of economic (particularly industrial) growth after 1951 was the incentives generated by partition. Chapter 3 showed that growth in manufacturing over the first five years of the decade was met almost entirely by import substitution, and that towards the end of the decade domestic demand became the leading source of growth, with import substitution remaining significant. This pattern is evident in the near-complete import substitution that Pakistan achieved in many basic consumer goods industries over the 1950s. This chapter showed that the policy complemented the incentives of partition, and was consistently orientated towards promoting import substitution in manufacturing.

Evaluation of efficiency, 1950/51 to 1959/60

By the early 1960s measures of the efficiency of manufacturing in Pakistan showed significant distortions. By 1963/64 the value added in manufacturing due to protection was 33% in consumer goods, 70% in intermediate goods, and 61% in investment and related goods. The crucial industries, cotton and jute textiles, had 68% and 65% of value added due to protection. Numerous industries were found even to have negative value added at world prices. Such industries included sugar, silk and art silk textiles, apparel, plastic goods, sports goods, electrical appliances, motor vehicles, and tanning (Lewis 1970: 80–1). Negative value added implies that the value added in the industry was negative when input and output prices are both calculated at the world/free trade values. These measures of inefficiency have been widely used as a proxy for the degree to which subsidies and protection allowed Pakistani producers to use the wrong inputs, produce inefficiently and produce in the wrong sectors.

The high prices of production need not indicate inefficiency, but rather the high profits described earlier in this chapter, and so are a measure of redistribution from consumers to manufacturers. There are about 39 industries for which data on actual and 'fair' prices were available in the early 1960s. They indicate the prevalence of abnormal profits in these industries, with the actual price being higher than the fair price by an extent varying from 8% to 32% (Islam 1967: 228). Making allowance for excess profits and the overvaluation of the exchange rate, implies that between 50% and 60% of all industries and between 40% and 54% of products were actually competitive, as against 10% of the industries and 5% of products in the absence of such adjustments (Islam 1967: 229).

Chapter 3 indicated that there were distinct signs of diversification in Pakistan's economy: a rising share of output and employment accounted for by industry at the expense of agriculture (Lewis 1969: 4, 1970: 9; Khan 1999: 99; Kemal et al. 2006: 295); and rapid growth, in particular of the large-scale manufacturing sector (Afridi 1985: 464; Kemal 1999: 161; Kemal et al. 2006: 271). The pessimistic view sees this process as having been driven by policy intervention that shifted Pakistan into inefficient industries whose existence was wholly dependent on protection and subsidies. Earlier, this chapter showed that, first, the principal determinant of the share of production in total supply of each industry was the importance of domestically produced raw materials used as inputs in production. Policy, in the form of tariff protection, was much less influential (Lewis 1969, 1970). Second, the industrial structure, far from being an aberration of distortionary policy choice, was, by the late 1950s, increasingly resembling a 'typical' LDC (Lewis 1970). This evidence suggests that output growth within the manufacturing sector was not grossly distorted by economic policy during the 1950s. Policy raised the domestic market price of all manufactured goods above the c.i.f. price by similar percentages, so the resulting pattern of investment was dominated by real costs. Distribution of manufacturing output among industries would not have been much different if policies have been more neutral and less favourable to manufacturing generally (Lewis 1970).

Over the 1950s there was a drastic decline in export earnings from traditional exports, raw jute, raw cotton, hides and skins, raw wool and tea. These products were increasingly used by domestic industry: raw cotton, wool and jute by the textile industry, and hides and skins by the leather industry (Lewis 1970). Sectors in which output growth and import substitution had been rapid emerged as significant exporters by the late 1950s, including food products, cotton textiles, footwear, soaps, miscellaneous manufactures (especially sports goods and surgical instruments), jute textiles, leather products, some chemical products (e.g. paints and varnishes) and some metal products and machinery lines (sewing machines, fans, hardware, and utensils) (Lewis 1970: 120). The share of consumer goods in imports (such as cotton yarn and cloth) declined, and the share of capital and intermediate goods (such as machinery and transport equipment, and iron and steel products) increased (Lewis 1969: 6). Pakistan was following a growth trajectory consistent with comparative advantage, first beginning to industrialise, based on processing domestically occurring raw materials for a domestic market, then exporting, based on those same sectors and importing capital goods.

We would expect Pakistan to have been producing at high cost relative to more established industrial countries by the end of the 1950s, even were the structures of production to have evolved in accordance with comparative advantage. What is important is what was happening to relative costs and productivity.

Comparative costs are defined as the ratios of ex-factory prices of specific domestic products to c.i.f. prices of closely competing imports. Using data from the Pakistan Tariff Commission for 115 industries over a 15-year period (1951 to 1966), Islam (1967) measured comparative costs. For 20 out of 21 manufactured products, domestic costs had fallen relative to c.i.f. costs; in five or more there was a fall of between 40% and 60%, and in four a fall of 60% or more (Islam 1967). Table 5.2 shows that comparative costs declined by various measures between the early and late 1950s. Generally, cost ratios were lowest for consumer goods and higher for capital and intermediate goods (Islam 1967: 217).

Table 5.2 Comparative cost ratios

	1951–55	1956–60
(A)	Average Values 1.56	Average Values 1.40
(B)	1.65	1.62
(C)	Median Values 1.43	Median Values 1.40–1.42

Source: Islam 1967: 216.
The cost ratios are based on ex-factory prices without indirect taxes.
(A) unweighted, simple averages of individual industry ratios.
(B) ratios are based on the number of products produced by each industry as weights.
(C) ratios are based on the number of products as weights for deriving the cost ratios of each major industry group; these are then weighted by the values of output of each major group of industry.

Were there to exist strong elements of learning-by-doing, we would anticipate older firms to have lower comparative costs. There is no clear relation between the age of a firm in Pakistan (in the mid-1960s) and its comparative cost ratio at the aggregate industry level, or when disaggregating (into consumer, intermediate and capital goods) (Islam 1967: 222). Such evidence is not conclusive, as the composition of industries in different age groups is different, and different industries are likely to have different periods of infancy.[6] Lewis (1970) disagrees, and argues that it was those industries that had been established the earliest and had the earliest import substitution that showed declining relative prices. These included, he argued, edible oils, cigarettes, cotton textiles, soaps, matches, pharmaceuticals and metal products.

Some evidence on efficiency comes from data on the physical operations of industrial plants. A study of the jute industry by the Food and Agriculture Organisation (FAO) showed that output (in weight) of cloth per loom in Pakistan more than doubled between 1954 and 1959. Some of this difference stemmed from a higher proportion of automatic looms and of new machinery in Pakistan, but the main difference was in the more intensive use of machinery. Firms in Pakistan utilised their comparative advantage in lower labour costs and compensated for scarce capital by working several shifts. Per-shift figures suggest that, after an average of only five years of operation, Pakistan's physical efficiency was little different from other countries' (Papanek 1964: 64–5). There was still enormous scope for efficiency gains in industry by the end of the 1950s. For example, there was considerable excess capacity in Pakistan. About 60% of the industries examined worked below 40% of their installed capacity (Islam 1967: 230). This was due to learning problems, not to a fundamentally wrong choice of technique of production. Only around 5% of total investment was reported to be operating at less than full capacity due to a shortage of skilled labour by 1958 (Papanek 1967: 108).

Table 5.3 shows that productivity measures in cotton yarn improved substantially over time, though remained low in 1959. Improvement was most marked in low-quality yarn, where the textile industry had the longest experience of production.

More general measures of productivity show positive signs of learning over the 1950s, in industry if not agriculture. There were signs of labour productivity growth over the 1950s. Between 1951 and 1961 in East Pakistan output per worker declined by 14% in agriculture, and increased by 49% in industry; in West Pakistan output per worker declined by 6% in agriculture, and increased by 11% in industry. The greater share of agriculture meant these figures implied a drop of 8% in output per worker in East Pakistan and a drop of 5% in West Pakistan (Farooq 1973: 302–3). Other figures

Table 5.3 Output of yarn per cotton spindle (ounces per spindle per sheet)

Quality of Yarn	India 1948	Pakistan 1952	Pakistan 1959
10s	7.74	–	10.78
20s	5.20	4.50	5.35
30s	2.80	2.80	3.00
40s	2.20	1.80	1.95
80s	0.90	–	0.89

Source: Papanek 1967: 65.

show no change in labour productivity between 1955/56 and 1959/60, though some rather dramatic fluctuations between these two dates cast some doubt on their reliability (Wizarat 2002: 82). The productivity of capital shows steady improvement after the late 1940s. The capital-output ratio declined from 4.9 in 1947/48 to 3.6 in 1958/59 (Papanek 1964: 478). Using two measures of TFP for large-scale manufacturing, Wizarat finds that an index increased rapidly from about 70 in 1955/56 to 100 in 1959/60, and inputs increased rapidly, but were surpassed by output growth (2002: 76–7).

For agriculture, there were generally disappointing indications of learning. Growth was resolutely based on using more labour, rather than raising productivity. There was a steady increase in total area farmed and in the amount of irrigated land. Growth was based on increased use of inputs, more water, fertiliser, tube-wells, tractors, and credit (Khan 1999: 108). There were some investments in large irrigation projects (Thal Development, Lower Sindh Barrage, Taunsa Barrage, Kurian Garahi Project) that brought new land into cultivation with a long lag, but did little to increase productivity in existing land (Ahmed and Amjad 1984).

In agriculture, between 1953/54 and 1959/60 the aggregate input index increased at an annual compound rate of 2.4% (labour, land and capital all increasing), the value added index rose annually by 0.9%, and TFP declined by 1.5% annually (Wizarat 1981: 433). Output per hectare (yield) either stagnated or declined slightly for wheat, maize and sugar cane, increased steadily for rice, and showed a sharp (30%) increase for cotton lint (Khan 1999: 105–6). In aggregate terms, there was some improvement in the performance of agriculture over the 1950s. The annual growth of crop production increased from 0.33% between 1950 and 1955, to 1.91% between 1955 and 1960. This was caused partly by an increase in the growth of inputs (from 1.64% to 2.40% p.a.) and partly by a slowdown in the rate at which productivity per acre was declining (from -0.91% to -0.14% p.a.). As a result, TFP decline slowed from -1.31% to -0.48% p.a over the two time periods (Chaudhry et al. 1996: 530). The slow growth of output and productivity in agriculture in the 1950s still represented a significant improvement over the pre-independence period. Between 1941/42 and 1950/51, for example, output had grown by only 0.05% p.a. (Kurosaki 1999: 161–4).

The (political) role of the state, 1951/52 to 1958/59: institutions

This section focuses on institutions that may or may not allow the state to overcome the inherent conflicts associated with economic growth. The institutions of autonomy and repression (the civil service and the military) were reconstructed quickly after independence. There is no consistent evidence that this relative autonomy allowed the government to implement policies over the 1950s in general and systematic accordance with long-term goals. The state failed in its efforts to promote inclusionary institutions. Labour remained badly organised and, despite falling/stagnating real wages, posed no threat to the state and accumulation over the 1950s. The state also failed in its efforts to reduce political mobilisation based around the issue of language – the next chapter shows that this had severe long-term implications. The relative failure of the political party system is an important part of this explanation and a stark contrast to India. There was no successful attempt to project any unifying ideology. The episode of growth was not sustainable. The exhaustion of opportunities for import substitution was limiting further growth solely to expansion of (slow-growing) domestic demand. Without sufficient autonomy or the development of inclusive institutions to absorb groups, it was unlikely that the state would have been able to sustain growth through an aggressive export-orientated strategy, or through deepening the pattern of import substitution to more capital-intensive and technologically demanding segments of industry, or pushing the growth of agriculture.

Institutions to manage conflict: autonomy and repression

The institutions of autonomy and repression were reconstructed quickly in the aftermath of independence; these included the civil service, the military, and the constitution.

There were few Muslims in senior positions in the civil service in the areas of British India that became Pakistan. For example, Muslims comprised 52.2% of the population and 19.35% of those in government service in the Punjab; 94.1% and 24.2%, respectively, in NWFP; and 87.4% and 10.5% in Baluchistan (Talha 2000: 9). In Pakistan the Indian Civil Service (ICS) was resurrected in the form of the Civil Service of Pakistan (CSP), where 500 members held commanding positions over 500,000 government employees during the 1950s and 1960s. Training and initial recruitment was controlled by the autonomous Public Services Commission, which was manned by CSP officers. The CSP was 'almost a caste on its own' (Alavi 1983: 67). The CSP had 'an extraordinary esprit de corps', whose members provided mutual support and solidarity and supported a legitimating myth of guardianship. In the 1950s the bureaucracy was the dominant element in a ruling military-bureaucratic oligarchy and was especially dominant over the political leadership formally in power. This was a legacy from reforms to the British Indian administration in the early 1920s. Under a 1921 Act, Indian Ministers were permitted to hold minor portfolios in provincial government. British civil servants had then acted to ensure their own dominance over the newly emerging political classes, and the trend continued after independence. The creation of the post of Secretary General after independence gave a bureaucratic office holder direct authority over every secretary of every ministry in Pakistan. The Secretary General presided over a Committee of Secretaries of Ministries that effectively formulated and co-ordinated policy as a super-cabinet, and so reduced the power of the political leadership. (Alavi 1983: 75).

The army was likewise reconstructed after independence. One estimate is that there were only 100 Muslim officers of the rank of captain and above in the British Indian army that opted for Pakistan, and none of these was above the rank of colonel. Almost 500 British officers were still present as late as 1951 when the first Pakistani (Ayub Khan) became commander in chief. Training was similar in spirit to that of the bureaucracy. The Pakistan Military Academy, and later Air Force Academy, were modelled on Britain's Sandhurst, with an independent board responsible for selection and a General Headquarters responsible for the administrative affairs of the various armed services (Hashmi 1983). While the bureaucracy was the dominant institution of state until 1954, after that date the military began to increase its influence.[7] After the dismissal of the Mazimuddin government in 1953, General Ayub Khan was appointed as a minister in the new government instead of retirement as rules demanded. Ayub was granted a further extension in 1958. The closer connections with the USA wrought by signing the CENTO treaty further enhanced the role of the military (Siddiqa 2007). Ayub Khan, for example, as commander in chief negotiated directly with Washington to secure the military aid programme of 1953/54 (Ali 2008). The final indication of the supreme role of the military was the military coup of 1958 and subsequent transfer of Pakistan's capital from Karachi to the garrison town of Rawalpindi in 1960 (Jaffrelot 2002).

In 1956 a constitutional bill was placed before the constituent assembly; its preamble defined Pakistan as an Islamic republic. It was based on a federal constitution and British-style parliamentary system. Far from providing checks and balances, it was a 'veritable time bomb' (Jalal 1990: 215). The power of the President was far greater than that typical in parliamentary systems and reflected the domestic strength of the military and civil service and weakness of party politics. The President was elected by the national and provincial assemblies for a maximum of two five-year terms. The President was subject to impeachment proceedings, but this required a very high (three-fourths) majority. Although the President was compelled to appoint a Prime Minister likely to command a majority in Parliament, executive authority was vested in the President, who also had the authority to intervene in cabinet discussion and faced no compulsion to accept cabinet advice/decisions. The President had the ability to appoint and dismiss the cabinet. The President had the authority to issue legal ordinances when Parliament was not in session and to use emergency powers to dismiss the assembly and rule by ordinance for an indefinite period. The same powers were replicated by the Governor over provincial governments and assemblies. The President was also the supreme commander of the armed forces (Jalal 1990; Afzal 2001).

There is no consistent evidence that this relative autonomy allowed the government to implement policies over the 1950s in general and systematic accordance with long-term goals. The first planning attempt was the Six Year Development Programme of 1951–7, which was drawn up over three months in 1950. The plan was little more than a general statement about goals and a list of specific projects. The Economic Appraisals Committee in 1952 gave an authoritative statement of government policy, but it contributed little in the way of planning. The first comprehensive efforts at planning began in 1953, with the appointment of a Planning Board with a staff of foreign advisors. The board drew up the First Five-year Plan scheduled to run from 1955 to 1960. The plan and its analysis were largely ignored until being more formally abandoned after the military coup in 1958 (Lewis 1969: 11). If unable to align policy with long-run economic goals, the autonomy of the state can be seen more narrowly in its ability to push through certain policies. Some writers, such as Burki (1999), have emphasised the role of historical accident (the decision not to devalue in 1949 and the Korean War) in enabling and promoting the shift to import substitution industrialisation. Others, such as Amjad (1983: 260), disagree and emphasise the role of emerging political and economic interests. He argues that the shift to import substitution industrialisation in the early 1950s was motivated by changing interests among merchant capital. Much of the profits earned by traders during the Korean War were spent on importing industrial machinery (especially textile machinery). So equipped, argues Amjad, the traders then pushed the government into providing them with the tariffs and subsidies necessary to become industrialists. There is a problem with this argument noted (also) by Amjad (1983: 261). How can we explain the general bias against agriculture throughout the 1950s, when landowners were clearly a dominant social group? This anomaly becomes clear if we accept that the bureaucracy and later the military were relatively autonomous of other social groupings. The decision to promote industry at the expense of agriculture was not due to the balance of class forces, specifically merchant capital over landowners, but to a decision carried out by a relatively autonomous state. The large landowners, for example, with few exceptions (the Qureshis of Sagoda and Hotis), did not themselves enter industry.

Leftwich (2000) notes that a key feature of developmental states is 'bureaucratic power'. The relative autonomy of the state is shaped by the creation of a 'powerful, professional, competent, insulated, career based bureaucracy' independent of the vagaries of short-term politics and able to formulate goals of long-term planning. In Pakistan the bureaucracy-military was certainty able to subvert the elected institutions of the state. Soon after independence, elected state-level governments were dismissed, the first being the government of Khan Sahib in NWFP by Jinnah, and seven months later the government of Khuro in Sindh (Noman 1988). Another example is that in 1953, despite his budget having been approved overwhelmingly by Parliament a few days before, the government of Nazimuddin was dismissed by the Governor General Ghulam Mohammed. Nazimuddin was replaced by Bogra, the pro-American Pakistani ambassador in Washington, a marginal political figure from East Pakistan (Jalal 1990: 180).

The state never managed to achieve the status of a developmental state[8] and could be better characterised as a 'fearful state', which saw pluralism as a sign of weakness, preferred coercion to co-option, was conscious of its own lack of legitimacy, and fearful of subversion by ethnic and subaltern forces (Talbot 1998). Prospective elections in 1958 would likely have been won by the Awami League in East Pakistan and Qaiym Muslim League in West Pakistan. The coup d'état of October 1958 was not a seizure of power. Mirza as President and Ayub as army Commander-in-Chief already held effective power. Rather, it marked the dismissal of the politicians who had provided a facade of parliamentary government and the dismantling of the constitutional apparatus through which new political forces were emerging and challenging bureaucratic power (Alavi 1983). Ayub was concerned that the first general election scheduled for April 1959 might have produced a coalition that would take Pakistan out of the security pacts and to a non-aligned foreign policy (Ali 2008), or that power would end up being transferred away from the West Pakistani bureaucratic-military to East Pakistan (Noman 1988).

The army seized power in October 1958 on the initiative of President Mirza, and within a few weeks the President himself had been deposed. Within six months all political parties and trade unions had been banned, and Progressive Newspapers Limited (the largest chain of opposition newspapers) had been taken over by the government (Ali 2008).

Institutions to manage conflict: inclusionary

The Indian state experienced similar problems at independence: a vast, heterogeneous population whose expectations of material gains and capacity to mobilise had been heightened by a long independence struggle. In McCartney (2009a) it was argued that the principle reason that the Indian state was able to overcome the inevitable conflicts associated with (rapid) industrialisation was an inclusive institution – the Congress party.

The Indian Congress was, through the efforts of Gandhi, organised into 21 units in conformity with major linguistic boundaries. There was a concerted effort to decentralise the party with branches down to local level (Menon 2003: 63–76). This hierarchical structure allowed the party to develop a system of factions that provided a system of co-ordination between the various levels of politics and government. By contrast, the Muslim League had very little organisational strength in the areas of future Pakistan; the party's main strength lay in Bengal, Uttar Pradesh and the Muslim University at Aligarh.

Bardhan argued that Congress 'provided a subtle and resilient mechanism for conflict management and transactional negotiations among the proprietary classes' (1984: 77). The central leadership provided a system of mediation and arbitration and inter-level co-ordination in the party. The person of Nehru provided the ultimate arbiter.[9] For a brief while, Jinnah offered an equivalent. Jinnah had a genius for building the broad coalition that created Pakistan, the urban gentry, rural notables and biraderi, professional associations, bazaar and artisans. Jinnah was able to override factional and parochial identities and, as did Gandhi and Nehru, bring together vertically structured patron-client and kinship networks and urban associations (Jones 2003). While in India the mantle of Gandhi passed to Nehru who remained as Prime Minister for seventeen years, Jinnah was dead within a few months after independence.

After independence the Indian Congress system retained a flexibility in incorporating a diverse array of the elite into its ranks. The Muslim League, by contrast, retained a rigidity and instead was more inclined to confront those who contested its hegemonic claims. Liaquat Ali Khan said in October 1950, 'the formation of new political parties in opposition to the Muslim League is against the interest of Pakistan' (Talbot 1998: 93). Without a domestic political base, the migrant political leadership relied on the military and bureaucracy, rather than incorporating local notables within the Muslim League (Jalal 1995). In East Pakistan political trouble flared when Jinnah appointed Nurul Amin as Chief Minister over the head of the provincial league. With no domestic political base, Amin had to increasingly rely on support from the centre and a group of non-Bengali civil servants. By February 1952 there was a General Strike in Dacca, students were killed and the army was called in. The provincial Muslim League was faced with mass defections, and support for Amin's ministry disappeared. Those of the elite incorporated into the Indian Congress were then subject to the hierarchy, conflict management procedures and transactional negotiations of the system. Votes were in turn delivered by local-level bosses acting as political intermediaries between the party and electorate. By contrast, the Muslim League had little organisational machinery linking the central leadership with those exercising power at the provincial and local levels. Those in power at the centre were either politicians with no identifiable bases of support, or civil servants. Pakistan, with its federal structure and absent national party organisation, lacked a means to facilitate two-way communication between government and different levels of society, hindering efforts at national integration. In the Indian Congress, new leaders were accommodated as both cause and effect of the party's endemic factionalism. New groups were incorporated to reinforce the positions of existing leaders. Successful leaders were those skilful in rewarding diverse factions and communities (Weiner 1971). Soon after independence the Working Committee of the Muslim League postponed all internal elections. Erosion of the political process was not just a consequence of the chaotic factionalism of the Muslim League, but that process was sacrificed to the desire to construct a strong central authority (Jalal 1990).

The Congress system allowed groups losing out from the pattern of economic development to be incorporated and compensated at minimal cost. There was nothing equivalent in Pakistan. Examples discussed here include the labour and language movements.

In 1946 the incoming Congress government was faced by a left-led labour uprising. The strikes were led by the All-India Trade Union Congress, a large and militant union federation. A new federation, the Indian National Trade Union Congress (INTUC) was formed and affiliated to Congress. Every affiliated organisation was compelled to submit to arbitration when industrial disputes were not resolved by negotiation. Under patronage of the government, the INTUC grew rapidly to become the largest labour organisation in the country. In return for accepting these institutional arrangements, working conditions were regulated by government legislation. Strike activity quickly dropped down to pre-war levels, and radical labour ceased to be a threat, even as the development strategy nibbled away at real disposable income. In Pakistan, the government attempted to likewise form a labour organisation that would agree to prioritise rapid economic development. Many of the leftists leaders of the East Pakistan Trade Union Federation (renamed the All Pakistan Trade Union Federation in 1949) were successfully isolated and the union was brought into line with the more accommodating Pakistan Federation of Labour in West Pakistan. The union of these two organisations in the All Pakistan Confederation of Labour (APCOL) in 1950 was largely achieved through the efforts of Dr A.M.Malik, an important leader in undivided India and president of the East Pakistan organisation. In 1950 Malik was appointed Labour Minister in the Central Government for the primary purpose of bringing the labour movement into a centralised body under government influence. Efforts at incorporation soon faltered, and the government resorted to cruder tactics. By 1954 the total membership of the registered trade unions of the PTUF was 410,755, or about 10% of the organised workers of East and West Pakistan. Because the PTUF was most active in the Punjab, a Punjab Labour League was promoted by the government in 1949 with the purpose of attracting workers away from the Communist-led unions. The Punjab Labour League proved to be ineffective and it was dissolved in 1954 (Shaheed 1983: 273). Other methods were used to try and neutralise the PTUF. The president, Mirza Ibrahim, was arrested and imprisoned in 1948 for fomenting 'illegal' strikes. Faiz Ahmed Faiz, president of the PTUF in 1948–51 was arrested in 1951 on the charge of conspiracy to overthrow the government and he remained in prison until 1954. The General Secretary of the Federation, Mohammed Afzal, was in jail in 1954–55. In 1954 the Communist Party was banned, and the PTUF, as designated as the labour arm of the CPP, was also banned (Shaheed 1983). Organised labour was no real threat to the central government during the 1950s. This was more due to chance and the failures of union organisation than conscious efforts at incorporation on the Indian model or state repression. At the time of independence unions were weak; in most cases they had been branches of all-India organisations, with no independent existence, and most were run by leaderswho migrated at the time of partition. The union system progressively fragmented. Between 1951 and 1958 there was a large increase in the number of registered trade unions, but little increase in membership. In December 1951 there were 309 registered trade unions with a membership of 393,137, and in June 1958 there were 635 trade unions with a membership of 376,029 (Ahmed and Amjad 1984). Although the government failed in its efforts to incorporate the labour movement, the labour movement was unable to mount any challenge in the 1950s. The number of man days lost due to disputes increased from the late 1940s to a fairly low plateau between 1954 and 1958 (with a drop in 1955); this was mirrored by the number of workers involved in disputes. After 1958 both indices dropped sharply (Wizarat 2002: 231).

'At independence the inherited state boundaries in South Asia were based on the vagaries of British colonisation, leaving large minority languages stranded in numerous states. Language in both India and Pakistan had/has a crucial material aspect. Proficiency in an officially recognised language was needed for those aspiring to public employment or for entry to higher education. In India such language issues led to large opposition movements in the 1950s in much of the South, particularly Tamil Nadu. There was a fear that the language riots would escalate into full-blown secessionist demands. The central state sought to avoid direct conflict and approached the problem with clear guidelines, based on arbitration and mediation with local leaders. The informal mechanisms of the Congress party organisation and its decentralised reach proved crucial in this process. The party centre promoted and supported strong state leaders to ensure mutual compromise on language issues. In 1955 the States Re-organisation Committee published its report and the southern states were re-organised in a manner that brought their boundaries into closer conformity with traditional linguistic regions. Somewhat later in 1960 Bombay province was split into Maharashtra and Gujarat, in 1966 Punjab was re-organised and Haryana created. The political heat was removed from the language movement and its nascent leadership incorporated into the Congress party at senior levels, which then retained political power in all these new states in the 1962 elections" (McCartney 2009a: 114). The contrast with Pakistan is striking: in 1951 the Constituent Assembly rejected that Bengali be used alongside Urdu as a national language, though over half of the population spoke Bengali and only 7% Urdu. Urdu was the mother tongue of a small minority and its choice reflected the prominent role in the Pakistan movement of the Urdu-speaking landed gentry and intelligentsia of northern India and was a symbol of centrally driven national integration (Bose 2004). The West Pakistani press and leadership declared the Bengali language issue to be the creation of Hindus and communists and part of a conspiracy to break up Pakistan. A general strike and deaths from police action at Dhaka University in 1952 generated Bengal's first martyrs and a direct line to the massive political mobilisation in the 1960s, and eventually independence in 1971. The language issue became a convenient hook on which to mobilise opposition, in large part owing to the inept and brutal handling of the issue by the state (Rahman 1997; Talbot 1998; Jaffrelot 2002).

The Indian Congress monopolised government from the centre and states down to village panchayats, which facilitated its ability to accommodate new leaders and groups. In the 1952 elections Congress received 45% of votes in the national elections and

42% of votes in the assembly elections; in 1957 this rose to 48% and 45% respectively. This translated into over 70% of seats in the Lok Sabha and control of almost every state government. In power, Congress monopolised the spoils of patronage from sugar co-operatives, banking corporations, and the government allocation of resources – licences, fertilisers, seeds and road construction. The monopoly of patronage resources made it rational for groups and patrons to remain within the party, even if they were not gaining short-term benefits. The exit option deprived them of any prospect of benefits. By contrast, the Muslim League suffered electoral collapse soon after independence. In the 1954 East Pakistan provincial election the ruling Muslim League won only 10 of 309 seats. The election was won by the United Front, a six-party alliance of convenience. It marked the disintegration of the Muslim League in Bengal and fragmentation of politics in the state. The victorious United Front government was soon dismissed from office and replaced by Governors Rule, and the state was subject to a wave of repression and arrests (Afzal 2001). In September 1956, despite still having a majority in the national assembly, Chaudhuri Mohammad Ali resigned and the Muslim League was finally eliminated from government in the centre and provinces.

Institutions to manage conflict: ideology

Pakistan never managed to construct any ideology that could act as a unifying element in state construction and national integration and remained a country in search of a national identity. After independence, language and religion opened a 'Pandora's box' of conflicting identities (Talbot 1998). Pakistani nationalism was imposed from the top. Consistently, the state regarded all dissent as a law and order problem, rather than a political issue (Talbot 1998). Society was compelled to accommodate itself to a state with uncertain structures of authority and only vague claims to legitimacy. The 1956 Constitution contained a few Islamic provisions, but an ideology of state-promoted Islam never came to replace the localised practice of the religion: in the Punjab and Sindh landlords continued to combine the functions of local religious leaders as pirs and sajjada nashins (Jalal 1990).

6 An episode of growth, 1960/61–1969/70

Summary of chapter findings

The period from 1958 to 1968 is often known as 'The Decade of Development' and is viewed by many with striking optimism, 'the period beginning approximately in 1958, and extending to date, has witnessed a change from almost hopeless stagnation to ebullient expansion that is rare in the annals of the less developed world (Papanek 1967: x).

The chapter is divided into three parts, each focusing on one particular role that the state has in promoting economic growth. These roles relate to finance, production and institutions. The underlying hypothesis here is that the state needs to be successful in all three to initiate and sustain an episode of growth.

The first section shows that the government of Pakistan aimed to mobilise an increased surplus, but that such aims met with limited success as savings and tax revenue increased from low to not-quite-so-low levels. As in the 1950s, the bulk of the increase in the surplus came from foreign capital inflows. The state proved well able to sustain high profit rates in the private sector, complementing traditional trade and exchange rate policies with reforms to corporate taxation and anti-union policies. The second section examines the role of the state in achieving a productive use of the surplus in both the public and private sectors. The principal sources of growth were domestic demand and a green revolution in agriculture, while export growth also contributed. There is evidence of high levels of inefficiency and low productivity in both industry and agriculture at the outset of this period. Production was very capital-intensive, and there were few signs of labour-intensive growth. There were indications of learning over the 1960s; relative costs of production were declining, and labour, capital and overall (TFP) productivity increased. The third section focuses on institutions that may or may not allow the state to overcome the inherent conflicts associated with economic growth. In the early years the autonomy of state policy making was enhanced by a more repressive stance with regard to groups such as newspapers, students and unions. The 1962 Constitution also strengthened the power of the central Presidency. This autonomy was reflected in more coherent planning and agricultural policy making. The episode of growth had its successes. A more autonomous state was able to intensify the more *ad hoc* process of import substitution of the 1950s through policies that sustained profitability in the private sector. The state was also able to push industry into upgrading the structure of production, through high levels of investment and successful learning, and also to push industry into high value-added niches in world export markets. The episode of growth was economically sustainable. By the late 1960s this autonomy gradually declined and policy became increasingly determined by political criteria. The state failed in its efforts to promote inclusionary institutions. Social change unleashed by the green revolution, urbanisation and industrialisation was not accommodated by Ayub's system of 'Basic Democrats' or, later, by the return to party-based politics. The attempt to project a modernist ideology had no substantial effect.

Recap from Chapter 3

The statistical analysis in Chapter 3 showed that GDP growth averaged 6.8% p.a. between 1960/61 and 1969/70. Growth was more balanced compared with the 1950s; there was a notable acceleration in the growth of agricultural output, which easily surpassed population growth. Growth in the large-scale manufacturing sector revived after showing signs of slowing in the late 1950s. Concerns included a general slowdown after the mid-1960s and growing disparities in income levels between West and East Pakistan. Structural change continued, with agriculture continuing to decline in its share of output and employment. Domestic demand was the most important source of growth throughout the decade.

Limitations of alternative explanations

Liberalisation

There is one strand of argument that sees rapid growth in the 1960s as having been a consequence of a more liberal policy environment (and greater political stability) – in particular, that the Free List and Export Bonus System (EBS) marked an important shift from direct to more flexible and market-orientated indirect controls (Papanek 1967: 127).

Placing imports of industrial raw materials and spare parts on a Free List in January 1964 was a much-heralded liberalising measure, the 'greatest single step toward import liberalisation taken since the imposition of detailed licensing in 1953' (Thomas 1966: 516). The Free List was started in 1964, when four (iron and steel) products were de-licensed with the backing of a US loan, and was extended to include some 60 items by the end of 1965. The Free List led to immediate falls in prices of included goods and easier access to raw materials for business. These liberalising benefits (which in any case occurred several years after the breakpoint in growth in c. 1960) were soon over. The Aid to Pakistan Consortium was cancelled in June 1965, and in September Pakistan went to war with India; the resulting decline in foreign exchange availability led to items on the list being subject to renewed administrative controls (Amjad 1982). Between 1964/65 and 1966/67 for Pakistan as a whole there had been no change in the average markup (43%) on imported commodities, and the markup on items included on the Free List actually increased, from about 30% to 43%. The most significant increase was for intermediate goods, where the markup increased from 26% to 67% (Alamgir 1968: 49).

The Export Bonus System (EBS) was introduced to compensate for the overvaluation of the rupee. The EBS permitted exporters of manufactured goods to retain a portion of their foreign exchange earnings in the form of bonus vouchers, which could be used to purchase imports on the bonus-import list or be freely marketed at a (typically, large) premium (Hecox 1970). The EBS reduced the number of individual decisions required of officials, who no longer had to determine who got an import licence and for what commodity. Freer imports under the bonus vouchers permitted more flexibility in the system; for example, an industrialist could access imported spare parts by buying a bonus voucher. The EBS introduced new and offsetting non-liberal elements to trade policy and resulted in a complex system of multiple exchange rates. The lists of commodities on which a bonus was allowed, the number of commodities that could be imported under the scheme, and the rates of bonus were all determined directly and in detail by administrative decisions. The rates of bonus and the resulting rates of protection were highly discriminatory and arbitrary and were changed frequently. There is no basis for assuming that the new system produced a structure of relative prices significantly more rational than that prevailing under the regime of widespread import licensing (Griffin and Khan 1972).

Tariffs were increased. Between 1959/60 and 1965/66 import tariffs increased from 35% to 70% on essential consumer goods, from 99% to 180% on luxury consumer goods, from 81% to 114% on capital goods, and from 14% to 34% on machinery and equipment. Most of this increase occurred between 1959/60 and 1960/61 (Lewis 1965: 474, 1970: 68; Thomas 1966: 532). Further increases occurred in the mid- and late-1960s (Thomas 1966: 518; White 1974: 133). There were also tighter controls on access to trade credit after July 1964 (Thomas 1966: 518).

A summary measure of trade policy (anti-export bias) was calculated by Mahmood and Qasim (1992). The liberalisation measures of the early 1960s did not reduce the anti-export bias of the effective exchange rate. Table 6.1 shows that the effective exchange rate for exports did increase steadily over the 1960s, but this was countered

Table 6.1 Effective exchange rates (EER) of imports (M) and exports (X)

Year	EER^M	EER^X	EER^M/EER^X
1959–60	11.13	7.85	1.42
1960–61	11.16	7.98	1.40
1961–62	11.22	7.92	1.42
1962–63	11.50	7.61	1.51
1963–64	11.90	7.63	1.56
1964–65	12.88	8.13	1.58
1965–66	13.39	8.17	1.64
1966–67	13.40	7.75	1.73
1967–68	14.07	7.80	1.80
1968–69	14.75	8.23	1.79
1969–70	14.77	8.40	1.76
1970–71	14.94	8.92	1.67

Source: Mahmood and Qasim 1992: 885.

by a more rapid increase in the effective exchange rate for imports, which implied that the anti-export bias actually increased between 1959/60 and 1967/68.

The world economy

Measures of the external terms of trade offer some support for the view that a positive shock from the world economy could have behind the acceleration of growth in the early 1960s. According to one measure, between 1959/60 and 1964/65 the price index of imports declined from 100 to 97 and that for export prices rose from 100 to 120, implying that the ratio of export to import prices increased from 100 to 124. For this series, though, this rise occurred well after the increase in economic growth. The ratio of export to import prices had only increased from 100 in 1959/60 to 104 in 1962/65 (Papanek 1967: 15). According to another series, there was a much more immediate increase in Pakistan's external terms of trade, from 100.0 in 1959/60 to 137.4 in 1960/61 (mainly due an increase of 47% in the unit values of exports) – although there was an equally sharp decline, to 106.6 in 1962/63 (again, mainly due to a decline in the unit value of exports) (Lewis 1970: 126).

There is good reason to believe that the role of foreign trade was simply too small for this improvement in the external terms of trade to have much aggregate influence. The ratio of exports to GDP stagnated at 4.5% between 1960 and 1965, then declined to 3.7% by 1970; that of imports fell from 10.7% to 10.6% and 7.6% over the same period. The ratio of total trade to GDP declined steadily, from 15.2% in 1960, to 15.1% in 1965 and 11.3% in 1970 (Husain 1999: 324).

The (economic) role of the state, 1960/61 to 1969/70: finance

The government of Pakistan was very candid about its development strategy. In the Second Five-year Plan it declared, 'Direct taxes cannot be made more progressive without affecting the incentives to work and save. The tax system should take full account of the needs of capital formation, it will be necessary to tolerate some initial growth in income inequalities to reach high levels of saving and investment. What is undesirable is a wide disparity in consumption levels. Tax policy should, therefore, be so orientated as to direct a large part of high incomes into saving and investment rather than consumption' (Maddison 1971: 136).

These aims met at best only limited success; savings and tax revenue increased from low to not-quite-so-low levels. The fierce contemporary praise by some of Ayub's regime was rather misplaced, 'In the face of its pitiful resource and capital endowment at independence, and in comparison with other countries, Pakistan's performance was outstanding' (Papanek 1967: 2). Private savings in particular showed no sustained increase, despite a gradual expansion of the financial sector. The bulk of the increase in the surplus came from foreign capital inflows, which reached 10% of GDP by the mid-1960s. The state proved well able to sustain high profit rates in the private sector, complementing traditional trade and exchange rate policies with reforms to corporate taxation and anti-union policies.

The mobilisation of savings, 1960/61 to 1970/71

There are various estimates of total savings over the 1950s: 5.6% of GNP in 1959/60 to 7.4% in 1961/62 (Power 1963: 130); 5.9% of GNP in 1959/60 to 9.5% in 1964/65 (Griffin 1965: 609); 7.1% of GNP in 1959/60 to 13.6% in 1969/70 (Lewis 1965: 464); 7.6% of GDP in 1959/60 to 10.6% in 1964/65 (current prices) or 9.6% (1959/60 prices) (Papanek 1967: 280–1); 7.88% of GNP in 1961 to 11.10% in 1970 (current prices) (Ahmed and Amjad 1984: 291); and 9.25% of GDP in 1960/61 to 12.95% in 1970/71 (Qureshi et al. 1997: 895). There is general agreement that savings increased from low to not-quite-so-low levels; some estimates even have savings falling back from peaks reached in the mid-1960s. Most estimates found savings rates in West Pakistan to be approximately double those in East Pakistan (Amjad 1982: 18; Ahmed and Amjad 1984: 80).

The role of the state in mobilising domestic savings

As usual, there are various estimates of the total tax revenue of the government. Total tax revenue increased from 6.2% of GNP in 1959/60 to 8.4% in 1964/65 (Lewis 1965: 409); from 7.0% of GNP in 1960/61 to 8.8% in 1967/68 (Ahmed and Amjad 1984: 261); from 6.1% of GNP in 1959/60 to 8.2% in 1964/65 and 9.1% in 1969/70 (Husain 1999: 176); and from 4.2% of GDP in 1959/60 to 6.4% in 1969/70 (Pasha and Fatima 1999: 204). As with savings, there is general agreement that tax revenue increased from very low to not-quite-so-low levels. What buoyancy there was in the tax system over the 1960s came from a high revenue elasticity of excise duties (2.28) to GDP growth. Revenue from excise duties increased from 0.9% to 3.0% of GDP over the 1960s. The revenue elasticity of direct taxation to GDP growth was low (0.87), and revenue from income and wealth taxes correspondingly dropped from 1.0% to 0.6% over the 1960s (Khan 1973: 422, Pasha and Fatima 1999: 204).

By the early 1960s income and corporate taxes were on a declining trend and contributed no more than 15%–20% of total tax revenue, while indirect taxes accounted for some 70%–75% (Khan 1973: 430). The marginal tax rate on taxable income in 1968/69 began at 2% and reached a ceiling of 70% at R100,000 (White 1974). The exemption level was around sixteen times average income (Griffin 1965). Income taxes also exempted a high proportion of high income individuals by not taxing agricultural income and granting 'earned income relief'. The income tax system granted exemptions on income used to pay for life insurance; to educate children; to maintain a scooter or automobile; for dividend income; and for rents from a newly constructed residence (Lewis 1964; White 1974). In 1964/65 only 113,826 individuals paid personal income taxes, which represented less than 1% of households in the country (White 1974). Corporation tax rates remained high, and the basic rate fell from 65% in 1959/60 to 60% from 1960/61 onwards (Lewis 1970: 61). Again, there were numerous exemptions. The most important was an exemption in the form of a tax holiday to 'approved' industrial undertakings, especially those based on indigenous raw materials. This condition was relaxed in 1964/65 and tax holidays were granted to firms using indigenous raw materials, exporting, in a risky sector, or contributing to agricultural development.

By the early 1960s nearly 50% of corporation tax revenue was exempted through tax holidays (Lewis 1970). The depreciation rules in effect over most of the 1950s and 1960s also had the effect of raising after-tax profits across the board. The exemption from import duty payments on imported inputs applied to most export industries (Lewis 1970).

A wealth tax was introduced into Pakistan following the recommendations of the Taxation Enquiry Committee of 1959. Under the Wealth Tax Act of 1963 all movable and immovable wealth was subject to a tax with a basic exemption of R1m. Land revenue in the two decades before 1972 had contributed about 30%–55% of provincial tax revenue, though this represented no more than about 3% of crop income. In 1967 West Pakistan raised the basic revenue rates by 25%. These measures had little impact on revenue. Crop value added more than doubled during the 1960s green revolution, whereas land revenue increased by only about one-third (Khan 1999: 131). During the 1960s the marginal rate of taxation on land revenue was estimated to be only 0.002% (Khan 1973).

The process of economic growth interacted with the tax system to undermine revenue mobilisation. Imported goods subject to high tariffs were replaced more quickly by domestic production, so tax incidence shifted towards lower-taxed imports. The export tax on raw jute and on raw cotton encouraged the domestic use of those commodities and resulted in revenue loss. The tax losses from changing economic structure and import substitution were a high proportion of overall tax revenue (Lewis 1970: 133).

Estimates of government consumption expenditure were low and fairly stagnant over the 1960s: 6%–6.5% of GDP (Pasha and Fatima 1999: 209), or 7%–10% in East Pakistan and 8%–10% in West Pakistan (Amjad 1982: 18). There was little change in subsidies (0.1%) or general administration throughout this period (Pasha and Fatima 1999: 209), and defence expenditure increased, from 5.3% of GDP in 1966 to 6.9% in 1971 (Hashmi 1983: 159), or 3.3% of GDP in 1959/60 to 3.8% in 1969/70 (Pasha and Fatima 1999: 209), but perhaps not as much as one would have imagined under the auspices of a military government in the aftermath of the 1965 war with India.

Fiscal policy was largely conservative throughout the 1960s; growth of government spending was kept within the limits permitted by growth in revenue and capital receipts, so that deficit financing was never more than 2.6% of GNP (Ahmed and Amjad 1984: 261). The net impact of fiscal policy was that public savings rates increased from 0.1% of GNP in 1959/60 to 2.4% in 1964/65 (Lewis 1965: 466), or by another estimate, there was a milder upward trend from a higher starting base, from 2.11% in 1960/61 to 3.15% in 1968/69, before falling sharply (Qureshi *et al.* 1997: 895).

The role of the state in creating institutions to mobilise private sector savings

There was no sustained increase in private savings over the 1960s, with the total increasing from 7.01% of GDP in 1960/61 to a peak of 16.69% in 1964/65, then declining to 7.74% in 1970/71. Corporate savings increased steadily, with fluctuations, from less than 0.95 to 1.26% over the same period. Household savings showed no trend, and fluctuated wildly (between 0.65% and 13.75% of GDP), sufficiently so as to shed doubt on the veracity of the data (Qureshi et al. 1997: 895).

State efforts were more successful in continuing the shift of savings from the informal to the formal sector. By the mid-1960s large parts of Pakistan's economy remained outside the formal monetised economy. Sample survey in Dacca reveals that as much as 42.5% of personal savings in the urban sector were in the form of gold and ornaments, consumer durables and housing (Griffin 1965: 609). Non-monetised investment declined from 16% of total investment in 1959/60 to less than 7% in 1964/65 (Papanek 1967: 283).

The State Bank of Pakistan (SBP) (established in 1947) made continuing efforts to develop the formal financial sector. The number of bank branches increased sharply, from 1,298 in 1964, to 3,418 in 1971 (Zaidi 2005). There is little evidence on the depth of the monetary system before 1961, but some indication that the system was deepening. There was rapid expansion of the money supply in the 1960s, alongside price stability, indicating growth in money demand (Ansari 1999). Financial depth is measured as broad money[1] divided by nominal GDP lagged by one year. Financial depth averaged 36.14% between 1961 and 1970 (Khan et al. 2005: 824). The ratio of bank deposits liabilities to GDP averaged 23.25%, of currency to GDP 16.06%, of private sector credit to GDP 19.6%, and of stock market capitalisation to GDP 8.42% (Khan and Qayyum 2007: 15). The ratio of M2 to GDP averaged 49.5% between 1961 and 1970 (Husain 1999: 179).

The slow growth of household savings despite the deepening of the financial sector can in part be explained by the general policy of financial repression (Khan 1988). The rate of interest was low over the 1960s, with the maximum rate of interest on fixed long-term deposits rising from 3.4% to 7%, while the returns on investment were as high as 15%–25%. The deliberate policy of keeping interest rates low discouraged financial asset accumulation and contributed to the slow development of the market for bonds and fixed securities (Islam 1972). There is a general agreement that there was a positive relation between the real interest rate and savings (Qureshi 1981; Khan et al. 1992; Khan and Hassan 1998).

The role of the state in mobilising foreign savings

External assistance is the missing link from low domestic savings to high investment to high growth (Hasen 1998). The share of investment financed by own savings declined from 81.8% in 1960/61 to 72.1% in 1963/64 in East Pakistan, and in West Pakistan from 61.7% to 57.8%. In both cases the growing discrepancy was caused by faster increases in investment than savings (Lewis 1970: 146). Donors responded well to the pro-Western, stable dictatorship of Ayub Khan. In 1960 the Aid to Pakistan Consortium was established to coordinate aid flows.[2] In 1960 Pakistan signed the Indus Basin Treaty with India, which unlocked donor financing for large irrigation investments (Hasen 1998), and over the 1960s a large share (20%) of foreign resources went to financing the Indus Basin Works (Papanek 1967). Increases in foreign resources were sometimes the result of specific changes in economic policy. The clearest example was the advent of the Free List in 1964, which was financed by a $100m. loan from the

USA. The Government Works Programme was financed by special foodgrain shipments under (US) Public Law 480 (Papanek 1967).

External assistance increased markedly relative to the 1950s, from 2.8% of GNP in 1959/60 to 6.6% in 1964/65, and then fell back to 3.8% in 1969/70 (Islam 1972: 503), or rose from 2.75% of GNP in 1961 to 8.79% in 1964, and then declined to 3.61% in 1970 (Ahmed and Amjad 1984: 291). Alternatively, in 1959/60 grants and loans financed around a third of total imports ($241m. out of $657m.), and in 1964/65 around a half ($657m. out of $1,291m.) (Papanek 1967: 308). By substituting the scarcity price for the official price of foreign exchange, it can be shown that the dependence on foreign assistance was far greater than implied by the official statistics. Griffin and Rahman make such adjustments and find that the ratio of 'true capital inflow' to 'true investment' was 15.7% in East Pakistan and 74.5% in West Pakistan (1972: 194).

There were problems with this capital inflow. Much of this aid was tied to purchases from the donor country. By the end of the 1960s most loans bore around 6% interest. Empirical evidence suggested that tied procurement raised this to around 15%–25% (Griffin 1965: 615, Khan 1968). A sample of 20 tied project loans in 1967 revealed a weighted average cost of 51% over international competitive bidding (Alavi 1983: 526). The share of grants as a share of total assistance declined from 54% between 1955 and 1960, to 40% between 1960 and 1965 and 26% between 1965 and 1970 (Rashid 1983: 180). Between 1955 and 1960 only $3.6m. of loans and credits from the USA were repayable in dollars, whereas between 1965 and 1970 this had increased to $819.4m. (Rashid 1983). This marked a worsening in the rate of interest, and repayment terms increased debt servicing from 3.6% of export earnings in 1960/61 to 9.9% in 1964/5 and 19.2% in 1969/70 (Griffin and Rahman 1972: 190).

Beyond the macroeconomic problems and costs associated with large-scale aid inflows, a very common unifying hypothesis to explain Pakistan's growth and development has been that Pakistan was/is dependent on foreign aid inflows. Foreign aid often came attached with institutions that were intended indirectly to influence/assist policy making in Pakistan. The Ford Foundation supported the establishment of the Development Advisory Service at Harvard in 1952, which worked with the Planning Commission from 1962 to 1970. After 1965 the Ford Foundation ended its direct support and was replaced by the World Bank and USAid. The launch of the Pakistan Institute of Development Economists (PIDE) was supported by the Ford Foundation (Naseem 2002). This has led to all sorts of allegations – that policy making was heavily influenced by the USA in particular, or even that such dependence left Pakistan and its development model very vulnerable. Some argued that the 'entire social and economic system, and the planning exercise which is its manifestation, is supported and sustained by foreign assistance' (Griffin 1965: 621) and that the entire edifice had been built upon these large doses of foreign capital, their reduction threatened the entire system (Amjad 1983: 264). Such views see a 'dependent' Pakistan with a development strategy entirely contingent on the goodwill or caprices of donors; in particular, 'US priorities determined Pakistan's domestic and foreign policies from 1951 onward' (Ali 2008: 251). The Ayub years are the most commonly cited example of this supposed dynamic at work. In response to Ayub's pro USA foreign policy stance during the Cold War, it is argued that a surge of capital inflows generated an investment-led boom until 1965, then declining capital inflows (related to the war with India in 1965) led to economic slowdown and debilitating domestic conflict over the more limited foreign largesse. Between 1960 and 1965 a government sanction for an investment project brought with it the ability to obtain the necessary foreign exchange from PICIC or IDBP. Such loans were significantly below the market interest rate. PICIC and IDBP financed about 40% of total gross investment in the early 1960s and provided about 70% of the foreign exchange component of investment for such loans. After 1965 only 18% of total investment was financed through loans from PICIC and IDBP (Amjad 1982). After 1965 infighting among the monopoly capitalists increased as there were no longer enough new investment projects to be divided up amongst them. For example, the fertiliser plant to be set up in the third FYP was delayed for almost three years because they could not decide who should set it up (Amjad 1983; Hasen 1998).

There is little general evidence for this specific argument. Over a longer period of time it is difficult to establish any one-way relationship between capital inflow and domestic savings/investment. During the first half of the 1950s there were years that witnessed a negative relationship between capital inflow and domestic savings, and in the 1960s the relationship seemed to turn positive. The causal relationship is difficult to assess (Islam 1972). Using more rigorous econometrics over a longer time period, there seems to be little generalised evidence that GDP growth in Pakistan has principally been of the (externally) dependent variety. There is a general and widespread (if not total) agreement that domestic savings have been negatively impacted by foreign capital inflows. Khilji and Zampelli (1991), for example, find that between 1960 and 1986 aid to Pakistan was strongly fungible, and the bulk of foreign aid was used to finance consumption expenditure. Mahmood and Qasim (1992) find that foreign capital inflows had a positive impact on public sector savings, but a negative impact on private sector savings. Khan *et al.* (1992) find that foreign capital inflows have a negative impact on savings.

Finally, in response to the declining flows of aid from the USA, Pakistan quite quickly completely re-orientated its foreign policy and sources of aid – hardly the actions of a cowed and dependent economy. The rapid increase in US arms deliveries to India during and after the 1962 war with China led to a deterioration of USA–Pakistan relations. Pakistan made a subsequent effort to improve relations in particular with China and other socialist countries. Between 1963 and 1965 there were numerous visits by official delegations and heads of governments between Pakistan and China; Ayub visited both China and the USSR. Increased trade and aid closely followed the improvement in Pakistani relations with socialist countries. In January 1963 Pakistan and China signed their first trade agreement. In 1963 an air transport agreement gave Pakistan International Airlines (PIA) a lucrative and virtual monopoly on China's air link with the world. This was followed by the first barter agreement between China and Pakistan, which was signed in September 1963. In 1963 and 1964 Pakistan also signed a number of trade agreements with the USSR. In August 1963 Pakistan received a $30m. loan from the USSR and in 1964 a $60m. loan from China. Socialist aid increased dramatically after 1965, when loans and grants from five socialist countries totalled $444m. (rising from 3.2% of all loans and grants received in the previous five years, to 15%). China was the largest donor, with some $260m., but Czechoslovakia ($40.1m.), Poland ($9.8m.), USSR ($93.0m.), and Yugoslavia ($33.7m.) also contributed (Noman 1975: 327). Between 1965 and 1966 China became a significant source of arms supplies, ending the virtual monopoly of the USA. In 1968 an agreement was signed to import Soviet arms (Noman 1975). While year-to-year fluctuations remained large, the three-year annual average value of trade with the socialist countries grew at the rate of 20% p.a. between 1959/60 and 1969/70. The share of such trade in Pakistan's total trade rose from 4.5% at the turn of the decade to nearly 14% by the end of the decade (Noman 1975: 322).

The role of the state in influencing private sector profitability

The government strategy was to channel resources to those groups with a high average and marginal savings rate. In practice, this meant transferring resources from rural masses to a small class of urban industrial entrepreneurs (Griffin 1965: 603). The surplus accumulated and available for investment would then be guided into high-priority projects through the use of indirect monetary and fiscal controls. These domestic resources would be supplemented with large imports of foreign capital (grants, loans, and private foreign investment). The Third Five-year Plan stated, 'There was a considerable transfer of savings from the agricultural to the industrial sector ... as terms of trade were deliberately turned against agriculture through such policies as licensing of scarce foreign exchange earned primarily by agriculture to the industrial sector, compulsory government procurement of foodgrains at low prices to subsidise the cost of living of the urban industrial workers, generous tax concessions to industry and lack of similar incentives for commercial, agricultural investment' (Griffin 1965).

There is some evidence of differences in the propensity to save from different incomes in the early 1960s.[3] Scattered sample and survey evidence suggests that corporate savings from gross pre-tax profits were something over 50%, and the share of gross savings from pre-tax gross profits increased from 70% to 74% between 1958 and 1963 (Lewis 1970: 54). Unincorporated enterprise or small-scale business also seemed to have very high ratios of savings to income (Lewis 1964). The aggregate marginal savings rate was estimated to be between 15% and 20% over the 1960s (Lewis 1965: 408). The efforts of policy makers had less aggregate impact than is often assumed. Despite efforts to shift income to the urban-industrial economy, by 1963/64 about three-quarters of total savings from all-Pakistan originated from rural areas (Bergan 1967: 186). Earlier, this section showed that corporate savings never much surpassed 1.5% of GDP over the 1960s.

In the late-1950s/early-1960s the tax system was reformed to further benefit the corporate sector. Depreciation allowances were made significantly more generous, and firms were allowed to defer tax payments, which was equivalent to giving interest-free loans. A tax holiday scheme was started in 1959, which granted complete exemption from income tax to new undertakings, provided they used local raw materials and reinvested 60% of their profits. In 1960 these conditions were extended so that existing firms expanding production could enjoy such privileges. There were numerous other exemptions, such as for banks and insurance companies, publicly listed companies, and companies involved in processing food, and for income earned abroad. In practice, less than about 30% of corporate profits were taxed. Even those eligible were subject to significant arrears. In 1964/65 legally recognised accumulated tax arrears were twice as large as direct tax payments, and only 75% of the direct taxes assessed that year were actually paid (Papanek 1967: 193; White 1974: 164; Amjad 1982: 35). While the level of gross profits (see later in this section) approximately doubled between 1959 and 1963, the level of retained earnings increased by about 150%. This reflected these reforms of corporate taxation (Haq and Baqai 1967: 298).

The incoming military government of Ayub Khan had a clear strategy to advantage profits at the expense of labour. The Industrial Disputes Ordinance of 1959 aimed to curtail the right to strike. Nearly all major industries were declared to be 'essential industries where strikes were forbidden', these included railways, post, telegraph, water, ports, defence, and telephones. Cement, iron and steel, sugar, leather and leather goods, vegetable oils, electrical equipment were declared 'essential for the time being'. The number of strikes fell drastically in the early years of the martial law government[4] (Shaheed 1983; Ahmed and Amjad 1984). There is some evidence that real wages in industry and particularly in the cotton textile sector fell in the early 1960s (Khan 1967: 326). There is also evidence of a sharp increase in hours worked in all industries, importantly including textiles in the early 1960s (Khan 1967: 331).[5] In East Pakistan labour's factor share declined from 37.6% in 1959/60 to 26.0% in 1962/63 in all industries, from 37.0% to 43.8% in cotton textiles, and from 42.3% to 29.5% for jute textiles. In West Pakistan for all industries there was a small decline, from 34.1% to 33.8%, and in cotton textiles from 38.4% to 36.1%. By factor, the share of wages in the large-scale manufacturing sector declined from 34.9% in 1959/60 to 18.3% in 1965/66, then increased slowly to 21.6% in 1970/71 (Wizarat 2002: 165).

The most important influence on relative prices by the mid-1960s was still the exchange and import control system. The domestic prices of agricultural goods were strongly influenced by the (overvalued) exchange rate received by exporters. Manufactured goods were primarily imported or competed with imports, and the restriction of imports raised domestic prices of manufactured goods. The reduction of agricultural prices was reinforced by the use of export taxes on raw jute and cotton. The relative price of agriculture remained at the low levels that it had experienced by the end of the 1950s. By one measure, the net barter terms of trade increased from 100.64 in 1956–59 to 107.99 in 1960–63, then slowly declined to just below 100 in the last years of the decade. By another measure, it rose from 98.16 in 1956–59 to 113.78 in 1964/67, and declined slightly over the rest of the decade. Strong output growth and stable relative prices implied that the income terms of trade increased, from 92.25 in 1956–59 to 204.05 in 1970–73 (Qureshi 1985: 367–9). A third estimate has the intersectoral terms of trade (three-year moving average: 1959 = 100) increasing from 98.76 in 1956–59 to 112.10 in 1964–67, then declining to 104.9 in 1969–72 (Kazi 1987: 87). Finally, the net barter terms of trade (1959/60 = 100) declined from 104.6 in 1964/65 to a low of 96.6 in 1968/69, then increased slightly to 99.4 in 1970/71 (Ali 2004: 509).

The policy structure generated an average price mark up of 50%–60% over the landed costs of imports. There were differences between the average mark ups on consumer goods (53%) and those on raw materials (39%) and capital goods (37%) (Pal 1964, 1965). Alamgir updated the work by Pal and estimated the excess of domestic wholesale prices over the landed cost of imports for both Karachi and Chittagong from November 1966 to February 1967. The overall average scarcity premium on imported commodities into Pakistan was 38.6%; on consumption goods it was 22%; on intermediate goods 51.5%; and on capital goods 43.4%. In each case, for those items subject to licensing, the mark up was significantly higher (1968: 44). Both Pal and Alamgir found that a considerable amount of the differentials by type of good was accounted for by the type of licence under which the good was importable. The licensing authorities decided on the commodities to be imported, determined the ceilings for the value of imports of individual items, groups of items and industries, and allocated the amount earmarked for each item to individual importers (Naqvi 1964). This crucially implied that 'profit allocation' was in the hands of the state (Sayeed 2002).[6] Getting the foreign exchange at the official rate via a system of licensing also provided the investor with the opportunity to over-invoice the cost of machinery and then remit the foreign exchange at the market rate (Griffin and Khan 1972; Amjad 1982). The typical magnitude of over-invoicing in 1966 was 10%; by 1970 this has increased to 20% (Winston 1970).

There are various ways of measuring the net impact of government policies. Between one-half to two-thirds of actual value added by domestic manufactures was the result of policy distortions to the price structure. Industry could purchase inputs at less than the world price, due to the overvalued exchange rate or export tax on important inputs such as raw jute and cotton, and sell its output for considerably more than the official price (due to the EBS) (Lewis and Guisinger 1968; Lewis 1969). 'Effective subsidy' can be defined as the percentage of value added in industry due to the multiple pricing of foreign exchange for inputs and outputs. In 1963/64 effective subsidy rates were 88% in cotton textiles, 46% in footwear, 80% in jute textiles, 85% in leather tanning, 58% in sewing machinery, and 48% in sports goods (Lewis 1970: 130). Guisinger and Kazi (1978) estimate the impact of government policies (low rates of interest, overvaluation of domestic currency, low tariffs on machinery imports, tax holidays and accelerated depreciation) on the market and 'rental' cost of capital for the 1960s. They estimate the 'real' rental value of capital by excluding market distortions, by calculating shadow prices for foreign exchange and interest, and by eliminating the cost-reducing effect of fiscal incentives. Capital equipment used in the large-scale manufacturing sector was mostly imported during the 1960 to 1971 period. For the years 1962/63 to 1964/65 the market cost of capital was only 25% of its 'real' price. During the Five-year Plan period the market cost increased to 34% (but 25% for those firms eligible for the new eight-year tax holiday) (Guisinger and Kazi 1978: 394).

There is a general consensus that profits in the 1960s were high, but lower than in the 1950s. Annual profits of 50%–100% on investment in the early 1950s gave way to profits in the range of 20%–50% in the 1960s[7] (Papanek 1967: 33, 39). Amjad measured the weighted average of profitability for companies quoted on the Karachi Stock Exchange (KSE) in 1961–65 and 1966–70 (excluding 1967). He found that profitability declined from 23.1% to 21.2% as measured by gross profits (minus interest) divided by net worth, from 21.1% to 17.3% for gross profits divided by net assets, and from

17.9% to 15.8% for the price-cost margin (1982: 67). By these three measures of profitability, profits in cotton textiles declined from a range of 31.3%–26.1% in 1961 to a low of 15.8%–19.2% in 1966, then revived to 19.3%–26.4% in 1969, before declining again in 1970. These patterns in profitability were heavily influenced by the variation in both the bonus rate and volume of exports for cotton textiles (Amjad 1982: 70). Haq and Baqai found a slight decline in profits in the early 1960s. Measured by the ratio of gross profits to gross sales, profits declined from 19.7% in 1959 to 18.2% in 1963; measured by the ratio of profits to gross capital employed, profits declined from 14.2% in 1959 to 13.4% in 1963; and, finally, measured by the ratio of profits to paid-up capital, profits declined from 33.6% in 1959 to 34.7% in 1963 (1967: 291). There is little evidence on state-owned enterprises. For the state-owned power sector, though, there is a general decline in profitability. Comparing 1964–65 with 1965–70 for WAPDA, the net profit margin on sales before interest increased, from 31.49% to 34.98%, and the return on capital before interest increased, from 3.34% to 3.57%. Other measures of profitability (net margin on sales after interest, return on capital after interest, etc.) declined for WAPDA. For KESC, all measures of profitability showed decline (Ghafoor and Weiss 2001: 122–3).

There is consistent, if scattered, evidence to link the high (if declining) profits of the 1960s to investment and growth by the corporate sector. Griffin estimates that roughly 15% of the value of agricultural output, when measured in local prices, was transferred to urban areas, though he argues that some 63%–85% of this was dissipated in the form of higher urban consumption (1965: 613). Others find more positive links. The cotton textiles and cigarette industries had been among the most highly protected and profitable industries in the early 1950s, accounting for nearly half of all value added in industry by 1958 (Papanek 1967). Amjad (1976, 1982) found that the boom in private industrial investment, especially in the cotton and jute industry in the early 1960s, was related to increased profits and sales. Profits, he found, became more important as a source of financing investment in the later 1960s, as the availability of foreign capital declined and firms had to rely more on internal financing. In a representative sample of the corporate sector Haq and Baqai (1967) found that internal sources of financing (profits) accounted for about 50% of investment. White (1974) finds a positive and significant relation between the growth of assets by firm between 1964 and 1968 and firm profits. Almost half of the industrialists in Pakistan in 1959 had emerged from trading, a much greater proportion than either from agriculture or existing industrial backgrounds[8] (Lewis 1970: 48). Industrial policy in Pakistan over the 1950s and especially 1960s was to push this tiny merchant capitalist class into industry. Survey evidence reveals that expected profits were the most important motivation for individuals entering large-scale industrial production in particular, and all industries in general. This was reinforced by a general perception that low profits were being earned in trading (Lewis 1970: 49).

There are various estimates of total investment in Pakistan: investment increased from 10.9% of GDP in 1959/60 to 15.8% in 1964/65 (Griffin 1965: 609); from 10.8% of GDP in 1959/60 to 17.3% in 1964/65 (at current prices) and from 10.8 to 17.0% (at 1959/60 prices) (Papanek 1967: 280–1); from 9.3% of GNP in 1959/60 to 16.9% in 1964/65 and 13.3% by the end of the 1960s (Amjad 1982); from 12.41% of

GNP in 1961 (current prices) to 17.52% in 1964, then 14.31% in 1970 (Ahmed and Amjad 1984: 291); from 8.5% of GDP in 1958/9 to 14% in 1968/9 (Hasen 1998); from 13.6% of GDP in 1959/60 to 22.8% in 1964/65, then 15.8% in 1969/70 (Kemal 1999: 158); and from 13.81% of GDP in 1960/61 to 22.34% in 1964/65 and 15.61% by 1969/70 (Kemal et al. 2006: 303). There is disagreement over the magnitudes, but a consensus over the pattern: a rapid rise in the first half of the 1960s, then a sharp decline.

The role of the state in influencing FDI

There are only rough estimates for FDI in Pakistan over the 1960s. The SBP estimated the total liabilities of firms and companies registered or incorporated outside Pakistan, Pakistani Joint Stock Companies having foreign participation, partnerships having foreign participation, net holdings of foreign securities by Pakistani nationals, Pakistani firms and companies operating abroad, and deferred payments. These estimates are based on a survey that was carried out annually. Crude estimates of the percentage of corporate business controlled either directly or indirectly by foreigners show that the share declined from 30% in 1962 to 15% in 1967. The SBP estimated that FDI averaged R80m. p.a. over the 1960s. Manufacturing increased its share of FDI from 29% in 1960 to 40% in 1967. In agriculture, all foreign investment has been in the form of reinvested earnings and, in utilities, where a sizeable stock of FDI existed, there was no new FDI after 1960. Total remittances (profits, dividends, royalties, trademarks, and technical fees) made through the SBP to private foreign investors averaged about R135m. p.a. between 1964/65 and 1967/68. These figures implied that remittances were some 50% greater than inflows of FDI (Chaudhry 1970).

There is reason to believe that positive spillovers from even this low level of FDI would have been negligible. Radhu conducted a sample of technology agreements with foreign countries over the 1960s, and most (64%) tended to be in more technologically complex industries, such as machinery chemicals or oil refining (1973: 365). A large proportion of these technology agreements had clauses that were likely to hinder the realisation of spillover benefits to the domestic economy. In the sample, 32% of the agreements had export-restriction clauses and another 8% of the agreements only permitted exports subject to the approval of the foreign firms. The purpose of such restrictions was probably to safeguard third export markets of parent companies. This would have limited the scale of production to the small local market and made it harder to realise scale economies. A total of 44% of agreements had tie-in clauses, which meant that all equipment and materials (imports) had to be purchased from the foreign collaborator or through them. These clauses and resulting over-pricing of intermediate inputs increased the cost of production and probably the import intensity of investment. Another common restrictive clause was that, on termination of an agreement, the local company should discontinue immediately the manufacture and sale of the products and all the technical information, process details and equipment supplied by the foreign collaborator should be returned. In the sample, 46% of the agreements contained such clauses. The implications of these conditions were that technical experience gained by the local firm during the period of agreement became useless upon termination of the agreement (Radhu 1973). Predictably, Shabbir and Mahmood (1992) find that between 1959/60 and 1987/88 there is no significant correlation between FDI and GDP.

The role of the state in allocating credit to small firms

The state had a very definite bias in favour of promoting growth among large firms. Small firms continued to have more trouble getting funds from commercial banks and, when they did so, it was allocated on less favourable terms. A 1969 Survey of Small and Household Industries showed that 86% of machinery used by small firms was produced domestically. In the late 1960s small firms paid 83% (compared to around 25% for large firms) of the market price for imported machinery (Guisinger and Kazi 1978: 396). In a sample of 173 small-scale firms related to the agricultural sector in the Punjab between 1968 and 1970 Child and Kaneda found no instance of credit from a government agency for establishing a firm and that virtually all firms derived their expansion capital from re-invested earnings, supplemented in a few cases by personal/family savings. The West Pakistan Small Industries Corporation was an agency established to promote small businesses and was the source of three loans of R20,000–R30,000 (three years' duration). The benefitting firms had between 30 and 60 employees, so they were hardly small firms (1975: 254).

The role of the state in allocating resources to projects essential for development

Public investment in West Pakistan rose from 7.0% of GDP in 1959/60, to 9.8% in 1964/65, then fell to 7.5% in 1969/70. In East Pakistan, the trend was continually upwards, from 3.2%, to 6.5%, to 7.0%, over the same years (Amjad 1982: 18). There was a sharp shift in public investment/development expenditure from West to East Pakistan in the early 1960s. Between 1955/56 and 1959/60, 70.2% had been allocated to West Pakistan, while between 1960/61 and 1964/65 this had fallen to 55.2% (Lewis 1970: 157). The government undertook large-scale infrastructure projects over the 1960s, particularly water and power projects in West Pakistan. The Tarbela dam, completed in 1971, proved to be a crucial asset as oil prices later increased rapidly (Hasen 1998). There had been very little development of energy over the 1950s. In 1947 Pakistan had only two small hydroelectric power stations with a total installed capacity of 57 MW; 46 MW of extra capacity had been added by 1958. During the 1960s hydroelectric power capacity expanded to 267 MW by 1964/65 and installed thermal capacity rose from 39 MW in 1959 to 560.5 MW in 1965 (Husain 1999).

For statistical tests using data from the 1960s, there is agreement that public investment had a positive (crowding-in effect) on private investment (Khan 1988; Hyder 2001).

The public sector development banks PICIC and IDBP provided almost 70% of the foreign exchange component of total investment projects sanctioned, and projects of these institutions accounted for about 65% of total investment sanctioned between 1960 and 1965, and 60% between 1965 and 1970 (Amjad 1982: 56). Almost 65% of loans disbursed by the PICIC in the period between 1958 (inception) and 1970 went to 37 monopoly houses, with 13 of the larger monopoly houses getting about 70% of this amount (Amjad 1982: 50). Cotton and jute textiles and sugar refining were the most important areas in which PICIC operated in the early 1960s (Lewis 1970: 103). The IDBP was established in 1961 with a mandate to serve smaller investors. However, over 30% of loans disbursed by the IDBP in the 1960s went to 30 monopoly houses and, of these, seven accounted for 70% of this amount (Amjad 1982: 50).

The Pakistan Industrial Development Corporation (PIDC) had been established in the 1950s to pioneer investments in sectors that, although important, the private sector was unwilling to enter. As time elapsed many of these projects were sold to the private sector. This policy of disinvestment played a crucial role in establishing some of the major industrial houses, especially in East Pakistan. Adamjee, Dawood, Amin, Crescent, Isphani, and Karim were all beneficiaries of disinvestment in East Pakistan. In West Pakistan, Saigol bought the Jauharabad Sugar Mill and Dawoods took over the Burewala Textile Mills from the PIDC (Amjad 1983: 237).

After the mid-1960s Ayub made a concerted effort to build up a Bengali bourgeoisie. Some Bengali contractors were given government contracts at inflated rates, providing substantial profits for re-investment. There was also encouragement to nascent industrialists with generous loans and official support.[9] The IDBP would advance two-thirds of investment funds required, the East Pakistan Industrial Development Corporation would provide half of the remaining amount, and even some of the remaining one-sixth would come from the National Investment Trust (state sponsored), and Investment Corporation of Pakistan. East Pakistani industrialists often needed barely 10% of the required capital. Such efforts were reasonably successful in raising the profitability of investment in East relative to West Pakistan (Amjad 1982: 68).

The (economic) role of the state, 1960/61 to 1969/70: production

This section examines the role of the state in achieving a productive use of the surplus in both the public and private sectors. The principal sources of growth were domestic demand and a green revolution in agriculture, while export growth also contributed. There is evidence of inefficiency and low productivity in both industry and agriculture at the outset of this period, patterns of production were very capital intensive, and there were few signs of labour-intensive growth – Pakistan was not following a pattern of production based on its comparative advantage. There were, though, indications of learning over the 1960s: relative costs of production were declining, while labour, capital and overall (TFP) productivity increased.

Domestic demand

There was a distinct shift in the sources of growth after the early 1960s. Between 1959/60 and 1963/64 domestic demand accounted for 95.7% of manufacturing growth, export expansion accounted for only 4.6%, and import substitution -0.3%. Between 1963/64 and 1970/71 the contribution of domestic demand fell to 60.0%, that of export expansion increased to 15.0%, and of import substitution to 25.0%

(Kemal 1999: 164). In terms of the aggregate contribution, between 1959/60 and 1963/64 45.1% of all growth in manufacturing came from domestic demand in consumption goods, followed by 30.6% of all growth coming from domestic demand in investment and related goods, and, third, 10.8% from domestic demand in intermediate goods, with no other cause being responsible for more than 6% of aggregate growth (Lewis and Soligo 1965: 106; Lewis 1969: 49). This pattern differs from the then norm among equivalent developing countries. Chenery and Taylor (1968) found that, typically, import substitution accounted for about one-half of the growth in manufacturing output.

In the 1950s (Chapter 4) there had been strong import substitution. The process of import substitution in basic manufacturing industries had been largely completed by the end of the 1950s. For consumer industries such as sugar manufacturing, edible oils, footwear, textiles and matches the percentage of domestic production in total supply was near 100% in 1959/60 (Lewis 1969: 116–17). The implicit exchange rate[10] in the early 1960s was significantly better for firms producing import substitutes, than for those making exports (Lewis 1970: 59). Luxuries and semi-luxuries received the greatest incentives for domestic production. While there was near equality between export and domestic sales incentives for jute textiles, despite the efforts at promoting exports for cotton textiles, the primary incentive was still for import substitution (Lewis 1965: 479).

Despite these incentives for some industries, rapid growth in domestic demand reduced the degree of self-sufficiency. Between 1959/60 and 1963/64 the percentage of domestic production in total supply fell from 96.6% to 78.3% in edible oils, 73.0% to 61.1% in food manufacturing, and from 82.7% to 45.5% in wood and furniture manufacturing. In tea manufacturing, a small decline in the percentage of domestic production in total supply, from 99.4% in 1959/60 to 98.7% in 1963/64, was accompanied by a collapse in the export orientation of the industry, from 22.8% of production being exported in 1959/60 to 0% in 1963/64 (Lewis 1969: 116–17).

Sources of growth: diversification of exports

The export bonus system (EBS) was introduced in January 1959 to provide an incentive to increase manufactured exports. Over the 1960s there was indeed a diversification of exports away from the traditional primary exports, raw jute and raw cotton.

Between 1960/61 and 1964/65 exports grew by 15.66% p.a. and imports by 21.13%. In value terms, exports increased from $114m. to $239m. and imports from $457m. to $772m. (and the deficit from $343m. to $533m.). Between 1964/65 and 1969/70 exports continued to grow, from $239m. to $338m., while imports declined (with fluctuations) from $772m. to $640m. (and the deficit from $533m to $352m) (Kemal et al. 2006: 305). Raw jute (47%.3 to 38.6%), raw cotton (17.7% to 12.0%), hides and skins (3.1% to 2.5%), raw wool (4.7% to 3.4%), tea (4.7% to 0.4%) were traditional exports that experienced declining shares of total exports (Lewis 1970: 120). Most of the industries in which exports were significant in the early 1960s were ones in which import substitution had occurred during the 1950s. For example, by 1963/64, for jute textiles, the percentage of domestic production in total supply was

100.0% and the percentage of production exported 86.4% (Lewis 1969: 116–17). In some categories of industries (e.g. metal products or chemicals) exports had emerged despite domestic production being a low share of total domestic supply. Industries exporting a significant share of domestic production included cotton textiles, footwear, miscellaneous manufactures (especially sports goods and surgical instruments), jute textiles, leather products, some chemical products (e.g. paints and varnishes) and some metal products and machinery lines (sewing machines, fans, hardware, and utensils) (Lewis 1970: 118).

Net foreign exchange earnings as a percentage of export f.o.b. values were very high in industries that were intensive in the use of domestic inputs. Such industries included jute pressing (99.75%), cotton ginning (97.07%), chemical fertilisers (96.04%) and tea (89.25%). Some export 'successes', though, were very import intensive, such as jute textiles (67.43%), footwear (59.38%), cotton textiles (55.62%), leather goods (45.28%), and woollen textiles (47.37%). The near-complete import substitution in matches looks something of an illusion given its very high import intensity (49.71%). Other industries in which Pakistan was engaged in ongoing import substitution were likewise very import intensive: basic metals (33.28%), electrical machinery and appliances (43.22%), transport equipment (47.64%), rubber products (44.94%), and metal goods (43.27%). None of these industries actually lost foreign exchange in a net sense (Soligo and Stern 1966: 44). Studies also found that the EBS reduced exports of raw cotton and jute, but led to significant net gains in export revenue from higher exports of manufactured cotton and jute (Ahmad 1966). If the bonus rates had been determined with respect to their impact on the level of foreign exchange earnings, then the focus should have been on net earnings. By contrast, in Pakistan over the 1960s the industries with the highest import requirements were the ones receiving the highest bonus rates (Soligo and Stern 1966: 49). The Export Performance Licensing Scheme was also poorly structured to act as an incentive to exporters to maximise net foreign exchange earnings. Exporters were given access to subsidised foreign exchange, so the scheme encouraged the excessive use of relatively expensive imported inputs (Hecox 1970: 41). A second factor that reduced the impact of the high rates of export growth on economic growth was that the total trade ratio to GDP declined steadily, from 15.2% in 1960, to 15.1% in 1965 and 11.3% in 1970 (Husain 1999: 324). Despite these factors, export growth was enough to account for 15% of overall GDP growth in the latter part of the 1960s, as this chapter showed earlier. Shirazi and Manap (2004) unusually find a positive link from exports to GDP growth between 1960 and 2004.

Sources of growth: a green revolution in agriculture

Over the 1960s the growth rate of total value added in agriculture was around 6% p.a. Agriculture was the largest contributor to economic growth over the 1960s, its share increasing from 23.95% of GDP growth between 1960 and 1965 to 36.72% between 1965 and 1970 (Burney 1986: 584–5). This was almost entirely due to the rapid growth of 'major crops', which benefited from green revolution technology. Despite the emphasis on manufacturing, its growth contribution was only half that of agriculture in the second part of the 1960s.

Government support to agriculture was largely unsuccessful in the 1950s. By 1960, for example, only 10% of cultivators had visited demonstration plots and less than 5% had used the services of the extension staff. Guaranteed and improved seed for jute was sufficient for less than 2% of total acreage in 1960. There was also a big discrepancy between the willingness of cultivators to use fertiliser and the government's ability to make it available on credit (Papanek 1967: 164).

Over the 1960s this changed. The government gave farmers greater incentives to produce and invest in new technology, and they responded. Distribution controls and compulsory procurement were replaced by support prices for foodgrains. Export duties for cotton were reduced. Large-scale public investment in storage and irrigation increased the availability of irrigation water by 40% over the 1960s. An estimated in excess of 31,500 tube-wells were installed in West Pakistan by 1965. About one-third of the additional water from wells was provided by the public sector over the 1960s, largely due to improved performance of the WAPDA; private tube-wells contributed two-thirds of the additional water (Papanek 1967: 180). The use of fertiliser increased by 35%–40% p.a. between 1967 and 1970, much of this being imported. In both East and West Pakistan the improved performance of government machinery (WAPDAs, ADCs and Agriculture Departments) resulted in more effective programmes for improved seeds, plant protection and water management (Papanek 1967: 180). A public sector monopoly at the retail level was replaced by a successful role for the private sector in distribution (Papanek 1967, Hasen 1998). The change in government policy was a major factor in the rapid increase of agricultural production in the 1960s (Papanek 1967: 182). Limited statistical analysis, for example, shows that in the 1960s, especially after 1965, increased irrigation water rather than the terms of trade had the more significant positive effect on farm output (Kazi 1987).

An evaluation of efficiency, 1960/61 to 1970/71

Some were scathing, 'Pakistan has been neglecting agriculture relative to industry, and has been producing the wrong industrial goods in the wrong way and, moreover, has been doing so inefficiently' (Griffin and Khan 1972: 26). Policy intervention may lead to an inefficient allocation of resources through improper choice of techniques, factor proportions, or input mix, or may alternatively redistribute incomes/profits to those in industry. We have already seen earlier that profits were extremely high in Pakistani industry. There are numerous studies that do agree that Pakistani industry over the 1960s was characterised by inefficiency.

The rate of effective protection is defined as the percentage by which value added at domestic prices exceeds value added at world prices. Industries with negative value added at world prices in 1963/64 included sugar (133%), cotton textiles (1,900%), silk and art silk textiles (488%), wearing apparel (116%), plastic goods (170%), sports goods (108%), electrical appliances (144%), motor vehicles (150%), and tanning (150%). The simple average for consumer goods was 67%, for intermediate goods 30%, and for investment and related goods 39% (Lewis 1970: 80–1). Negative value added implies that the value added in the industry was negative when input and output prices are both calculated at the world/free trade values. Cotton textiles (68%) and jute textiles (65%) were two of the most important industries in Pakistan and showed that around two-thirds of value added was due to protection. Both were export-orientated industries receiving a price of foreign exchange higher than the official rate through the EBS, and both used raw materials at lower cost due to export taxes on raw cotton and jute (Soligo and Stern 1965; Child 1968; Lewis 1970; Little et al. 1970).

Ikram (1973) attempts to compute the gains/losses to Pakistan's economy from exporting a unit of manufactures and contrasts these results with the gains made by the private importer for 1968/69. The latter are based on costs and returns at market prices, while the estimation of social profitability involves the valuation of resources at opportunity cost (shadow prices). Some of the items show a loss (i.e. a cost-benefit ratio in excess of unity) when valued at shadow prices: this occurs for 5 out of 19 items, including some important manufactured exports (hessian, yarn and sewing machines). In general, there is little correlation between social and private benefits. Good government policy that corrected for market failures would have ensured that high rates of private profitability coincided with high social profitability. This is true in the case of radios, cement, and leather. There are several instances where greater subsidies to production, to raise private profitability in line with social profitability, would have been warranted: carpets, footwear, and leather – interestingly these were all successful export industries. The worst cases are those six instances of industries that were privately profitable, but generated social losses (yarn, hessian, backing, sacking transistors, and sewing machines). There are numerous other instances of private profitability being higher than social benefits, hence industries that should have had subsidies reduced or taxes increased (Ikram 1973: 167).

There is no evidence that the stock market contributed to the efficient allocation of resources over the 1960s. Husain and Mahmood find that after 1960/61 there is almost zero correlation between changes in real consumption, changes in real investment or changes in real GDP and stock prices. Any causal relationship that did exist tended to run from macroeconomic variables to stock prices: fluctuations in macroeconomic variables cause changes in stock prices, but not vice versa. The stock market was not a leading indicator of economic activity (2001: 111).

There is a general perception that the underpricing of capital in Pakistan over the 1960s led to the selection of an excessively capital-intensive production structure. Some studies, such as Islam (1970), examined factor intensity by defining as labour intensive (capital intensive) all industries that have value added per employee less (more) than the average value added per employee for the manufacturing sector in Pakistan as a whole. This only measures factor intensities of industries relative to each other in Pakistan. It does not help answer whether factor proportions chosen by the industries in Pakistan were optimum, given factor endowments. Khan (1970) estimates capital intensity for large- and medium-scale industries for 1962/63. The three sectors that stand out with unusually high capital intensities are fertiliser (in both the regions), paper (which is concentrated in East Pakistan), and petroleum products (located in West Pakistan). Some very rough estimates, argues Khan (1970), show that capital intensities tended to be higher in both regions of Pakistan than for Japan, and in some sectors were close to those in the USA. To measure capital intensity in the late 1960s, Kemal (1976) used three criteria, capital-labour ratios, capital-output ratios, and capital-value added ratios. Kemal (1976) finds that paper, chemicals and non-metallic mineral products industries (according to all three criteria) are the most capital-intensive industries, and that tobacco manufacturing, leather, and footwear are the least capital-intensive industries. Textiles and transport equipment industries are very capital intensive according to the first two criteria, but about average on the basis of the last criterion. Food manufacturing is very capital intensive on the first and the last criteria, but about average on the second criterion. Kemal (1981) found that capital-output ratios in Pakistan were among the highest in the world. Zahid et al. (1992) found that industry in Pakistan between 1960 and 1986 was generally capital intensive, including textiles as well as more obvious examples, such as steel, machinery and transport equipment, with the principal exception being drugs and pharmaceuticals.

There is no evidence that Pakistan as a 'labour surplus' economy was experiencing labour-intensive growth over the 1960s. There was a sharp slowdown in employment growth in large-scale manufacturing in the 1960s: from 11.7% p.a. between 1955/56 and 1959/60 to 2.0% between 1962/63 and 1969/70. Over the 1960s capital inputs grew by 2.83% p.a. and labour inputs by 0.78% p.a. (Kemal et al. 2006: 306). Between 1960 and 1965 45.48% of GDP growth in Pakistan came from increased factor inputs (7.93% from labour and 37.55% from capital), while between 1965 and 1970 the contribution of factor inputs declined to 41.87% (labour 10.18% and capital 31.69%) (Burney 1986: 578). Over the entire decade, Srinivasan agrees, labour inputs accounted for only 11.18% of GDP growth (2005: 499). Evidence on shares of wages supports this finding. The share of wages and salaries in net output fell throughout industry in 1965/66 relative to 1955, for example in food manufacturing, from 33.4% to 13.6%, in textiles, from 40.3% to 29.7%, in leather and leather products, from 30.8% to 17.1%, in printing and publishing from 67.2% to 34.4%, in industrial chemicals from 29.5% to 16.3%, in rubber products from 42.7% to 23.9% and in total manufacturing, from 37.4% to 21.4% (Wizarat 2002: 168).

The underlying assumption in any discussion or critique about the correct 'factor intensities of production' is that there is a choice between alternative techniques, embodying different degrees of labour intensity, and that in this case Pakistan had adequate policy instruments to regulate the choice of technology in the public and private sectors. There is very little relevant empirical analysis. What does exist suggests that there were limited options to switch to more labour-intensive methods of production in the industrial sector. Kemal (1981, 1982) finds that the elasticity of substitution between capital- and labour-intensive techniques in a number of industries was rather low and insignificant. In important industries, such as sugar, tobacco, textiles, and chemicals, he finds that there were only negligible possibilities for substitution between capital and labour.[11] Ahmed (1982) suggests that the measures of elasticity of substitution produced by Kemal were biased downwards due to the irrelevance of the production functions in LDCs and the nature of the data employed in the study. There are also questions about the reliability of measures of the capital stock (Norbye 1978). Zahid et al. (1992) confirms the earlier findings, that, except for drugs and pharmaceuticals, the elasticity of substitution for all the industries measured was less than one, suggesting that industries in general have a tendency towards fixed input-output coefficients.

A key reason for the fact that Pakistan was constrained in its choice of production techniques was that it remained import dependent in technology, so that it was limited to factor intensities developed to produce for large, high-income markets. Some took a rather dismissive view of technological change in agriculture in particular over the 1960s, arguing that it was capital intensive and mechanised and required the development of heavy engineering and chemical industries (Alam 1983). Others have highlighted the absence of an indigenous technological effort. Of the 17,486 patent applications filed in Pakistan between 1955 and 1969, for example, only 5% of them were Pakistani, and the annual share showed no sign of rising over this period (Radhu 1973: 367). Others take a more optimistic view and see instead the growth of a small-scale engineering industry that supplied key durable goods inputs to agriculture, such as diesel engines, pumps, and strainers. This, they argue, was a good example of successful agriculture-industry interaction using appropriate technology. Child and Kaneda surveyed 173 firms (of the estimated 533 firms in the industry) in 1969–70: 103 of these firms were established between 1958 and 1968, and only 18 pre-dated 1947. The industry used 'appropriate' technology. Strainers, for example, were constructed entirely by manual labour using iron strips, rivets and a hammer to form a pipe-shaped cage, which is wrapped with coir (coconut fibre) string. The coir string strainer was very simple and effective, in contrast to the relatively expensive brass strainers used in high quality tube-well installations (1975: 251). Diesel technology was predominantly a copy of an English engine from the 1920s. It was adapted by about one-third of firms to suit local conditions of production, reducing the engine speed and enlarging the water jacket to suit the hot Punjabi climate. The engine was 'not a masterpiece of engineering but functions well and is economically a triumph' (1975: 257).

Other than correcting for a wrong choice of technique, a second policy-induced means by which capital intensity might be raised related to the fact that firms were operating at a low level of capacity utilisation. Underutilisation of capacity was widespread across industrial sectors in the mid-1960s. Roughly, capacity utilisation tended to be higher in the more low-technology, labour-intensive, export-orientated sectors such as cotton textiles (68.73%) and leather (62.75%), and lower in more high-technology, capital-intensive sectors such as electrical machinery (16.13%), chemicals and pharmaceuticals (18.68%), and transport equipment (21.35%). However, overall capital goods industries tended to have higher (34.1%) capacity utilisation than did consumption goods industries (28.7%) (Winston 1971: 50). A later study shows that, of 60 industries surveyed in 1967/68, 32 had capacity utilisation rates of between 0% and 40%, and only 14 rates of between 60% and 100%. Capacity utilisation was low in many industries typically found in LDCs. Capacity utilisation in 1967/68 was 75% in cotton textiles, 13% in steel rerolling, 44% in sewing machines, 39% in electric motors, 39% in leather tanning, 30% in pharmaceuticals, 92% in cement, 41% in matches, 22% in food processing, 86% in cigarettes, 21% in edible oils, 60% in plywood, 16% in paper, 28% in soaps and detergents, 28% in salt, 57% in fertilisers, and 29% in textile machinery (Kemal and Alauddin 1974: 242).

It is easy to exaggerate the aggregate impact of high-technology, capital-intensive sectors in Pakistan's 1960s economy. Industrial output in Pakistan was dominated by those industries typical of an LDC, such as cotton and jute textiles, leather products, shoes and soaps. More generally, Pakistan's share of domestic production in total supply was below that for a 'typical' country (of 100m. people and approximately $75 per capita annual income) in most industries in the early 1950s and approached 'normal' shares in the late 1950s and early 1960s (Lewis 1969).

There is some evidence that dependence on imported raw materials reduced capacity utilisation in the 1960s, but little evidence that demand was a constraint (Kemal and Alauddin 1974: 242). A more likely explanation is that Pakistan had developed an industrial structure for which it simply did not yet have the skills, education and experience to operate efficiently. There is some limited evidence that high levels of comparative (relative to imports) costs in the mid-1960s were related to higher skill levels and capital intensity of the industry (Islam 1967). In 1959 Pakistan had few chemical or engineering industries; most existing units were for the manufacture of cotton or jute products. In the 1960s Pakistan created advanced chemical, petrochemical, pharmaceutical, and heavy engineering industries and extended the world's largest irrigation system. Few highly-trained Pakistani scientists and engineers took part in these projects, and their maintenance was done on a turnkey basis. There is little evidence that new industries were properly utilising available skills. Successive governments had increased the funding of science and engineering. The Federal Government of Islamabad and the Karachi University created science departments with sophisticated research facilities. Throughout the 1960s, though, there was minimal demand for qualified personnel from science and engineering, and graduates tended to accept jobs unrelated to their training, or migrate to the industrial countries (Alam 1983). There is little evidence of significant improvements in human capital over the 1960s: the literacy rate, for example, showed only slight improvement between 1961 and 1971, from 18.4% to 21.7% overall, and from 26.9% to 30.2% for men and from 8.2% to 11.6% for women (Zaidi 2005: 394).

There is little evidence therefore to suggest that Pakistan chose the wrong industries or could easily have adopted more labour-intensive methods of production in those industries. Even if we accept that Pakistan had an inefficient industrial sector in the early-1960s, problems with which were manifest in high costs and low value added, it is important to examine the evolution of those costs over time. If firms are engaged in a process of learning-by-doing, we would expect to see comparative cost ratios declining over time.

There is first some reason to believe that the studies of inefficiency discussed earlier were unduly pessimistic. By using more disaggregated data than earlier studies, Kemal (1974) found that the ratio of the share of manufacturing at world prices to that at domestic prices increased substantially. Another bias arises from the underestimation of outputs and overstatement of inputs in the data reported by firms to reduce recorded profits and hence tax assessments. Noman found data for seven items produced by four firms showing actual and reported production for 1967/68. The four firms were subsequently nationalised (in the early 1970s), and the new management was able to obtain both sets of records. All the firms understated output; actual output was higher by margins of up to 50% (1991: 852). This would imply that other studies had substantially underestimated value added at world prices in manufacturing.

Using data from published and unpublished reports of the Pakistan Tariff Commission on 115 industries between 1951 and 1966, Islam (1967) examines the comparative (to imports) costs of about 359 products.[12] Measuring average cost ratios (by three different methods of weighting) and correcting for the relative overvaluation of the currency, by 1961–66 Islam finds that 26 out of 62 industries had average cost ratios below one, and so were competitive relative to competing imports. Consumer goods had an average cost ratio only slightly higher than one (1.03) (Islam 1967: 225). If the factor costs do not represent scarcity prices, but contain large monopoly rents as a result of institutional factors and imperfect markets, a high price is not an index of comparative inefficiency, as discussed earlier in this chapter, but represents a transfer from consumers to the factors employed in the industry concerned. There are about 39 industries for which data on actual and 'fair' prices are available. Making allowance for this as well implies that between 50% and 60% of all industries and between 40% and 54% of industrial products were competitive by the mid-1960s (Islam 1967: 228).

Islam finds that there does not appear to be any clear relation between the length of time a firm has been in operation and comparative cost ratios (1967: 222). This is weak evidence against the learning-by-doing hypothesis. It is likely that different industries have different periods of infancy, and some develop competitive efficiency earlier than others. Cost ratios may turn unfavourable even when there is an improvement in efficiency and productivity in the domestic industry, because the costs of competing imports fall faster. To estimate the impact of learning-by-doing, Kemal (1979) uses two alternative indices of 'doing', gross investment and cumulative output, and uses them as variables to help explain the growth of value added. Kemal finds that learning coefficients are positive and statistically significant in 12 out of 16 industries. In two more industries the coefficient is positive, but not statistically significant. Lewis (1970) finds that it was consumption goods industries that showed declining relative prices over time. They had been established earliest, had the earliest import substitution and in many cases had begun to export by the late 1950s and early 1960s. The goods with the greatest decline in relative prices from the mid-1950s to the mid-1960s were edible oils, cigarettes, cotton textiles, soaps, matches, pharmaceuticals and metal products. Of these, cotton textiles, pharmaceuticals, soaps, and some metal products were exported by the 1960s. Ghafoor and Weiss found that the unit cost of public sector electricity fell over the 1960s by four methods of measuring cost in both WAPDA and KESC (2001: 126).

There is only limited evidence on the efficiency with which public sector enterprises operated. Table 6.2 shows that the growth of power generation experienced a clear slowdown in the late 1960s compared to the early 1960s. The evidence on the efficiency with which capacity was used is ambiguous, as system losses for both WAPDA and KESC increased after the mid-1960s, while, for WAPDA, generation as a percentage of installed capacity increased in the second half of the 1960s, and,for KESC, it declined.

There are a number of partial measures of productivity for the 1960s that all point to learning. Kemal finds that the capital-output ratio for the industrial sector declined from 0.730 in 1959/60 to 0.559 in 1969/70. For food manufactures, the ratio declined from 0.397 to 0.392, for tobacco manufactures, from 0.568 to 0.210, for textile manufacturing, from 1.111 to 0.747, for leather and leather products, from 0.416 to 0.113, and for footwear and other apparel, from 0.285 to 0.213. Other, more

Table 6.2 Selected indicators for evaluating the performance of state-owned electric power industry in Pakistan, 1961–71

Years	Growth in Power Generation (%)			System Losses (%)			Generation Capacity Factor (%)		
	WAPDA	KESC	Power	WAPDA	KESC	Power	WAPDA	KESC	Power
1960–65	26	17	24	26	17	24	34	47	36
1966–71	15	14	15	31	19	28	45	42	44

Source: Ghafoor and Weiss 2001: 19.

capital-intensive sectors shared this general decline: the ratio for manufacture of transport equipment fell from 1.324 to 0.752, for basic metals industries, from 1.109 to 0.469, for manufacture of chemical and chemical products, from 1.537 to 1.061, and for electrical machinery, from 0.971 to 0.597[13] (1976: 355). Amjad agrees, and finds that the capital-output ratio declined from 3.04 for 1960/61 to 1964/65, to 2.64 for 1964/65 to 1969/70 (1986: 767). Papanek finds likewise, that the capital-output ratio declined from 3.5% in the 1950s to 2.6% in the 1960s, and in the latter period was distinctly lower than in India (4.1%) (1991: 628). An important reason, and supporting evidence, is the general increase in capacity utilisation. Zaidi finds that capital utilisation in consumer goods industries increased from 47.87% in 1960/61 to 62.61% in 1965, and was 57.80% in 1965/66 and 68.13% in 1967/68. In intermediate goods, the respective figures were 21.60%, 66.45%, 62.07% and 54.42% and in capital goods, 25.33%, 39.11%, 30.23% and 55.76% (2005: 154).

There is limited evidence of an improvement in another partial measure, labour productivity. Output per worker in the manufacturing sector increased by about one-third over the 1960s, and value added per worker by about two-thirds (Kemal 1976b: 357–8). An index of labour productivity increased from 100.0 in 1959/60 to a peak of 169.58 in 1965/66, then fell steadily to 113.63 in 1970/71 (Wizarat 2002: 82).

The most comprehensive and complete proxy measure for learning and upgrading is the growth of TFP. Table 6.3 shows that there was rapid, if very variable, growth of TFP over the 1960s. There is general agreement among other authors.[14] Srinivasan (2005) finds that TFP growth between 1960 and 1970 was 3.39% overall, 4.00% in agriculture and 4.26% in manufacturing. Khan (2005) finds that TFP grew by 2.4% over the 1960s. Kemal *et al.* (2006: 306) find that TFP growth over the 1960s was 3.39%, and in manufacturing 4.26%. (Cheema 1978: 48) finds that TFP growth (measured by value added) over the 1960s was rapid in rubber (8.66%), tobacco (3.43%), textiles (6.20%), basic metals (8.60%), printing and publishing (5.85%), leather (9.09%), and electrical machinery (6.76%), and moderate or negative in food manufacturing (0.53%), paper (-8.09%), chemicals (-1.58%), and metal products (2.40%). (Zaidi 2005: 102) finds that TFP growth compared very favourably with other developing countries, such as Korea, 1960–73: 8.3%; Argentina, 1960–70: 2.64%; India, 1959–76: 0.00%; Thailand, 1963–77: 1.50%; Mexico, 1960–70: 3.01%; and Brazil 1960–70: 0.75%.

There was enormous scope for catch-up growth in agriculture in Pakistan. Table 6.4 shows that, in the early 1960s, productivity (yield per hectare) was lagging that of other LDCs by some distance in the principal crops.

Chapter 3 demonstrated that there was a significant increase in agricultural growth in the 1960s relative to the 1950s. Earlier, this chapter showed the very large contribution made by agriculture to overall GDP growth over the 1960s. The new dwarf varieties of grain accounted for most of this increase, and between 1966 and 1969 wheat and rice production in West Pakistan increased by 79% and 61%, respectively. There is broad agreement that the 1960s also witnessed significant gains in TFP in agriculture. TFP growth increased from 3.70% p.a. between 1960 and 1965, to 9.5% between 1966 and 1970 (Wizarat 1981), or, respectively, from 2.97% to 6.26% and

Table 6.3 Growth rate of total factor productivity, 1960–70 (in %)

Industries	TFPG
Food processing	2.17
Tobacco manufacturing	8.19
Textile manufacturing	5.27
Footwear and apparel	1.30
Paper and paper products	-8.71
Printing and publishing	5.68
Leather and leather products	9.60
Rubber and rubber products	12.64
Chemicals and chemical products	-2.31
Non-metallic minerals	-2.83
Basic metal industries	8.13
Metal products	1.52
Non-electrical machinery	2.81
Electrical machinery	5.65
Transport equipment	0.90
Miscellaneous	10.95
Total	5.06

Source: Zaidi 2005: 101.

Table 6.4 Yield per hectare performance for main crops in main producing countries, 1961–65

	Wheat (kg/hectare)	Rice (kg/hectare)	Cotton (kg/hectare)	Sugar cane (kg/hectare)
World	1,209	2,040	957	49,394
Pakistan	833	1,417	783	34,247
India	835	1,480	388	44,807
Mexico	2,085	2,290	1,717	61,530
Brazil	707	1,607	627	43,332
China	882	2,780	903	54,555
USA	1,700	4,374	1,488	88,001
Egypt	2,621	5,307	1,764	90,061

Source: Ali 2005: 741.

from 2.67% to 3.49% (Ali 2004), or 4.0% over the the decade of the 1960s as a whole (Srinivasan 2005, Kemal *et al.* 2006). Looking at specific crops, the importance of productivity/yield increases in agriculture is made further apparent. Between 1961/62 and 1970/71 the production of rice increased by 8.81% p.a., driven by yield increases of 5.65% p.a. Over the 1950s yield had declined by 0.23% p.a. Over the same two decades the yield figures for wheat were, respectively, 4.21% and 1.53% (Kurosaki 1999: 164). The contribution of TFP to overall output growth increased from 38% in the first five years of the 1960s to 87% in the second five-year period (Ali 2004: 499; Srinivasan 2005, Kemal *et al.* 2006). The yield of wheat increased from 863 kg/hectare in 1964/65 to 1,083 kg/hectare in 1970/71, that of rice from 996 kg/hectare to 1, 464 kg/hectare, of sugar cane from 37,113 kg/hectare to 36,426 kg/hectare, and of cotton from 258 kg/hectare to 313 kg/hectare (Ali 2004: 509).

There is reason to believe that the growth of human capital over the 1960s was more relevant to the needs of agriculture than the equivalent for industry. Between 1960 and 1965 two new agricultural universities were established, and teaching facilities were improved at three other agricultural colleges. This trend continued into the Third Five-year Plan, and enrolment at agricultural universities almost doubled from 2,000 in 1964/65, to 4,000 in 1967/68. The Agricultural University as Faisalabad played a significant role in developing HYVs for Pakistan in rice and wheat (Alam 1983).

The (political) role of the state, 1960/61 to 1969/70: institutions

This section focuses on institutions that may or may not allow the state to overcome the inherent conflicts associated with economic growth. In the early years the autonomy of state policy making was enhanced by a more repressive stance with regard to groups such as newspapers, students and unions. The 1962 Constitution also strengthened the power of the central Presidency. This autonomy was reflected in more-coherent planning and agricultural policy making. The episode of growth had its successes. A more autonomous state was able to intensify the more *ad hoc* process of import substitution of the 1950s through policies that sustained profitability in the private sector. The state was also able to push industry into upgrading the structure of production through high levels of investment and successful learning, and also to push industry into high-value-added niches in world export markets. The episode of growth was economically sustainable. By the late 1960s this autonomy gradually declined, and policy became increasingly determined by political criteria. The state failed in its efforts to promote inclusionary institutions. Social change unleashed by the green revolution, urbanisation and industrialisation was not accommodated by Ayub's system of 'Basic Democrats' or, later, by the return to party-based politics. The attempt to project a modernist ideology had no substantial effect.

Institutions to manage conflict: autonomy and repression

The 1959 coup d'etat was not a seizure of power. Power was already in the hands of the coup makers. The coup was about dismantling the parliamentary apparatus, through which state power had been legitimated but was threatened in the advent of an election being held under the new 1956 Constitution (Alavi 1983). For the industrialists, the threat from the feudal classes loomed, with general elections to be held at end of 1958: there was a widespread belief that they would be returned to political power and so would undermine the government's pro-industrial strategy (Amjad 1983: 263). There was a short shock effect after the military coup in 1958, based on its novelty and severity, and the popularity of the army (Afzal 2001). The military government suppressed criticism through press restrictions, which were subsequently consolidated in 1960 into the Press and Publications Ordinance. The government took over a major newspaper (Progressive Papers Ltd). All political organisations, such as political parties, student bodies, and professional associations, were banned, and elected institutions from the National Assembly down were abolished. Martial Law Regulations/Orders led to the disqualification (until December 1966) of over 3,000 politicians. The Public Conduct Scrutiny Rules were used to purge the bureaucracy of corrupt and undesirable figures, and 128 senior civil servants were removed from service. The East Pakistan Public Safety Ordinance 1958 and West Pakistan Public Safety Order 1960 enabled the government to prosecute anyone endangering public safety and public order. University Ordinances banned students and teachers from participating in political activity.

A Constitutional Commission was established to investigate the problems of governance from the 1950s. The commission concluded that excessive state interference in the regions, a lack of well organised and disciplined political parties, and lack of responsible leadership led to breakdown in 1958. The commission recommended a Presidential system with a bicameral legislature to exercise restraint on the President, and also a Vice President and a two-term maximum. The eventual (new) constitution promulgated on 1st March 1962 ignored the report and represented a strengthening of the more repressive aspects of the state (Huntingdon 1968). A strong Presidency (with a maximum of two terms) was established with a unicameral legislature. The President was given power over the most important appointments. The constitution did not separate the executive from the legislature, but instead gave the President substantial powers over the legislative process. The President could assume even greater legislative powers during an emergency in consequence of internal disturbance or external aggression. The centre was given absolute power over the provinces. The National Assembly was empowered to legislate on items in the provincial list when authorised, or on the grounds of national interest in regard to Pakistan's stability (Afzal 2001). Ayub did not impose a military regime. Only a month after the coup, the military regime withdrew into the background, and on 11th November 1958 troops were ordered back to barracks and to stop assisting civilian authorities. After the coup a civilian (Aziz Ahmad) was appointed Secretary General of the Government and Deputy Chief Martial Law Administrator (Alavi 1983). Over the 1960s there was only very limited induction of military personnel into the civil service (Afzal 2001).

The strengthening of the coercive apparatus of the state did increase the degree of autonomy of policy making and implementation by the state.[15] This autonomy continued to be exercised (except perhaps in agriculture) in a fairly *ad hoc* manner and over time the degree of autonomy showed notable signs of ebbing.

The machinery of planning did strengthen its capacity and autonomy over the 1960s. The planning agencies at the centre and with the two provincial governments became extremely influential, probably more so than any other central planning or economic staff in the developing world (Papanek 1967: 85). By the mid-1960s they were consulted on all important economic decisions and received backing from the Prime Minister, Minister of Finance and President. One of their highly valued functions that increased their leverage over other government agencies was their ability to prepare the professional documentation required by various foreign and international agencies (Papanek 1967). Government planning during the 1960s was more influential, but in terms of investment allocation remained *ad hoc*. The total investment sanctions for the Second Five-year Plan were committed within 18 months of the plan starting (Child 1968; Amjad 1982). The machinery of government policy making even so remained rather chaotic. Decisions on import controls and the allocation of import licences were made by the Chief Controller of Imports and Exports (CCI&E) who was located in the Ministry of Commerce. Decisions on tariff rates were made by the Central Board of Revenue and Tariff Commission until well into the Second Five-year Plan period.

Some labour legislation during the 1950s had been favourable to organised labour, for example the Industrial Disputes Act 1947 was amended in 1956 to provide quicker remedies for labour disputes. In October 1958 the new military government repealed the Industrial Disputes Act 1947 and replaced it with the Industrial Disputes Ordinance 1959. The aim of the new legislation was to prohibit the right to strike. Nearly all major industries were declared to be essential industries where strikes were forbidden, including railways, post, telegraph, water, ports, defence, and telephones. Others, such as cement, iron and steel, sugar, leather and leather goods, vegetable oils, and electrical equipment were declared 'essential for the time being'. Under the Revised Labour Policy, all disputes that could not be resolved collectively with the aid of a Conciliation Officer were automatically referred to an Industrial Court for a decision, which was legally binding on both parties. The government promulgated a new Presidential Ordinance in March 1963 banning the publication of any news items relating to strikes or industrial unrest (Shaheed 1983). There is evidence that the government did affect the trend in wages over the 1960s, but was unable to evolve a systematic policy with regard to wage levels and wage increases (Guisinger and Irfan 1974). As with the case of planning, government labour policy was distinguished by its *ad hoc* nature. Between 1962 and 1963 there were several increases in wages for civil servants. At around the same time the government began to intervene more directly in the wage rate for unskilled labour in the private sector, through the establishment of Minimum Wage Boards under the Minimum Wage Ordinance of 1961. In cotton textiles this led to the wage floor of the least skilled increasing by 30% (Guisinger and Irfan 1974: 374). Not surprisingly, this undermined more general efforts to control wage levels in industry, and trade unions began to push for comparable wage increases. The number of strikes had fallen sharply during the early years of martial law, then more than doubled during 1963 and 1964, with 69,000 workers involved in 1962, and 218,000 in 1963 (Ahmed and Amjad 1984). In 1962 a successful strike in a Karachi tobacco company gave the labour movement the impetus to establish an alternative labour organisation, the Mazdoor Rabita (Workers Coordination) Committee. This undermined the government-sponsored APCOL. The organisation attracted militants previously working underground and also those working with the existing pro-government labour organisations. A subsequent strike in the textile sector was organised by the newo movement in 1963. The strike was initially opposed by police firing, which affected industrial units in Karachi for eight days in March. The strike met with initial success and an unprecedented promise of higher pay. Management later refused payment to all workers and, in response, faced more protest/strikes. The government responded by arresting 800 workers, including all the top leaders, and forced labour to resume production. In 1964, with preparations being made for a general election, the government wanted to project an image of broad-based political support in both urban and rural areas, and trade unions were granted concessions in the form of increased wages and more favourable decisions in the Industrial Courts (Guisinger and Irfan 1974; Shaheed 1983). A renewed upsurge of strike activity in the late 1960s saw the number of man-days lost to disputes increase from 226,778 in 1967 to 1,220,377 in 1969 (Wizarat 2002: 231). This time the government responded more quickly with concessions and sought to improve labour conditions and wages. The money wage of all production workers increased by 26% between 1967/68 and 1969/70 (Guisinger and Hicks 1978: 1276).

Government intervention in agriculture was sustained, consistent and successful. The increase in agricultural growth after 1959, and especially after 1965, was due to the green revolution technology package of HYVs, chemical fertilisers, and pesticides. The increase in water availability from irrigation/tube-wells was estimated to be responsible for 50% of the output gain (Zaidi 2005: 29). The Agricultural Development Bank of Pakistan followed a liberal credit policy and provided numerous loans to farmers to set up private tube-wells. The number of tube-wells increased from a few hundred in 1960 to 75,000 in 1968. In the 1960s two semi-autonomous Water and Power Development agencies (WAPDAs) were established in each province. They were less bound by rigid bureaucratic practices, had good staffing levels and made extensive use of outside consultants. The substantial Indus Basin Replacement Works was completed ahead of schedule by the mid-1960s. The East Pakistan WAPDA was slower in getting started, but by the mid-1960s was beginning to show progress (Papanek 1967: 156). Water availability (measured in million acre feet–MAF) increased from 63.87 MAF in 1965/66 to 75.5 MAF in 1969/70, and fertiliser offtake from 1,087.2 nutrient tonnes–N/T in 1964/65 to 283,200 N/T in 1970/71 (Ali 2004: 509). The number of tractors increased from 2,000 in 1959 to 18,909 in 1968 – this was facilitated by generous credit from the ADBP (Zaidi 2005). The agricultural research system in Pakistan includes research organisations both at federal and provincial level, while extension is largely carried out by the provincial agricultural departments. The 1960s green revolution was founded on adaptive research experiments by the research institutes and dissemination of results by extension agencies, which together were responsible for the rapid spread of HYVs in wheat and rice. By 1969/70 more than half of Pakistan's irrigated area (6m. acres) was cultivated with the improved seeds. Ali adds together provincial and federal data to generate a total research expenditure series for the period 1960–96 and examines its relation with agricultural productivity. The marginal internal rate of return on research and extension investment he estimates at 88% (2005: 738).

The state had acquired more autonomy by the early 1960s, but had achieved this in a context where it had little legitimacy. There was very little effort to reflect 'popular will' in the highest echelons of government. Of the 16 ministers who served Ayub, four came from services and one was a journalist, the remaining 11 were ex-Muslim League members, eight of whom had contested and lost the elections of 1954. Of the four governors of East Pakistan during the Ayub decade, two were Pathans from the civil service and military, the last being an East Pakistan civil servant who lasted for seven years (though even he depended on patronage from Ayub for his position) and who had contested and lost the 1954 election heavily enough to forfeit his deposit (Maniruzzaman 1971: 231). Conscious of lacking legitimacy, the elite retained a profound fear of subversion by ethnic and subaltern forces. This was an enduring problem and gave rise to what some theorists have labelled the 'fearful state', in which pluralism was seen as a source of weakness. The ruling elite tended to adopt policies of coercion, rather than co-option, in dealing with sub-nationalist movements (Talbot 1998).

In autumn 1968 there were widespread disturbances throughout the country, including massive labour unrest. The 'fearful state' responded with a mix of crude repression and concessions. In January 1968, for example, Ayub's government announced the existence of a conspiracy to make East Pakistan an independent state, and Sheikh Mujib, previously in prison with little protest, became a heroic Bengali martyr (Jones 2003). Baluchis had a long-standing resentment that settlers (most of whom had migrated from the Punjab during the British days) controlled more than half the urban property and some mines in Baluchistan, and their advantage in education drew heavily on Baluchistan's limited quota for admission to government services. There was a popular sentiment in Baluchistan that martial law had further undermined regional rights, and so some Baluch tribes, especially those in Kalat Division, revolted against the government, and within six months 15,000 armed troops were involved (Talbot 1998).

This domestic conflict (rather than a decline in foreign capital inflows after the mid-1960s) has been directly linked to the economic slowdown of Pakistan in the Third Plan Period (1965–70). The Pakistan state increasingly lacked, argued Khan (2000b), the ability to enforce conditionalities on its help to industry and was unable to enforce the allocation of credit for the acquisition of high technology. In the mid-1960s, in response to the upsurge in resistance from excluded social groups, the government responded by increasing allocations to capitalists with the most significant political connections – an emerging class of political entrepreneurs. In particular, a large proportion of industrial investments were relocated to East Pakistan. While total investment continued to increase up to 1968, it was the greater political motivation behind its allocation that led to growth rates declining after the mid-1960s (Khan 2000b).

Institutions to manage conflict: inclusionary

By 1970, 41 industrial houses controlled almost 80% of the private domestic assets of both non-financial and manufacturing companies quoted on the KSE. In West Pakistan for the entire large-scale manufacturing sector, 41 houses accounted for 41.7% of industrial assets and 52.3% of private domestic assets. Of these, the 10 largest industrial houses controlled 24.8% of all assets and 31.1% of private domestic assets. In East

Pakistan, 16 industrial houses accounted for 27.7% of all industrial assets and over 51% of all private domestic assets (Amjad 1983: 241). Banks controlled by seven industrial families accounted for 60.3% of all bank deposits in Pakistan. There were close relations between many of the families: there were 103 cases in which one family had at least one member on the board of directors of at least one company of another family (White 1974: 82–3). A Credit Inquiry Commission in 1959 found that 60% of all bank credit went into 222 accounts (White 1974: 42). It may be tempting to dismiss the importance of industrial concentration; by 1967/68 large-scale manufacturing contributed only 8.2% to GNP (White 1974). This would be wrong. 'The Ayub era presents us with a clear paradox. The decade which saw relative political stability, sustained economic progress, and fairly co-ordinated economic policy-making also left large parts of the population feeling dissatisfied even in West Pakistan (Hasen 1998: 143). More important than the dry statistics on inequalities was the widespread perception that large fractions of the population had been bypassed by rapid economic growth and industrialisation, that the process was somehow unfair. The declaration of Mahbubul Haq, the Chief Economist of the Planning Commission, in April 1968 that 22 families controlled 66% of industrial wealth and 87% of banking and insurance, even if dubious statistically, chimed with popular feeling (Ahmed and Amjad 1984).

There was a realistic perception that the top ranks of the industrialists were closed off to newcomers. With few exceptions, the top houses were the same in 1961 and 1970: the top three remained, Adamjee, Saigol and Dawood. The industrial families were strongly represented by minority groups (Memons, Bohras, Khojas) who had migrated from India mostly from Kathiawar and had experience in trade before partition. The two Punjabi families in the big five (Saigols and Colony) came from Chakwal and Chiniot. The Saigol Group, before partition, had been engaged in small business in Calcutta, and the Colony Family was also well established before partition (Papanek 1967: 41; Papanek 1972; Griffin and Khan 1972; Alavi 1983; Amjad 1983). Regression analysis shows that the capital goods licences received by a family over the 1960s were positively related to the assets that it controlled in 1961 (White 1974).[16] Sindhis did not figure in the famous 22 families that came to dominate the commercial and industrial sectors of the economy. The Sindhi political elite felt marginalised under the One Unit scheme[17] and had a 'settler' problem as land released from newly constructed barrages was being allotted mainly to military and civil service men, most of whom were Punjabis (Maniruzzaman 1971; Talbot 1998). Ayub had recruited his ruling oligarchy from a narrow social/regional base, while the excluded middle classes denied entry had been the organisers of political opposition (Alavi 1974: 76). A network of 15,000 civil servants and 500 top military officers had shared in the allocation of licences and posts in public corporations (Jalal 1995). Policy reform efforts at redistribution had minimal impact.

In the budget of July 1963, the government proposed an extra tax on corporations that had gone public by listing their shares on the KSE, but that still had over 50% of their shares in fewer than 20 hands. This was true of 89 of the 119 non-government-controlled listed companies. The stock market fell sharply, and the government suspended the proposal (White 1974: 42–3). The proposal was kept 'live' and in 1968 the government issued a 'grandfather' exclusion to all firms already listed, but insisted that all new firms must offer over 50% of their shares to the public or face the tax. Ayub in the foreword to the Third Five-year Plan (1965–70) declared, 'it will be our firm policy to prevent excessive concentration and wealth in the hands of the few' (White 1974: 43). The rest of the plan was silent on the concentration issue, except for a declaration that the disinvestment of government-controlled industries should be done by converting them into public companies with a larger number of shareholders (White 1974). It took the downfall of Ayub in 1969 for Pakistan's first Monopoly Control Ordinance to be passed into law. The Fourth Five-year Plan (1970–75) devoted a considerable amount of space to the problem of industrial concentration, overall ownership and control concentration, and consequent mal-distribution of income and wealth. Ayub's efforts had only a minimal impact. There was only a very slight decline in industrial concentration in 1970 relative to 1961. In West Pakistan in 1961, 13 houses controlled 30% of assets and 20% of production of the large-scale manufacturing sector, whereas in 1970, the same number of houses controlled about 27% of assets and 17% of production. Concentration for the major industrial product, cotton textiles, also showed a slight decline. In 1961 nine industrial houses controlled 50% of cotton textile production; in 1970 the same number controlled about 40%. The top five controlled 37.3% of textile production in 1961, and their share came down to 30% in 1970 (Amjad 1983: 245).

Ayub's government made some attempts to appease East Pakistan. The Raisam Award of 1952 was reviewed, and East Pakistan was subsequently given 50% of income and corporation tax, 60% of sales tax and 60% of the export duty of jute. The Pakistan Industrial Development Corporation (PIDC) and Pakistan Agricultural Corporation and Railways were bifurcated and brought under provincial control (Afzal 2001). East Pakistan's share of public sector outlays increased gradually from 38% in 1960/61 to 54% in 1967/6, and its share of development loans to provincial governments increased from 47% in 1960/61 to 67% in 1967/68 (Maniruzzaman 1971). Thomas found that established importers first dominated the allocations of Open General (import) Licences (OGL), but that between January and June 1964 the share allocated to newcomers increased to 65.38%. The big increase was in East Pakistan, where OGL newcomers received in this period 150% more licences than in January to June 1963. East Pakistan also received a higher increase of goods on the Free List (1966: 520). Such policies had no impact on stemming the growth of regional inequality. GDP per capita was higher in West than East Pakistan by 32% in 1959/60, 45% in 1964/65 and 61% in 1969/70 (Bergan 1967; Ahmed and Amjad 1984).

Land reforms in 1959 failed to alter the skewed pattern of land ownership. Senior military and civil officials gained privileged access to agricultural and urban land (Jalal 1995). According to the 1972 Census of Agriculture, 2% of agricultural holdings (those with over 100 acres) accounted for 28% of the land.[18] In addition, 9% of the smallest holdings had no more than 1% of the farm area (Alavi 1983).

Ayub's direct efforts to ameliorate perceptions of economic inequalities were largely failures. His government had two principal structures to act as politically integrating mechanisms. The first was the system of basic democracies; the second was a belated return to party politics.

One aspect of the political settlement was the 'Basic Democrats', which was the principal means to provide for popular participation in politics. A multi-tiered hierarchical structure was established. At the base were the Union Councils, which averaged ten members (one member per thousand population) and were elected by universal suffrage (the Basic Democrats). Above these, the Thana (East Pakistan) or Tehsil (West Pakistan) Councils, composed of the chairman of the Union Councils, plus an equal number of appointed official members. The Union and District councils were responsible for development of agriculture, industry and community and could impose local taxes. The Basic Democrat system reintroduced the nineteenth-century idea of political tutelage through indirect elections and the official nomination of representatives. The 1959 Basic Democrat elections proved quite successful in bringing into the Union Councils and Town Committees groups that had hitherto been excluded from local politics. These included small and middling business entrepreneurs, grain commission agents and government contractors. These individuals came from middle agricultural families, were recent migrants to towns and retained strong rural links (Jones 2003). It appeared that the system had proved effective both in integrating new groups and in providing a support base for Ayub. In the first elections to the Union Councils held in 1959 and 1960, 50% of eligible voters participated. Of the 80,000 Basic Democrats, the majority were new to politics and over 50,000 had a background in agriculture. The elections had brought politics, previously almost exclusively an urban activity, to rural areas and created a class of rural activists (Huntingdon 1968: 252). Ayub received 95% of the vote in the first election for President among the Basic Democrats in January 1960. The Basic Democrats also chose the partyless members of the National and Provincial Assemblies in 1962 (Talbot 1998).

Over time it became clear that the Basic Democrats had not established a sufficiently encompassing popular base for the regime. Ayub had failed to appreciate the degree to which his own development policies would ignite social change and hence political demands. The process of migration and urbanisation unleashed by the green revolution and industrialisation put an intolerable strain on the political system (Jones 2003). New industries had grown up in Lahore, Lyallpur, Mutan, Hyderabad and other cities and formed growing centres of a new working class (Shaheed 1983). Over the 1960s there was a rapid growth of small towns (Burki 1974: 754). Small towns tended to grow most rapidly in areas with extensive agricultural techniques that generated a need for a more dispersed type of urban community (Burki 1974: 755). Rapid growth in agriculture was related both to mechanisation and to substantial out-migration from (in particular) Punjabi villages over the 1960s. Landless labourers migrated to cities and towns in search of employment. Landlords formed a large proportion of out-migrants, particularly in small towns (Burki 1974: 757). Over the 1960s towns were increasingly servicing the agricultural districts. Rapid growth in agriculture prompted the growth of a small-scale engineering industry, which supplied key durable goods inputs such as diesel engines, pumps and strainers. This growth of industry was concentrated in various centres around the Punjab region. These small labour-intensive, constant returns to scale industries required the type of capital and labour that could be provided by landlords on the one hand and landless labour on the other (Burki 1974). The 1970 election saw a high correlation between voting for the PPP and the area under Mexican varieties of wheat (Zaidi 2005: 32). In the 1970 election, in the Punjab the PPP had its strongest showing in towns and secondary cities that had been most affected by the green revolution. Lyallpur city gave the PPP its best vote of any major urban area. Lyallpur had also experienced rapid industrial growth based mainly on textiles, but also including chemicals, pharmaceuticals, construction, and synthetics. There was also a significant stratum of middle and small enterprises, from traditional artisans to foundry industries (Jalal 1995; Jones 2003). The Muslim professional class had done well since independence, largely displacing the Hindus and British, and by the late 1960s there were 350,000 teachers, the number trebling since independence. The number of doctors had increased from 6,000 to 16,000 (Maddison 1971). In contrast to this socio-economic ferment, a survey of the Basic Democracies in East Pakistan showed that some 80% were from the middle or wealthy landlord farmer class (Maniruzzaman 1971: 225; Jones 2003: 35). The balance had shifted, and there were gains in parliamentary representation in the National Assembly for middle farmers at the expense of large landowners (Jones 2003: 52).

The second means to promote political integration was a belated and half-hearted attempt to return to party politics. In July 1962 Ayub's government legalised party organisation to regularise a situation in which party activity had unofficially resumed outside the legislature. In September 1962 pro-government politicians formed into the Convention Muslim League, which drew largely on the Muslim League 1956 Constitution. Ayub became the party president in December 1963. The top-down Convention Muslim League was little more than a coterie of sycophants and scarcely existed outside the legislature. The party was largely bypassed in the 1964/65 elections, and Ayub mobilised his support through the bureaucracy. In the elections, Ayub won 63.3% of the Basic Democrats; in Karachi his opponent, Fatima Jinnah, took 55% of the vote (Talbot 1998; Jones 2003). With no political party to act as an institution of integration, Pakistani politics remained an ephemeral process, based on shifting allegiances and personality, rather than ideology or party institutionalisation (Talbot 1998). As the Basic Democrats faded into oblivion during the 1969 agitation, there was nothing to replace them.

The uprisings of November 1968 were based on two broad pressures for structural change. The first, the demand for greater access to the policy-making functions of government, and the second the demand for the downward redistribution of power to the provincial elite. These demands stemmed from the rise of newly emergent (particularly urban) groups, the political marginalisation of established urban groups, and the perception of excessive centralisation to a narrow elite in government. In East Pakistan the Six Points of the Awami League represented the aspiration of a rising Bengali middle class (Jones 2003). The November Movement spread from Rawalpindi to other large cities and small towns and was almost entirely an urban phenomenon. The first phase, in late 1968, was carried out by students, shopkeepers, lawyers, and politicians, with these groups relying on existing organisations, such as Bar Associations, Students Unions, Merchant and Market Committees, and political parties. None of these groups had been successfully integrated into the Ayub system. The second phase, which occurred in early 1969, was the most violent and saw organised labour enter the protest in West Pakistan. Ayub met the protest with a barrage of concessions, a return to parliamentary democracy, the undertaking that he would not seek re-election, the release of political prisoners, and the withdrawal of the conspiracy case against Sheikh Mujib. In March 1969 Ayub stepped down from government and there was another military coup (Maniruzzaman 1971; Jones 2003). With the only institutions to manage conflict consisting of the most extreme institution of repression – the army – the civil administration had no other option but to acquiesce in the coup.

Institutions to manage conflict: ideology

Ayub attempted to rule with some sort of modernist ideology. During the constitutional debate up to 1962 he had worked closely with a secularising elite and made only minimal consultations with religious figures. At first, Ayub had tried to remove 'Islamic' from the constitution and referred only to the 'Republic of Pakistan'. The fragility of his modernist agenda was revealed by the speed with which he backed down and re-inserted 'Islamic' into a 1963 constitutional amendment. Ayub never found an ideological hook to weld together Pakistan and grappled unsuccessfully with the enduring problem of 'creating Pakistanis.' (Maniruzzaman 1971: 237).

7 An episode of stagnation, 1970/71–1991/92

Summary of chapter findings

The chapter is divided into three parts, each focusing on one particular role that the state has in promoting economic growth. These relate to finance, production and institutions. The underlying hypothesis here is that the state needs to be successful in all three to initiate and sustain an episode of growth.

The first section shows that the domestic surplus mobilised by the state after 1970/71 was stagnant, but compensated for by international capital inflows. Total savings stagnated; this was true for both public and private sector savings, the former being linked to stagnant tax revenues and the latter to a slowdown in the growth of the domestic financial sector. Savings remained below investment; the gap was filled by international capital inflows. A poor record of corporate profitability was not explained by the relative growth of the state. There was substantial expansion in public investment under Bhutto, which supported growth throughout this period. The second section examines the role of the state in achieving a productive use of the surplus in both the public and private sectors. This section shows that Pakistan did not follow a growth pattern based on its (labour-intensive) comparative advantage. There are indications of dynamic learning/upgrading: both capital and labour productivity improved significantly, and the capital-intensive path of growth in agriculture alleviated some key constraints in the sector and supported rapid growth. The performance of state-owned enterprises contributed to productivity growth. The broader measure of productivity, TFP, showed improvement, particularly in the 1980s. The third section focuses on institutions that may or may not allow the state to overcome the inherent conflicts associated with economic growth. The elections of 1970 and rise of the PPP gave Pakistan a chance to re-assert the supremacy of the democratic (integrative) over the repressive (autonomous) institutions of the state. Early efforts to reduce the role of the military and civil service were short lived, and Bhutto came to depend on both; the coup of 1977 was a continuation of such trends. The PPP failed in its possible role as an inclusionary institution – it was gradually taken over by more conservative groups and failed to incorporate the groups emerging in a changing society. The 1973 constitution, despite its federal structure and formal decentralised structure, was undermined by the centralising and anti-democratic instincts of Bhutto. The rule of Zia further strengthened the power of the central political leadership. The emergence of a two-party democratic system in the 1990s failed to promote institutionalisation of social groups and exacerbated conflict. Zia tried to implement a more ideological approach (Islamisation) to the management of Pakistan, but succeeded only in exacerbating conflict. After a hiatus in the early 1970s, the repressive institutions of the state re-emerged under Bhutto and were formally re-established in power with the military coup of 1977. By domestic criteria, this episode of stagnation (though quite successful, judged in terms of average growth rates) probably was sustainable. The government lacked the developmental autonomy or inclusionary institutions or ideology to promote a real development drive. The government in the 1980s was secure enough in power to rule, and able to mobilise sufficient resources and utilise them productively enough, to keep GDP at a reasonable rate. The end of the episode we can trace to exogenous factors, the death of Zia in that ever-mysterious plane crash, the rise of neo-liberalisation, and the worldwide democratic upsurge that gave Pakistan no option other than to return to competitive party politics and adopt a neo-liberal programme of reforms. This combination pushed Pakistan into a further episode of stagnation, as we will see in Chapter 8.

Recap from Chapter 3

The statistical analysis in Chapter 3 showed that GDP growth averaged 5.6% p.a. between 1970/71 and 1991/92. This was a creditable average, if a significant decline relative to the previous decade. Growth of manufacturing and especially agriculture increased in the 1980s, relative to the 1970s. Over these two decades the industrial sector remained highly concentrated, and the output share of traditional industries dependent on indigenous raw materials accounted for over 60% of value added, though the share was declining over time. There was no shift, as in the newly industrialising economies of Asia, into metal products and machinery.

Limitations of alternative explanations

The world economy

The 20% fall in the terms of trade between 1969/70 and 1971/72, when combined with a total trade dependence of Pakistan's economy equal to 15%, was not enough to account for the structural decline in GDP growth rates in 1970/71. Over time, the world economy had potentially more influence. The trade dependence of Pakistan's economy increased dramatically over the first half of this period. The share of imports in GNP rose from 9.1% in 1971/72 to 20.8% in 1979/80, and the share of exports from 6.0% to 10.0%, hence the trade ratio increased from 15.1% to 30.8% (Nawab *et al.* 1984: 104). There was little change over the 1980s; the trade ratio in 1990 was 31.1% (Husain 1999: 324).

The terms of trade were generally unfavourable to Pakistan throughout the 1970s. The unit value indices for imports increased from 155.9 in 1971/72 (1969/70 = 100) to 802.8 in 1979/80, and for exports from 129.1 to 673.4. As a result, the terms of trade declined from 100.0 in 1969/70 to 82.8 in 1971/72, rose to 106.4 in 1973/74, fell to 66.7 in 1974/75 and rose slowly to 83.9 in 1979/80 (Nawab et al. 1984: 107). The rise in the international price of wheat affected Pakistan's terms of trade, and between 1972/73 and 1975/76 imports were running at over 1m. tonnes p.a. Rising prices (and import volumes) of petroleum products meant that, by the end of the 1970s, the value of kerosene, diesel oil and crude petroleum accounted for over 21% of the total value of imports (Nawab et al. 1984: 121).

Sarmad (1992) built a computable general equilibrium (CGE) model of Pakistan's economy that allows us to quantify more exactly the impact of the world economy. The negative impact of external shocks in the mid/early 1970s on the current account was not as significant in Pakistan as in other LDCs. In Pakistan the process of adjustment was underwritten by a dramatic increase in remittance inflows. Recession in high-income economies (and hence reduction in world trade growth) was offset by a rising share of the booming Middle East market. Between 1974 and 1982 Pakistan's share of Organisation of the Islamic Conference (mostly oil exporters) exports increased from 14% of its own exports to 24.4%. Higher interest rates and renewed world recession in the late 1970s was cushioned by access to low-interest, long-term loans.

Liberalisation

Liberalisation cannot explain the episode of stagnation after 1971/72. The era of Bhutto (beginning the episode of stagnation), often associated with a big increase in state intervention, also contained important liberalisation measures. There was more state intervention during the Zia era than many commentators have allowed for.

It is often overlooked that the advent of Bhutto saw a number of distinctive liberalisation measures. Between 1971/72 and 1975/76 the Pakistani rupee was devalued by 130%,[1] import restrictions were abolished for over 300 commodity items, the Export Bonus System (EBS) was abolished, tariff rates were lowered on intermediate and capital goods, and the degree of cascading tariff in the tariff system was reduced. The trade bias index (effective exchange rate for imports divided by the effective exchange rate for exports) declined from 1.67 to 1.23 (Mahmood and Qasim 1992: 885). Bhutto's government was not anti-private property per se – it was, rather, particular capitalists who fuelled its ire. Nationalisation, for example, did not touch foreign capital.[2] In 1976 the National Assembly passed a law (the first in Pakistan's history) exempting foreign capital from future nationalisation. Those capitalists that were expropriated were given liberal compensation. The Habibs received R36.31 for each share originally valued at R5 (Ahmed 1982: 110). In the manufacturing sector, nationalisation often had the effect of absorbing the losses of the private sector in units that had become uneconomical following the abolition of subsidies like the EBS (Ahmed 1982: 110).

The political change in 1977 saw a 'comeback' of the private sector, if not yet outright liberalisation (Ahmed and Amjad 1984). The early aim of Zia's government was to revive confidence in the private sector, and relevant policies included denationalisation of some public sector industries (agro-based industries and some small engineering units), protection of the rights of investors, opening certain heavy and basic chemical and cement industries to private sector investment, and fiscal and other incentives (tax holidays, reduced import duties and income taxes, the setting up of EPZs, and reduced interest rates for industrial investment). It is easy to exaggerate the significance of this process. There had been a sharp increase in the percentage share of the public sector in non-agricultural GDP in the early 1970s, from 6.6% in 1970/71 to 11.5% in 1974/75; under Zia there was actually a continued (if slower) increase to 14.3% in 1984/85, then a very slight fall to 13.7% by 1987/88. In particular, the share of government in trade increased from 7.9% in 1974/75 to 30.2% in 1987/88, with the increase coming entirely during the Zia era (Naqvi and Kemal 1991: 111). Despite the opening of the non-bank financial sector for private investment in the mid-1980s, by 1990 public sector banks and non-bank financial institutions held 74.7% of assets, 65.9% of advances and 93.8% of investments (Khan et al. 2005: 822). Even by the late 1980s there was no clear shift towards privatisation.

A more obvious process of deregulation and liberalisation was begun during the Sixth Five-year Plan (1983–88) under Zia. The scope of investment licensing and tariffs on raw materials, intermediate goods, and capital goods was reduced. Some quantitative restrictions on imports were replaced by tariffs. The average level of tariffs and their dispersion was reduced, from 70% in 1979 to 30% in the late 1980s. Again, this had limited effects. Between 1976/77 and 1987/88 the rupee again became overvalued (it was pegged to an appreciating dollar), different duty rates were imposed for commercial and industrial users, and other quantitative restrictions on imports and export subsidies were extended. The trade bias index increased from 1.23 in 1976/77 to a peak of 1.56 in 1980/81, after which some trade liberalisation measures were introduced, then it declined to 1.39 in 1982/83, before increasing to 1.54 in 1987/88 (Mahmood and Qasim 1992: 885). By the mid-1980s Pakistan was still a relatively heavily protected economy, and 31.6% of its imports faced tariffs of between 10% and 50%, and 22.5% tariffs of over 50% (James and Naya 1990: 213). Implicit effective protection rates (IEPR) in the manufacturing sector in 1980/81 were still as high as 66% (Naqvi and Kemal 1991).

The (economic) role of the state, 1970/71 to 1991/92: finance

This section shows that the domestic surplus mobilised by the state after 1970/71 was stagnant, but compensated for by international capital inflows. Total savings stagnated; this was true for both public and private sector savings, the former being linked to stagnant tax revenues and the latter to a slowdown in the growth of the domestic financial sector. Savings remained below investment; the gap was filled by international capital inflows. This process left Pakistan more independent than is often argued by commentators. A poor record of overall corporate profitability was not explained by the relative growth of the state. State enterprises performed well over this period. There was substantial expansion in public investment under Bhutto, which supported growth throughout this period.

The mobilisation of savings, 1970/71 to 1992/93

The level of gross domestic savings declined from 13 % of GDP in 1971, to 9.9% in 1972/73, and to a low of 3.8% in 1974/75, and then increased to 8.5% in 1975/76, declined further to 6% in 1980, and then slowly increased to over 10% by the early 1990s[3] (Ahmed and Amjad 1984: 97; James and Naya 1990: 204; Khan 1993: 1068; Husain 1999: 331). The marginal rate of savings over this period was no more than about 15%, less than half that in Korea and less than two-thirds that in India (Nawab et al. 1984: 56–7; Hasen 1998).

The role of the state in mobilising domestic savings

Public sector savings showed some improvement over the 1970s, rising from -0.5% in 1972/73 to 0.7% in 1975/76 (Ahmed and Amjad 1984: 97). There were a few successful few years: public savings reached 4.17% of GDP in 1980/81 (Qureshi et al. 1997: 895), but the subsequent decline was dramatic, and public savings bottomed out at -4.7% in 1988/89, before recovering somewhat to -1.5% in 1992/93 (Bilquees 2003: 189).

Table 7.1 shows that total tax revenue increased as a proportion of GDP in the early and late 1970s, but was flat from the early 1980s. The jump in the tax ratio in the early 1970s was due to a sharp rise in customs duty, mainly reflecting the rupee devaluation of 1972/73 and consequent rise in the rupee value of exports. Excise duties continued to show rapid growth, partly due to reduction in tax evasion after nationalisation of industries, and partly as a result of an increase in tax rates. Revenues from income taxation also showed rapid growth in the 1970s, reflecting a change in fiscal policy, specifically the large-scale withdrawal of tax holidays. Rising revenue from income, wealth and sales taxes in the 1980s was largely offset by reductions in revenue from excise duty after 1979/80, or from customs duty after 1989/90. Rising revenue from sales tax in the latter 1980s was due to the withdrawal of exemptions at the import and manufacturing stages and to higher rates. Rising revenue from income taxation occurred in the early 1990s, despite falling personal and corporate tax rates, due to effective broadening of the tax base through reforms involving withholding and presumptive taxes on various sectors and various streams of income (interest, rent, exports, etc.) (Pasha and Fatima 1999).

Table 7.1 Tax to GDP ratio overall and for individual taxes of the central government (%)

Year	Income and Wealth Tax	Customs Duty	Excise Duty	Sales Tax	Surcharges	Total Taxes
1969–70	0.6	2.3	3.0	0.5	–	6.4
1970–75	1.5	4.5	3.5	1.0	–	10.5
1979–80	2.5	5.9	4.5	1.1	–	14.0
1984–85	2.2	5.5	3.6	1.1	0.8	13.2
1989–90	2.0	6.4	2.9	2.4	1.3	15.0
1994–95	3.4	4.6	2.6	2.6	1.3	14.5

Source: Pasha and Fatima 1999: 204.

Pakistan was consistently unable to generate more than 14% of GDP in tax revenues. This was due to three enduring weaknesses, a narrow and distorted tax system, the over-reliance on indirect taxes, and weak tax administration (Bilquees 2004; Zaidi 2005). It was estimated that, at the beginning of the 1990s, if all allowances were used by an individual, the exemption limit for income taxation would be over twelve times average income. Only 1m. out of a population of over 130m. then paid income tax (Husain 1999: 138). Despite efforts to raise revenue from direct taxes, indirect taxes raised over 80% of total revenues between 1974/75 and 1990/91, more than half of this being from customs revenue and the bulk of the rest from central excise duties (Nawab et al. 1988: 77; Pasha and Fatima 1999: 207; Bilquees 2004: 76). In the late 1970s, 84% of collections from excise duties came from sugar, POL, tobacco, vegetable products, and cement (Ahmed and Amjad 1984).

No serious attempt over this period was made to increase taxes on agriculture, even though revenue bore no relation to the general increase in incomes and land prices since the mid-1970s. The average tax would then have been around 1%–1.5% of net income (Khan 1991: 462). The ratio of land revenue to value added by crops declined from 0.58% in 1980/81 to 0.45% in 1994/95 (Zaidi 2005). A tax on immovable wealth was introduced in 1963, but agricultural land was exempted in 1970 for those landowners whose only source of income was agriculture. In 1977 the PPP abolished land revenue and replaced it with a uniform and universal national income tax. After the military coup, Zia suspended, then cancelled, the policy, and the former tax exemption on agriculture income was restored in 1979. In 1993 a caretaker government removed the wealth tax exemption for agriculture. In 1994 the PPP government re-introduced several deductions to reduce the impact of the wealth tax. The wealth tax on agriculture only yielded a tiny amount of revenue, an estimated R15m. from 2,000 individuals in 1988/89. In 1982/83 the federal government introduced the ushr levy on Muslim landowners in lieu of land revenue. Ushr revenue was collected and distributed by the local Ushr and Zakat committees; it yielded R177m. in 1982/83, R256m. in 1984/85, and R210m. by 1987/88.

The problems with revenue raising at the central level were replicated at the provincial level, with notably worse tax administration, and taxes generally being more inelastic with respect to growth in their revenue-raising potential (land revenue), being difficult to collect (property taxes), or being undermined by the growing strength of an Islamic movement (excise and entertainment taxes). Provincial governments made a distinct effort to mobilise tax revenue in the early 1990s, removing exemptions, increasing rates on stamp duties, motor vehicle tax, paddy fees, cotton duty, and electricity, and switching from specific to ad valorem taxes. There was considerable growth after 1990/91 in revenues, especially in Sindh and NWFP (Zaidi 2005: 221). Land revenue was a tax on land that generated income and was assessed and collected by the provincial government. In 1988/89 collected land revenue was 2.8% of total revenue from direct taxes (Khan 1991).

Gillani was an optimist about the tax system. He found the elasticity of tax revenue with respect to GDP growth between 1971/72 and 1982/83 to have been greater than one for both total (1.26), indirect (1.24) and direct (1.44) taxes (1986: 170). Bilquees finds instead very low elasticities; his methodology (for example testing for stationarity, rather than using simple OLS) and data marked an improvement over Gillani. He found that, for total tax revenue, excise duty, sales tax, and customs duty, revenue elasticity was less than one in the short and long run, while income tax at least rose above one in the long term (2004: 85). Mukarram estimated the elasticity of the tax system after 1980/81: for the whole tax system, he estimated 0.64; and specifically for customs duty, 0.32; direct taxes, 1.61; excise duty, 0.47; and sales tax, 0.99 (2001: 81). Other studies find the elasticity of the total tax system declining in the 1980s, relative to the 1970s, for all major taxes (except sales tax); for income and corporate taxation they were below unity throughout, while excise duties and customs duties fell from above to below unity (Husain 1999: 181, Zaidi 2005: 219). By the early 1990s the tax base for direct taxes was extremely narrow (yielding only about 2% of GDP). It could have been broadened by eliminating some 180 income tax exemptions and by gradually phasing out numerous tax credits and industry-specific tax holidays (Khan 1993: 1074).

Total (central and provincial) government expenditure increased from 24.53% of GDP in 1971/72 to 32.01% in 1972/73, declined steadily to 22.10% in 1981/82, then fluctuated around 26% until 1992/93. This pattern hid sharp changes in the composition of total spending: current expenditure increased from 11.32% in 1971/72 to 20.30% in 1992/93; development spending declined from 12.67% in 1971/72 to 5.70% in 1992/93 (Ahmed and Amjad 1984: 261; Qureshi *et al.* 1997: 897–8). As a share of consolidated federal and provincial government expenditure, current expenditure increased from 68.1% in 1971/72 to 62.7% in 1980/81 and 75% in 1990/91. Despite the long military dictatorship, this was not due to rising defence expenditure. Defence spending rose from 7.5% of GDP (56.3% of total expenditure) in 1971/72 to a peak of 7.8% (39.8%) in 1987/88, then declined steadily to 7.3% in 1992/93 (35.7%) (Pasha and Fatima 1999: 213).[4] Nor was this due to rising subsidies or the general cost of government. Subsidies increased from 0.1% of GDP (0.9% of total central government expenditure) in 1969/70 to a peak of 2.4% of GDP (13.9%) in 1984/85, then declined to 1.5% (8.7%) in 1994/95 (Pasha and Fatima 1999: 209–10). Pasha *et al.* use a much broader measure of subsidies[5] and find that there was little change from 1972/73 (6% of GDP) to the mid-1990s (5% of GDP) (2002: 632–6). General administration costs increased from 1.0% of GDP in 1969/70 to 1.8% in 1975/76, then declined steadily, reaching 0.9% in 1994/95 (Pasha and Fatima 1999: 209). The decline after the early 1970s was related to the reduction in the real wages of civil servants (Qureshi and Bilquees 1977: 329); costs of government continued to decline even after 1977 when civil service wages were increased (Bilquees 1992). Much of this rise in current expenditure was due to a higher interest burden on the (growing) public debt. Debt servicing increased from 1.3% of GDP (19.6% of total central government expenditure) in 1969/70, to a peak of 8.9% (44.6%) of GDP in 1989/90, then declined slowly to 8.3% (46.9%) by 1994/95 (Pasha and Fatima 1999: 209). Rising interest payments were not due (in the 1980s) to higher interest rates. The real cost of public debt was relatively low in the 1980s, and external debt (3.4%) and domestic debt (0.5%) combined to cost around 2.5%; these figures fell to -0.9%, -0.3% and -0.5%, respectively, in the early 1990s. It was only as the 1990s wore on that the cost of debt became prohibitive, when financial sector liberalisation, initiated in

1989, shifted government debt raising to a full market-based auction programme (Zaidi 2005: 248). The principal reason for the growth in interest payments (and hence current expenditure) was the growth in the volume of the domestic debt, which increased from 2.1% of GDP in 1980/81 to 52.2% in 1999/00 (Zaidi 2005: 230). Pakistan was entering the foothills of a debt trap, as current expenditure and deficits were being driven by the interest costs on the growing stock of government debt. The overall deficit declined from 9.7% in 1978/79, to 5.3% in 1981/82, then increased steadily to 8.0% in 1992/93 (Bilquees 2003: 186; Zaidi 2005: 442).

The role of the state in creating institutions to mobilise private sector savings

Private savings fluctuated around a low level in the 1970s, reaching a low of 5%–6% in 1974/75 and a high of 12.67% in 1977/78; there was no obvious trend. There was a jump in private savings in the early 1980s, to 14.72% in 1982/83; the level then fluctuated until 1992/93 in the range of 12%–16%. Most of these fluctuations were driven by changes in household savings. The other component, corporate savings, mostly remained in the range 1.00%–1.60% over the entire period (Ahmed and Amjad 1984: 97; Qureshi et al. 1997: 895; Bilquees 2003: 189).

In 1974 the largest banks in Pakistan were nationalised and consolidated into a 'big five', Habib, National, Muslim Commercial, United, and Allied Banks; between them they had 7,500 branches and dominated the financial services industry. After nationalisation there was a major drive to expand the banking system led by these 'big five'. Between January 1974 and March 1976 the number of bank branches increased by 54%, deposits by 80%, loans by 65%, and bank employees by 35% (Ahmed 1982). The number of bank branches increased from 3,418 in 1971, to 6,737 in 1977, and to 7,404 in 1990 (Zaidi 2005). Despite this, Table 7.2 shows that there was little in the way of financial development between 1970 and 1990, or relative to the 1960s. The ratios of broad money, stock market capitalisation and private sector credit to GDP were stagnant, while ratios of total deposit liabilities and broad money to GDP declined. The M2/GDP ratio was stagnant after 1970, showing little change between 1971–80 (44.2%) and 1981–90 (45.6%) or 1991–96 (44.6%) (Husain 1999: 179).

The paradox of an expanding financial system by physical measures (number of branches) and a stagnant system by financial measures (table 7.2) can be reconciled by reference to the government's monetary policy. In the 1970s and 1980s the budget deficit was rising steadily (see earlier note), and during this time between 20% and 50% of the deficit was being financed by borrowing from banks (Qureshi et al. 1997: 897–8; Zaidi 2005: 231). As a share of GDP, budgetary support from the banking system declined, with fluctuations, from 4.4% in 1978/79 to 0.1% in 1988/89, and then increased dramatically, to between 4% and 6% of GDP in the three years to 1992/93 (Zaidi 2005: 231). To reduce the cost of its borrowing, the government repressed the financial system through forcing the banks to hold low-return government debt (Khan 1988). Between 1973 and 1977 real interest rates were estimated to be -10.5%, and between 1978 and 1982 -2.9%. Negative real interest rates discouraged disintermediation from the informal sector, where nominal rates of return were substantially higher, to the formal banking sector. By the late 1980s the ratio of deposits to

Table 7.2 Indicators of financial deepening (%)

Indicators	1961–70	1970–80	1981–90	1990
Broad Money/GDP[1]	34.03	33.90	34.02	32.27
Total Deposit Liabilities/GDP[2]	23.52	34.47	32.36	27.91
Amount of Clearing House/GDP[3]	90.74	97.70	111.63	126.88
Currency/M_2	45.13	32.29	32.28	37.56
Currency/GDP	16.06	13.53	13.29	14.73
Private Sector Credit/GDP	19.60	19.24	21.45	19.92
Stock market Capitalisation/GDP	8.42	4.08	3.75	4.68

Source: Khan and Qayyum 2007: 15.
1 Broad money (money plus quasi-money). Broad money includes the sum of currency outside the banks plus demand, time, savings and foreign currency deposits of residents other than the central government.
2 Total bank deposit liabilities are equal to liquid liabilities minus currency in circulation – without deducting currency in circulation we are left with primarily a measure of monetisation, not financial depth.
3 The amount of money cleared through cheques by clearing house can be used as an indicator of financial services development.

GDP began to decline absolutely (Khan 1999). Using data from this period, Iqbal (1993) finds that there is a positive and significant relationship between household savings and the real interest rate. Khan and Hasan (1998) find a positive relation between the real interest rate and money demand. Khan and Qayyum (2007) find a positive and significant relation between the real interest rate and financial development. Nasir and Khalid (2004) disagree and find an insignificant link from interest rates to savings.

More narrowly successful was the growth of banking for the agricultural sector. A 1972/73 survey showed that 90%, and a 1985 survey that 68%, of credit to agriculture was provided by non-institutional sources (Zaidi 2005: 63). This decline was in part due to the expansion of bank services, such as the specialised rural financial institutions, like the Zarai Taraqiate Bank Limited (ZTBL), formerly the Agricultural Development Bank of Pakistan (ADBP). ZTBL was the largest source of institutionalised credit; after the mid-1990s it provided more than 64% of total credit, with most loans being long term and many going towards buying tractors (Zaidi 2005).

The role of the state in mobilising foreign savings

Between 1970 and 1992 Pakistan was heavily dependent on external resource inflows as investment remained significantly higher than savings. The net national balance reached a peak of -10.4% of GDP in 1975, then fluctuated between about -3% and -7% of GDP until 1992. The principal reason was the significant negative balance of the public sector that invested heavily (over 8% of GDP), but saved little (1%–2% of GDP). The private sector was consistently, if not enough to compensate, in surplus between these years (Naweb et al. 1984: 69; James and Naya 1990: 204; Qureshi et al. 1997: 899–900). Among comparable Asian developing countries over the 1970s and 1980s, Pakistan tended to have lower levels of investment, significantly lower levels of domestic savings and consequently a significantly higher need to access external savings (Qureshi et al. 1997: 894).

The need for capital inflows is usually complemented with other rather *ad hoc* evidence to bolster views of Pakistan as 'dependent'. Limited survey evidence shows that much of this aid was tied to imports from the donor at prices of up to 157% over world prices (Rashid 1983: 183–4). Such dependence, argue some, was the key dynamic in Pakistan, and such views see a 'dependent' Pakistan, with a development strategy entirely contingent on the goodwill or caprices of donors; in particular,.US priorities determined Pakistan's domestic and foreign policies from 1951 onward' (Ali 2008: 251). This was reflected in Bhutto's book, *The Myth of Independence*, where he argued instead for a foreign and domestic policy independent of the great powers. This view was largely mistaken for being synonymous with the Bhutto era and, though there was more truth in it during the 1980s, it remained exaggerated.

For the first two years of Bhutto's rule (1971 to 1973) Pakistan's foreign policy was dominated by the legacy of the conflict with Bangladesh. Pakistan was internationally isolated, publicity about the war was very negative, and India held 90,000 prisoners of war. The USA had pressed the World Bank to withhold aid until Pakistan recognised Bangladesh. At first this isolation intensified, Pakistan severed ties with countries recognising Bangladesh and withdrew from the Commonwealth after recognition by Britain. Far from the situation driving Pakistan into greater dependence, the effort to stave off early recognition of Bangladesh by Muslim countries became a proactive foreign policy process by Bhutto, and he embarked on a 12-day tour of 14 countries in the Middle East, and later visited China and the USSR. In 1972 China vetoed the entry of Bangladesh to the UN and contributed to the first heavy-engineering projects in Pakistan – the Heavy Mechanical Complex and Heavy Foundry and Forge near Taxila (Raza 1997). The USSR pressed for Pakistan to negotiate with India and to accept Bangladesh, but agreed to fund a steel mill. Pakistan withdrew from SEATO in 1972, but balanced this by acting as a go-between for US National Security Advisor Henry Kissinger's visit to China. In February 1975 Bhutto visited the USA and President Ford lifted the arms embargo. From defeat in 1971, Pakistan quickly recovered, and in April1972 Bhutto negotiated with India in Simla, where the existing line of control was accepted. At the Islamic Summit in February 1974 Pakistan recognised Bangladesh without having to involve India, and the remaining prisoners of war were released. The process of normalisation went forward quite quickly after 1974. In January 1976 the first Bangladeshi ambassador to Pakistan arrived, and trade and shipping agreements were signed in April. A Pakistani bank opened in Dacca, and in October a Bangaldeshi bank opened in Karachi. Telephone and telegraph links were re-established and provisions made to exchange TV programmes. With relations with India normalised, ambassadors were exchanged, a trade agreement signed, mail and telecommunication links restored, freight and passenger traffic by air and rail begun, and overflights again permitted. In 1976 there were also significant foreign policy breakthroughs with Afghanistan. Following Prince Daud's seizure of power in July 1973, the Afghan government tried to exploit a perception of Pakistan's isolation, reactivated the issue of Pakhtoon nationalism and established links with Pakistani NAP politicians. With Pakistan's international standing carefully enhanced by June 1976, Daud invited Bhutto to

Kabul, and the two governments agreed to suspend hostile propaganda against each other and pursue peaceful coexistence (Syed 1977).

This greater degree of foreign policy independence was reflected in a striking diversification of trade and aid. Pakistan was very successful in boosting exports from an annual value of $700m. during the last four years of united Pakistan to over $1bn in 1973/74, despite losing markets in Bangladesh. The most significant breakthrough came in exports to Muslim countries. The share of eight major Muslim trade partners (Iran, Iraq, Libya, Indonesia, Saudi Arabia, Abu Dhabi, Kuwait, Dubai) increased from 6.6% in 1969/70 to 24.8% in 1973/74 (Ahmed 1982: 194). Pakistan has been a major recipient of OPEC aid: in 1974/75 those Muslim countries pledged $896m., or 51.4% of the record aid commitment of $1,744m. made to Pakistan by various donors. Iran agreed to provide $580m. over a three-year period. By comparison, the USA committed $194m. The USSR concluded its largest ever donor programme, pledging $214m. for a steel mill near Karachi. Between 1971/72 and 1974/75 there were rapid increases in lending from the Asian Development Bank (ADB) for agriculture (Ahmed 1982). After 1970, loans from China increased from nothing to $217.4m., and from socialist countries (plus Austria and Denmark) from $155.2m. to $748.5m. (Rashid 1983). The share of gross aid disbursements from the traditional developed 'consortium countries' declined from 86.88% in 1969/70 to 41.97% in 1979/80 (Naweb et al. 1984: 103). This last figure demonstrates that Bhutto had substantially achieved his aim of building a degree of independence from the 'great powers'.

The downfall of Bhutto was linked by some to US displeasure at his efforts to develop a nuclear weapon and the USA's re-assertion of Pakistan's dependent status. The US Carter administration in the mid-1970s certainly put more emphasis on human rights, nuclear non-proliferation and narcotics – all of which generated more pressure on Pakistan. Instead of backtracking, in March 1979 Pakistan (and Iran) terminated their membership of CENTO. The USA responded in April by cutting off all non-food aid (not Public Law 480) and began to pass various laws to restrict aid to countries trying to develop weapons. This culminated in the 1985 Pressler agreement, which required annual certification by the President that Pakistan did not have a nuclear device, and without which Pakistan could not receive US foreign aid. In December 1979 the Soviets invaded Afghanistan. Pakistan's increased importance and relative independence was demonstrated by the rejection of President Carter's offer of $400m. in aid by President Zia as 'peanuts'. In 1980–81 President Reagan concluded an aid package worth $3.6bn over six years (Burki 1988, 1991, 1999; Baxter 1991).

The purely financial aspects of foreign relations were generating alarmism by the late 1970s. In 1979/80 'debt servicing alone cost almost 2.5 times the amount of non-project aid, and national debt had reached $8.7bn a 300% increase over ten years' (Naweb et al. 1984). External debt 'increased further to $30bn in 1995 raising the debt to GDP ratio and debt servicing ratio[6]' (Hasen 1998). Despite the long-standing and heavy dependence on foreign savings, there was no indication that Pakistan was facing an international debt crisis and sliding into financial dependency. Table 7.3 shows that external debt indicators were generally improving from the early 1970s to the mid 1980s; there was some worsening after this time, but not to levels unprecedented in Pakistan's recent history.[7]

The average maturity period of loans declined from 28 years between 1972/73 and 1976/77, to 27 years between 1977/78 and 1987/88 and 22 years between 1988/89 and 1992/93, and the average grant element from 48% to 42% and 37% over the same period. The average interest rates (respectively, 4%, 5% and 5%) were low and remained so (Khan 1997: 948). Pakistan's long-term debt in 1992 was 57% below what one might expect, given its per capita GDP (in purchasing power parity) and population (Khan 1997).

The most important mechanism for overcoming financial dependence from the early 1970s onwards was remittance income. In the late 1960s the government of Pakistan adopted an official policy of encouraging the large-scale export of manpower to the Middle East as a means of earning foreign exchange. The Bureau of Emigration was set up in 1969 to facilitate overseas employment (Ahmed 1982). The key breakthrough was the re-orientation of Pakistan's foreign policy under Bhutto towards a pro-Middle Eastern line and the sharp rise in the price of oil in the early 1970s. This combination left workers from Pakistan ideally placed to acquire visas and employment in sectors like construction in the dollar-laden Middle East. This line was continued by Zia. If he lacked the flair and élan of Bhutto when conducting foreign policy, he made up for it by a strong commitment to Islam and a very practical approach to foreign policy in the Middle East – military protection. By 1983 there were around 30,000 military personnel in the Middle East, about 20,000 of them in Saudi Arabia (Baxter 1991). By the late 1970s more than half the armed forces of the Sultan of Oman were believed to be mercenaries from Baluchistan (Ahmed 1982: 195).

In 1970/71 total private remittances were probably negative, but by 1977/78 they had risen to $1.1bn, and commodity exports increased from $589m. to $1.3bn over the same period. There was a further dramatic rise in remittance flows after the late 1970s, to $2,038m. in 1980, peaking at $2,925m. in 1983, then slow declining to $1,860m. in 1988 (James and Naya 1990: 208, Husain 1999: 331). Table 7.4 demonstrates the rising share of remittances in GNP and in total foreign exchange earnings, as well as relative to the trade gap over the 1970s. By the late 1970s workers' remittances dwarfed net aid inflow and generated as much foreign exchange as exports.[8]

Table 7.5 shows that the importance of remittances in covering very substantial trade deficits continued into the 1980s and early 1990s. The peak year was in 1982/83 when workers' remittances from the Middle East alone reached 9.39% of GDP (Amjad 1986: 763).

Though helping to avoid dependence and largely funding the trade deficit, there is little evidence that remittances or capital inflows more generally were utilised in a

Table 7.3 External debt indicators

	1971–75	1976–80	1981–85	1986–90
Debt–GNP Ratio	48.8	46.6	40.3	48.4
Debt–Export Ratio	397.7	276.6	200.3	241.5
Debt–Service Ratio	20.2	19.3	18.8	24.6
Interest–Export Ratio	7.6	7.7	7.5	9.4

Source: Husain 1999: 335.

Table 7.4 Workers' remittances, 1970/71–1979/80

Years	As Percentage of GNP	As Percentage of Total Foreign Exchange Earnings	As Percentage of Net Aid Inflow	As Percentage of Trade Gap
1970/71	0.5	5.6	–	9.7
1971/72	1.0	12.9	–	32.7
1972/73	2.0	11.9	76.4	99.4
1973/74	1.7	9.7	46.2	29.2
1974/75	2.0	14.2	27.9	18.7
1975/76	2.7	18.6	43.1	34.2
1976/77	4.1	28.7	95.3	44.9
1977/78	6.8	40.8	239.9	78.7
1978/79	7.1	39.4	307.7	64.3
1979/80	7.5	36.7	214.1	69.3

Source: Nawab et al. 1984: 97.

Table 7.5 Components of balance of payments, 1980–2002 (% of average GDP)

Year	Exports	Imports	Trade Deficit	Workers' Remittances
1980–85	8.96	18.72	9.74	8.30
1985–90	11.28	17.10	5.82	5.94
1990–95	13.52	17.8	4.28	3.2

Source: Zaidi 2005: 165.

developmental manner. Remittances tended to be diverted to consumption and the purchase of real estate, and to fulfil social obligations such as the Hajj and weddings. Investment tended to account for only a small share of workers' remittances (Nawab et al. 1984: 99; Tsakok 1982: 322; Amjad 1986).[9] The general finding in the statistical literature is that aid inflows increased consumption rather than savings and investment (Khilji and Zampelli 1991; Chishti and Hasan 1992; Khan et al. 1992; Mahmood and Qasim 1992; Khan and Rahmin 1993; Iqbal 1993, 1994, 1997).[10]

If not pro-actively utilised by the state in a developmental manner, remittance income did have an important indirect effect on the economy. As much as 46% of the national net increase in consumption between 1976 and 1985 may have been accounted for by remittance income, which clearly had a macroeconomic impact in stimulating domestic demand and was reflected in the more rapid growth of the small-scale sector in the 1970s (see Chapter 3). Sectors such as small-scale manufacturing, construction, transport and communication and wholesale/retail trade responded strongly to this demand. Many new industries opened, most in the small-scale sector. Examples included the plastic industry producing tableware, utensils, water-coolers, containers and toys. Others in the engineering industry included those producing appliances such as desert coolers, washing machines, and gas cookers. Traditional industries such as fans, sewing machines, and bicycles experienced much higher demand growth (Amjad 1986).

The role of the state in influencing private sector profitability

In large-scale manufacturing there was an increase in the wage share relative to profits in the early 1970s, from 20.5% in 1969/70 to 26.0% in 1975/76; it thereafter declined to around 20%–22% for period until 1990/91. There was no great shift over the entire 20-year interval (Wizarat 2002: 165). There are two possible reasons for the fall in profit share in the 1970s, higher prices of wage goods and labour policy.

There is no clear evidence of an emerging domestic wage goods constraint. The most important wage good for Pakistan was agriculture. The net barter terms of trade for agriculture did increase from 103.4 (1969 = 100) in 1970/71 to a peak of 114.2 in 1973/74, then fluctuated at this level until 1981/82 (Kazi 1987: 83). The shift after 1972/73, though, was largely a result of the dramatic price increase in the export crops (rice, cotton) following the devaluation of the rupee in May 1972, increased subsidies on agricultural inputs, and increased world prices of primary commodities. There was no major trend in the domestic net barter terms of trade over the 1970s and early 1980s (Qureshi 1985: 367–8). We would expect a wage goods constraint to be visible as rising wage shares in more labour-intensive economic sectors. However, during the 1970s there was no general tendency for wage shares to increase in labour-intensive, relative to capital-intensive, industries (Afridi 1985: 474; Wizarat 2002: 168).

The second possible explanation is that this early shift in income distribution to wage earners was related to the introduction of a new labour policy by the Bhutto government. This was matched by rises in government salaries concentrated among the lowest paid. Over time, slower economic growth and high inflation led to an erosion of these early gains. Real wages in industry and construction increased up to about 1976 (Ahmed and Amjad 1984; Guisinger and Hicks 1978). Real wages of government employees fell after 1975/76 (Qureshi and Bilquees 1977: 331; Guisinger and Hicks 1978: 1273, 1276; Irfan and Ahmed 1985). The declining wage share after the mid-1970s is difficult to reconcile with labour migration to the Middle East. It is easy to link this to the sharp rise (10%–20% p.a.) in real wages that occurred for construction workers after the mid-1970s (Tsakok 1982: 321). Irfan and Ahmed (1985) find that a time series regression of real wages of production workers in six manufacturing industries in the Punjab shows that real wages were strongly correlated with the stock of labour in the Middle East. The peak of migration occurred in 1981 (Bilquees 1992: 1248).

From the early 1970s the public sector became involved in new and basic industries, such as edible oils, petrochemicals, fertiliser, pesticides, petroleum refining, non-metallic mineral products, cement, iron and steel, engines, motor vehicles, and ship building (Rauf 1994). By 1987/88 public industrial enterprises accounted for 13.8% of value added and 17.9% of investment in large-scale manufacturing, but only 2% of GDP. More broadly, there was a sharp increase in the percentage share of the public sector in non-agricultural GDP in the early 1970s, and under Zia there was a continued (if slower) increase to 1984/85, then a very slight fall thereafter (Naqvi and Kemal 1991: 111). Despite the opening of the non-bank financial sector for private investment in the mid-1980s, by 1990 public sector banks and non-bank financial institutions held 74.7% of assets, 65.9% of advances and 93.8% of investments (Khan et al. 2005: 822). This growth of the public sector did not have an adverse impact on corporate profitability (contrary to popular assumption). Using a sample of eight important public sector enterprises[11] accounting for more than 70% of the output originating in public enterprises in 1987/88, gives an average pre-tax return on net equity, paid up capital, and fixed assets of 10.0%, 7.8% and 9.3%, respectively. Excluding Pakistan Steel, the average return on net equity, on paid up capital, and on fixed assets was 27.2%, 25.0%, and 23%, respectively. These latter figures are significantly higher than the rate of interest paid on government debt. Naqvi and Kemal found no systematic difference in the profitability of industries in which both the public and private sectors had a substantial presence (tractors, fertiliser and cement) (1991). Mahmood and Sahibzada found no particular trend in the profitability of public sector enterprises in large-scale manufacturing, though such returns remained above the costs of public debt (1987: 798–9).

Table 7.6 shows that profitability of the state-owned electricity sector according to various measures declined in the mid-1970s, revived in the late 1970s and early 1980s and ended in the early 1990s at a level similar to that in the early 1970s. Making correction for government subsidies and access to cheap foreign exchange (replacing actual interest rates with a notional real annual capital charge of 10% of capital assets) shows the power sector to be extremely unprofitable. This indicates clearly the impact of government policy on profits.

As in the 1960s (Chapter 6), trade policy continued to exert an influence on profits. There is some evidence relating the two for the late 1980s. Table 7.7 shows that effective rates of protection (ERP) tended to decline between the years 1988 and 1993, and that there is in general a clear positive relation between the changes in the ERP and private returns.

We may have expected to see a decline in the profitability of the private sector in Pakistan in the early 1970s. The nationalisation programme of the PPP government was intended to reduce levels of concentration and hence 'exploitative profits' of the private corporate sector. The position of the industrial houses was further affected by the loss of assets in East Pakistan. The principal industrial houses lost a large share of their assets, Saigol: 68.8%; Habib: 69.8%; Adamjee: 40.0%; Fancy: 89.7%; Valika: 66.1%; and Rangoonwala: 100.0% (Amjad 1983: 256). The control of assets in the large-scale manufacturing sector showed a drop from 41.7% for 41 houses to 31% for 39 houses. In practice, nationalisation had little impact on industrial concentration. Industrial houses still controlled a reasonably large section of private domestic assets and private domestic production of the large-scale manufacturing sector. Their continued role was owing to their dominating position in cotton textiles and sugar industry – the latter, for example, contributed almost one-third of total value added in the large-scale manufacturing sector (Amjad 1983). The concentration ratio[12] of 273 large-scale firms mainly (though not exclusively) listed on the Karachi Stock Exchange increased from 55.62% in 1967, to 59.01% in 1970 and 61.79% in 1973 (Sharwani 1976). There is good reason to believe that profits will be related to the market power (as proxied by firm size) of industrial enterprises. Sarmad (1984) finds to the contrary that profit rates of enterprises in Pakistan between 1977/78 and 1981/82 were negatively related to firm size. Sharwani finds that profits according to two measures declined, from 39.04% and 39.04% in 1967, to 19.77% and 18.63% in 1973 respectively. Econometric analysis

Table 7.6 Various concepts of net profit margin on sale of state-owned electric power industry in Pakistan, 1960–95

Years	Net Profit Margin on Sale before Interest (%)			Net Profit Margin on Sale after Interest (Actual) (%)			Net Profit Margin on Sale after 10% Opportunity Cost on Capital (%)		
	WAPDA	KESC	Power	WAPDA	KESC	Power	WAPDA	KESC	Power
1966–71	34.98	26.40	35.17	4.51	19.24	10.71	-63.61	-26.25	-52.75
1972–77	26.15	8.20	25.28	-1.32	-0.38	1.50	-98.94	-88.58	-90.66
1978–83	48.72	18.09	42.85	29.86	9.31	25.93	-42.34	-45.65	-44.21
1984–89	33.46	17.01	31.77	15.54	5.27	14.82	-37.38	-50.65	-35.90
1990–95	39.40	13.74	36.29	19.93	0.07	17.53	-26.43	-34.95	-28.88

Source: Ghafoor and Weiss 2001: 122.

Table 7.7 Impact of trade reform on effective protection and profitability, 1988–93 (in %)

	Pre-Reform		Post-Reform	
	EPR	Private Returns	EPR	Private Returns
Chemical				
Paper and paper products	-8	12	24	26
Basic industrial chemicals	70	9	1	-5
Fertilisers	23	14	3	9
MMF	29	9	0	3
Other chemical products	10	27	19	32
Rubber and plastics	19	13	32	18
Glass and ceramics	6	11	20	15
Subsector	20	14	13	12
Engineering				
Basic metals	25	7	48	14
Metal products	19	12	11	10
Mechanical machinery	58	19	24	9
Electrical machinery	-13	14	30	31
Electronics	-31	2	16	16
Transport equipment	-1	7	24	13
Subsector	12	11	27	15
Textiles				
Cotton spinning	-5	20	12	26
Weaving and finishing	45	16	22	10
Cotton made-ups	9	18	3	16
Woollen products	93	6	17	-5
Jute products	38	16	21	12
Subsector	13	17	12	16

Source: Zaidi 2005: 155.

shows a strong relation between concentration ratios and both measures of profitability in 1967 and 1970, but little or no relation after 1970 (1976: 280). Relatively small shifts in profits occurred, with a massive drop in real private industrial investment, which by 1976/7 was only about 40% of the level in 1969/70; this was compensated to some extent by increases in small-scale investment, which increased by 20%–25% over the same period (Hasen 1998: 213). This was related to the changing nature of public investment discussed later in this chapter.

Ahmad and Chaudhry (1987) find that over the early 1980s there was a negative trend in net income from the major agricultural crops. For rice, cotton and sugar cane, input prices increased faster than output/market prices.

The role of the state in allocating credit to small firms

The government certainly made an effort to help small firms gain access to credit. By the time of the Sixth Five-year Plan, the small-scale sector benefited from numerous incentives and benefits. These included the exemption of cottage industries from central excise and sales taxes. A number of financial institutions had been either encouraged, or were created with a dedicated mandate, to supply small firms with credit. These included the nationalised commercial banks, the Small Industries Corporations, The Industrial Development Bank of Pakistan, and the Small Business Finance Corporation. There is a general lack of data on the impact of these institutions. What evidence exists, though, shows that loans from these institutions were not very significant. A UNIDO study found that less than 2% of Pakistan's small-scale industry units had received financing from banks. There remained credit barriers for small-scale firms, with collateral guarantees, lengthy procedures, and detailed paperwork (Malik and Cheema 1986; Zaidi 2005).

The role of the state in managing flows of FDI

Earlier, this chapter showed that Bhutto made concessions to foreign capital, and this trend was generally continued under Zia. These changes had little impact. FDI increased from a total of $41m. between 1970 and 1974 (0.53% of gross capital formation) to $138m. between 1975 and 1979 (0.98%), $322m. between 1980 and 1984 (1.22%), and $764m. between 1985 and 1989 (2.31%). (Atique *et al.* 2004: 709). FDI was not a significant component of capital inflow. The share of FDI in total foreign capital inflows increased from 6.77% in 1970/71, to 6.96% in 1980/81 and 8.62% in 1990/91 (Shah and Ahmed 2003: 698).

There is very little work on the economic impact of FDI in Pakistan over this period. Khan and Rahmin (1993) find domestic savings to be positively correlated with FDI, and foreign loans negatively so. The results hint at a more favourable impact of FDI than other forms of capital inflow, but the results do not, for example, consider the question of causality in the relationship. Shabbir and Mahmood (1992) find that between 1959/60 and 1987/88 there is no significant correlation between FDI and GDP, Ahmad *et al.* (2003) find a positive relation between 1972 and 2001, and Atique *et al.* (2004) find the growth impact of FDI to be greater under export promotion regimes rather than import substitution regimes between 1970 and 2001.

The role of the state in allocating resources to projects essential for development

Gross domestic investment increased very slowly, from 16% of GDP in 1971, to 13% in 1974, 18.5% in 1980, 18.0% in 1990, and 20.5% in 1992/93 (James and Naya 1990: 204; Khan 1993: 1068; Husain 1999: 331; Kemal 1999: 158; Wizarat 2002: 29; Kemal *et al.* 2006: 312). This slow increase disguised a dramatic change in the composition of investment. The share of public investment in total investment increased rapidly in the early 1970s, from 49.9% in 1970/71, to 71.5% in 1975/76, and then declined slowly to the end of the decade, reaching 68.0% in 1979/80 and 49.7% in 1988/89 (Naweb *et al.* 1984: 64; James and Naya 1990: 206). The share of development spending in total federal spending increased from 19.1% in 1971/72 to a peak of 44.6% in 1976/77, then declined to 35.6% in 1979/80 (Nawab *et al.* 1984: 83). Rising public investment in the early 1970s was largely due to the large-scale manufacturing sector; the share of total public investment going to this sector increased from 5.3% in 1969/70 to 24.1% in 1976/77. Public sector investment was focused in long-gestation, capital-intensive projects that included the Pakistan steel mill, sugar, cement, fertiliser and textile factories. Public investment was also almost entirely responsible for a construction boom in the first half of the 1970s (Hasen 1998). Public investment in agriculture declined mainly with the completion in the early 1970s of the Indus Basin project (Nawab *et al.* 1984: 66; Afridi 1985: 465).

Over the 1970s and 1980s there were indications that the growth potential of this effort was undermined by inefficient utilisation. This period saw significant expansion of capacity in power. In the 1970s public investment aimed to reduce oil imports by exploring for gas and oil, building a nuclear plant and exploring hydro potential in the upper reaches of the Indus and Jhelum. Production kilo wattage tripled over the 1980s, and between 1980 and 1996 power use per capita increased from 139kg to 243kg. By 1990 power generation capacity was above the average of low-income countries. Power losses, though, at 25% of production, remained very high (Husain 1999). The number of telephone lines per thousand of population increased from 3 in 1978 to 18 in 1996. This expansion was state led; the public sector retained a monopoly under the Telegraph and Telephone Department in the Ministry of Communications until 1990. By the early 1990s Pakistan had a higher telephone density than most Asian nations, but a very high rate of fault, more than ten times higher than in Indonesia, Turkey, Brazil, Malaysia, or Egypt. (Husain 1999). By the 1980s the railway system had 130,000 employees and 8,800 km of track. However, there was little expansion, as track length was barely changed from the 8,574km in 1960. Since the late-1970s the number of locomotives, wagons, and passengers carried and freight handled had declined by 30%–60% (Husain 1999). There were concerns that the expansion of public investment under Bhutto was motivated by political populism. Under Bhutto, the Planning Commission lost its role in policy co-ordination, and project and programme review, leading to a loss of consistency in investment projects and intersectoral balance (Hasen 1998). An example is the Lowari Tunnel (the all-weather link from Chitral), which was budgeted at $200m. and intended to connect the Northern Areas with the rest of Pakistan. The project was motivated by political, rather than economic, criteria and aimed to reduce the strength of Wali Khan's NAP members in the Frontier Province. The Karachi steel mill had been abandoned in the 1960s with the view that it had little economic justification; it was revived in the 1970s with Soviet financing as a prestige project guided by foreign policy considerations (Burki 1980).

There has been some work on crowding in of private investment in the Pakistan context. The general finding is that public investment has a positive impact on private investment (Khan 1988; Hyder 2001; Naqvi 2002; Ahmed and Qayyam 2007), though some argue the opposite (Ghani and ud Din 2006).

The (economic) role of the state, 1970/71 to 1991/92: production

This second section examines the role of the state in achieving a productive use of the surplus in both the public and private sectors. Exports made a marginal contribution to GDP over this period. There is evidence that Pakistan did not follow a growth pattern based on its (labour-intensive) comparative advantage. Production was capital intensive, and there were no indications of labour-intensive growth. There were indications of dynamic learning/upgrading, as both capital and labour productivity improved significantly, and the capital-intensive path of growth in agriculture alleviated some key constraints in the sector and supported rapid growth, particularly in the 1980s. The performance of state-owned enterprises contributed to productivity growth. Broader measures of productivity (TFP) showed improvement particularly in the 1980s.

Sources of growth: export growth

There was a temporary boom in exports from Pakistan in the early 1970s, aided by the 1972 devaluation and the 1972/73 world commodity price boom. High inflation quickly reduced the effect of the 1972 devaluation, and high import taxation continued to generate an anti-export bias (Hasen 1998). Between 1970 and 1977 Pakistan's share of world exports fell from 0.2% to 0.11%. Export growth increased again after the late 1970s. Between 1969/70 and 1976/77, and then from 1977/78 to 1986/87, export growth of primary products (including fuels) increased from 6.8% to 9.4%, manufactures increased from 7.3% to 14.0%, and invisibles declined from 12.6% to 11.1% (Papanek 1991: 610). Total exports increased from $420m. in 1970/71 to $2,365m. in 1979/80. Imports rose even more rapidly, from $757m. in 1970/71 to $4,740m. in 1979/80. The overall trade balance improved in the very early 1970s, even showing a modest ($20m.) surplus in 1972/73, though over the rest of the decade it worsened reaching -$2,375m. in 1979/80 (Kemal et al. 2006: 313). Exports continued to grow rapidly over the 1980s, from $2,858m. in 1980/81 to $4,954m. in 1989/90, while imports grew less rapidly, from $5,409m. in 1980/81 to $6,935m. in 1989/90. The overall trade balance reached a peak of -$3,415m. in 1984/85, then dropped to around -$2bn for the rest of the decade (Kemal et al. 2006: 322). Export growth declined, when measured in current prices (US$), from 22.35% in the 1970s, to 8.55% in the 1980s, but increased when measured in constant prices (Rs), from 2.75% to 8.44% (Kemal et al. 2006: 284). After all this export growth, Pakistan's share of world markets had reached only 0.18% by 1990 (Kemal et al. 2006: 286–7).

There was little diversification in the overall composition of exports; the share of the top ten export items increased from 72% in 1969/70 to 80% in 1979/80. Some traditional products declined, such as cotton yarn, from 15.8% to 8.7%, and cotton cloth, from 16.0% to 10.3%, while raw cotton rose from 13.0%, to 14.2% but fluctuated dramatically (owing to rises and falls in international commodity prices), reaching a high of 28.3% in 1971/72 and a low of 2.6% in 1976/77. Some manufactured goods showed steady increases: carpets and rugs from 3.4% to 9.4%, readymade garments from 1.2% to 3.1%, while others declined: sports goods from 1.9% to 1.0%, and leather from 6.8% to 5.4%. The major increase occurred in rice, from 5.8% to 17.9% (Naweb et al. 1984: 116). Naweb et al. are optimists about the 1970s; they argue that this period saw rapid growth of 'new' export products. The lack of a structural change in the composition of exports over the 1970s, they argue, was due to the fact that, while export growth of 'new' manufactured goods (26.6% p.a.) was rapid, structural change did not occur, as exports from the traditional sector continued to be successful (24.8%) (1984: 111). Over a longer period, this optimism is unwarranted. Mahmood and Akhtar (1996: 697) analysed the change in Pakistan's export performance between 1984/85 and 1992/93 by decomposing the actual changes in exports into four effects, the world trade effect (export growth due to expanding world export markets), the commodity composition effect (when exports are concentrated in commodities for which world demand growth is more favourable than the growth of world trade), the market distribution effect (whether destination markets are growing relatively faster), and the competitiveness effect (a residual, reflecting the differences between the actual export growth and the growth that would have occurred if a country had maintained its share of exports of each commodity to each country).

The world trade effect was positive throughout, with almost 50% of the increase in exports explained by a general rise in world exports. The commodity composition effect was negative throughout. The commodity composition of Pakistan's exports did not change much over time and remained concentrated in traditional commodities such as raw cotton, rice and semi-finished textile products, for which world demand only grew slowly. The share of cotton manufactures declined in the 1970s, but increased in the 1980s, and by 1995 accounted for 60% of total manufactured exports. Other traditional exports, such as carpets, leather manufactures and carpets, declined in importance and became quite marginal by the 1990s (Husain 1999: 327; Nabi 1999: 178; Akbar and Naqvi 2000: 580). Classifying exports on the basis of competitive advantage showed that, by the early 1990s, 99.5% of Pakistan's exports were in labour-intensive sectors. Pakistan's share of science-based, resource-intensive, scale- intensive, or differentiated products was essentially zero (Nabi 1999: 185). Within cotton manufactures, exports from Pakistan have been concentrated in low-value-added products. In 1998 finished garments fetched an average of $5 per pound as compared to US$1.40 in the case of cotton yarn. The share of cotton yarn in Pakistan's exports increased from 26.30% in the 1980s to 41.90% between 1990 and 1996; the share of cotton cloth actually fell, from 29.89% to 29.19% over the same period (Khan 1998: 600–2). Pakistan by the early 1990s was among the top five cotton producing countries, although its cotton yield and quality of production remained low by world standards. By the early 1990s the Pakistani textile industry was still living on cheap, low-quality cotton, fiscal, monetary and commercial policy incentives, and trade barriers for its survival (Khan 1998). An exception, if small still in aggregate terms, was exports of surgical instruments. Since the mid-1980s export growth in real terms for Pakistan's surgical instrument sector (based in Sialkot) averaged roughly 10% p.a., while total export sales by the mid-1990s reached $125m., 80% of which was earned from high-income markets in the USA and Western Europe. Pakistan by then held 20% of world trade in this sector. Nadvi (1999b) found that 60% of a sample of firms he had interviewed, both large and small, had upgraded into higher value-added products. The competitiveness of Sialkot producers had pushed many German firms (industry market leaders) to enter into joint venture production agreements with Sialkot partners. The market distribution effect was positive and increasing over this period. The positive sign reflects the growth of exports to more rapidly growing markets, such as Hong Kong, Singapore and Thailand, and the relative decline in exports to destinations such as Sweden, Switzerland and Saudi Arabia. The competitiveness effect became a large contributor to growth towards the end of this period. The competitiveness effect of traditional exports, except rice and cotton, remained positive and improved; the effect was negative for non-traditional exports, such as toys, games and sporting goods, medical instruments, and fish and fish preparations.

Between 1980/81 and 1988/89 export expansion accounted for 10.20% and import substitution 10.10% of manufacturing growth, and between 1988/89 and 1991/92 the contribution of export expansion increased to 37.90%, while import substitution fell to 1.70% (Kemal 1999: 164). There is no evidence of exports leading economic growth between the 1970s and 1990s (Ahmed et al. 2000; Akbar and Naqvi 2000). Shirazi and Manap (2004) unusually find a positive link from exports to GDP growth between 1960 and 2004.

Evaluation of efficiency

If lacking the very detailed studies on the efficiency implications of trade protection for the 1960s, there are indications of inefficient production for this period. Kemal, for example, measures the social costs of trade protection, defined as the increase in the share of manufacturing sector in the GDP due to protection, measured at world market prices. Total costs, he finds, were 9.9% of GDP in 1980/81 (1999: 168). Parikh et al. conducted a sample survey in Peshawar in the NWFP in 1990/91. They found a discrepancy between observed costs and lowest possible costs that was due to both technical and allocative inefficiencies. On average, they found that 11.5% of total cost could have been reduced without any loss in output. (1995: 680).

There is no evidence that the stock market contributed to the efficient allocation of resources over the 1960s. Husain and Mahmood find that between 1960/61 and 1989/90 there is almost zero correlation between changes in real consumption, changes in real investment, or changes in real GDP with stock prices. Any causal relationship that did exist tended to run from macroeconomic variables to stock prices: fluctuations in macroeconomic variables cause changes in stock prices, but not vice-versa. The stock market was not a leading indicator of economic activity (2001: 111).

There is good evidence to suggest that Pakistan used very capital-intensive methods of production during this period. During the 1970s, for example, there was a significant and widespread decline in the elasticity of employment with respect to real GDP growth. Employment growth in large-scale manufacturing had been nearly 12% p.a. in the latter half of the 1950s; it fell continuously thereafter, from 2.0% p.a. in the 1960s, to 0.8% p.a. in the 1970s and 3.0% p.a. in the 1980s. The growth of value added showed no similar pattern, increasing by 18.7%, 14.9%, 22.6% and 14.6% over the same four time periods (Wizarat 2002: 169). Alternatively, over a different time period, again in large-scale manufacturing, output growth increased from 4.3% p.a. between 1970 and 1976, to 12.3% between 1976 and 1981, while over the same years, growth of production workers declined from 4.9% to -1.1% p.a. (Irfan and Ahmed 1985: 431). Kemal (1981) found capital-output ratios in Pakistan to be one of the highest in the world. Zahid et al. (1992) found that industry in Pakistan between 1960 and 1986 was capital intensive. This included textiles as well as the more obvious examples, steel, machinery and transport equipment. In agriculture the number of tractors increased five-fold between 1973 and 1983. In construction the extensive use of conveyor belts, vibrators, crushers, and mixers is suggestive of the widespread displacement of labour in this sector (Irfan and Ahmed 1985). Ali and Hamid disaggregate contributions to growth for agriculture and manufacturing between 1972/73 and 1994/95. Overall, the largest contribution was from capital. Capital's share in total growth of output in the agricultural sector was 61%, and labour's share 18%. The share of capital in manufacturing output and value added was about 60% and that of labour about 10% (1996: 224). Between 1955 and 1991 Wizarat finds that the percentage contribution to growth in large-scale manufacturing was 73.41% from capital and 16.43% from labour (2002: 98). Kemal et al. find that the growth of the capital stock contributed 50% of overall growth in the 1970s and 43% in the 1980s (2006: 324, 323). Labour could have contributed more; much of the growth in human capital was lost to migration. The great majority of official temporary migrants consisted of skilled masons, carpenters, plumbers, mechanics, electricians, and technicians. By the late 1970s there was an emigration/new supply ratio of 37:100 of doctors. Most of the senior professors of Pakistan universities likewise became migrants (Ahmed 1982: 201–2).

As with the manufacturing sector, growth in agriculture over this period was very capital intensive. Capital inputs to agriculture increased by 12.0% p.a. between 1972/73 and 1987/88, those for land by only 0.5% and for labour by 2.0% (Sabir and Ahmed 2003: 7). There were massive increases in agricultural inputs over the 1970s: fertiliser, from 307,700 tonnes in 1969/70 to 1,044,100 in 1979/80; water availability at the farm gate, from 75.5 MAF to 94.1 MAF; the number of tube-wells in operation, from 86,754 to 179,153; and the number of tractors in operation from 29,659 to 131,159 (Naweb et al. 1984: 147; Kazi 1987: 91; Chaudhry 1990: 295). Between 1976/77 and 1979/80 water availability was both higher and more consistent, partly because of releases from the Tarbela Dam. This capital-intensive pattern continued into the 1980s: water availability rose from 89.32 MAF in 1977–80 to 127.45 (MAF) in 1992–95; fertiliser offtake from 879,200 metric tons to 2,524,000 metric tons; and cropped area from 19.21m. hectares to 22.77m. hectares (Ali 2004: 509).

There are two means of refuting this criticism, first that there is some evidence that there was less discretion in choice of technique than such criticisms allow for and second, that the methods of production that were chosen generated learning and upgrading. Making judgements about methods of production in an economy that is too capital intensive makes an implicit assumption that elasticities of substitution are such that removing 'policy distortions' will allow firms to change methods of production. Given that Pakistan had high capital-output ratios and is often assumed to be a labour-surplus economy, this would imply that a re-allocation of resources to labour-intensive activities and a switch over to labour-intensive techniques of production would have been instrumental in raising the growth rate. Kemal (1976) found that substitution possibilities between capital- and labour-intensive methods of production were rather limited. In sugar, tobacco, textiles, and chemicals, which were all important industries in Pakistan by the end of the 1970s, there were negligible possibilities of substitution between capital and labour. Ahmed (1982) suggested that Kemal's measures of elasticity of substitution were biased downwards. Norbye (1978) argues that measures of the capital for Pakistan were very unreliable. Kemal (1982) refuted these criticisms and found support in Zahid et al. (1992), who found the elasticity of substitution for industries were less than one, suggesting that there was a tendency to fixed input–output coefficients.

Partial measures of efficiency show no clear pattern over this period. Afridi finds that capital efficiency measured in terms of the value added-capital ratio declined in the small-scale sector between 1970/71 and 1976/77 and improved in all other size classes. Between 1976/77 and 1980/81 this measure improved in the small and small-medium sectors, whilst declining in all other sectors. Capital efficiency in the aggregate improved from 1970/71 to 1976/77, and declined from 1976/77 to 1980/81 (1985: 468). Mahmood and Siddiqui found that capital productivity grew by 2.20% between 1972 and 1975, by -2.50% from 1975 to 1980, by 4.14% from 1980 to 1985, by 4.79% from 1985 to 1990, and by 0.51% from 1990 to 1995 (2000: 10). Kemal et al. found that capital productivity grew by 2.28% in the 1970s and by 2.64% in the 1980s (2006: 314, 323). Estimates of the capital-output ratio find it falling from about 3.5 in the first half of the 1970s, to around 2.5 in the second half of the decade and stabilising at this level into the 1980s (Papanek 1991: 628; Amjad 1986: 767; Khan 1993: 1076). This improvement is something of a puzzle, as there is little evidence of any increase in the most productive type of investment – private corporate investment, which generally declined, but remained at no more than 1% of GDP over the 1970s and 1980s (Zaidi 2005: 298). Even this probably exaggerates the total. The price of investment goods rose sharply in the 1970s, and a deflator for gross domestic investment rose from 100 in 1969/70 to 412.96 in 1979/80 (Naweb et al. 1984: 63).

Wizarat has estimated labour productivity and finds it collapsing over this period. Her index (1959/60 = 100) declined from 126.92 in 1969/70 to 40.56 in 1980/81 and 15.38 in 1990/91 (2002: 82). Such extreme results are not found elsewhere in the literature. Mahmood and Siddiqui, for example, found labour productivity growing at 1.72% between 1972 and 1975, 5.27% from 1975 to 1980, 8.31% from 1980 to 1985, 5.90% from 1985 to 1990, and 4.60% from 1990 to 1995 (2000: 10). Malik and Nazli find that labour productivity showed an increase after the mid- to late-1970s, from 1.7% between 1971/72 and 1978/79, to 4.3% from 1978/79 to 1986/87, and 4.14% from 1986/87 to 1990/91. In manufacturing the increase for the same period was sharp, from -1.1%, to 7.16%, to 9.16%; it was steady in agriculture (at 0.2%, 2.3% and 4.34% respectively); it fluctuated in construction (1.6%, 3.0%, and 0.37%); and declined in finance (7.8%, 6.7% and 2.04%) (1999: 336). There were signs of growth in the stock of human capital over this period. After 1972 the Bhutto government made a conscious effort to expand capacity in higher education. Between 1972 and 1976 four new, general universities were established, raising the total to 12. Centres of Excellence in five scientific disciplines were established at different universities. By 1976 over 27,000 students were enrolled at the 12 universities, over 6,000 of whom were accounted for by the engineering and agricultural universities. Affiliated colleges had an enrolment of over 84,000 (Alam 1983). There was a steady rise in education expenditure after 1981, from 1.4% of GDP in 1981/82, to 2.4% in 1992/93 (Siddiqa 2007: 163). Total literacy in Pakistan increased from 21.7% in 1972, to 26.2% in 1981, and 34.9% in 1990; the corresponding increases in male and female literacy were: 30.2%, 35%, and 15.1% and 11.6%, 16% and 20.9% (Zaidi 2005: 394). A proxy for human capital (average years of schooling of total population aged 25 and over) grew relatively rapidly during this period, by 3.2% in the 1970s, and 4.2% in the 1980s (IMF 2002: 10).

There is evidence that the capital-intensive pattern of growth in agriculture was removing key bottlenecks to growth and so, given the circumstances of agriculture in the early 1970s, this was a more efficient means of promoting growth than more labour-intensive options. The enduring problem of agriculture in Pakistan in the 1970s had been low productivity, rather than a labour shortage. It was estimated that, given sufficient supplies of agricultural-capital inputs and their adequate utilisation, average farm productivity could have been more than doubled, and in some cases tripled (Nawab et al. 1984). The supply of fertilisers in the early 1970s was sufficient to meet only 30% of requirements, and less than 10% of cropped area was covered by plant protection. The annual supply of irrigation fell short by more than 40%. The public provision of credit and extension services was also in short supply. Such inputs are highly complementary, for example, the coefficient of correlation between inputs of tractors, fertiliser and water is 0.996 (Nawab et al. 1984: 27). The increased use of tractors was found to induce the greater use of fertiliser and so raise the productivity of wheat-based agriculture (Salam 1981). As a result, partial measures of productivity in agriculture (yields) also showed improvement over this period. Cotton, which accounted for about 20%–30% of the value added of major crops in the 1980s, did well in the 1980s, touching annual yield growth of over 5% p.a. after 1985. Sugar cane, which made up about 13% of the value added of major crops, also began to experience a yield increase after 1985, after a long period of stagnation. The livestock sector also showed rapid growth after 1985 (Ali 2004). Productivity growth per acre, after being negative in the early 1970s, was consistently between 2% and 2.5% p.a. until the early 1990s (Chaudhry et al. 1996: 53). Table 7.8 shows that the yields of all major crops increased from the late 1970s to the mid-1990s, this increase being much higher for cotton and wheat, than for either rice or sugar cane.

As rapid as these yield increases were, only in the case of cotton was there some indication of Pakistan catching up with world yield performances, though this sector was particularly significant, as much of Pakistan's export-orientated textile sector was dependent on raw cotton inputs (Ali 2005: 741).

A final 'partial' measure of performance is that of the state sector. As a consequence of the Bhutto nationalisations, by 1977 the government had become involved

Table 7.8 Yield level of major crops and imports inputs, 1972–95

Year	Wheat kg/h	Rice kg/h	Cotton kg/h	Sugarcane kg/h
1977–80	1,457	1,583	304	37,075
1980–83	1,628	1,697	347	37,841
1983–86	1,658	1,632	396	36,496
1986–89	1,719	1,635	547	40,198
1989–92	1,885	1,539	648	41,883
1992–95	1,973	1,675	529	45,304

Source: Ali 2004: 509.

extensively in production. By the 1990s there was a widespread impression that state ownership had left an inefficient and loss-making industrial sector and that this specifically explained the alleged decline in productivity growth of the industrial sector in the 1970s (Malik and Cheema 1986; Talbot 1998; Husain 1999). However there is 'little doubt that state owned enterprises performed better than the overall manufacturing sector from Bhutto onwards' (Zaidi 2005). Between 1972/73 and 1981/82 state-owned enterprises outperformed private sector enterprises in terms of production, labour productivity and overall productivity; labour productivity, for example, increased by 52% for public sector industries and only 27% for those remaining in the private sector (Zaidi 2005: 147). Naqvi and Kemal (1991) found in a study of eight corporations running state-owned enterprises that capacity utilisation was high in the public sector (39 out of 60 enterprises had capacity utilisation rates exceeding 75%) and that profits were not due to high rates of protection or restrictions on the entry of new firms, but to better performance and superior productive efficiency. The World Bank reviewed the performance of public sector enterprises between 1972/73 and 1976/77. It found that labour productivity was higher in these units than in the manufacturing sector as a whole. The return on investment tended to be low, averaging about 6% before interest, which was low relative to the cost of borrowing. Private enterprise, though, did little better: the rate of return (after interest but before tax) for a sample of 242 companies on the Karachi Stock Exchange was 5.3% in 1972/73 and 4.1% in 1973/74. There was a sharp improvement in labour productivity and pre-tax profits of the state-owned sector after 1977. The improved profitability was not due to higher prices or accounting changes. Between 1976/77 and 1979/80 the production index increased from 162 (1972/73 = 100) to 262, and the employment index from 133 to 123, and as a result the index of real output per worker increased from 122 to 213. Much of this improvement was due to the spectacular growth of the National Fertiliser Corporation and Petroleum Corporation (Ahmed and Amjad 1984: 225).

There was a general improvement in the performance indices of the state-owned electric power industry over this period. Table 7.9 shows that system losses[13] declined overall after 1972–77, but increased for KESC, and that generation capacity improved steadily for both WAPDA and KESC. There is no real trend in unit costs of production, measured in various ways for either WAPDA or KESC (Ghafoor and Weiss 2001: 126).

Table 7.9 Selected indicators for evaluating the performance of state-owned electric power industry in Pakistan, 1972–95

Years	System Losses (%)			Generation Capacity Factor (%)		
	WAPDA	KESC	Power	WAPDA	KESC	Power
1972–77	34	22	32	46	42	45
1978–83	32	23	31	50	48	48
1984–89	26	26	26	52	50	50
1990–95	23	33	26	54	50	52

Source: Ghafoor and Weiss 2001: 119

The most common general measure of productivity growth is TFP. Kemal *et al.* find TFP growth of 0.82% in the 1970s and 2.45% in the 1980s (2006: 314, 323). There is broad agreement with these numbers from other works, with TFP growth rising from 1.3% p.a. in the 1970s to 2.5% p.a. in the 1980s (IMF 2002: 10), or by 0.73% in the 1970s and 2.1% in the 1980s (Khan 2005: 391), by 2.8% between 1972/73 and 1987/88 (Sabir and Ahmed 2003: 9), by 2.0% between 1972/73 and 1977/78, by 3.7% between 1977/78 and 1982/83, and by 2.8% between 1982/83 and 1987/88, and then falling to 1.0% between 1987/88 and 1992/93 (Pasha *et al.* 2002: 6), by 2.08% between 1972 and 1975, by -0.75% from 1975 to 1980, by 4.84% from 1980 to 1985, by 4.92% from 1985 to 1990, and by 1.36% from 1990 to 1995 (Mahmood and Siddiqui 2000: 10).[14]

Kemal *et al.* find TFP growth in manufacturing increasing from 2.01% in the 1970s to 5.3% in the 1980s, and in agriculture falling from -0.77% to -1.32% (2006: 314, 323). Other estimates for agriculture are more optimistic. Ali finds that TFP growth in agriculture was slower (1.2%–1.6%) in the 1970s and first half of the 1980s, then accelerated in the second half of the 1980s and 1990s (2004: 498–9). Pasha *et al.* find that TFP growth in agriculture increased from 0.4% between 1972/73 and 1977/78, to 2.7% between 1977/78 and 1982/83, 1.9% between 1982/83 and 1987/88, and 2.7% between 1987/88 and 1992/93 (2002: 7). Chaudhry *et al.* find similar patterns, but lower rates of growth (1996: 530).[15]

In the public sector between 1961 and 1995 TFP declined by 1.65% p.a. for KESC and increased by 1.52% p.a. for WAPDA, implying growth of 0.37% overall (Ghafoor and Weiss 2001: 129).

The (political) role of the state, 1970/71 to 1991/92: institutions

The elections of 1970 and the rise of the PPP gave Pakistan a chance to re-assert the supremacy of democratic, rather than repressive, institutions of the state. Early efforts to reduce the role of the military were quickly over, and Bhutto came to depend on the military; the coup of 1977 was a continuation of such trends. Bhutto likewise tried to strengthen the relative power of the PPP over the civil service; again, this attempt failed. The PPP failed in its possible role as an inclusionary institution, and it was gradually taken over by more conservative groups and either ejected or failed to incorporate the groups emerging in a changing society. The 1973 constitution, despite its federal and formally decentralised structure, was undermined by the centralising and anti-democratic instincts of Bhutto, and these trends were further strengthened by Zia. The emergence of a two-party democratic system in the 1990s failed to promote institutionalisation of social groups and exacerbated conflict. Zia tried to implement a more ideological approach (Islamisation) to the management of Pakistan, but succeeded only in exacerbating conflict. After a hiatus in the early 1970s, the repressive institutions of the state re-emerged under Bhutto and were formally re-established in power with the military coup of 1977. By domestic criteria this episode of stagnation (though quite successful judged in terms of average growth rates) probably was sustainable. The government lacked the developmental autonomy or inclusionary institutions or ideology to promote a real development drive. The government in the 1980s was secure enough in power to rule, and able to mobilise sufficient resources and utilise them productively enough, to keep GDP at a reasonable rate. The end of the episode we can trace to exogenous factors, the death of Zia in that ever-mysterious plane crash, the rise of neo-liberalisation and the worldwide democratic upsurge that gave Pakistan no option other than to return to competitive party politics and adopt a neo-liberal programme of reforms. This combination pushed Pakistan into a further episode of stagnation as we will see in Chapter 8.

Institutions to manage conflict: autonomy and repression

The secession of Bangladesh gave Bhutto the opportunity to curb the power of the military and strengthen the democratic/inclusionary institutions of government. Bhutto introduced a three-person committee, including himself, General Tikka Khan and General Imtiaz Ahmad, to approve all promotions and transfers above the rank of Brigadier-General. Bhutto attempted to distribute top military positions to officers without known group loyalties. The command of the armed forces was divided between three persons. The Chief of Staff (Zia ul Haq) was put in charge of strategy and coordination between the army, navy and airforce. The military advisor to Bhutto (General Tikka Khan) was made responsible for internal security. The Secretary of Defence (General Fazal Muqeen Khan) was placed in charge of administration. Within four months 24 officers had been sacked, and the Chief of Army staff replaced by General Tikka Khan, who was himself replaced by Zia-ul-Haq in 1976 (Ahmed 1982; Burki 1980).

Instead of gaining autonomy of action, Bhutto became increasingly reliant on the army. The downward spiral towards the 1977 coup began very quickly. Army officers were exempted from the 1972 land reforms. The army were in action in July 1972 in response to language riots in Sindh and again soon after in labour disturbances in the Landi and Korangi areas of Karachi. In April 1972 a tripartite accord signed between PPP and opposition parties in Baluchistan and NWFP allowed the opposition to form state governments. In February 1973 the state government of Baluchistan was dismissed, and an armed revolt began in May. Baluchistan had grievances over low levels of per capita income (40% below the Punjab), lack of industry and transfer to the central government of revenues from its extensive gas and other mineral resources. Out of 830 higher civil service posts in Baluchistan, only 181 were held by Baluchis. Bhutto's government failed to address these grievances and alienated the moderates among the Baluchi leadership by dismissing the provincial governments (Noman 1988). The army's involvement in Baluchistan significantly undermined the attempt to establish civilian supremacy, and rather than engaging with political demands through the political system, this represented another attempt to promote national integration by force. The army had previously intervened in Baluchistan in March 1948 and October 1958. A more successful subsequent programme of electrification, roads and other infrastructure saw the province restored to normalcy in the 1980s (Talbot 1998). The failure of democracy in 1977 and reversion to military rule saw commentators defining Pakistan in terms of the dominance of institutions of repression and autonomy; it had a 'political economy of defence' (Jalal 1990).

The military takeover by Zia in 1977 crystallised the hegemony of the military. In the late 1970s the military rolled over civil society institutions. Zia banned all major sources of public protest, including labour and student unions. Laws were changed to allow the prosecution of newspaper editors for publishing stories against the interests of the regime. The ISI gained strength through the 1980s because of its close involvement in the Afghan war. The ISI was also involved in the formation of opposition parties, Islami Jamhoori Ittihad (IJI) and Muhajir Qaumi Movement (MQM), to counter the PPP. Other safeguards for the armed forces included the Eighth Amendment to the 1973 constitution, which empowered the President to sack a government, become supreme commander of the armed forces, and appoint the heads of the three services and chairman of the JCSC.

Academia and universities between the 1970s and the 1990s failed to provide any consistent lobby for reform. The government retained a monopoly or tight supervisory control on all academic institutions and academic journals. Publishing businesses did not survive other than through government purchases and patronage, since libraries and academic institutions were government owned and syllabi were prescribed by the government. Policy prescriptions, particularly in the 1990s, originated from either donor-initiated consultancy work or from the staff of multilateral financial institutions (Ul Haque 1999).

The dominant role of the military outlived the military dictatorship. In February 1989 Benazir appointed a committee to review the role and relationship of the military intelligence agencies in a democracy. Based on its findings, she chose to try and exert greater civilian control. The ISI had played a key role against her during the Zia years and in creating the alternative IJI electoral alliance before the elections. In May 1989, against the advice of the COAS, she replaced the ISI chief, Lieutenant General Hamid Gul. Instead of appointing a serving officer, the new head was retired Lieutenant General Shams ur Rahman Kallu (Shafqat 1996). The new head was virtually boycotted by the ISI, which continued to work against the Bhutto governments of the 1990s (Talbot 1998). In 1990 there was a constitutional crisis over who had the authority (the President or Prime Minister) to appoint the Chairman of the Joint Chiefs of Staff Committee. The issue originated from the impending retirement of Admiral Sirohi at the end of his three-year term in 1991. Under threat of Presidential dismissal under the Eighth Amendment, Benazir retreated, looking 'inept and powerless' (Akhund 2000: 70). In June 1990 Benazir tried to intervene to extend the term of Lieutenant General Alam Jan Mehsud, the corps commander in Lahore, but the army selection board did not agree. In August 1990 Benazir's government was dismissed on the grounds of corruption, inefficiency, and misconduct of power. Benazir's attempts to exert greater control over the military had played a key role in this decision (Waseem 1992; Shafqat 1996).

In 1973 Bhutto abolished the Civil Service of Pakistan (CSP) and merged it into a uniform all-Pakistan grade structure. In the early years of the Bhutto government, 1,300 officials were purged on the grounds of corruption, though the purpose was rather to promote bureaucrats loyal to the Bhutto regime. Bhutto instituted the principal of lateral entry at all levels of the administration and diplomatic services. Viqar Ahmad, the first non CSP officer to hold the key post of Secretary Establishment in the

Central Government, was placed in charge of senior appointments and overseeing the entire bureaucracy, working on direct orders from Bhutto (Alavi 1983: 76). These aims did not weaken the role of the bureaucracy as an institution of autonomy. The nationalisation programme after 1972 widened the scope for patronage and placed enormous new demands on the managerial role of the state, the main beneficiaries being the civil service. During the rule of Zia, the CSP was not formally restored, but survived informally with the same esprit de corps as before. Key jobs were returned to ex-CSP officers. Some things had changed. While Ayub had relied on the civilian bureaucracy in the 1960s, Zia shifted the nature of the state to a more military character (Jalal 1995). By the early 1980s the Federal Public Service Commission and all but one Provincial Services Commission were headed by army officers, and 10% of all posts at every level were filled by army officers through the principle of lateral entry. Retired generals filled seven ministerial posts, and four retired generals held posts of Secretaries of the Central Government in charge of Ministries. Ex-army officers had been appointed to numerous posts at lower echelons of government, most critically as Joint Secretaries in ministries with control over appointments and transfers. Retired major generals tended to prefer appointments as heads of state corporations where there was much greater scope for patronage and nepotism (Alavi 1983). Military personnel were invited to serve on the boards of companies and even today many large businesses and enterprises are owned by retired military officials who joined the ranks of the industrialists under Zia (Zaidi 2005).

The PPP also functioned as another institution of repression. The Federal Security Force (FSF), created in 1972, directly accountable to Bhutto, was intended to reduce the political role of the military (Talbot 1998), and after May 1973 it was used to disrupt meetings and rallies of political parties opposed to the PPP (Noman 1988). Those not joining (Wali Khan and Bizenjo), or defecting from the PPP (Ghulam Mustafa Khar and Haneef Ramay, both former Chief Ministers of the Punjab who joined the CML), frequently faced prosecution, for among other things treason and treachery (Syed 1977). The opposition were hindered from engaging with the electorate. The government's imposition of section 144 (prohibiting the assembly of five or more persons and/or use of a public address system) often precluded the meetings, processions, and rallies of the opposition (Syed 1977: 182). The mass media, mostly under government control, ignored the statements and activities of the opposition.

Institutions to manage conflict: inclusionary

The ultimate responsibility for creating the institutional base for a democratic structure rested with the PPP. It needed to create a structure that met two objectives, to integrate the minority ethnic groups into the framework of state power and develop representative institutions at all levels of society. The PPP was founded in September 1967. The party initially aspired to revive Jinnah's coalition of nationalist and radical social forces and add to them the social and interest groups that had emerged in the post-independence period. The largest social component of the PPP were the students, middle-class professionals, organised labour, and small businessmen (Jones 2003: 120). Like the Muslim League, the PPP emerged as a broad-based movement held together by a single dominating figure (Ahmed 1982; Talbot 1998). It is easy to see the potential of the PPP. Bhutto came to power at a time when the loss of Bangladesh had generated a crisis for the ruling classes; he possessed immense authority and legitimacy as the first elected government in Pakistan's history. But the weaknesses of the PPP were also evident at the outset. The PPP won only 81 of 138 seats in West Pakistan, 62 of those in the Punjab, most of the rest in Sindh, and none in the regional or national election in Baluchistan (Talbot 1998).

These weaknesses were overcome as the PPP initially proved adept at attracting defectors from other parties. The members of the Qayyum Muslim League defected to the PPP after 1970, when their leader became Bhutto's interior minister. There were also substantial defections to the PPP from the CML and the JUI, including veteran CML leader Sardar Shaukat Hayat. The banning of the NAP in 1975 opened the way for numerous NAP legislators to defect to the PPP (Syed 1977). Bhutto had not permitted the PPP to become an ideological party, nor for party ideologues to dictate policy choices. Bhutto took care to balance socialists with conservatives and pragmatists. In 1974, for example, in a party re-organisation in the Punjab, he appointed Meraj Khalid, a moderate, as president of the provincial party organisation, Nasir Rizvi, a conservative landlord from Multan, as secretary-general, and Taj Langah, a radical socialist, as deputy secretary-general. Bhutto also had a number of successes in reconciling Islamic groups to his rule. Bhutto invited the Imam of the Prophets mosque in Madina, and later the Imam of the mosque at the Ka'aba, to Pakistan in the spring of 1976. Later in the year the government sponsored and funded an international conference on the life/work of the prophet. For the first time in Pakistan's history, the central cabinet included a Minister for religious affairs. By 1976 this balance began to tilt in favour of the conservatives, as provincial governments were placed under nawabs and landed aristocrats. The nawab of Bahawalpur came out of retirement to become governor of the Punjab, and Nawab Sadiq Husain Qureshi of Multan became the Chief Minister. Dilawar Khanji, the former Nawab of Qalat, continued as governor of Baluchistan, and Ghulam Mustafa Jatoi, the Sindhi landlord, remained Chief Minister. The central cabinet lost prominent socialists, such as Sheikh Rashid (Syed 1977).

Bhutto's government mobilised on the promise of benefiting labour. In April 1972 new laws gave greater worker participation in management, the right to appoint an auditor to inspect firms' accounts and records, an increased (from 2% to 4%) share in profits, reduced strike notification time, welfare funds for housing, free education up to matriculation for one child of each worker as the responsibility of the employer, provision for old age pensions, compulsory group insurance for workers for death and injury, and the right to written reasons in case of dismissal. In August 1974 the PPP passed a cost of living ordinance for both public and private sectors, giving the government powers to compel inflation-adjusted salary increases (Ahmed and Amjad 1984; Guisinger and Hicks 1978). As we saw earlier, real wages increased up to the mid-1970s, then fell thereafter. The upsurge of strike activity manifest in the late 1960s peaked in 1972, when 2,018,308 man-days were lost to disputes in manufacturing (involving 361,149 workers), then gradually declined throughout the decade, reaching 200,865 man-days (49,093 workers) in 1977 and 54,730 man-days (24,710 workers) in 1980/81. There was some resurgence, albeit at lower levels, to a peak of 690,872 man-days

(22,409 workers) in 1982/83, then a decline throughout the rest of Zia's time in office, to 179,351 man-days (8,231 workers) in 1988/89, and a new peak of 582,964 man-days (116,306 workers) in 1991/92 after the advent of democracy (Wizarat 2002: 231).

A new constitution came into effect in August 1973 that promised to end national integration based on coercion and replace it with an acceptance of plurality, diversity and decentralisation. The constitution provided for an independent judiciary and guaranteed fundamental rights. It was strongly federal in structure, with a bicameral legislature elected by direct vote and an indirectly elected Senate. The constitution gave more power to smaller provinces (provinces were equally represented in the Senate), created a Council of Common Interests and a National Finance Commission to advise on the distribution of federal revenues (Afzar 1991). After long previous wrangles about the proper role for Islam in Pakistan, the 1973 Constitution successfully attempted to project the 'social gospel and dynamic spirit of Islam' (Raza 1997: 182) by including Islam as a practical and ethical religion, not a set of prohibitions and injunctions. For example, the constitution accepted the right to property, but gave parliament the right to determine compensation for compulsory acquisition and to legislate on the maximum limits of property holdings. These promises meant that the constitution was passed with a near unanimous vote among the nine parties of the national assembly comprising, variously, left, religious and regional groups (Afzar 1991).

After 1973 there was a slow dissipation of the federal structure and checks and balances, 'True to tradition, he [Bhutto] centralised power and circumvented the carefully designed federal arrangements' (Raza 1997: 182). Bhutto's fatal flaw was his failure to share power (Ali 2008). There were seven amendments to the constitution between 1974 and 1977. These included enabling the government to 'ban political parties operating in a manner prejudicial to the sovereignty/integrity of Pakistan', 'restricting the high court in respect of preventive detention', and increasing the capacity of the government to make discretionary (rather than seniority-based) appointments of Chief Justices (Raza 1997). Civil liberties and provincial autonomy were legally overridden by extraordinary powers accorded to rulers for 'reasons of state'. Such measures during the Bhutto era included the Prevention of Anti-National Activities Ordinance (1973) and the Suppression of Terrorist Activities Act (1975). Opponents were also detained under the Defence of Pakistan rules (Noman 1988; Talbot 1998). The decentralisation of power promised by the federal structure of the constitution was replaced by Bhutto's growing domination of the provinces (Raza 1997: 260). In February 1973 the government of Baluchistan was removed, and in August its leaders were arrested under the Emergency powers of the 1973 Constitution. The Chief Minister of Sindh was removed at the end of 1973. In February 1975 the NAP, the governing party of the NWFP, was banned and its members arrested, and President's rule was imposed on the province.

The PPP faced a serious problem in making the transition from a movement to a well-structured party of government. New groups joined the PPP, but were not then subject to any formal elected structures. The expansion of the party fermented instead factionalism and clientelism. Most factional conflict based on biraderi rivalries, as with the Muslim League in the 1940s. The PPP, for example, expanded into rural areas of the Frontier by securing support from local landowners and tribal leaders. This provided a more secure power base for the party, but also intensified existing institutional/organisational weaknesses created by Bhutto's patrimonialism by importing particularist cleavages into the party (Talbot 1998). The factionalism of the 1970s proved to be far harder for the PPP to contain and manage than that in the 1940s for the Muslim League. There were numerous new social forces to accommodate by then. The number of teachers, for example, by the late 1960s had trebled since independence to around 350,000, and rapid increases also occurred in the number of lawyers and doctors (Maddison 1971). This process had been manifest in the relatively fast growth of small towns in the 1960s. Rapid growth of the agricultural sector in the 1960s had promoted the growth of a small-scale engineering industry to supply durable inputs (engines, pumps, etc.) to agriculture. This growth industry was concentrated in various centres around the Punjab region (Burki 1974: 759). By 1972 the population of small and medium towns (with an average size of less than about 80,000 inhabitants) had increased to over six million, or 37% of the total urban population (Burki 1974: 753). These groups had been mobilised first by the Basic Democracies of Ayub Khan (Chapter 5), and then by the anti-Ayub agitation after 1968. Integration efforts in one area by the PPP led to corresponding fragmentation elsewhere. Within three years of forming the government, the PPP was purged of its left wing. Rapidly, on assuming office, the PPP struck back against organised labour, and in reaction to labour conflicts the police were ordered to fire on workers attempting to seize or burn factories. The decline of the left and labour was linked to Bhutto's effort to cultivate the Punjabi landed elite. By 1976, 28 of the 33 leading aristocratic families of the Punjab had representatives in the PPP (Noman 1988: 104). Efforts to integrate the Sindhis, through the passing of the Sindhi language bill in July 1972, which elevated the language to that of an official provincial language, and a quota system for educational institutions, ran up against opposition from Mohajirs. In 1978 the All Pakistan Mohajir Student Organisation (the precursor of the MQM formed in 1984) was formed partly to oppose such reforms (Raza 1997; Rahman 1997; Talbot 1998).

Some integration efforts simply failed. The stated aim of many of Bhutto's land reforms in 1972 was to transfer ownership from a small minority and induct a substantial number into the ranks of the propertied. Land ceilings were lowered in 1972 from their 1959 levels, and exemptions from earlier land reform efforts were removed. A striking difference was that land resumed would not receive compensation. Land resumed was to be distributed free to landless tenants. There were also efforts to shift to landlords the burden of paying land revenue and water rates. All peasants having received land under 1959 reforms had dues written off. Less than 0.01% of total farm area in the country was resumed, and eventually 50,548 persons benefited from the redistribution of 308,390 acres, only 1% of landless tenants and small owners benefited (Burki 1980; Zaidi 2005).

Integrating all these various groups into the PPP, subjecting them once inside to the socialisation effects of party rules and procedures, and incorporating them into government proved, for Bhutto, ultimately impossible, 'The disjuncture between the state and other social forces under populism was unsustainable for the simple reason that pay-offs required to maintain stability were not there' (Sayeed 2002: 225). Without the necessary patronage resources or party organisation, the PPP finally depended on the charisma of Bhutto, but 'even his genius at debate and his deft political manoeuvring could not indefinitely hold at bay mounting provincial and socio-economic pressures, frustrations and discontent that kept Pakistan's most crowded urban centres and depressed rural backwaters boiling with linguistic and ethnic violence' (Wolpert 1993: 196).

There was hope in 1988 that the return of Benazir would bring about a new era, where a modern party system would increase government legitimacy and compel politicians towards the compromise, consensus and coalition building of party politics. Instead, the governments of the 1990s used very selective legal accountability to intimidate the opposition, and the oppositions denied and strove to deny the ruling party any legitimacy. Neither Bhutto nor Sharif for most of the 1990s had the two-thirds majority in the central parliament to repeal Zia's constitutional amendment that left the President able to dismiss at will federal and provincial elected assemblies. The two political alliances were unable to co-operate for fear of a repeal being used to cement their own exclusion from power (Akhund 2000). Politics became so conflict ridden, that the process of parliamentary legislation all but ceased, and legislation was restricted to that which could be passed by Presidential ordinance.

The 'two-party alliance system' that emerged from the democracy of the 1990s was unstable, weak and chaotic. The PPP in 1988 won only 92 from 204 National Assembly seats, and they were stuck with the MQM (13 seats) as an alliance partner, which made any resolution of the problem in the Sindh difficult. In 1989 the MQM defected to Nawaz Sharif to support a no-confidence vote against Benazir's government. The Punjab was the main power base of the IJI or Islamic-Democratic Alliance, the opposition to the PPP. This alliance comprised the Nawaz Sharif and Junejo Muslim Leagues and eight other parties and was held together by little more than hostility to the PPP. The opposition won office in the Punjab. Throughout her first term Benazir's government was stuck in a bitter power struggle with the state government of the Punjab, which formed a parallel administration, requesting civil servants for example not to implement federal policies (Talbot 1998). As well as formal political opposition, Benazir was also the least powerful of a troika during her first period in office, after the army chief and President. The President retained those 'viceregal' powers granted to Zia under the constitution giving him the freedom to act at will in all major areas, particularly those related to the armed forces, foreign policy and judicial appointments. Benazir was permitted to take office conditional on the army retaining a veto of Afghan policy, defence expenditure and service conditions (Akhund 2000).

The 1990 election confirmed a number of well-established trends; the MQM continued to dominate urban Sindh, and Baluchistan politics was dominated by tribal leaders of regional parties. There was only a 1% difference in the vote share of the PPP and Muslim League (Nawaz)-dominated coalitions, but a big difference in their seats, 45 to 105 in the national assembly (Talbot 1998). Nawaz after 1990 showed a greater ability to deal with inter-provincial disputes. His government was able to solve some long-standing disputes, such as in March 1991 the apportionment of the Indus waters (Waseem 1992; Yasmeen 1994). Despite having the support of the Presidency, the old Zia establishment, and a secure power base in the Punjab, the new ruling coalition proved as incompatible as the old, and tension existed between the PML and ANP, and the JI and both the MQM and JUP. Again, much of the government's time took the form of pursuing a personal vendetta between Sharif and Bhutto. In May 1991 Benazir's husband Asif Zardari was charged with murder. Pakistan continued to be riven by endemic lawlessness and ethnic violence, and Karachi became a battleground between rival MQM factions, Sunni and Shia militants, and drug barons (Waseem 1992; Talbot 1998).

The long-standing tradition of politics being seen as a zero-sum game in Pakistan continued into the 1980s and 1990s, with an enormous upsurge in ethnic and sectarian violence in numerous parts of the country (Zaidi 1999). Weinbaum (1996) argues that this entire era was marked by a 'crisis of authority' in which the opposition and large numbers of their supporters saw any government in power as illegitimate both for how they gained office and the way they used power, and those in office typically saw their opponents as guilty of treasonous acts. Politics in Pakistan remained highly personal and emotional, constructive dialogue was largely absent, and political competition revolved around the desire to belittle and humiliate opponents.

Institutions to manage conflict: ideology

The Zia period marked a qualitative change in the relationship between state and society, the critical difference being ideological. In 1977 Zia's government initiated a process of Islamisation and attempted to convert Pakistan into a theocratic society. A comprehensive moral code gradually permeated social, political and economic life, and the powers of government were used to force obedience. In 1978 Zia announced that the legal system of Pakistan would in future be based on the Nizam-i-Mustafa (law of the prophet) and the ultimate aim was that shariah would be the basis of all law. In 1978 Zia decreed the establishment of special shariah courts to adjudicate cases brought under shariah law. In 1979 Islamic punishments were imposed for the commission of several crimes, including drinking, theft, and prostitution. The rules of evidence were more stringent in Islamic courts. This worked against women, and rape trials from secular courts became guilty verdicts for adultery in shariah courts. In 1984 an Ordinance was issued concerning rules of evidence in matters of financial dispute, with evidence of two women being equal to that of one man and, in situations of claims for retribution and compensation, women were given less status. In 1981 a Ramadan Ordinance instigated a system of fines/imprisonment for those eating, smoking or drinking in public. Quranic, Islamic and Pakistan studies were made compulsory, and textbooks were revised to conform to an official discourse. In February 1980 the government announced plans for implementation of an Islamic economic system, introducing Zakat and interest-free banking. There were numerous instances of petty legislation, such as the ban on pigeon flying in Lahore in 1981, or an attempt to ban kite flying (Qureshi 1980; Noman 1988; Hasen 1998; Talbot 1998; Jaffrelot 2002; Ali 2008).

This process presented two problems: who would make the decisions and what Islamic school of law would be followed? Islam in Pakistan (as elsewhere) was a mix of different groups and interpretations. Islam was divided by the Sunni and Shia (the latter 10%–25% of population) divisions. Then, in turn, the majority of the Shia belongs to the Ithna Ashari division, and a minority to the Ismaili (Aga Khan). One consequence of the Islamisation policy was to open up rifts between the Sunni and Shia. The Shia, for example, opposed the compulsory levying of Zakat, which they had always regarded as voluntary. In 1979/80 the Shia expressed opposition through violence and defying the martial law ruling against demonstrations. Zakat was eventually withdrawn as a compulsory requirement for Shia in 1981 (Jalal 1990; Baxter 1991; Jaffrelot 2002). The greatest tension was through the state's legalistic imposition of Islam and the humanist traditions of Sufism; this was particularly explosive in Sindh, where Sufism had always been an integral component of regional cultural identity. The Pirs of Sindh were eventually to play a leading role in the opposition Movement for the Restoration of Democracy (MRD) in the 1980s. Islam never provided the ideological cohesion that Zia's government hoped for; instead, state-sponsored Islamisation intensified sectarian divisions within Pakistani Islam, and the cultural pluralism and the rich inheritance of South Asia could not be forced into the straightjacket of a self-proclaimed ideological state (Talbot 1998: 286).

Under Zia the military co-opted the religious right, in particular the Jama'at. The Jama'at had always been a semi-secret, conspiratorial organisation of trained/disciplined cadres giving priority to organisational efficiency and loyalty over numerical strength. Its ideology stood for a certain version of fundamentalist Islam, defence of private property, and a unitary Pakistan with a strong centre that denied the existence of separate nationalities. This ideological stance captured some common ground between the urban petty bourgeoisie and the bureaucratic-military elite. The Jama'at had given up on gaining electoral power after receiving less than 5% of the vote in 1970. The generational shift from the British-trained, secular officers, to the less literate, more socially and religiously conservative from the small towns of the Potwar region led to the army becoming under Zia more susceptible to the puritanical ideology of the Jama'at. Since the 1970 elections the Jama'at had been successful in infiltrating other civic institutions, in particular students and educational institutions, and the vernacular press. The Jami'at, the student front of the Jama'at became the largest and most disciplined student organisation in the country (Ahmed 1982). Early expectations by Ahmed (1982), among others, that the Jama'at would provide the military government with their public persona and ideological cover were misplaced, and pro Jama'at elements in the officers corps played a less crucial role in government than expected. The Jama'at was effective, but remained so small that its presence in government in no way gave the government a representative or legitimate character. The zeal and discipline of Jama'at cadres were unable to offset the continued popularity of the PPP and heterodox traditions of Islam (Ahmed 1982).

Zia was always afraid of party-based elections; his ideological efforts were never enough to overcome the appeal of Bhutto's PPP. The elections for local bodies held in September 1979 were won by many PPP candidates, even though it was formally held on a non-party basis. This created a reasonable fear in Zia's mind that the planned November 1979 national and provincial elections would lead to a PPP victory (Jalal 1990; Burki 1991). The elections were cancelled, and subsequent elections such as the 1985 provincial and national assembly elections were also held on a non-party basis. Zia's longevity rested not on Islamic discourse or ideology. Zia learned from Ayub and made sure to keep his army officers loyal. Ayub had delegated military affairs to Yahya

Khan; Zia retained control. Senior military commanders had to accept the principle of job rotation and fixed-period assignments. Rotation and fixed-term appointments were scrupulously adhered to, except for Zia, whose post as Chief of Army Staff (COAS) was extended in 1980, 1984 and 1988. Zia never relinquished the post of COAS (technically subordinate to the Defence Minister), to which he was appointed by Bhutto in March 1976. Zia stayed on as COAS even after martial law was lifted and Junejo became Prime Minister (Burki 1988, 1991), 'Until his death in a mysterious air crash in August 1988 Zia remained as ringmaster of a subservient, fragmented, highly monetised, corrupt and violent political system (Jalal 1995: 107).

8 An episode of stagnation, 1992/93–2002/03

Summary of chapter findings

The chapter is divided into three parts, each focusing on one particular role that the state has in promoting economic growth. These relate to finance, production and institutions. The underlying hypothesis here is that the state needs to be successful in all three to initiate and sustain an episode of growth.

The first section shows that the state found it increasingly hard to mobilise a domestic surplus after 1992/93. Total savings were stagnant, and the state failed to increase its own contribution. Foreign capital inflows increased, but at high cost. The stock market played no role in mobilising savings, there is little evidence to suggest any increase in corporate profitability, FDI remained very low, and public investment showed signs of becoming less productive over this episode. The second section examines the role of the state in achieving a productive use of the surplus in both the public and private sectors. There are indications that the episode of stagnation is linked to deflationary macroeconomic policy after the late 1980s. There is mixed evidence on indicators of efficiency in Pakistan, in industry, banking, and public investment. Exports remained stuck at the low end of the market; there were few indications of learning or upgrading. Broader measures of productivity (TFP) declined in the 1990s relative to the 1980s. The third section focuses on institutions that may or may not allow the state to overcome the inherent conflicts associated with economic growth. The relative autonomy of the state declined drastically over the 1990s, and party politics led to an upsurge in uncontrolled and chaotic factionalism that undermined the clarity and coherence of policy making. The main political parties frequently turned to the military to find allies in politics; this undermined the institutionalisation of democracy. Inclusionary or ideological institutions to manage conflict were non-existent. Pakistan over the 1990s was locked into a destructive episode of stagnation with no internal means to exit.

Recap from Chapter 3

The statistical analysis in Chapter 3 showed that GDP growth averaged 3.7% p.a. between 1992/93 and 2002/03. There is a widespread perception, if not backed by rigorous statistics, that growth was gradually slowing (Wizarat 2002: 18). Growth of agriculture and services showed little change in the 1990s relative to the 1980s. The growth rate of manufacturing slowed sharply in the 1990s relative to earlier decades, and the small-scale sector showed more resilience than the large-scale sector. The share of agriculture and services increased marginally over the 1990s. There was little change in the share of manufacturing in GDP, which increased (with some fluctuations) marginally.

Limitations of alternative explanations

The world economy

After having stagnated since 1970 the trade ratio (exports plus imports as a share of GDP) started to rise after 1985. Between 1985 and 1996 the share of exports in GDP increased from 8.0% to 14.7%, and of imports from 19.0% to 19.8%, increasing the potential of the world economy to impact on growth in Pakistan (Husain 1999: 324). The greater exposure to the world economy magnified the impact of external shocks in the mid-1980s. The decline in remittances during 1987–90 was the single most important factor leading to deterioration in the current account deficit, despite significant improvement in external variables and export expansion. The adjustment burden was not responsible for the slowdown and was manifest, not in expenditure reduction (deflation), but in expenditure switching; changes in domestic absorption variables were small. Devaluation and improved incentives led to adjustment through export growth, rather than import decline (Sarmad 1992: 866).

Liberalisation

The episode of stagnation after 1992/93 was (perhaps) paradoxically associated with the promise and practice of liberalisation. The Seventh Five-year Plan (1988–93) was commissioned at the same time as World Bank/IMF-induced conditionality was accepted. This culminated in a three-year agreement scheduled to run from 1988 to 1991. Future industrial policy was outlined in a letter of interest, which committed the government to substantial liberalisation. These measures included, deregulation of business, raising the investment sanctioning limit, phasing out industrial location policies over a three-year period, providing infrastructural facilities at economic costs, selling shares in public sector enterprises, and substantial trade liberalisation (Zaidi 2005). Substantial trade liberalisation occurred after 1987 and continued to the eve and beyond of this period. The maximum tariff was reduced from 225% in 1986/87, to 70% in 1994/95, to 25% in 2001/02, with the number of tariff slabs declining from 14 to 4 over the 1990s. The average tariff on dutiable imports (excluding duty-free imports) fell from 23% in 1996/97 to 17% in 2001/02. The rupee depreciated by about 10% annually against the dollar over the 1990s (Anwar 2000; Din *et al.* 2003; Zaidi 2005). Pakistan's progress in trade liberalisation exceeded those requirements under its WTO commitments, (Anwar 2000: 8).

The (economic) role of the state, 1992/93 to 2002/03: finance

This section shows that the state found it increasingly hard to mobilise a surplus after 1992/93. Total savings were stagnant. The public sector barely increased its contribution; higher revenues from income taxation were offset by reduced revenue from trade taxation. Foreign capital inflows did increase, but at rising cost, and domestic savings were increasingly in the form of high-cost and volatile foreign currency deposits. The stock market played no role in mobilising savings, there is little evidence to suggest any increase in corporate profitability, FDI remained very low, and public investment showed signs of becoming less productive over this episode.

The mobilisation of savings

Private savings showed no trend change in the early 1990s: from an average of 12.71% of GDP in the 1980s, there was a slight increase to over 13% by 1993/94, then a decline to 11.24% in 1995/96. The bulk of private savings and the principal influence on these patterns were from the household sector, which accounted for more than 90% of the total. Corporate savings were consistently ranged from 1.3% to 1.5% of GDP in the early 1990s (Qureshi *et al.* 1997: 895).

The role of the state in mobilising domestic savings

One of the key aims of the various structural adjustment programmes (SAPs) begun at the end of the 1980s was to reform the tax system. One significant and enduring problem was the low income elasticity of the tax system, estimates of which had declined significantly in the 1980s relative to the 1970s (Husain 1999: 181; Zaidi 2005: 219). By the end of the 1980s the tax system was raising only 13%–14% of GDP, much lower than in other LDCs. The SAPs sought to broaden the tax base and increase the elasticity of the system, shift the incidence of taxation from indirect taxes to consumption, and raise the contribution of income tax. In the years to 2002/03 some progress had been made. As shares of GDP, income tax revenue increased from 1.7% in 1989/90, to 3.5% in 2002/03, customs duties from 5.7% to 1.6%, excise duties from 2.6% to 1.1%, and sales tax from 2.2% to 4.6% (Bilquees 2004: 76; Zaidi 2005: 218). Indirect taxes did decline in relative importance: sales tax increased its share of total taxation from 9% to 43%, customs duty declined from 43% to 15%, and central excise duty from 31% to 10%. Direct income taxes increased from 17% to 32%. The sales tax was more broadly based than central excise duty. There had been a gradual reduction of exemptions of various imported and domestically produced goods. The sales tax was extended from manufactures and importers to the level of wholesalers and retailers for some products. Between 1983 and 2002/03 the balance between indirect and direct taxes had shifted from 83:17 to 67:33 (Fatima and Ahmed 2001: 508; Bilquees 2004: 76; Zaidi 2005: 217).

Revenue from income tax did increase, but there remained many problems. Income tax continued to have poor coverage, a narrow base with many exemptions (savings, agriculture, exports, etc.), and income tax procedure was badly integrated with company law. The exemption from taxation of gross income according to some estimates was about twelve times average income (Husain 1999: 138). By 2002/03 there were no more than 1.5m, income taxpayers from a population of 150m. (Zaidi 2005: 218). The 1990s can be characterised by efforts to offset the revenue losses from import liberalisation rather than making progress at increasing tax revenue (Fatima and Ahmed 2001: 507). Tax revenue remained unchanged over the 1990s at around 12% of GDP (Mukarram 2001: 76; IMF 2004: 47).

The democratic governments of Benazir and Nawaz found it continually difficult to close tax exemptions by extending rates and coverage due to domestic opposition from business (Anwar 2000; Fatima and Ahmed 2001). For example, in 1993 the caretaker government removed the 1970 exemption of agricultural land for the purposes of wealth tax. The incoming PPP government in 1994 introduced several exemptions that reduced the impact of the wealth tax. In 1994/95 the ratio of land revenue to value added by crops was estimated to be 0.45% (Khan 1999; Zaidi 2005). Even after more than a decade of tax reform, the income elasticity of tax revenue remained below one, both in the aggregate and, in some studies, for each component separately (income, customs, sales, etc.) (Mukarram 2001; Chaudhary and Hamid 2001; Bilquees 2004).

The problems with central government taxes were generally echoed at provincial level. Provincial governments made similar efforts to raise tax revenue after 1991, through removing exemptions and increasing rates on stamp duties, motor vehicle tax, paddy fees, and cotton duty. There was some effort to switch from specific to ad valorem taxes. Some provinces, such as Sindh and NWFP, achieved considerable growth in revenues (Zaidi 2005: 221).

Total expenditure as a share of GDP did decline, from 26.0% of GDP in 1992/93 to 23.90% in 1995/96. The bulk of this decline was due to reduced development expenditure, which declined steadily during the 1990s, from 7.6% of GDP in 1991/92 to a low of 1.7% in 2000/01, then increased somewhat to 2.2% in 2002/03. Defence spending declined from 6.0% of GDP in 1992/93 to 3.4% in 2002/03, and the rate of decline actually increased after the 1999 military coup (Siddiqa 2007: 163).[1] Subsidies (defined as cost of provision minus user charges) increased over the 1990s in irrigation, roads, primary and secondary education (they were stable in higher education), curative health, and water supply and sanitation. Total subsidies reached around 5% of GDP by the end of the 1990s, although only around 40% of this total was to goods that could be classified as 'merit goods' (Pasha et al. 2002: 631–7).

High levels of debt at the end of the 1990s left Pakistan's public finances vulnerable to shocks. Short-term debt comprising mainly treasury bills held by the SBP and Commercial Banks comprised 49% of all domestic debt by 2002/03. Unfunded debt through voluntary savings schemes (mainly the National Savings Instruments) comprised a further 28% of total government debt and offered very high tax-free yields (Zaidi 2005: 230). In general, the domestic debt profile worsened over this period. The ratio of total public debt servicing to tax revenue, total revenue, total expenditure and current expenditure increased between 1993/94 and 2001/02, before showing a sharp improvement in the year to 2002/03 (Zaidi 2005: 245). In 2001/02 public debt stood at 98% of GDP, and interest payments accounted for 6.6% of GDP, or almost 30% of public expenditure (Fatima and Ahmed 2001: 514; IMF 2002; Wizarat 2002: 30; Zaidi 2005: 230).

The result was some reduction in the government budget deficit, from 8%–9% of GDP in the 1980s, to 8% in 1992/93, to 6.3% in 1995/96. This was less progress than promised; the 1988 IMF agreement required that the fiscal deficit be reduced from 8.5% in 1987/88 to 4.8% in 1990/91. Towards the end of this period the budget deficit declined rapidly, from 5.4% in 1999/00, to 3.7% in 2002/03 (Fatima and Ahmed 2001: 507; Zaidi 2005: 442).

The net result of stagnating tax revenue and reduced public expenditure was that public sector savings increased slightly in the early 1990s. From an average of 1.6% of GDP in the 1980s, public sector savings increased from 1.50% of GDP in 1992/93 to 2.49% in 1995/96 (Qureshi et al. 1997: 895).

The role of the state in creating institutions to mobilise private sector savings

Reforms to the financial sector were initiated in 1989 with a World Bank loan, and were implemented throughout the 1990s, increasing in speed after 1997. The features of the strategy were to shift to market-based monetary and exchange rate policies, and from direct state intervention to an indirect regulatory approach. These reforms were conducted in parallel with the introduction of market-based government debt instruments (IMF 2002). Policies were intended to make it easier to mobilise private sector savings, including the granting of licences for private banks after 1992, and the privatisation of two of the five nationalised banks between 1991 and 1993 (the Muslim Commercial Bank (MCB) and Allied Bank (ABL)), and in September 2002 United Bank Limited (UBL) was sold to a foreign group. Despite these efforts, the public sector remained dominant throughout the 1990s. The share of state-owned bank assets as a share of total assets declined sharply over the 1990s, from 92.2% in 1990 to 64.1% in 2001, before rising steadily, to 71.0% in 2004 (Khan et al. 2005: 824).

The switch from administratively to market-determined interest rates promised to help re-intermediate savings through the formal financial system (Hasen 1998; IMF 2002; Zaidi 2005). Various scholars have unearthed a positive relation between interest rates and savings or other measures of financial sector development (Iqbal 1993; Khan and Hasan 1998; Khan and Qayyum 2007; Nasir and Khalid 2004). There is mixed evidence on financial sector development over the 1990s. Financial savings increased from 45% of GDP in 1992/93, to over 60% in 2001/02. Most of the increase in financial savings was absorbed by the attractive government National Savings Schemes (NSS), which grew from 11.3% to 23.4% of GDP over the same period. Savings accumulated in banks were more or less stable over the period (IMF 2002: 54). One measure of financial depth is broad money[2] divided by nominal GDP lagged by one year. Financial depth remained stagnant (around 41%) between 1970 and 1990, then declined steadily, from 39.20% in 1990 to 36.70% in 2001. Deducting currency in circulation from this total may give a better measure of financial depth (as opposed to monetisation). This measure showed a steady decline from 1970 to 1990, then rose to reach its 1970s level in 2000 (Khan et al. 2005: 824). The ratio of broad money to GDP increased from 32.27% in 1990 to 38.59% in 2000. Total bank deposit liabilities (liquid liabilities minus currency in circulation) increased from 27.91% of GDP in 1990 to 37.51% in 2000 (Khan and Qayyum 2007: 15). The biggest change was in the composition, not the volume, of savings. The opening up of foreign currency deposits led to a substantial portfolio shift, and by June 1998 such deposits accounted for US $11bn or 40% of total bank deposits. The SBP provided heavily subsidised foreign exchange cover to foreign bank branches, giving banks attractive margins, and was instrumental in determining this shift (Husain 1999).

The role of the state in mobilising foreign savings

Throughout the 1990s Pakistan showed a consistent pattern of a government deficit being partly absorbed by the surplus in private sector savings over private sector investment, with the remainder (3%–5% of GDP) spilling over into the current account deficit (Qureshi *et al.* 1997: 899–900). The current account deficit remained high throughout the 1990s, peaking at 7.1% in 1992/93, then declining, and then rising to another peak of 7.2% in 1995/96. In the late 1990s the current account deficit improved sharply, from 4.1% in 1998/99, to a surplus of 3.8% in 2002/03 (Wizarat 2002: 27; Zaidi 2005: 346).

The 1990s marked a significantly more difficult decade in which to acquire foreign capital on reasonable terms. The Iraqi invasion of Kuwait in 1990 led to a fall of remittance income (and a fall of exports to Gulf States). The withdrawal of Soviet troops from Afghanistan in 1989 and the collapse of the USSR in 1991 led to the ending of US aid in 1990, when George Bush refused to certify that Pakistan was not in violation of the Pressler agreement.

In May 1998, after nuclear tests, the USA and Japan imposed sanctions, and lending from the World Bank, IMF, G-8 and ADB was halted (Burki 1999). The inflow of official grants declined steadily over the 1990s, from $325.6m. in 1990/91 to $124.6m. in 1999/2000, and the relative share of debt-creating inflows increased (Shah and Ahmed 2003: 698). To some extent this process was slowed by Benazir's charm offensive and democratic credentials, which at times led to improved relations with the USA. Under her first government, several hundred million dollars of military equipment that Pakistan had paid for but not received was released. Under her second government, the Brown amendment to the Pressler law was ratified by President Clinton in 1996. The Brown amendment alleviated some of the Pressler sanctions and allowed $370m. of military arms and spare parts to be delivered to Pakistan (Talbot 1998). The general exception was relations with the World Bank. Between 1990 and 1995 the World Bank financed $2.5bn of new inflows. The World Bank focused on trade policy, energy pricing, agricultural prices, financial sector reform, privatisation and support to public sector expenditure priorities. Despite the failure to meet conditionalities, lending increased in 1993–95 relative to 1990–92 (Hasen 1998).

To promote intermediation and to attract funds held abroad by Pakistani nationals, non-resident Pakistanis were allowed to open foreign currency accounts (FCAs) with Pakistani banks that were freely transferable abroad. These accounts were exempted from income and wealth tax, and no questions were asked about the source of foreign exchange. Those holding FCAs could also obtain rupee loans against such accounts (Khan et al. 2005). Foreign currency deposits and portfolio inflows played a vital role in financing the external deficit after 1991. Between 1992 and 1996 portfolio flows totalled $2bn; half of this was accounted for by the sale abroad of publicly owned shares in PTC. Between June 1991 and June 1996 $4bn was deposited in domestic foreign exchange accounts. Such deposits were large (ten times as big), relative to foreign exchange reserves. The cost of attracting such deposits was very high, and they reduced the ability of the SBP to control the money supply, such assets constituting 20% of the monetary base by the end of 1996 (Hasen 1998). The inflow of workers' remittances was rarely enough over this period; only in 1991/92 did the inflow of remittances (3.0%) cover the current account deficit (2.8%) (Wizarat 2002: 27). The inflow of external resources fluctuated around a rising trend over the 1990s, from 4.1% of GDP in 1992/93, to 6.89% in 2001/02 (Fatima and Ahmed 2001: 507).

After 1996 there were some concerns that Pakistan was heading for an external debt crisis, as measures of external debt showed a worsening. Total foreign debt increased from $20bn in 1990 to $43bn in 1998, then constituting almost 50% of GDP. The debt-export ratio increased from 241.5 in 1986–90 to 277.8 in 1997, and the debt service ratio increased from 24.6% to 30.9% and the interest-export ratio from 9.4% to 11.1% over the same years (Husain 1999: 335; 2003). This is an exaggeration, as there was no looming international debt crisis at the end of the 1990s. Debt measures substantially improved. The ratio of external debt servicing declined from 55.4% of export earnings in 1997/98 to 28.8% in 2002/03, and from 34.9% to 16% of foreign exchange earnings over the same period (Zaidi 2005: 245). Total external debt as a share of GDP was declining gradually, from 62.8% in 1997/98 to 61.7% in 2000/01. Of this total, 50.6% was medium- and long-term public and publicly guaranteed debt and 45.4% was project and non-project aid; only 1.1% was from commercial banks and 1.5% Eurobonds and construction bonds (IMF 2002: 117).

There are clear indications of policy trade-offs. Regression analysis shows that both FDI and foreign loans were inversely correlated with domestic savings. Results show that every additional percent of foreign loans as a proportion of national income resulted in a decline of about one-third of a percent of average savings, and vice versa (Khan and Rahmin 1993).

The role of the state in influencing stock markets

Capital market reforms were started in 1994, and accelerated after 1997, supported by the Asian Development Bank. The three regional stock market exchanges in Pakistan were modernised in 1997 and made subject to more transparent regulations. An independent regulatory authority, the Securities and Exchange Commission of Pakistan (SECP), became operational in 1999. After 1999 the SBP was increasingly focused on banks, and the SECP became the sole regulator of non-bank financial institutions (NBFIs) (IMF 2002). The government pursued various reforms that impacted on the stock market, such as incentives for foreign portfolio investment, expansion of the range of financial intermediation, improvements in the system of underwriting and pricing of initial public offers, and attempts to eliminate corporate malpractice (Khan 1999). Pakistan over the 1990s had one of the most open stock markets in the world, and policy makers retained an enduring commitment to attracting portfolio investment from overseas investors (Khan 1999).

The number of companies listed on the Karachi Stock Exchange (KSE) increased from 300 in 1986, to 775 in September 1996, and 689 in 2004 (Zaidi 2005). In the first half of the 1990s the KSE was one of the best performing stock markets in Asia. The market reached peaks in December 1994. Over these years there was a boom in secondary market activity, which encouraged the primary/new issues market. Fresh funds from public subscriptions peaked at R34bn in 1994 (Khan 1999). Stock market capitalisation to GDP increased from 4.68% in 1990 to 10.24% in 2000, declined to 8.15% in 2001, and increased rapidly to 15.48% in 2003 (Khan and Qayyum 2007: 15).

Despite these numbers, there is little evidence that the stock market contributed in a significant manner to mobilising resources (or, as this chapter later shows, to efficiently allocating resources). The stock markets lagged behind the banking system and non-bank financial system. Between 1980 and 1990 on average only 5%–6% of private funds were mobilised through the stock market. Over the 1990s the average amount raised through new issues was R7–9bn, compared to R75–80bn from deposit mobilisation by the commercial banking system (Khan 1999: 231). The KSE was characterised by low turnover and thin markets. The thinness resulted from the structure of equity ownership in the country, as well as passive investment strategies of institutional investors, insider dealing by brokers, and the inefficiency of regulatory authorities to police corporate malpractice. Investors also had to cope with a very poor dividend records of listed companies (Khan 1999). One exception was the link between remittances inflows and the stock market after 2001, though this was not related to any domestic fundamentals. In October 2001 the US government passed the Patriot Act, tightening regulatory powers to combat corruption, and money laundering. Traditional forms of remitting money to Pakistan through the Hundi lost out, relative to more formal channels; there was a surge of savings sent back to Pakistan. In 1999/2000 Pakistani-Americans sent back $80m., and between July 2002 and February 2003 remittances equalled $856m. Between September 2001 and September 2003, the KSE rose by 250% (Zaidi 2005).

The role of the state in influencing private sector profitability

Studies of corporate sector profitability all but disappear during the 1990s. Despite some measures of liberalisation over the 1980s, the effective rates of protection for 1991/92 show that farmers growing wheat, rice, and cotton were facing negative effective protection rates, and that sugar was the only crop with a positive rate of protection. This continued, if at a lower rate, the policy of transferring resources from agriculture to other economic sectors. The estimate of the transfer from agricultural producers for the four major crops was about R19bn in 1992/93, or 6% of agricultural gross product, though this was a decline from 14% in 1984–87 (Husain 1999: 347).

There were distinct efforts to improve the profitability of state owned enterprises towards the end of the 1990s. Employees of Pakistan railways were reduced from 104,185 in 1997/98, to 92,500 in 2000/01; there was a large increase in revenue receipts and a sharp fall in operating losses. Pakistan International Airways showed a sharp improvement in its net operating balance between 2000 and 2001, through increased revenue and falls in fuel costs (and capital expenditure). Pakistan Steel Mills reduced its number of employees from 20,625 in 1998/99 to 14,407 in 2000/01, raised revenues and so improved its operating balance (IMF 2002: 98–9).

Return on banking sector assets declined from 0.8% in 1992 to 0.0% in 2001, while return on equity, with more extreme fluctuations, declined from 18.2% in 1992 to -0.1% in 2001. If credit losses were properly provided for, nationalised banks would have had negative net worth over the 1990s (IMF 2002: 51). Large fluctuations in measures of profitability since the mid-1990s seem to mostly reflect the large provisions for non-performing loans and, later, the impact of the freeze on foreign currency deposits, which deprived banks of a very profitable activity (IMF 2002). Foreign banks made up about 20% of the banking sector and accounted for two-thirds of industry profits, up from 20% in the mid-1980s (Husain 1999). A lack of profitable lending opportunities is supported by evidence that shows banks did not utilise ample opportunities to increase lending. Banks remained very liquid, and liquid assets declined only very slowly, from over 40% in the early 1990s to around 35% by 2001. This was true even though a combination of the gradual reduction in the Cash Reserve Ratio (CRR) and Statutory Liquidity Ratio (SLR) imposed on banks by the SBP, the development of banks refinancing through the SBP discount window, and repo operations, significantly reduced banks' legal and practical liquidity needs (IMF 2002).

The role of the state in managing flows of FDI

Numerous policy changes were implemented over the 1990s to encourage the inflow of FDI. The requirement of government approval for FDI was removed, except in the case of a few industries. Foreign equity participation of up to 100% was allowed, and foreign investors were allowed to purchase equity in existing enterprises. Foreign investors were allowed to negotiate terms and conditions of payment of royalties and technical fees. Remittances of the principle and dividends from FDI/portfolio investment were permitted without prior clearance from the SBP. In 1994 the Pakistani rupee was made convertible, restrictions on some capital transactions were partially relaxed, and foreign borrowing and certain outward investments were allowed. In addition, there were a pro-active set of investment incentives, including credit facilities, fiscal incentives and visa policy (Anwar 2000; Khan et al. 2005).

In response, there was a steady, if unspectacular and fluctuating, increase in FDI after 1990. FDI increased from $277.72m. in 1990/91, to $514.85m. in 1995/96 and $456.00m. in 1999/2000. As a share of total inflows, this represented an increase from 6.96% to 41.90% (Shah and Ahmed 2003: 698). This was nothing compared to the $40bn p.a. that China was attracting in FDI over the same period (Naughton 2007: Ch7). Ahmad et al. (2003) and Atique et al. (2004) find a positive relation between FDI and GDP growth during during this period.

The role of the state in allocating resources to projects essential for development

The state substantially retreated from the role of directly allocating resources to projects essential for development over the 1990s. Banks were given greater discretion over the allocation of their lending portfolios by reductions in the CRR and SLR. The government competed on more open terms for credit through open market auctions for government debt. Various subsidised credit schemes were eliminated, or their rates gradually linked to market interest rates. Development Finance Institutions (DFIs) had been set up in the 1960s with the objective of providing long-term finance at affordable rates. The majority of DFIs were government owned or had a government equity stake. By 1995 there were 15 DFIs. Political influence over lending had encouraged poor asset-liability management; this was reflected in a concentration of loan portfolios to a narrow enclave of borrowers whose credit-worthiness reduced loan quality, and an estimated 30% of the lending portfolio of DFIs was non-performing by 1989. DFIs' own financing was so heavily subsidised that it reduced any incentives to build a deposit base. Over the 1990s DFIs were either closed down or else pushed into becoming regular banks (Khan 1999; Zaidi 2005)

There was no positive impact on investment, and total investment declined steadily from 20.5% of GDP in 1992/93 to 14.9% in 1998/99. Private investment remained stable up until 1997/98 (at 9%–10% of GDP), before falling to 8.3% in 1998/99 (Wizarat 2002: 29). There was no significant privatisation of investment. The share of public (private) investment increased from 44.25% (47.50%) in 1992/93 to 52.19% (37.09%) in 2001/02 (IMF 2002: 55; Kemal *et al.* 2006: 330).

There are various reasons for this poor outcome. One is that the government failed to correct its budget deficit until after 2000. Much of the pool of private savings was absorbed by the government. In 1992/93, 58% of the government's deficit was financed by borrowing through the banking system; this declined to 18% by 1994/95 (or from 4.7% to 1.4% of GDP) (Zaidi 2005: 231); it increased to 57% in 1996/97, before falling again (Qureshi *et al.* 1997: 897–8; Fatima and Ahmed 2001: 516). The heavy demand for funds by the government, with a stagnant supply (savings) and liberalised interest rates, helped push up the borrowing cost for private investors. The real (weighted averaged) lending rate increased steadily over the 1990s, from an average of 1.98% between 1990 and 1995 to 10.9% in 2000; it remained high, before falling sharply after 2003 (Khan and Qayyum 2007: 13).

Alternative means of financing investment remained poorly developed. The stock market (as discussed earlier) and the bond market remained marginal. Historically cheap bank finance available to the corporate sector undermined the growth of a domestic bond market. The first major bond issue, in 1988, by a non-financial institution in Pakistan (WAPDA) was motivated by government fiscal difficulties. Since then, WAPDA made more issues, and a small number of other companies did likewise. Discount houses have emerged to trade such bonds, and a credit rating agency to value them. The bond market remained small. The tax structure did not encourage companies to access debt markets, and revolving short-term finance or concessional loans from overseas donors remained the preferred options. The poor disclosure record of listed companies means that investors found it difficult to assess the viability of debt issues (Khan 1999).

Government development spending (slightly more than what is classified as 'public investment') had risen to a peak of 7.5% of GDP in 1991/92, then declined to 4.3% of GDP in 1995/96, reached a low of 1.7% in 2000/01, then increased somewhat to 2.2% in 2002/03(Qureshi et al. 1997: 897–8; Wizarat 2002: 29; Zaidi 2005: 442). There is reason to believe that even this declining level of public investment became less productive over the 1990s. Political pressures in the choice of projects and implementation arrangements became increasingly evident. Governmental institutional capacity for review and appraisal of projects was weakened. For the People's Work Programme, roads, and energy development, formal approval procedures were often bypassed. By the end of 1996 there were R700bn of projects ongoing, compared to an annual resources availability of R85–90bn. Despite these evident problems, in 1996 large new projects were added – including the Lahore Light Rail Transit and a major rehabilitation of Pakistan steel mills – many of doubtful economic and financial availability. The *ad hoc* nature of decision making probably reached its nadir under Benazir Bhutto's second government (Hasen 1998). There is some limited case study evidence that shows that tax concessions distorted decisions, rather than encouraged productive private investment (Ahmed and Ahsan 1997). Lower levels and declining productivity of public investment reduced its crowding in effects on private investment. There has been some work on crowding in of private investment in the Pakistan context. The general finding is that public investment has a positive impact on private investment (Khan 1988; Hyder 2001; Naqvi 2002; Ahmed and Qayyam 2007), though some argue the opposite (Ghani and ud Din 2006).

The (economic) role of the state, 1992/93 to 2002/03: production

This second section examines the role of the state in achieving a productive use of the surplus in both the public and private sectors. There are indications that the episode of stagnation is linked to deflationary macroeconomic policy after the late 1980s, and then to a lack of learning and upgrading. There is mixed evidence on indicators of efficiency in Pakistan, in industry, banking, and public investment. Exports remained stuck at the low end of the market. Broader measures of productivity (TFP) worsened over the 1990s relative to the 1980s.

Sources of growth: deflation

The liberalisation at the end of the 1980s can be linked to the episode of stagnation after 1992/93. Between 1980/81 and 1988/89 the combination of domestic demand and import substitution accounted for 90% of manufacturing growth, and export expansion for the remainder. Weakening domestic demand caused by fiscal retrenchment and higher interest rates between 1988/89 and 1991/92 reduced the contribution of domestic sources to only 62% of manufacturing growth. Devaluation and export orientation increased the contribution of export expansion to manufacturing growth to nearly 40% (Kemal 1999: 164) – even though export growth was lower in the 1990s relative to the 1980s.

Evaluation of efficiency, 1992/93 to 2002/03

There are various case studies showing that industrial sectors in Pakistan were inefficient over this period. Burki and Terrell (1998) conducted a study of manufacturing firms in Gujranwala. They find relatively low levels of technical efficiency (a composite measure of pure technical efficiency and scale efficiency), ranging from a low of 71% in knitting mills, to 94% in china and ceramics, with an average of 86% for the entire sample. About 46% of the firms exhibit increasing returns to scale, while only 16% of the firms operate at decreasing returns. This implies that a primary source of scale inefficiency is operating at less than the optimal level of production. Din et al. (2007) use data envelope analysis to examine the outputs produced for a given level of inputs in 101 large-scale manufacturing industries for the years 1995/96 to 2000/01. Overall, the mean efficiency score increased from 0.58 in 1995/96 to 0.65 in 2000/01, indicating an improvement in efficiency of the large-scale manufacturing sector. There remained in 2000/01 considerable room for improvement. In 1995/96 the least efficient industries were sports and athletic goods, surgical instruments, leather and leather products, manufacturing of textiles, and apparel. All these industries are export orientated. By 2000/01 a remarkable turnaround had been shown by the sports and athletic goods, which was then among the top five most efficient industries. Textiles made only marginal improvements over these years. There has been a decline in the efficiency of other non-metallic mineral products, tobacco manufacturing, transport equipment, other chemical products, pottery, china and earthenware, and glass and glass products. Over the 1990s one clear success story was the Sialkot cluster of surgical instrument manufacturers. Since the mid-1980s export growth in real terms averaged roughly 10% p.a., and total export sales exceeded $125m. by the mid-1990s, over 85% of which went to high-income markets in USA and Western Europe. Pakistan has 20% of world trade in this sector. In interviews, a majority of firms had reported improvements in quality standards; such rising quality had motivated many leading German firms to enter into joint venture production agreements. There has been a clear link between upgrading and improved firm performance (Nadvi 1999a and b).

There is mixed evidence linking financial liberalisation and efficiency. The interest rate spread increased from 4.4% in 1992 to a peak of 9.6% in 2002, before declining. This reflected limited competition in the banking sector, continuing inefficiencies, and the increasing cost of provisioning for NPLs. The quality of bank assets did not markedly improve between 1992 and 2001, and the ratio of non-performing loans to total gross loans remained close to 20% (Husain 1999; Rizvi 2001; IMF 2002: 51; Khan and Qayyum 2007: 13). Hardy and di Patti find that measures of efficiency in the banking sector (cost and revenue efficiency and profitability) increased in some public sector banks over the 1990s and improved relative to other banks. Public sector banks could still be classified as inefficient by the end of the 1990s (2001). Rizvi used eight measures of productivity and efficiency in the banking-financial sector and found efficiency on a marginally declining trend for 37 scheduled banks between 1993 and 1998 (2001). Iimi finds that the impact of financial liberalisation on the five major public sector banks from 1997 onwards was varied. Technical efficiency improved for HBL and NBP and declined or fluctuated for UBL, IDBP and NDFC

(2003). Jaffry *et al.* use panel data from 114 Pakistani (and Indian) banks covering 1985 to 2003. The variables they used included the total quantity of labour hours used, wages, loans, investment, deposits, number of branches, fixed assets, and a time trend representing exogenous rates of technical change. They calculate individual bank-specific efficiencies by year, size classes, types of ownership and countries. Efficiency, they find, improved over time, but remained very low. By adopting the most efficient standard, on average, public banks in Pakistan and India could have reduced their labour usage by almost 35%, private banks by 34% and foreign banks by 26% without suffering any loss in output (2006). Khan and Qayyam use data envelope analysis to measure the cost efficiency of the Pakistani banking system for 29 banks between 1998 and 2005. Efficiency was found to have declined in 2004 relative to 1999 for all groups (domestic, foreign, and big banks), and the average efficiency score was higher for domestic banks than for all banks until 2000 and higher for foreign banks until 2004 (2007).

Earlier, this chapter showed that there was reason to believe that public investment was becoming less productive over the 1990s. By the end of the decade there were some indications of a change and signs of increasing productivity in key public sector industries, such as Pakistan Railways, Pakistan International Airways and Pakistan Steel (IMF 2002: 98–9).

There is no evidence that the KSE provided useful signals for investors: trading activity and hence price formation were related, not to any fundamentals, but to existing trends in prices (Farid and Ashraf 1995: 654; Ali and Mustafa 2001; Husain and Mahmood 2001; Hameed and Ashraf 2006).

Between 1992/93 and 2002/03 the number of cotton textile mills increased from 284 to 363, the number of spindles from 5,493,000 to 9,216,000, the number of spindles working at end of period from 4,754,000 to 7,623,000, and total cloth production from 292.9 (m.sq mtr) to 576.6 (m.sq mtr) (Government of Pakistan 2010). Growth was combined with (in terms of the number of spindles) a fall in capacity utilisation from 86.5% to 82.7%. By the end of the 1990s around 70% of Pakistan's yarn production was coarse yarn cotton and only 3% fine and super-fine. Pakistan is one of the largest exporters of cotton yarn in the world, but its low value means that Pakistan captures only 5% of the export market. Pakistan remained a dominant producer of low-cost and low-quality cotton fabrics. In particular, textile yarn and its manufacture constituted between 71% and 85% of Pakistan's exports to its four major high-income trading partners (USA, UK, Germany and Japan) between 1990 and 1995 (Akhtar and Malik 2000). Lall (1999) demonstrated that the growth of world markets was higher for more technologically sophisticated products over the 1990s. Fitting this pattern, the growth rate of exports from Pakistan slowed from the 1980s to the 1990s, from 8.55% to 6.11% p.a., when measured in current prices (US$), and from 8.44% to 5.15% when measured in constant prices. Pakistan's share in the world export market increased from 0.18% in 1990 to 0.28% in 1997 (Husain 1999: 327; Zaidi 2005; Kemal *et al.* 2006: 284). The competitive and low-value-added niche in which Pakistan's textile firms remained led to them performing poorly on the stock market over the 1990s, with most textile units operating at a loss and not declaring any dividends (Khan 1998: 605).

Mahmood catalogues patterns of Revealed Comparative Advantage (RCA) for Pakistan between 1990 and 2000.[3] There are some reasons for optimism, and signs of sectors that may exhibit longer-term export growth. Over this period, 20 of the top 25 RCA products were labour intensive, and 20 of the 25 were from the textiles and clothing sector. The RCA for cotton is more than 70 (2004: 546). Some exports are 'competitively positioned'. These are exports with RCAs greater than unity and showing consistent improvement over time. Out of the 978 product lines examined, 222 are competitively positioned; 34.7% of these are from the textiles and clothing sector, and 23.9% from chemicals. There is some cause for optimism; the increasing specialisation in chemicals does reflect structural change in manufacturing towards more highly value added sectors. There are similar trends in other relatively skilled-labour and technology industries, such as base metals and articles, machinery and mechanical appliances, and measuring and musical instruments. In the main, these are traditional industries that continue to base their comparative position on low wages and easily available raw materials. 'Threatened product lines' have RCAs greater than unity, but the indices are declining over time. This includes 56 product lines, 6% of the total, a third of which are from the textiles and clothing sector. The most significant RCA decline occurred in jute products, which was likely due to extra government help being extended to producers in India and Bangladesh. Of some concern is the inclusion of sports goods in this section, which was a major export earner for Pakistan over the 1990s. 'Emerging products' are those with an RCA of less than unity, but improving their relative position in export markets. This may indicate a promise of future export potential. This includes 349 product lines, or 36% of the total, and includes relatively technologically advanced manufacturing sectors, such as chemical machinery and mechanical appliances, base metals and articles, and chemical products. 'Weakly positioned products' are those with an RCA of less than unity that is declining, and such products include those similar to the previous category, base metals and articles, chemicals sector, and machinery and mechanical appliances. The sectors with future export potential in the chemicals sector are important. The chemicals sector recorded total world trade of $595bn in 2001, and after a decade of rapid growth it has increased its share of world trade from 8.7% in 1990 to 9.9% in 2001.

Lower GDP growth rates were driven by factor accumulation, not productivity. Between 1972/73 to 1987/88 and 1987/88 to 2001/02 the contribution of factor accumulation to growth in manufacturing increased from 1.5% to 2.5%, in services from 5.2% to 5.5%, and for overall GDP from 3.1% to 3.6% (Sabir and Ahmed 2003: 9). The physical capital stock grew by 4.4% between 1991 and 1996, and by 3.7% between 1996 and 2001 (IMF 2002: 10). There is some indication that labour quality improved over this period. In absolute terms, the 1990s saw the best performance in improving literacy rates in post-independent Pakistan. Total literacy increased from 34.9% in 1990 to 47.1% in 1999/2000 (for males, from45.1 to 59% and for females, from 20.9 to 34.4%) (Zaidi 2005: 394). A measure of human capital grew by 3.0% between 1991 and 1996 and by 4.0% between 1996 and 2001 (IMF 2002: 10). In a sample of five large Asian countries, Pakistan is second only to Bangladesh (beating India, Nepal, Sri Lanka and India) in the contribution of improved labour quality to

GDP growth, at 0.51% (of the 4% growth in average GDP) between 1989 and 1995, and 0.45% between 1995 and 2003 (Srinivasan 2005: 494).

Growth of TFP slowed after the late 1980s, from 2.8% between 1972/73 and 1987/88 to 0.7% between 1987/88 and 2001/02 (Sabir and Ahmed 2003: 9). Slow growth of TFP over the 1990s is confirmed by other studies: 0.7% (Pasha *et al.* 2002: 6); 0.6% (Khan 2005: 391); 0.78% (Kemal *et al.* 2006: 333). Other estimates show a fall in TFP growth over the 1990s: from 0.6% between 1991 and 1996 to -0.5% between 1996 and 2001 (IMF 2002: 10); or from 0.76% between 1989 and 1995 to 0.52% between 1995 and 2003 (Srinivasan 2005: 494). Estimates for manufacturing are quite close: 1.4% (Pasha *et al.* 2002: 7); 1.9% (Sabir and Ahmed 2003: 9); and 1.64% (Kemal *et al.* 2006: 333). Estimates for agriculture are more mixed: 1.7% (Chaudhry *et al.* 1996: 53); 4.2% (Pasha *et al.* 2002: 7); 2.6% (Sabir and Ahmed 2003: 9); and 1.52% (Kemal *et al.* 2006: 333).

The (political) role of the state, 1992/93 to 2002/03: institutions

This third section focuses on institutions that may or may not allow the state to overcome the inherent conflicts associated with economic growth. The relative autonomy of the state declined drastically over the 1990s, and party politics led to an upsurge in uncontrolled and chaotic factionalism that undermined the clarity and coherence of policy making. The main political parties frequently turned to the military to find allies in their political struggle; this undermined the institutionalisation of democracy. Inclusionary or ideological institutions to manage conflict were non-existent. Pakistan over the 1990s was locked into a destructive episode of stagnation with no internal means to exit.

Institutions to manage conflict: autonomy and repression

It was hoped that the democracy, in conjunction with a new generation of young leaders, would be able to achieve the greater degree of consensus in the operation of the political system necessary to establish the autonomy of the elected political/civil institutions over the bureaucratic-military oligarchy (Malik 1996). Instead, both the PPP and Muslim League turned to alliances outside the political system, often but not always the military, in order to find allies in their struggle with each other. The military's intelligence apparatus was adept at alternately encouraging, offering to help, and exploiting divisions between the political actors (Siddiqa 2007). The Muslim League in particular co-operated with the IJI to destabilise PPP governments. After winning the 1993 elections, the PPP government was faced with widespread street protests by the religious political parties (who themselves gained 8% of the vote and 3 out of 327 national assembly seats). The PPP did not seek alliance with moderates either from within the democratic political system or among other Islamic groups to, for example, repeal the Hudood Ordinance, but, rather, appeared to compete with the extremists in being ever more confrontational over Kashmir (Malik 1996), and using (rather than repealing) blasphemy laws to intimidate religious minorities (Talbot 1998). Despite its evident promise for consolidating democracy, both the PPP and Muslim League failed to co-operate on a vote to repeal the Eighth Amendment of the 1973 constitution, for fear that the one would use it to consolidate their own rule at the other's expense. During the 1990s the MQM often held the balance of political power in the centre. For example, in the 1988 national elections, the PPP won 93 seats (from 207), the IJI 55 and the MQM 13. Competitive wooing of the MQM by the PPP and IJI eventually contributed to an escalation of violence in Karachi. This absent autonomy can be seen in the process of law making. The uncontrolled factionalism of the national assembly meant that parliament had little role as a legislative body, and most bills were enacted through Presidential Ordinance (Talbot 1998). Autonomy was only ever discovered briefly during the non-democratic interludes of the 1990s. The various caretaker governments between elected governments tended to be noted for quite vigorous policy reform. In 1993 Moeen Qureshi (a former World Bank official) was imported as caretaker Prime Minister. His government introduced major economic reforms. These included operational autonomy for the SBP, the introduction of an agricultural income tax, a 6% devaluation of the rupee, and the removal of subsidies on ghee, flour and fertilisers. Incoming democratic governments tended to undo many such reforms when the moment of autonomy passed.

Democracy began in 1988 under a substantial khaki shadow. Hours before Benazir's inauguration as Prime Minister, Pakistan signed an agreement with the IMF. Benazir was permitted to take office on condition that she accepted the agreement. Benazir's government was likewise forced to relinquish control over important policy decisions, especially the control of the Afghan Jihad and administration of the military, accept Sahibzadah Yaqub Khan as Foreign Minister, and promise support to Ishtaq Khan in his bid to stay on as President (Nasr 1992). The democratic parts of the political system achieved their greatest opportunity for autonomy in 1996. The Muslim League then won 134 seats out of 204, including 107 from the Punjab. This gave Nawaz the two-thirds majority necessary to change the constitution. In April 1997 the 13th Amendment was passed by the two parliamentary chambers, which overturned four Articles of the Eighth Amendment. These related to the appointment of military leaders, the President's power to dissolve the national assembly, the governor's power to dissolve provincial assemblies, and consultation of the Prime Minister before nominating governors. awaz went further than securing autonomy for democratic actors in general and sought to cement his specific rule. The PPP was swamped with court cases. The Supreme Court was reduced from 17 to 12 members to curb its powers. The President was forced to resign and was replaced by Rafiq Tarar (a family friend) (Jaffrelot 2002).

Weinbaum (1996) argues that this entire 'democratic' era was marked by a 'crisis of authority', in which the opposition saw any government in power as illegitimate, both for how it gained office and the way it used power. The opposition would turn to religious extremists or the military to effect a non-democratic removal of the government. Those in office typically saw opposition to their government as akin to treason and used legal sanctions and court convictions, rather than political debate, to censor them. Between winning the national election in October 1993 and December 1995, for example, 140 cases of corruption had been filed against Nawaz Sharif and his family

(Shafqat 1996). In the process, democratic norms never took root, and politicians continually subordinated democracy to their own short-term ambitions for office.

The lack of relative autonomy and the inability to manage conflict can be seen in the incapacity of policymakers to implement policy over the 1990s. The 1996 annual transparency report rated Pakistan 54th from a sample of 55 countries. Governments were dismissed for incompetence and corruption in 1990, 1993 and 1996; no government filled a five-year mandate (Burki 1999). This was reflected in the declining capacity of the state to intervene meaningfully. Earlier, this chapter noted that the productivity of state development spending declined over the decade. This was also true of state social spending. There were declines (despite higher spending) in school enrolment and access to piped drinking water (Hasnain 2008). The Social Action Programme, which ran from 1992 to 2000, was the most concerted effort in the country's history to improve service delivery. Over these years the government and donor community spent a total of $9bn on the programme, with very poor results. In general, Pakistan improved its social indicators at a much slower rate than other countries with similar income levels (Easterly 2001b).

Institutions to manage conflict: inclusionary

Pakistan never managed to define an identity as part of which its inhabitants could be included. Ayub Khan tried 'modernisation' in the 1960s, Bhutto 'Islamic Socialism'; in the 1970s, and Zia 'Islamisation' in the 1980s. Without a constructive means for inclusion, and faced with a 'Pandora's box/of conflicting regional and linguistic identities', Pakistan's military-bureaucracy attempted to impose Pakistani nationalism from above. Three factors emerged as important, the tendency to regard all dissent as a law and order problem rather than a political issue, the manipulation and repression of popular forces by successive authoritarian regimes, and the uneven relationship between the Punjab and other regions (Talbot 1998). Another solution briefly flared in the 1990s, but well-institutionalised political parties failed to emerge. Political parties have the capacity to absorb diverse groups into the organisation and, once inside, to subject and socialise them and their leaders to the processes of hierarchy, consensus, compromise and coalition building. The PPP and Muslim League over the 1990s were not organised political parties, but unstable and temporary amalgams of groups based on shifting allegiances and personality organised around temporary patron-client ties (Talbot 1998). The recognition of this potential and, for Pakistan in the 1990s, actual role of party politics was subject to a very insightful empirical study by Hasnain (2008). Between 1988 and 1999 Pakistan experienced its longest democratic interlude, yet social services for the majority of voters (the poor) showed negligible improvement. Elected politicians over the 1990s seemed adept at providing patronage/targeted favours to small numbers of privileged groups, rather than providing general public goods that would benefit the majority of citizens, such as clean water or literacy, improving basic education. In Sindh, for example, there was a substantial increase in the number of teachers, but a decline in measures of educational quality. Hasnain (2008) found, using state-level data, that the higher the levels of fragmentation, factionalism, and polarisation, the greater the incentives for patronage and the poorer quality of general service delivery. His model explained both the low level of provision of general public goods and also the variability in provision across space. The party fragmentation of the 1990s increased the informational demand on voters, since there were more candidates and more messages to evaluate during election time, making it harder to link an improvement in service delivery with a particular politician. This increased the incentives on politicians to provide targeted benefits, rather than general public goods. Party organisation of the PPP and others was highly personalised, and those close to the leadership assumed positions of responsibility, rather than those winning internal elections. This personalisation promoted factionalism. Such factionalism did not provide party members with stable career prospects, and so politicians had a greater incentive to focus on targeted public goods to build a personal reputation that would carry across party lines. There was a high degree of candidate churning in Pakistani politics over the 1990s. A significant number of incumbents changed constituency or competed as members of other parties in provincial assemblies. This gave incumbents an incentive to establish a reputation for themselves among voters that transcended party identity and so created incentives to focus on particularised benefits. Party factionalisation was linked to the provision of targeted, rather than general, public goods. In more ethnically divided parts of Pakistan the provision of general public services would have provided fewer political benefits than targeted benefits to particular ethnic groups. So again, polarisation was linked to the provision of targeted, rather than general, public goods.

Institutions to manage conflict: ideological

The PPP in its early incarnation offered an inclusionary ideology. Soon after acquiring office in the early 1970s it was flooded with new members from the landed elite; they were welcomed, and with them their dependents, to cement PPP power in rural Pakistan. In response, the left ideologues were purged. Zia subsequently put a lot of effort into his ideology of 'Islamisation', perhaps more sincere than Bhutto's socialism and longer lasting, but it was likewise unsuccessful. Over the 1990s the PPP had a tendency to append 'People's' to any patronage-orientated policy (such as the 'People's Work Programme') that in practice is designed to effect political transfers to build political support. The Muslim League has generally promised little more than patronage and a more competent and mildly more technocratic approach to government.

The most obvious social phenomenon in Pakistan today, argues Zaidi (2005), is a vibrant middle-class revolution. This transformation, he argues, has killed off any remnants of an encompassing ideology and redefined cultural, political, social and economic practices, identities and relationships. Consumerism, he notes, has spread rapidly to the smaller rural and semi-urban towns in Sindh, Punjab, and NWFP. The failed state has been replaced by private sector provision of education, health and security. Though this has heralded a move away from regionalism and nationalism into a more articulate and composite Pakistani identity, it marks 'an evolving, immature, crude, greedy, selfish, narrow-minded middle class, whose only pursuit is self-interest' (Zaidi 2005: 506).

One exception to this general trend was the MQM. After their formation in 1984 the MQM represented one of the most successful political formations in South Asia.

Historically, the Mohajir community was a loose affiliation of disparate groups that traced their presence in Pakistan to migration at the time of partition. The MQM are an extremely well institutionalised, highly disciplined and even semi-fascistic organisation. The MQM have been highly successful in mobilising the Mohajir community around issues of discrimination in employment and admission to educational institutions, and persecution by the provincial government (composed of native Sindhis) and by the Punjabi-dominated federal bureaucracy and army. This search for identity reached its climax in 1986–88, when the MQM launched a crusade through regular ideological meetings. The MQM have dominated the politics of urban Sindh since winning power in 1988. They have attained the status of creating a state within a state, but are constrained by their very specific appeal in spreading their dominance outside power centres like Karachi (Jalal 1995; Ahmar 1996).

9 An episode of growth, 2003/04–2008/09

Summary of chapter findings

The chapter is divided into three parts, each focusing on one particular role that the state has in promoting economic growth. These relate to finance, production and institutions. The underlying hypothesis here is that the state needs to be successful in all three to initiate and sustain an episode of growth.

The first section shows that the state was relatively successful in mobilising a surplus after 2003/04. The government was successful in raising savings, reducing current expenditure and imports, managing domestic and external debt, raising public and private corporate profitability and boosting public investment. These efforts faded noticeably as this episode wore on. The second section examines the role of the state in achieving a productive use of the surplus in both the public and private sectors. There were signs of efficiency and productivity improving from the very low levels achieved in the 1990s, but this improvement at most represented a better performance in the low-value-added end of traditional export markets, rather than upgrading to higher-value-added niches. The third section focuses on institutions that may or may not allow the state to overcome the inherent conflicts associated with economic growth. After 1999 the government passed power to a team of technocrats with the capacity and commitment to implement reforms. The best evidence of the new-found autonomy of policy makers was that, for the first time in its history, Pakistan was able to complete the 2000 standby arrangement with the IMF without delay or interruption. This section shows that the military coup temporarily strengthened institutions of autonomy and repression, but that this effect declined over time and there was no corresponding creation of inclusive institutions; hence, the episode of growth was ultimately unsustainable and would likely have faded even without the global financial crisis of 2008–10.

Recap from Chapter 3

The statistical analysis in Chapter 3 showed that GDP growth averaged 5.9% p.a. between 2003/04 and 2008/09. There was a gradual acceleration in the growth rate: starting in 2002–03 the rate of GDP increased, and eventually reached 9.0% in

2004/05. The government maintained that 2004/05 marked a significant break with the past and had set the economy on a new trajectory of growth (Burki 2007: 20). Such assertions are based on favourable changes in other macroeconomic aggregates. In 2003/04 inflation fell to the lowest level in 15 years, fiscal deficits to the lowest level in 20 years, remittances rose to record highs, exports crossed $10bn, and the stock market reached record highs (Zaidi 2005). Other authors question the sustainability of this 'episode', noting that rapid growth after 2003 rested on domestic consumption, not investment or exports (Burki 2007). Growth of agriculture remained positive through this episode, manufacturing growth peaked in 2004/05, slowed, then declined in 2008/09, and service sector growth was robust and positive throughout. After a sharp slowdown at the end of this episode, growth recovered in 2009/10. Between 2003/03 and 2008/09 the share of agriculture in GDP declined from 24.0% to 21.8%, that of manufacturing increased and that of services increased very slightly.

Limitations of alternative explanations

There are two debates about this apparent turnaround. One can be called 'the tough decisions hypothesis', which emphasises the successes of the Musharaff government after the military coup in 1999 in taking politically unpopular decisions that were to the collective (growth) benefit. The second, the 'good luck' hypothesis, emphasises in particular the suddenly favourable geo-political position in which Pakistan found itself after 11th September 2001. This, goes the argument, led to a dramatic improvement in Pakistan's external resource situation, and its economy floated upwards on a sea of capital inflow on very favourable terms. There has not yet been any effort to rigorously test these two hypotheses. The framework developed in this book does offer such a possibility. If the 'tough decisions hypothesis' were true, we should expect to see that the state around 2003 was better able to mobilise resources, both domestic and external, was better able to utilise those resources productively and had formed or revived institutions able to manage the conflict associated with development. Were the 'good luck' hypothesis to be correct, we would expect to see the greater mobilisation of resources to be an external, not a domestic phenomenon, and no change in the ability of the state to ensure that those resources were utilised more productively or any change in the ability of institutions to manage conflict.

The (economic) role of the state, 2003/04 to 2008/09: finance

This section shows that the state was relatively successful in mobilising a surplus after 2003/04. The government was successful in raising savings, reducing current expenditure and imports, managing domestic and external debt, raising public and private corporate profitability and boosting public investment. These efforts faded noticeably as this episode wore on. This section therefore offers some, if weak, support for the 'tough decisions hypothesis'.

The mobilisation of savings

Total savings rates were stagnant, or even slowly declining in the late 1990s (Husain 2003; Lorie and Iqbal 2005). National savings then increased rapidly, from 16.5% of GDP in 2000/01, to 18.6% in 2001/02, and a peak of 20.8% in 2002/03; they remained higher than in the 1990s, but slowly declined to 17.4% in 2006/07, then fell more rapidly with the economic problems at the end of this growth episode to reach only 14.3% in 2008/09 (Government of Pakistan 2009: 15).

The role of the state in mobilising domestic savings

The government made significant efforts to tackle problems with tax collection. A new Income Tax Ordinance was introduced in 2001, which allowed for self-assessment, more uniform tax rates, removal of non-adjustable withholding taxes, elimination of exemptions and detailed audit. A simultaneous tax survey and documentation drive in 1999/2000 generated an extra 134,000 income taxpayers and 30,000 new sales taxpayers. The Central Board of Revenues, long mired in inefficiency, corruption, lack of accountability, and excessive discretionary power, was reformed into a new system where contact between tax collectors and taxpayers was reduced, and the overall process was increasingly computerised and adjudication procedures were simplified (Husain 2003). These efforts had no positive effect on tax revenue: while total government revenue declined slightly from 14.8% of GDP in 2002/03 to 14.5% in 2008/09, tax revenue declined considerably, from 11.4% to 9.5% over the same years (Government of Pakistan 2010).

There were good indications that current expenditures were more successfully controlled over the early years of this episode. Current expenditure declined from 16.2% of GDP in 2002/03 to 13.3% in 2004/05, then increased steadily to 16.0% in 2008/09. Development expenditure did increase, but not by much, from 2.2% of GDP in 2002/03 to a peak of 4.9% in 2006/07, before falling again to 3.8% in 2008/09 (Government of Pakistan 2010). Oddly, given that there was a military government in power, defence expenditure declined steadily. Official defence expenditure declined from 4.8% of GDP (25.3% of revenues) in 1998/99, to 3.8% (19.6%) in 2002/03 (Husain 2003: 137). Some of this reflected an accounting exercise, whereby military pensions were moved out of the defence budget, which reduced recorded defence spending (Siddiqa 2007: 207). The decline continued from 18.1% of current expenditure in 2002/03, to 12.2% in 2007/08. From being 20% higher than development spending at the beginning of this episode, defence spending fell to two-thirds the level of development spending by the end. The biggest change was debt servicing, which consumed 52.5% of total government expenditure in 2001/02, declined to 24.4% in 2005/06, then slowly increased to 34.8% by 2008/09 (Government of Pakistan 2010: 59).

The reduction in the government budget deficit pre-dated this episode and showed improvement in its early years. Between 1999/2000 and 2002/03 the ratio of total public sector debt servicing to tax revenue declined from 90.3% to 54.8%, and to total expenditure from 71.5% to 42.3%. Total debt declined from 104.7% to 95.1% of GDP, domestic debt from 50.2% to 46.1%, external debt from 53.5% to 48%, and explicit liabilities from 2.4% to 1.0% over the same years (Zaidi 2005: 245). The deficit fell to a low of 2.3% in 2003/04, and then increased steadily to 7.6% in 2007/08. The negative rates of public saving from the 1990s were briefly reversed between 2003/04 and 2007/08, but never amounted to more than about 1% of GDP, and by 2007/08 the government had lurched back into public savings of -3.2% (Government of Pakistan 2010).

The role of the state in creating institutions to mobilise private sector savings

Liberalisation over the 1990s had led to substantial new bank entry. By 2003 14 new domestic private commercial banks and 16 private investment banks had been established, and 19 foreign commercial banks were operating in the country. Of the five big nationalised commercial banks, three had been privatised, and privatisation of the Habib bank was promised by the end of 2003, while 10% of the National Bank of Pakistan was floated on the stock exchange (Husain 2003). The emphasis during the Musharraf period was less on expanding the size and reach of the banking system, but rather on its quality. In particular, efforts were made to strengthen the capacity of the SBP for supervision and prudential regulation. The SBP implemented a computerised reporting system in exchange and debt management departments to monitor foreign exchange and money markets. The government also attempted to improve corporate governance and rules governing disclosure and transparency so as to assure the credibility of banks' financial statements. Banks were required to prepare financial statements in accordance with international accounting standards. The SBP made credit ratings compulsory for all banks and NBFIs from July 2001. Pakistan also moved to the Basle system of defining minimum capital requirements for banks (Husain 2003). As a complement, the licensing and regulatory environment for microcredit and rural financial institutions was relaxed; unlike commercial banks, these could be set up at district, provincial and national level, with varying capital requirements. By 2003 Khushali Bank (formed by domestic and foreign banks) and First Microfinance Bank had been set up (Husain 2003). New instruments to attract private savings were created. After long being neglected, the SBP made efforts to develop markets for long-term capital, launching, for example, the Pakistan Investment Bonds with maturity up to ten years, for which regular auctions took place. A market for corporate bonds also began to emerge (Husain 2003).

The reforms of the savings institutions gave investors confidence to re-intermediate savings, and measures of financial depth showed striking increases in these years. One measure of financial depth is broad money[1] divided by nominal GDP lagged by one year. Financial depth declined steadily, from 39.20% in 1990 to 36.70% in 2001, after which it began rapidly rising to 43.10% in 2003 and 49.20% in 2004. Deducting currency in circulation from this total may give a better measure of financial depth (as opposed to monetisation). This measure showed a steady decline from 1970 to 1990, and only exceeded its 1970s level in 2002, after which it rose rapidly (Khan et al. 2005: 824). The ratio of broad money to GDP increased from 32.27% in 1990 to 38.59% in 2000, then more rapidly to 46.99% in 2003. Total bank deposit liabilities (liquid liabilities minus currency in circulation) increased from 27.91% of GDP in 1990 to 37.51% in 2000, then declined to 30.43% in 2003 (Khan and Qayyum 2007: 15).

The role of the state in influencing stock markets

Efforts to revitalise the Karachi Stock Exchange (KSE) occurred in the early 2000s, following on from substantial reforms of capital markets in the 1990s. There were significant reforms in the areas of risk management, governance, transparency, and investor protection. The capabilities of the Securities and Exchange Commission of Pakistan were strengthened. New codes of conduct for dealers raised the net capital requirements for brokers, and established rules against insider trading and regulations to provide for mergers, acquisitions, takeovers, and liquidation of public listed companies. An acceleration of privatisation deepened and broadened the capital market. Between 2001 and 2005 the KSE index (end of year) increased from 1273.07 to 9556.61, and the daily turnover in share trading more than trebled, though the number of listed companies declined from 747 to 661 (Husain 2003; Hameed and Ashraf 2006). There was no change in the number of companies listed by 2008/09 (Government of Pakistan 2010: 172). The growth of the stock market contributed at the margin to the mobilisation of resources. Primary mobilisation raised new capital for firms equal to 1.9% of GDP in 2003/04, 1.0% in 2007/08 and 0.8% in 2008/09. In each year, it was barely a quarter of bank lending. However, in 2008/09 bank lending dried up almost completely (0.14% of GDP), and more was raised through the stock market (Government of Pakistan 2010: 175).

The role of the state in managing flows of FDI

There are few empirical studies of its impact, but it is reasonable to presume that FDI inflows were beneficial to Pakistan during this episode. FDI remained (for Pakistan) relatively high, at $3,305.9bn in 2007/08 and $3,042.1bn in 2008/09. The bulk of this was in infrastructure. In oil and gas explorations and communications, annual FDI inflows ranged between $400m. and $900m. p.a. Energy and telecommunications had been important constraints by the late 1990s, so this was probably desirable. Annual inflows of between $600m. and $940m. in financial business helped deepen the financial sector, as noted previously. There were minimal FDI inflows into the more directly productive sectors, such as textiles (around $25m. p.a.) and cement ($30–80m. p.a.) (Government of Pakistan 2009: 15).

The role of the state in mobilising foreign savings

By the end of the 1990s servicing the stock of debt crowded out other forms of public expenditure, and it consumed over 50% of budgetary revenues. Annual external debt service payments of $6–7bn were required every year (for a total external debt of almost $38bn by mid 2001), which was equivalent to two-thirds of export earnings.

After 11th September 2001, Pakistan gave assurances that it would help the USA in Afghanistan against the Taleban. This led to the rapid resumption of financial aid ties with the USA, World Bank and IMF, relations that had been suspended after Pakistan's nuclear tests in 1998. Musharraf was welcomed back into the international fold, and dozens of leaders visited Islamabad. On 23rd September President Bush waived key sanctions, and the USA voted in favour of the IMF negotiating a Poverty Reduction and

Growth Strategy with Pakistan that had been opposed a few days before (Zaidi 2005). In December 2001 relief was granted to the entire stock of $12.5bn debt owed to the Paris Club (18 key creditor countries). Pakistan benefited from lower interest rates and extended repayment periods. The net present value of the debt stock was consequently reduced by 50%, which saved $1.2–1.5bn in annual servicing costs after 2001.

There is one strand of thought that sees growth after 2002/03 as being dependent on this resumption of capital inflows and part of a longer term argument that sees growth in Pakistan as being ultimately dependent on favourable relations with the USA (Ali 2008).

There is more to the story than the vagaries of US goodwill. 11th September did lead to a dramatic shift in Pakistan's relations with the outside world that facilitated significant capital inflow. However, the strategy to reduce the burden of debt pre-dated 2001. In January 1999 the Paris Club had rescheduled $3.3bn of debt under the Houston terms; debt servicing and arrears were postponed. Between 1999/2000 and 2001/02 the government re-paid $4.5bn of commercial and short-term debt and made considerable efforts to build up foreign exchange reserves. The external position had been improving since 1999; 11th September accelerated an existing trend. Between 1999/2000 and 2001/02, the trade gap declined from $1.6bn to $1.2bn, and the current account shifted from a deficit of $1.9bn to a surplus of $2.7bn (Husain 2003; Zaidi 2005). There was a sudden surge in remittances from the USA, from $80m. in 1999/2000 to $1.2–1.7bn p.a. after 2001/02. Some have argued that this was a one-off shift in portfolios in response to tighter banking regulations in the USA after 11th September. The remittances from the USA continued unabated throughout this episode. Others have argued that much of this represented remittances from more established professionals in the USA, who were making economic investments in Pakistan (Burki 2007: 260). Higher oil prices towards the end of this episode led to higher remittances from the more traditional Gulf countries, in particular Saudi Arabia and UAE. This again was not related to 11th September. Total remittances increased from $2,389m. in 2001/02 to $7,811m. in 2008/09, or from 3.3% of GDP to 4.8%.

The trade deficit declined rapidly after the mid-1990s, from 5.7% of GDP in 1996/97 to 1.3% in 2002/03, and the surge in remittance income led to a surplus on current account between 2001/02 and 2003/04. This represented little more than a temporary blip. The main reason for the improvement was a temporary decline in imports, from 19.1% of GDP in 1996/97 to 14.8% in 2002/03. Exports remained unchanged at 12%–13% of GDP. After this date exports stagnated, falling to 10.9% of GDP in 2008/09, and imports surged to 21.5% of GDP in 2008/09. Increased remittances were not enough, and the economy faced a huge (5%–6%) current account deficit by the end of this period. Not surprisingly, whether measured relative to GDP, foreign exchange earnings, or foreign exchange reserves, there were signs that Pakistan's external debt situation was worsening towards the end of this episode (Government of Pakistan 2010: Ch8).

The role of the state in influencing private and public sector profitability

Public enterprise losses were substantially (around one-third of the total) responsible for the high fiscal deficits in the late 1990s and a large proportion of the bad debts of the state owned banks. Particularly large losses were made by WAPDA, KESC, Railways, PIA, Steel Mills, and the nationalised commercial banks. The government after 2000 successfully pushed Pakistan Steel, the Railways and PIA towards profitability. WAPDA and KESC continued to run up losses equal to around 1% of GDP (Husain 2003). One key reason for improved profitability was that the imports and pricing of petroleum products were linked to international prices (Husain 2003). This process continued throughout this episode, and between 2006/07 and 2007/08, despite declining output, public sector enterprises managed to increase profits by 160% on the back of only a 5% increase in sales (Government of Pakistan 2008: 52).

After 1999 Habib and United Banks underwent major restructuring, whilst still in the state sector, and by 2003 50% of staff had been retrenched, 600 branches closed and the cost to income ratio substantially reduced. The government set up an asset management company, the Corporate and Industrial Restructuring Corporation (CIRC), to deal with the NPLs of national commercial banks and DFIs. A loan recovery drive collected $500m. from the forced repayment of loans up to 2001/02. The overall health of the financial sector improved sharply, as was evident in measures of capital adequacy, asset quality, and profitability, and liquidity indicators. Nationalised commercial banks brought down their NPLs from 36.8% of total advances in June 1998 to 25% in June 2002 (Husain 2003).

Lorie and Iqbal argue that there was a significant improvement in the financial performance of the corporate sector (both private and public) after 2001. Between 2001 and 2003 the after-tax profits of corporations listed on the Karachi Stock Exchange rose by 1% of GDP. This improvement in profitability, they argue, was principally derived from efficiency gains and 'augured well for the sustainability of high growth rates' (2005: 3–4). This improvement was from a low base. In 2008, of 209 cotton and other textile firms listed on the KSE, only 69 were profit making and 37 paying dividends. Chemical and pharmaceutical firms had 34 listings, of which 26 were profit making and 20 dividend paying; for sugar and allied sectors, the figures were 37, 21 and 11, respectively (Government of Pakistan 2010: 174).

The role of the state in allocating resources to projects essential for development

Public investment showed a general upward trend over this episode, from 4.0% in 2002/03 to a peak of 5.6% in 2006/07, then a decline to 4.9% in 2008/09 (Government of Pakistan 2009: 15). Given the general finding that public investment has a positive impact on private investment (Khan 1988; Hyder 2001; Naqvi 2002; Ahmed and Qayyam 2007), the very similar patterns for private investment are not unexpected. Private investment increased from 11.3% in 2002/03 to a peak of 15.7% in 2005/06, then fell to 13.2% in 2008/09. Including stock changes, total investment in Pakistan broke through 20% of GDP for the first time since the mid-1960s (Government of Pakistan 2009: 15).

The government also acted to push the private sector to increase productive investment. Throughout the 1990s the commercial banks retained a large amount of liquidity and invested in safe government securities over and above the minimum levels they were required to. A key reason for this was the high interest payments on NSS. After 2000, banks and other financial institutions were barred from investing in the NSS and were forced to make resources available to the private sector (Burki 2007).

While focusing more on infrastructure, the government drew back from more directly productive investment. Traditionally, long-term investment in industry had been financed through public sector-owned and -managed Development Finance Institutions (DFIs). After 1999 the government shifted to a more market-based financial system, founded on banks and capital markets. Eleven existing DFIs were restructured through mergers, closure, liquidation and reorganisation. The largest DFI, the National Development Finance Corporation, was shut down, and its liabilities taken over by the NBP. Publicly owned DFIs were phased out, and PICIC, for example, became a privately owned company (Husain 2003).

The (economic) role of the state, 2003/04 to 2008/09: production

This second section examines the role of the state in achieving a productive use of the surplus in both the public and private sectors. Pessimistic views about the nature of growth, that it was solely consumption-led after 2003, are misplaced, as investment and exports at times continued to make important contributions. Growth was quite broad based, and services and industry grew relatively rapidly. Growth was supported by an emerging demographic dividend. There were signs of efficiency and productivity improving from the very low levels achieved in the 1990s, but this improvement at most represented a better performance in the low-value-added end of traditional export markets, rather than upgrading to higher-value-added niches. At most this provided weak evidence for the 'tough decisions' hypothesis outlined at the beginning of this chapter.

Sources of growth: domestic and international sources

Burki argues that the boom after 2003 rested on weak foundations, as it was based on consumption, not investment (2007:29). Lorie and Iqbal argue that growth that had been mainly export led before 2003/04 was thereafter largely domestic led, relying particularly on consumer demand (2005).

Table 9.1 shows that there was some truth in this view, though it was unduly pessimistic. The contribution of consumption (and investment) was very low between 2000/01 and 2002/03; net exports were indeed responsible for about half of GDP growth over this period. Between 2003/04 and 2005/06 consumption and, to a lesser extent, investment become important in driving GDP growth. Private consumption leads for the first two years, then public consumption. By 2006/07 investment has become the most important contributor to GDP growth. The contribution of investment belies the pessimism of Burki and Lorie and Iqbal. The slowdown in 2007/08 is mitigated by strong growth in public consumption, and the revival of 2008/09 is then dependent on private consumption but also on net exports.

Table 9.1 Composition of GDP growth (point contribution)

Flows	2000/01	2001/02	2002/03	2003/04	2004/05	2005/06	2006/07	2007/08	2008/09
Private consumption	0.4	1.0	0.3	7.1	8.7	0.8	3.4	-0.9	3.6
Public consumption	-0.5	1.2	0.6	0.1	0.1	3.9	-1.1	3.8	-1.8
Total consumption (C)	-0.1	2.2	0.9	7.2	9.4	4.7	2.3	2.9	1.8
Gross fixed investment	0.7	-0.1	0.6	-1.0	1.8	2.9	2.6	0.7	-1.2
Change in stocks	0.0	0.0	0.4	0.1	0.1	0.1	0.1	0.1	-0.1
Total investment (I)	0.7	0.0	1.1	-0.9	2.0	2.9	2.7	0.7	-1.2
Exports (goods and services) X	1.6	1.5	4.5	-0.3	1.7	1.8	0.4	-1.0	1.5
Imports (goods and services) M	0.3	0.4	1.6	-1.3	5.4	3.2	-0.5	0.6	-1.6
Net exports (X-M)	1.3	1.0	2.8	1.0	-3.7	-1.5	1.0	-1.6	3.2
Aggregate demand (C+I+X)	2.3	3.7	6.5	6.0	13.0	9.4	5.5	2.6	2.1
Domestic demand (C+I)	0.7	2.2	2.0	6.3	11.3	7.6	5.0	3.6	0.6
GDP MP	2.0	3.2	4.8	7.4	7.7	6.2	6.0	2.0	3.7

Source: Government of Pakistan 2008: 9, 2009: 12.

Sources of growth: services and industry

Table 9.2 shows that the principal sources of growth over this episode were services and also industry (manufacturing in particular). Growth slowed notably in 2007/08 and 2008/09, though GDP growth remained positive, unlike in many other countries in Asia. Service growth was quite robust.

Sources of growth: demographic dividend

The crude birth rate in Pakistan peaked at about 45 (per 1,000) in the late 1970s to early 1980s, and declined to 30 by 2006; by 2050 it is expected to be 16. The crude death rate declined from 24 in 1950 to approximately 8 by 2006, and is projected to continue declining to 2045. Population growth rates peaked in the 1980s, at around 3.5%; this declined to about 2% by 2006, and is forecast to fall further to 0.78% in 2050. These changes resulted in the proportion of the population that is of working age (15–64 years) rising from 52% in the late 1980s/early 1990s to 59% in 2006. This share is forecast to peak at 68% in 2045. The median age of the population in 2006 was only 20. The total labour force is forecast to increase from 175m. to 221m. This demographic dividend represents an enormous potential. The higher numbers of workers need to be absorbed by the labour market. The female labour force participation rate does show a slight increasing trend, but has continued to remain low over the last decade (Nayab 2006: 13). The impact on savings (and hence investment) works through the proposition that the working age population produce more than they consume (savings). Various studies in the Pakistan context have shown an inverse relation between the dependency ratio and savings (Khan et al. 1992; Siddiqui and Siddiqui 1993; Iqbal 1993) and one study has shown no relation (Husain 1996). A larger workforce will require relevant skills to be fully productive. In Pakistan currently, only about half the population is literate, and only 2.6% are educated up to graduate level; there are also strong concerns about the quality of education (Nayab 2006).

Evaluation of efficiency, 2003/04 to 2008/09

A lot of the growth during this episode was taking up enormous inefficient slack that had emerged in the economy during the years of slow, inefficient and low productivity growth of the 1990s. Even as late as 2008/09, Pakistani industry was running a long

Table 9.2 Sectoral contribution to GDP growth (%)

Sector	2002/03	2003/04	2004/05	2005/06	2006/07	2007/08	2008/09
Agriculture	1.0	0.6	1.5	1.4	0.8	0.24	1.00
Industry	1.0	3.8	3.1	1.1	2.1	0.45	-0.92
Manufacturing	1.1	2.3	2.7	1.6	1.5	0.91	-0.64
Services	2.7	3.1	4.4	3.3	3.9	3.41	1.92
Real GDP	4.7	7.5	9.0	5.8	6.8	4.10	2.00

Source: Government of Pakistan 2008: 8, 2009: 11.

way below capacity. Production, for example, was 63,273 units in cars (installed capacity 275,000), buses 408 (5,000), trucks 2,169 (28,500), and tractors 41,661 (65,000) (Government of Pakistan 2010: 49).

Textiles remained the key economic sector in Pakistan. In 2006/07 textiles accounted for 61.1% of exports, 46% of manufacturing output, 38% of manufacturing employment, and 8.5% of GDP. Over this episode the government made a substantial effort to promote the textile sector, launching the 'Textile Vision Strategy 2005' in 2000. The government established a separate Ministry of Textiles, launched a programme to reduce contamination in raw cotton, reduced tariffs on textile machinery imports to 5%, reduced sales tax and import duties on raw materials to zero, and gave a lot of direct assistance to promoting textile-related R&D. In response, imports of textile machinery reached $928.6m. in 2004/05, before declining to $212.0m. in 2008/09 (Government of Pakistan 2010: 46). Between 2002/03 and 2008/09 the number of cotton textile mills increased from 363 to 369 (down from 437 in 2005/06), the number of spindles from 9,216,000 to 10,514,000, the number of spindles working from 7,623,000 to 9,375,000, and total cloth production from 576.6m.sq mtr to 1,019.2m.sq mtr) (Government of Pakistan 2010). Output growth was thus combined, with the capacity utilisation of spindles increasing from 82.7 to 89%. Further attempts to promote the sector with soft loans and various export and other incentives for upgrading were undermined by IMF opposition expressed through the conditions attached to structural adjustment lending. The ambitious textile export promotion strategy was abandoned. Lorie and Iqbal argue that there were some more general signs of increased efficiency as measured by a decline in the capital-output ratio (2005).

There is little evidence that Pakistan was able to upgrade into higher-value-added sectors in exports. In effect, Pakistan resumed output growth near the bottom end of the textile market. Exports of textiles increased from $4,532m. in 2000 to $7,3186m. in 2008. Exports of clothing increased slightly from 47% to 53% of textile exports. Pakistan had not shared in the relative boom in clothing relative to textile exports more generally. World clothing exports had been the same as that of textiles in 1990, but, by 2008, clothing exports were 50% higher (Government of Pakistan 2010: 43). Between 2002/03 and 2008/09 the share of cotton manufacturers in total exports declined steadily from 63.3% to 52.2%. Again, there were no indications of diversification into higher-value-added exports. These high-value-added exports include leather, whose share of total exports declined from 6.2% to 5.4%, synthetic textiles, from 6.2% to 5.4%, and sports goods, from 3.0% to 1.5%. The principal gaining export sector over this period was rice, whose share increased from 5.0% to 11.2% (Government of Pakistan 2010: 93).

There is no evidence that the stock market contributed to the efficient allocation of resources during this episode. Hameed and Ashraf (2006) test for weak form efficiency (that prices of financial assets reflect all information contained in the past prices) in the KSE between December 1998 and March 2006. They find that stock price returns 'exhibit persistence and volatility clustering', and so reject the weak form efficiency hypothesis, as it is found that 'past information helps in predicting future prices'.

Institutions to manage conflict

This third section focuses on institutions that may or may not allow the state to overcome the inherent conflicts associated with economic growth. There was a widely held perception after 1999 that Pakistan was not a safe place to do business and that the state had failed in its basic duty to provide adequate protection. The USA, for example, continued to warn against travel to Pakistan for the period 2001 to 2006 (Burki 2007). Ali put it somewhat more pithily, the fading state was 'gradually being reduced to the level of a stagnant and treacherous swamp' (2008: 1). The failing state was reflected in deteriorating macroeconomic statistics. Between 1997/98 and 2000/01 GDP growth, investment, total savings, and development expenditure declined, and poverty and external debt increased. In May 1998 the government froze foreign currency deposits of non-resident Pakistanis after which home remittances declined to $500m. annually and FDI declined from $1bn to $400m. (Husain 2003; Lorie and Iqbal 2005).

After 1999 the government passed power to a team of technocrats with the capacity and commitment to implement reforms. Such efforts included the separation of policy and regulatory functions, formation of independent regulatory agencies, and in some cases the liquidation of defunct institutions (Husain 2003). The State Bank of Pakistan went through significant structural reforms to improve the operation of monetary management and strengthen its supervisory and regulatory mechanisms. The regulation of banking and non-banking sectors was placed in the hands of separate agencies. The Security Exchange Commission of Pakistan (SECP) later introduced reforms to strengthen the internal management of the corporations listed on the various stock exchanges (Burki 2007). The best evidence of the new-found autonomy of policy makers was that, for the first time in its history, Pakistan was able to complete the 2000 standby arrangement with the IMF without delays or interruptions.

This chapter has shown that, until the mid-2000s, the government implemented tough economic policies. The government was successful in raising savings, reducing current expenditure and imports, managing domestic and external debt, raising public and private corporate profitability and boosting public investment. There is also limited evidence that the resources mobilised were utilised productively. This did not last: by the mid-2000s efforts to mobilise resources were fading, tax revenue continued to stagnate, current expenditure and imports soared, public savings and the current account went into striking deficit, and indices of domestic and external debt showed marked worsening. This section shows that the military coup temporarily strengthened institutions of autonomy and repression that permitted early gains in mobilising and productively allocating a surplus. The ability of such institutions to maintain the autonomy of the state declined over time, and there was no corresponding creation of inclusive institutions. The episode of growth provides evidence that a military government was briefly able to take 'tough decisions', but that growth was ultimately unsustainable and would likely have faded even without the global financial crisis of 2008–10. There was evidence of the gradual decline in the surplus being mobilised as the autonomy of the state faded away.

Institutions to manage conflict: autonomy and repression

The military coup strengthened the traditional institution of autonomy and repression, the army. The army officer class remained united throughout the Musharraf dictatorship, The Pakistan army is half a million strong. Its tentacles are everywhere: land, industry, public utilities, and so on. It would require a cataclysmic upheaval (a US invasion and occupation for example) for this army to feel threatened by a jihadi uprising (Ali 2008: 180). The ousting of the chaotic political classes and military backing enabled a team of technocrats to implement the 'tough decisions' discussed in the previous section. As debated in the introduction to this chapter, growth was not simply due to good luck.

The continued autonomy of the army over time had increasingly non-developmental outcomes (Siddiqa 2007). The military, instead of supporting the autonomy of the state, gradually began to undermine it, utilising its privileged access to earn large profits. Through the Defence Housing Authorities (DHA), the military acquired public land cheaply and developed it for a substantial profit. An Army Welfare Trust (AWT) scheme at Sanjiani, Punjab, for example, cost $12.4m. to develop and showed a profit of $413m. There were similar DHA schemes in Rawalpindi and Park Town in Lahore. The various welfare trusts, such as the Fauji Foundation (FF) and AWT, were heavily involved in commercial ventures. The commercial viability of these trusts was dependent on preferential access to decision making and resource transfers from the government budget. Assessment based on available financial data for these ventures from 1998 to 2001 and audit reports of the government have established the fact that resources continuously leaked from the government to these companies, though they are supposed to operate in the private sector. For the AWT in 1999, the Sharif regime approved a guarantee of $43.1m., which was used to redeem an earlier guarantee of $68.96m. (Siddiqa 2007: 221). The Fauji Foundation was one of the first companies to enter the fertiliser market, gaining a 60% share of Pakistan's market, though this was based more on its ability to manipulate supply and prices for fertiliser. The military now comprises around 10% of the private sector (Siddiqa 2007: 236). The military has led to the political creation of monopoly-like situations in cargo transportation and road construction and has dominated fertiliser and cereal manufacture.

Typically, much of the autonomy granted to the state by military backing was squandered persecuting members of the previous government. After the military coup in 1999, Nawaz Sharif was exiled. In July 2003 the Bhuttos were convicted by a Swiss court of accepting $15m. from two Swiss companies, SGS and Cotecna. They were sentenced to six months in prison and ordered to return $11.9m. to the government of Pakistan (Ali 2008).

Institutions to manage conflict: inclusionary

Musharraf took some steps to spread the inclusionary net of government. Musharraf's government introduced local government decentralisation, transferring a significant amount of authority to elected people at the local level. The Nizams (mayors) elected by the people were supposedly closer to the citizenry than any other elected official (Burki 2007). Administrative and fiscal powers were devolved to new local governments, the districts or zilas (city districts in the four provincial capitals), tehsils (called towns in the four city districts) and union councils. The plan was implemented over 2001/02, and there was turnout of 52.5% in the first elections. In theory, devolution would make the district administration answerable to the chief executive of the district, rather than the provincial or central government authorities, potentially a major decentralisation. The formula for devolving resource to lower tiers of government and the conditions on these allocations was decided by the Provincial Finance Commission (PFC) and ultimately by the provincial governor. Members of the PFC were nominated by the provincial government. Lower tiers of government were given minimal ability to mobilise resources. Own funds of the district governments in Sindh account for only 1.3% of total revenue. The bulk of transfers were earmarked for salaries and could not be used for other purposes. District governments also had little control over staffing levels. The administrative structure under devolution left a substantial authority in the hands of centrally appointed civil servants. Devolution created the post of District Coordinating Officer (DCO), replacing the former Deputy Commissioner. The DCO lacks many of the legal powers of the DC, but still has significant executive and managerial authority (Keefer et al. 2003).

A long-standing concern is that a ruling landlord oligarchy at local level will gain control over the process of decentralisation, and it will be an exclusionary, rather than an inclusionary process. Easterly (2001b), for example, states that a ruling oligarchy would be unlikely to promote mass education for fear that more educated people will be more likely to demand political power (democracy). In the December 2000 elections the rural gentry were argued to have captured 70% of seats in local elections. Keefer et al. (2003) disagree and argue that local level political competition was more intense after 2000 than it had been in the 1990s. More competition, they argue, would have generated more uncertainty about election results and reduced the influence of special interests on candidate's positions. The uncertainty about the institutional characteristics of devolution would, though, make it more difficult for voters to verify whether candidate failure to fulfil promises is a result of shirking/incompetence or exogenous factors outside the candidates' control.

Ultimately, there were no signs of devolution being able to offer stable inclusionary government. In response, on 3rd November 2007 Musharraf suspended the 1973 constitution and imposed a state of emergency. All non-government television channels were taken off the air, mobile phone networks were jammed, and paramilitary units surrounded the Supreme Court. The Chief Justice convened an emergency bench of judges, who declared the new dispensation illegal and unconstitutional; they were removed and placed under house arrest. Several thousand civil rights activists and political activists were picked up, and lawyers were arrested all over the country. Unable to impose the autonomy of the state through repressive institutions and unable to create inclusionary institutions as an alternative, Musharaff allowed a belated return to party politics, just as had Ayub and Zia in years gone by. The national elections of February 2008 merely confirmed the fragmented nature of Pakistani politics.[2] In the election, the PPP won 120 of 342 seats in the National Assembly, the Sharif Muslim

League 90, the ANP 13, the Pro-Musharraf Muslim League 51, the MQM 25 and the religious coalition 6 (though Jamaat-e-Islami had boycotted the election) (Ali 2008).

Institutions to Manage Conflict: Ideology

There were no signs of any encompassing ideological dimension to Pakistan's government during this episode. After 2002 the MMA (a united front consisting of the Jamaat-i-Islam (JI) and the Jamait-Ulema-e-Islam (JUI) and four minor religious sects) governed the NWFP with a clear Islamicist ideology. The MMA lost heavily in the 2008 elections. The Islamist coalition won 15% of the national vote in 2002, and only 6% in 2008 (Ali 2008).

10 Conclusion

Implications for economic principles and policy

The conclusion outlines some of the more general implications for the study and practice of development economics of this specific case study of Pakistan. It examines the importance of four big themes, liberalisation, the role of a developmental state, external influences and the link between development and conflict, in explaining growth in Pakistan since independence.

Liberalisation

Orthodox neo-classical economics has derived two key propositions about economic growth. The first is that policy is the most important influence on economic growth, the second that a particular set of policies – neo-liberal reforms – will generate a faster rate of economic growth. The first of these propositions is for developing countries an optimistic one. If poor economic outcomes, in particular the rate of economic growth, is due to poor policies, changing policy will improve outcomes. The World Bank said of sub-Saharan Africa,

> The main factors behind the stagnation and decline were poor policies – both macroeconomic and sectoral – emanating from a development paradigm that gave the state a prominent role in production and regulating economic activity.
> (World Bank 1994: 20).

This first proposition, the primacy of policy, distinguishes orthodox economics from the recent work by a wide range of other scholars focusing on factors such as whether countries are landlocked, or have a tropical climate, the nature of the colonial state, endowments of land and natural resources, power relations in society, and the unequal status of a developing country in the world economy. This thesis supports the orthodox neo-classical view that policy is important over the medium term, but disagrees with the nature of what constitutes desirable policies. This thesis shows that the other policies of the Washington Consensus and later Good Governance agenda are not of first order importance in Pakistan in determining patterns of growth and stagnation over the medium term. Episodes of growth between 1951/52 and 1958/59 (Chapter

5), between 1960/61 and 1969/70 (Chapter 6) and between 2003/04 and 2008/09 (Chapter 9) were not associated with liberalisation. Liberalising efforts under President Zia (especially after 1983) were more half-hearted than many realise and were not associated with any increase in economic growth (Chapter 7). The very substantial liberalisation efforts at the end of the 1980s and early 1990s were associated with an episode of stagnation between 1992/93 and 2002/03 (Chapter 8).

A developmental state

This book started with the theoretical assumption that the state is important in both initiating and sustaining economic growth. This finding is contrary to neo-classical economics, which argues that economic growth is best promoted by reducing the economic role of the state through liberalisation and privatisation. This book provided extended evidence that episodes of growth in Pakistan since independence are linked to those times when the state was able to successfully mobilise and allocate resources through the state budget, the banking system, foreign sources, and public investment (finance), and to ensure that those resources were productively utilised in a process of learning and upgrading (production), and when the state was able to create institutions to manage the conflicts associated with development (institutions). Where the state was unsuccessful in these three roles, Pakistan was stuck in episodes of stagnation or episodes of growth that proved unsustainable. One very specific mechanism linking the state to episodes of growth was those occasions when the state was able to boost the profitability and investments of private sector business: a state-business development pact.

There is evidence for the state-business developmental pact across several of the episodes of growth and stagnation in Pakistan since independence. The episode of growth between 1951/52 and 1958/59 (Chapter 5) was associated with very high (50%–100%) profit rates that stimulated private sector investment and GDP growth. Profits were in part related to trade protection and exchange rate policy. The episode of growth between 1960/61 and 1969/70 (Chapter 6) was associated with a rise again in profits that was clearly linked with private sector investment. During this episode of growth the state complemented traditional trade and exchange rate policies with reforms to corporate taxation and anti-union policies. The episode of stagnation between 1970/71 and 1991/92 (Chapter 7) can be related to the rupture of the state-business developmental pact of the 1960s. The Pakistani bourgeoisie suffered severe setbacks after 1970, a precipitous fall in private industrial investment in industry, a rise of working class militancy supported by the PPP government (at least in the very early 1970s), and the ongoing nationalisation programme of the PPP. The latter had a profound impact, particularly with the takeover of the vegetable ghee industry in 1973, contrary to earlier assurances by Bhutto that the nationalisation programme had been completed. This rupture is easily linked to the collapse of private sector investment and episode of stagnation in GDP growth after 1971. There was perhaps likewise some evidence of a revival of the developmental-pact after the military coup of 1999 and episode of growth between 2002/03 and 2008/09 (Chapter 9). There was some evidence of improved profitability of state-owned enterprises, such as airlines and steel and also of the private corporate sector, but the subsequent link from profits to investment is less evident. The episode of growth was also related at various times to increased consumption and exports.

External influences

A very common unifying hypothesis to explain Pakistan's growth and development since independence has been its dependence on foreign aid inflows. Systematically, since 1951 domestic investment has exceeded domestic savings, and investment at the margin has been dependent on foreign capital inflows. The ebb and flow of capital inflows, according to many, has been a determining influence on growth rates, as well as exposing Pakistan to policy influence from donors: 'US priorities determined Pakistan's domestic and foreign policies from 1951 onward' (Ali 2008: 251). The most striking example in the literature is the Decade of Development (1958–68) under Ayub Khan. In response to Ayub's pro-USA foreign policy stance during the Cold War, it is argued that a surge of capital inflows generated an investment-led boom until 1965, when declining capital inflows (related to the war with India in 1965) led to economic slowdown and debilitating domestic conflict over the more limited foreign largesse.

Not only is there no good evidence to link episodes of growth with favourable circumstances emanating from the world economy, or episodes of stagnation with unfavourable circumstances, the entire hypothesis of 'dependent Pakistan' is simply not supported by the evidence. The episodes of growth between 1951/52 and 1958/59 (Chapter 5) and between 1960/61 and 1969/70 (Chapter 6) were not related to a sustained and favourable movement in Pakistan's external terms of trade. In both cases, external trade was simply too small in relation to the aggregate economy for the external terms of trade to have any significant impact on growth. There is evidence that Pakistan was heavily dependent on the USA in the earlier episode for aid, particularly military assistance. In the later period, Pakistan experienced a sharp fall in US aid after the mid-1960s. In response, Pakistan was able to quickly re-orientate its foreign policy and sources of aid, hardly the actions of a cowed and dependent economy. The episode of stagnation between 1969/70 and 1971/72 was associated with a sharp fall in Pakistan's external terms of trade, but once again Pakistan's trade ratio was too small for this to translate into a significant causal impact on aggregate economic growth. A computable general equilibrium (CGE) model developed by Sarmad (1992) shows that domestic policy over this episode was quite successful in mitigating adverse shocks from the world economy. The dependency hypothesis was largely mistaken for the Bhutto era and, though there was more truth in the argument during the 1980s under Zia, it remained exaggerated (Chapter 7). Bhutto continued the late Ayub policy of diversifying Pakistan's foreign policy (and hence trade and aid) away from narrow dependence on the USA. The downfall of Bhutto was linked by some to US displeasure at his efforts to develop a nuclear weapon and so to a re-assertion of Pakistan's dependent status. However, with the invasion of Afghanistan by the Soviet Union in 1979, Pakistan was able to reject initial US offers of aid and secured a huge subsequent increase. Reports of Pakistan sliding into dependency through an emerging debt crisis were greatly exaggerated. The most important mechanism for overcoming financial dependence from the early 1970s onwards was the enormous increase in remittance income. From the late 1980s, the trade ratio increased rapidly, meaning that the negative external shocks of the mid-1980s could have generated the episode of stagnation between 1992/92 and 2002/03 (Chapter 8). The decline in remittance income after 1987 likewise could have reinforced that impact. Sarmad (1992), using his CGE model, finds that domestic policy again successfully adjusted to such external shocks, and that stagnation was caused by changes in economic policy. A big and more contemporary argument is that Pakistan benefited from its suddenly favourable geo-political position after 11th September 2001. The argument runs that Pakistan's support for the US intervention in Afghanistan led to a huge surge in capital inflows and, as a result, Pakistan's economy floated upwards to success. Chapter 9 discusses this argument and finds the episode of growth between 2002/03 and 2008/09 was better explained by a stronger (military) government able to (briefly) successfully mobilise domestic resources, ensure they were utilised productively, and create institutions that were able to (again briefly) overcome the conflicts associated with economic development. The general statistical evidence fails to relate capital inflows to savings and investment (and hence growth). Relevant studies find that capital inflows (especially aid) increased consumption rather than savings and investment (Khilji and Zampelli 1991; Chishti and Hasan 1992; Khan et al. 1992; Mahmood and Qasim 1992; Khan and Rahmin 1993; Iqbal 1993, 1994, 1997).[1]

Development and conflict

This book took as a starting assumption the idea that conflict is an inherent part of the process of growth and development. The material side to this argument sees that economic development is concerned with shifting resources from low- to high-productivity areas. The mobility of some assets will be limited; owners will then face problems of obsolescence and unemployment. Those having sunk investments into physical capital, skills, contractual relationships, and political patronage are likely to resist change. The political side of this argument shows how growth and development lead to social and economic changes, such as urbanisation, increased literacy, industrialisation, and expansion of the mass media, that extend political consciousness and political participation. Traditional sources of authority (family and religion) are undermined, and new ones (civil servants and teachers) take time to gain legitimacy. Economic development also creates newly wealthy groups not assimilated into the existing social order. There is no guarantee that political institutions will emerge to absorb newly emergent groups and provide a stable institutional framework for the expression of political participation. Economic development and political stability are two very different and perhaps contradictory processes. Ignoring the role of conflict and its central place in growth and development would be to miss out on a central dynamic of Pakistan and its political economy since independence. The threat of conflict being unleashed by democratic elections in 1958 was a key driver of the military coup in 1958 (Chapter 5). The temporary cessation of conflict during the military dictatorships of Ayub (Chapter 6) and Musharraf (Chapter 9) allowed the state more autonomy and improved its ability to mobilise an economic surplus and utilise it productively. In both cases, the failure to maintain the capacity of repressive institutions to contain conflict or build integrating or ideological institutions to manage conflict led to the episodes of growth being ultimately unsustainable. The relative autonomy of the state declined drastically over the 1990s (Chapter 8), and party politics led to an upsurge in uncontrolled and chaotic factionalism that undermined the clarity and coherence of policy making. The main political parties frequently turned to the military to find allies in politics; this undermined the institutionalisation of democracy. Inclusionary or ideological institutions to manage conflict were non-existent. Pakistan over the 1990s was locked into a destructive episode of stagnation with no internal means to exit. The episode of stagnation between 1970/71 and 1991/92 (Chapter 7) was relatively successful in its ability to manage conflict; this was related ultimately to the realistic aspirations of Zia. After a hiatus in the early 1970s, the repressive institutions of the state re-emerged under Bhutto and were formally re-established in power with the military coup of 1977. By domestic criteria, this episode of stagnation (though quite successful judged in terms of average growth rates) probably was sustainable. The government lacked the developmental autonomy or inclusionary institutions or ideology to promote a real development drive. However, the government in the 1980s was secure enough in power to rule, and able to mobilise sufficient resources and utilise them productively enough, to keep GDP growth at a reasonable rate.

Notes

Introduction
1 3rd November 2010.

2 A methodological critique and framework
1 E.g. the legacy of Japanese colonialism (Kohli 1994), the class structure (Khan 2000b), a shift to outward orientation, etc. (World Bank 1993).
2 Solow (2001: 286) argues that this is not a problem: growth theory should be more explicitly concerned with the supply side of the macroeconomy (potential output), while deviations are demand driven (actual output).
3 The dates differ slightly from Rodrik (2003).
4 I am not aware of any study that models episodes of growth and stagnation as transitional Solow growth paths.
5 Often education (Romer 1986; Lucas 1988).
6 Also (Brock and Durlauf 2001: 235).
7 See (Easterly and Levine 1997; Kenny 1999). The term structural refers to a continuum from country-specific time-invariant variables, such as latitude and geography, to quantities that evolve slowly, such as population size and human capital, and finally to highly volatile series, such as black market premia, capital inflows, and the terms of trade.
8 Also the standard deviation of domestic credit growth.
9 The latter forms the centrepiece of Arrow's (1962) model of growth.
10 Adding a premium, for example, when reforms were conducted in the correct sequence: deflation before devaluation, liberalisation of the current account before the capital account, etc.
11 Sala-i-Martin (2001: 281) argues that this is really a problem of small samples; if the sample were large enough, all potential variables, with particular slopes/intercepts for each set of countries for all potential non-linearities, could be fitted into a regression.
12 Temple (1998: 338) suggests that this relationship is U-shaped.
13 Measured by Sachs and Warner (1995) index or the trade share in GDP.
14 This section is based on McCartney (2009a: Ch3).
15 One exception to this rule is a recent and very detailed statistical treatment of the Pakistani economy, which simply divided the period since independence into calendar decades (Kemal *et al.* 2006).

3 Episodes of growth and stagnation in Pakistan, 1951–2008
1 Grateful thanks to Grace Kite who did the crucial statistical work for this section. See Kite and McCartney (forthcoming).
2 These data are drawn from various publications by the Government of Pakistan, including the Economic Survey of Pakistan. The purpose of sharing a data source with a very recent study throws a spotlight on the different implications and findings of the methodology we use here.

3 For example, splitting the sample at 1960/61 would give us two time periods in the data: phase 1 would include 1951/52 to 1959/60 and phase 2 would include 1960/61 to 2008/09.
4 Very simply, mean(2)/mean(1).
5 The statistical significance of these shifts has not been tested. There was a statistically significant slowdown in industrial growth in India after 1965 (Varshney 1984; Ahluwalia 1985; McCartney 2009a).
6 Kemal uses different techniques to measure growth and correct for the effects of inflation. He broadly echoes these general results, in particular rapid growth of large-scale manufacturing in the 1960s. The exercise does show how growth rates can vary: his estimates for growth rates in tobacco manufacturing vary from 15% to 25% p.a. (1976: 360).
7 An episode of stagnation is defined as a 'statistically significant decline in the GDP growth rate'; the 5.6% average growth rate over the 1970s and 1980s is quite respectable by other standards.

4 Theoretical framework

1 This chapter is a revised version of the theoretical model found in McCartney (2009a).
2 Large industrialists, landowners, professional elite, military and civil bureaucracy.
3 Or 'confess', in the language of a typical prisoner's dilemma game.
4 'We may define primitive accumulation as the transfer of assets, most notably land, by non-market means, from non-capitalist to potentially capitalist classes, and usually with state compliance or mediation: by force majeure, whether via theft, eviction, or purchase at a nominal price' (Byres 2005: 83).
5 The last is not discussed here, due to its limited relevance outside a small number of Southeast/East Asian countries.
6 Public savings are defined as total government revenue minus public expenditure (net of public investment).
7 Taiwan had one of the largest state sectors outside the communist bloc (Wade 1990:176–7).
8 Such long-term financing institutions in India have included the IDBI, IFCI, and ICICI.
9 Amsden distinguishes between this 'information failure' and the 'imperfect information' discussed by Akerlof (1970) and Stiglitz and Weiss (1981).
10 This work has its genesis in the tradition of the infant industry phenomenon.
11 South Korea, Malaysia, Indonesia, Thailand and the Philippines.
12 The role of copper MNCs in the 1973 coup in Chile is an obvious example.
13 It could be that the price of labour needs to be negative in order for a country to have a comparative advantage in labour-using industries.
14 This is in the tradition of Stiglitz who takes Pareto Efficiency as the benchmark and government policy as a means to make the world look more like neo-classical theory. If there exists a wedge between social and private costs (an externality) taxation, subsidy or regulation can push the economy towards the overall social optimum. An optimal Pigouvian tax can replicate an 'efficient' allocation (Mas-Colell et al. 1995: 355).
15 Rodrik assumes that latent social conflict is measured by the depth of pre-existing social cleavages in a society; these can exist along lines of wealth, ethnic identity, geographic division, etc.
16 A stationary bandit is likely to charge higher taxes than a democracy and faces a greater problem with the uncertainty generated by securing dynastic rule and making a credible promise to protect property rights – how can a supreme autocrat be bound by an independent judiciary?
17 There are signs that the difference was narrowing by the late 1990s. The BJP gradually shifted its electoral strategy from mobilisation to alliances and electoral adjustments, increasing the influence of accommodation at the expense of ideology (Hansen and Jaffrelot 1998).
18 Through, for example, screenings of the Mahabaratha and Ramayana.

5 An episode of growth, 1951/1952–1958/1959

1 Lewis and Khan (1964) for example discuss how their various estimates of savings are derived.
2 The notion of 'normal' is taken from statistical work by Chenery (1960).

214 *Notes*

3 An implicit exchange rate is the ratio between the domestic wholesale price of a commodity in local currency (Rs 1.00 per yard of cloth) and the foreign price of the same item at the port of entry or exit, in some international currency (e.g. $20 per yard). The exchange rate implied by these prices is the implicit exchange rate for cloth. If this item were imported having been subjected to no duties or quantitative restrictions, then the implicit exchange rate would be equal to the official exchange rate between the two countries (Lewis 1968).
4 The narrowing of the gap between the implicit exchange rates for the two sectors after the mid-1950s is consistent, argues Lewis (1968, 1969), with the hypothesis that the growth process worked off the disequilibrium of Partition.
5 The wholesale prices of goods that the sector sells relative to the wholesale prices of the goods that it buys.
6 The more general weakness of using comparative cost data is that cost ratios may turn unfavourable simply as a result of the costs of competing imports falling faster on account of productivity growth in other countries.
7 The first coup plotters from the military (Major General Akbar Khan) had been arrested as early as 1951 (Jalal 1990).
8 A developmental state can be defined as one 'whose politics have concentrated sufficient power, probity, autonomy and competence at the centre to shape, pursue and encourage the achievement of explicit and nationally-determined developmental objectives, whether by establishing and promoting the conditions of growth, by organising it directly, or by a varying combination of both' (Leftwich 1995:401).
9 'Throughout the 1950s Nehru enjoyed unlimited, indeed, virtually unchallenged power over the Indian republic. He was the darling of India's people, the hero of his party, the unrivalled leader of his government' (Wolpert 1996:457).

6 An episode of growth, 1960/61–1969/70

1 Broad money includes the sum of currency outside the bank plus demand, time, savings and foreign currency deposits of residents other than the central government.
2 Its members included Belgium, Canada, France, Italy, Japan, Netherlands, UK, USA, West Germany, and the World Bank and its associates, including the IDA.
3 Later evidence shows that in the mid-1980s a greater proportion of households had positive savings among higher income deciles (Zaidi and De Vos 1994: 927).
4 However, they began rising strongly after 1963 and 1964.
5 Guisinger and Irfan (1974:367, 376) argue that the impact on wages and strikes of the Ayub government was mild and short lived.
6 However, the link between the Five-year Plans and the volume/destination of licences actually issued was usually rather loose (Lewis 1970:102).
7 Winston estimates that over-invoicing of imports contributed to higher real profits and that the rate of such manipulation increased over the 1960s (1970:175).
8 In late 1950s Karachi, 71% of small-scale and 82% of large-scale entrepreneurs were migrants from India (Lewis 1970:45). Minor Muslim communities (who were largely migrants from India) represented under 1% of the population, but controlled over half of industrial assets by 1959 (Lewis 1970:47).
9 Licences granted to the influential (relatives of bureaucrats/politicians) were often sold on to West Pakistani businessmen, the transfer succeeded only in transferring resources from consumers to rentiers (Alavi 1974:78).
10 Export taxes, import duties, sales and excise taxes, and the export bonus system introduced measurable distortions between world and domestic prices at the official exchange rate, termed 'implicit exchange rates'.
11 For the manufacturing sector as whole Kemal (1981) found that the elasticity of substitution between labour and capital was high and significant.
12 Crucial industries, such as cotton textiles, jute textiles, woollen textiles, and fertilisers, are not included in his analysis, since they were not subject to investigation by the Tariff Commission.

13 According to Kemal (1976b), the only industry with a rising capital-output ratio was the manufacture of non-metallic mineral products.
14 Wizarat as always offers an alternative so unusual that one must doubt her calculations: she shows that the TFP index for large-scale manufacturing increased from 100.0 in 1959/60 to 124.57 in 1964/65, then dropped to 108.39 in 1965/66, jumped again to 122.26 in 1966/67, then declined again to 102.15 by 1970 (2002: 76).
15 Some contemporary praise was a little excessive, 'More than any other political leader in a modernising country after World War II, Ayub Khan came close to filling the role of a Solon or Lycurgus or "Great Legislator" on the Platonic or Rousseauean model.' (Huntingdon 1968:251).
16 Only after the mid-1960s did this pact with incumbents begin to break down, and both began to support business entrants in an effort to reduce the concentration of control (Papanek 1967:91).
17 The 1956 reform that amalgamated all West Pakistan into one province, dominated by what had been the Punjab.
18 This is recognised as a gross underestimate, as large owners under-reported land for fear of land reform.

7 An episode of stagnation, 1970/71–1991/92

1 The effective devaluation was more like 60% once the abolition of various export incentives was accounted for (Kemal and Alvie 1975).
2 However, Chapter 5 did note that foreign capital was relatively insignificant in Pakistan by the late 1960s.
3 In 1990 the saving rate was approximately half that in India.
4 Estimates of defence expenditure in Pakistan are at best only approximates, but similar estimates are found in Hashmi (1983:159), Khan (2004), and Zaidi (2005:214).
5 Defined as total costs minus total revenues from user charges, where total costs include depreciation, interest costs, the salary bill and operations and maintenance costs (in 1997/98 prices).
6 The debt servicing ratio is the principal and interest costs of servicing the stock of foreign debt as a percentage of foreign exchange earnings.
7 With slightly different estimates/time periods, this conclusion is echoed in Nawab et al. (1984:101) and Khan (1997:949).
8 Sarmad (1993) argues that unrecorded capital flight also increased over the 1970s and 1980s.
9 Alderman (1996) is unusual and finds between 1986 and 1989 that almost all remittance income is saved by rural households.
10 Franco-Rodriquez et al. (1998) and Nasir and Khalid (2004) disagree.
11 These were Federal Chemicals and Ceramics Corporation, National Fertiliser Corporation, Pakistan Automobile Corporation Ltd, Pakistan Industrial Development Corporation, State Cement Corporation of Pakistan, State Engineering Corporation Ltd, State Petroleum Refining and Petrochem Corp, and Pakistan Steel Mills Corporation.
12 Measured as sales of the largest two firms as a percentage of total industry sales, using data collected from the Census of Manufacturing Industries.
13 System losses may be due to technical reasons such as unreliable and aging generation plants, low voltage transmission and distribution lines, and inappropriate location of grid stations, as well as non-technical factors such as inaccurate metering and billing, default payments, un-metered supplies, and theft through illegal connections.
14 Wizarat as ever is the sceptic; she finds a massive decline in productivity growth of the large-scale manufacturing sector. Using two methods, she measures the decline in TFP as -7.3/-4.0% over the 1970s and -6.8/-3.7% over the 1980s (2002:81).
15 Wizarat (1981:433) finds no increase in TFP in agriculture over the 1970s; growth, she finds, was entirely driven by increased factor inputs.

8 An episode of stagnation, 1992/93–2002/03

1 These figures provide an underestimate of the cost of the military sector; military pensions were moved out of the defence budget, which had the effect of reducing defence spending (Siddiqa 2007: 207). Resources also have a tendency to 'leak' from the government budget as subsidies and

216 *Notes*

  loan guarantees to army companies such as the Fauji Foundation, Frontier Works Organisation and Army Welfare Trust.
2 Broad money includes the sum of currency outside the bank plus demand, time, savings and foreign currency deposits of residents other than the central government.
3 The RCA index captures a country's world export share of a commodity compared with the country's total share in world exports. If a country's share of world exports of a particular commodity is greater than its share of world exports of all commodities, the RCA will be greater than one. A high value of the RCA indicates relative export specialisation.

9 An episode of growth, 2003/04–2008/09

1 Broad money includes the sum of currency outside the bank plus demand, time, savings and foreign currency deposits of residents other than the central government.
2 In December 2008, as Benazir was beginning her campaign against the military in Rawalpindi, she was assassinated (Ali 2008).

Conclusion

1 Franco-Rodriguez *et al.* (1998) and Nasir and Khalid (2004) disagree.

Bibliography

Acemoglu, D. (2002), *Why Not a Political Coase Theorem? Social Conflict, Commitment and Politics*, Department of Economics, MIT, Mimeo.
Acemoglu, D. (2003), 'Root Causes: A Historical Approach to Assessing the Role of Institutions in Economic Development', *Finance and Development*, 40:2, pp. 27–30.
Acemoglu, D. and J.A. Robinson (1999), *Political Losers as a Barrier to Economic Development*, Department of Economics, MIT, Mimeo.
Acemoglu, D., S. Johnson and J.A. Robinson (2001), 'The Colonial Origins of Comparative Development: An Empirical Investigation', *American Economic Review*, 91, pp. 1369–1401.
Afridi, U. (1985), 'Dynamics of Change in Pakistan's Large-scale Manufacturing Sector', *The Pakistan Development Review*, 24:3+4, pp. 463–78.
Afzal, M.R. (2001), *Pakistan: History and Politics, 1947–1971*, Karachi, Oxford University Press.
Afzar, K. (1991), 'Constitutional Dilemmas in Pakistan', in Burki, S.J. and C. Baxter (Eds) (1991), *Pakistan Under the Military: Eleven Years of Zia ul-Haq*, Boulder, Westview Press.
Aghion, P., R. Burgess, S. Redding and F. Zilibotti (2005), *The Unequal Effects of Liberalisation: Evidence from Dismantling the License Raj in India*, LSE, Mimeo.
Ahluwalia, I.J. (1985), *Industrial Growth in India: Stagnation Since the Mid-Sixties*, New Delhi, Oxford University Press.
Ahluwalia, M.S. (2001), 'State Level Performance under Economic Reforms in India', CREDPR, Working Paper No. 96, Stanford University, Centre for Research on Economic Development and Policy Reform.
Ahmad, B. and A.M. Chaudhry (1987), 'Profitability of Pakistan's Agriculture', *The Pakistan Development Review*, 26:4, pp. 457–69.
Ahmad, M.H., S. Alam and M.S. Butt (2003), 'Foreign Direct Investment, Exports and Domestic Output in Pakistan', *The Pakistan Development Review*, 42:4, pp. 715–23.
Ahmad, Q.K. (1966), 'The Operation of the Export Bonus Scheme in Pakistan's Jute and Cotton Industries', *The Pakistan Development Review,* 5:1, pp. 1–37.
Ahmar, M. (1996), 'Ethnicity and State Power in Pakistan: The Karachi Crisis', *Asian Survey*, 36:10, pp. 1031–46.
Ahmed, I. and A. Qayyam (2007), 'Do Public Expenditure and Macroeconomic Uncertainty Matter to Private Investment? Evidence from Pakistan', *The Pakistan Development Review*, 46:2, pp. 145–61.
Ahmed, M. (1982), 'Substitution Elasticities in the Large-scale Manufacturing Industries of Pakistan: A Comment', *The Pakistan Development Review*, 21:1, pp. 73–82.
Ahmed, Q.M. and S.M. Ahsan (1997), 'Tax Concessions and Investment Behaviour', *The Pakistan Development Review*, 36:4, pp. 537–62.
Ahmed, Q.M., M.S. Butt and S. Alam (2000), 'Economic Growth, Export and External Debt Causality: The Case of Asian Countries', *The Pakistan Development Review*, 39:4, pp. 591–608.

Ahmed, V. and R. Amjad (1984), *The Management of Pakistan's Economy, 1947–82*, Karachi, Oxford University Press.

Aitken, B.J. and A.E. Harrison (1999), 'Do Domestic Firms Benefit from FDI? Evidence from Venezuela', *American Economic Review*, 89:3, pp. 605–18.

Akbar, M. and Z.F. Naqvi (2000), 'Export Diverisification and the Structural Dynamics in the Growth Process: The Case of Pakistan', *The Pakistan Development Review*, 39:4, pp. 573–89.

Akerlof, G. (1970), 'The Market for Lemons: Qualitative Uncertainty and the Market Mechanism', *Quarterly Journal of Economics*, 86, pp. 488–500.

Akhund, I. (2000), *Trial and Error: The Advent and Eclipse of Benazir Bhutt'*, Karachi, Oxford University Press.

Akhtar, S. and F. Malik (2000), 'Pakistan's Trading Performance vis-à-vis its Major Trading Partners', *The Pakistan Development Review*, 39:1, pp. 37–50.

Alam, A. (1983), 'Science and Engineering Education', in Gardezi, H. and J. Rashid (Eds) (1983), *Pakistan: The Roots of Dictatorship: The Political Economy of a Praetorian State*, London, Zed Press.

Alamgir, M. (1968), 'The Domestic Prices of Imported Commodities in Pakistan A Further Study', *The Pakistan Development Review*, 8:1, pp. 35–73.

Alavi, H. (1974), 'The State in Post-Colonial Societies: Pakistan and Bangladesh', *New Left Review*, 74, July-August, pp. 59–81.

Alavi, H. (1983), 'Class and State', in Gardezi, H. and J. Rashid (Eds) (1983), *Pakistan: The Roots of Dictatorship: The Political Economy of a Praetorian State*, London, Zed Press.

Alderman, H. (1996), 'Saving and Economic Shocks in Rural Pakistan', *Journal of Development Economics*, 51, pp. 343–65.

Alesina, A. and D. Rodrik (1994), 'Distributive Policies and Economic Growth', *Quarterly Journal of Economics*, 109, pp. 365–490.

Alesina, A., R. Baqir and W. Easterly (1999), 'Public Goods and Ethnic Divisions', *Quarterly Journal of Economics*, 114, pp. 1243–84.

Ali, K. and A. Hamid (1996), 'Technical Change, Technical Efficiency, and Their Impact on Input Demand in the Agricultural and Manufacturing Sectors of Pakistan', *The Pakistan Development Review*, 35:3, pp. 215–28.

Ali, S. (2004), 'Total Factor Productivity Growth in Pakistan's Agriculture: 1960–96', *The Pakistan Development Review*, 43:4, pp. 493–513.

Ali, S. (2005), 'Total Factor Productivity Growth and Agricultural Research and Extension: An Analysis of Pakistan's Agriculture, 1960–96', *The Pakistan Development Review*, 44:4, pp. 729–46.

Ali, S.S. and K. Mustafa (2001), 'Testing Semi-strong Form Efficiency of Stock Market', *The Pakistan Development Review*, 40:4, pp. 651–74.

Ali, T. (2008), *The Duel: Pakistan on the Flight Path of American Power*, London, Simon and Schuster.

Amjad, R. (1977), Profitability and Industrial Concentration in Pakistan', *Journal of Development Studies*, 13:3, pp. 181–98.

Amjad, R. (1976), 'A Study of Investment Behaviour in Pakistan, 1962–70', *The Pakistan Development Review*, 15:2, pp. 134–53.

Amjad, R. (1982), *Private Industrial Investment in Pakistan 1960–1970*, Cambridge, Cambridge University Press.

Amjad, R. (1983), 'Industrial Concentration and Economic Power', in Gardezi, H. and J. Rashid (Eds) (1983), *Pakistan: The Roots of Dictatorship: The Political Economy of a Praetorian State*, London, Zed Press.

Amjad, R. (1986), 'Impact of Workers' Remittances from the Middle East on Pakistan's Economy: Some Selected Issues', *The Pakistan Development Review*, 25:4, pp. 757–85.

Amsden, A.H. (1989), *Asia's Next Giant: South Korea and Late Industrialisation*, Oxford, Oxford University Press.

Amsden, A.H. (1997), 'Editorial: Bringing Production Back in – Understanding Government's Role in Late Industrialisation', *World Development*, 25:4, pp. 469–80.

Amsden, A. (2001), *The Rise of 'The Rest': Challenges to the West from Late-Industrialising Economies*, Oxford, Oxford University Press.

Andrews, D. (1993), 'Tests for Parameter Instability and Structural Change with Unknown Change Point', *Econometrica*, 61, pp. 821–56.

Annett, A. (1999), *Ethnic and Religious Division, Political Instability and Government Consumption*, IMF, Mimeo.

Ansari, J.A. (1999), 'Macroeconomic Management: An Alternative Perspective', in Khan, S.R. (Ed.) (1999), *50 Years of Pakistan's Economy: Traditional Topics and Contemporary Concerns*, Karachi, Oxford University Press.

Anwar, T. (2000), *Impact of Globalisation and Liberalisation on Growth, Employment and Poverty: A Case Study of Pakistan*, State Bank of Pakistan, Mimeo.

Arrow, K. (1962), 'The Economic Implications of Learning-by-Doing', *Review of Economic Studies*, 29, pp. 155–73.

Arunatilake, N., S. Jayasuriya and S. Kelegama (2001), 'The Economic Cost of the War in Sri Lanka', *World Development*, 29:9, pp. 1483–1500.

Asiedu, E. (2002), 'On the Determinants of Foreign Direct Investment to Developing Countries: Is Africa Different?', *World Development*, 30:1, pp. 107–19.

Athukorala, P.C. and K. Sen (2002), *Savings, Investment and Growth in India*, New Delhi, Oxford University Press.

Atique, Z., M.H. Khan and U. Azhar (2004), 'The Impact of FDI on Economic Growth under Foreign Trade Regimes: A Case Study of Pakistan', *The Pakistan Development Review*, 43:4, pp. 707–18.

Baddeley, M., K. McNay and R. Cassen (2006), 'Divergence in India: Income Differentials at the State Level, 1970–97', *Journal of Development Studies*, 42:6, pp. 1000–22.

Bagchi, A.K. (1976), 'De-Industrialisation in India in the Nineteenth Century: Some Theoretical Implications', *Journal of Development Studies*, 12:2, pp. 135–64.

Bajpai, N. and J.D. Sachs (1999), 'Fiscal Policy in India's Economic Reforms', in Sachs, J.D., A. Varshney and N. Bajpai (Eds) (1999), *India in the Era of Economic Reforms*, New Delhi, Oxford University Press.

Balakrishnan, P. and M. Parameswaran (2007), 'Understanding Economic Growth in India: A Prerequisite', *Economic and Political Weekly*, July 14th, pp. 2915–22.

Balasubramanyam, V.N., M. Salisu and D. Sapsford (1996), 'Foreign Direct Investment and Growth in EP and IS Countries', *Economic Journal*, 106, pp. 92–105.

Baran, P. (1957), *The Political Economy of Growth*, London, Penguin.

Baran, P. and P.M. Sweezy (1966), *Monopoly Capitalism: An Essay on the American Economic and Social Order*, Harmondsworth, Pelican.

Bardhan, P.K. (1984), *The Political Economy of Development in India*, New Delhi, Oxford University Press (reprinted with new epilogue 1998).

Bardhan, P.K. (2001), 'Sharing the Spoils: Group Equity Development and Democracy', in Kohli, A. (Ed.) (2001), *The Success of India's Democracy*, Cambridge, Cambridge University Press.

Barro, R.J. (1990), 'Government Spending in a Simple Model of Endogenous Growth', *Journal of Political Economy*, 98:5, pp. S103–25.

Barro, R.J. (1991), 'Economic Growth in a Cross-section of Countries' *Quarterly Journal of Economics*, 106, pp. 407–431.

Barro, R.J. (1996), 'Democracy and Growth', *Journal of Economic Growth*, 1, pp. 1–27.

Barro, R.J. (1999), 'Determinants of Democracy', *Journal of Political Economy*, 107:6, pp. S158–83.

Basu, A. (2001), 'The Dialectics of Hindu Nationalism', in Kohli, A. (Ed.) (2001), *The Success of India's Democracy*, Cambridge, Cambridge University Press.

Bates, R.H. (2000), 'Ethnicity and Development in Africa: A Reappraisal', *American Economic Review*, 90:2, pp. 131–4.

Baxter, C. (1991), 'Pakistan Becomes Prominent in the International Arena', in Burki, S.J. and C. Baxter (Eds) (1991), *Pakistan Under the Military: Eleven Years of Zia ul-Haq*, Boulder, Westview Press.

Bergan, A. (1967), 'Personal Income distribution and Personal Savings in Pakistan, 1963/64', *The Pakistan Development Review*, 7:2, pp. 160–212.

Bernanke, B.S. (1983), 'Nonmonetary Effects of the Financial Crisis in the Propagation of the Great Depression', *American Economic Review*, 73, pp. 257–76.

Berthelemy, J-C. and L. Soderling (2001), 'The Role of Capital Accumulation, Adjustment and Structural Change for Economic Growth Take-Off: Empirical Evidence from African Growth Episodes', *World Development*, 29:2, pp. 323–43.

Bhargava, S. and V. Joshi (1990), 'Increase in India's Growth Rate: Facts and a Tentative Explanation', *Economic and Political Weekly*, 1st December, pp. M2657–61.

Bilquees, F. (1992), 'Trends in Intersectoral Wages in Pakistan', *The Pakistan Development Review*, 3:4, pp. 1243–53.

Bilquees, F. (2003), 'An Analysis of Budget Deficits, Debt Accumulation and Debt Instability', *The Pakistan Development Review*, 42:3, pp. 177–95.

Bilquees, F. (2004), 'Elasticity and Buoyancy of the Tax System in Pakistan', *The Pakistan Development Review*, 43:1, pp. 3–93.

Bils, M. and P.J. Klenow (2000), 'Does Schooling Cause Growth?', *American Economic Review*, 90:5, pp. 1160–83.

Bleaney, M.F. (1996), 'Macroeconomic Stability, Investment and Growth in Developing Countries', *Journal of Development Economics*, 48:2, pp. 461–77.

Block, S.A. (2001), 'Does Africa Grow Differently?', *Journal of Development Economics*, 65, pp. 443–67.

Blomstrom, M., R.E. Lipsey and M. Zejan (1996), 'Is Fixed Investment the Key to Economic Growth?', *Quarterly Journal of Economics*, 111, pp. 269–76.

Bloom, D.E. and J.D. Sachs (1998), 'Geography, Demography, and Economic Growth in Africa', *Brookings Papers on Economic Activity* 2, pp. 207–95.

Bose, S. (2004), 'Decolonisation and State Building in South Asia', *Journal of International Affairs*, 58:1, pp. 95–113.

Bose, S.R. (1968), 'Trend of Real Income of the Rural Poor in East Pakistan', in Griffin, K. and A.R. Rahman (1972), *Growth and Inequality in Pakistan*, London, Macmillan.

Brecher, R.A. and C.F. Diaz-Alejandro (1977), 'Tariffs, Foreign Capital and Immiserizing Growth', *Journal of International Economics*, 7, pp. 317–22.

Brock, W.A. and S.N. Durlauf (2001), 'Growth Empirics and Reality: What Have We Learned from a Decade of Empirical Research on Growth', *World Bank Economic Review*, 15:2, pp. 229–72.

Burki, A.A. and D.Terrell (1998), 'Measuring Production Efficiency of Small Firms in Pakistan', *World Development*, 26:1, pp. 155–69.

Burki, S.J. (1974), 'Development of Towns: The Pakistan Experience', *Asian Survey*, 14:8, pp. 751–62.

Burki, S.J. (1980), *Pakistan Under Bhutto, 1971–1977*, London, Macmillan Press.

Burki, S.J. (1988), Pakistan Under Zia, 1977–88, *Asian Survey*, 28:10, pp.1082–1100.

Burki, S.J. (1991), 'Zia's Eleven Years' in Burki, S.J. and C. Baxter (Eds) (1991), *Pakistan Under the Military: Eleven Years of Zia ul-Haq*, Boulder, Westview Press.

Burki, S.J. (1999), *Pakistan: Fifty Years of Nationhood*, Boulder, Westview Press.

Burki, S.J. (2007), *Changing Perceptions, Altered Reality: Pakistan's Economy under Musharraf, 1999–2006*, Karachi, Oxford University Press.

Burney, N.A. (1986), 'Sources of Pakistan's Economic Growth', *The Pakistan Development Review*, 25:4, pp. 573–87.

Byres, T.J. (2005), 'Neoliberalism and Primitive Accumulation in Less Developed Countries', in Saad-Filho, A. and D. Johnson (Eds) (2005), *Neo-Liberalism: A Critical Reader,* London, Pluto Press.

Caporaso, J.A. and D.P. Levine (1992), *Theories of Political Economy*, Cambridge, Cambridge University Press.
Chang, H-J. (1999), 'The Economic Theory of the Developmental State', in Woo-Cumings, M. (Ed.) (1999), *The Developmental State in Historical Perspective*, Ithaca, Cornell University Press.
Chang, H-J. and I. Grabel (2004), *Reclaiming Development: An Alternative Economic Policy Manual*, London, Zed Books.
Chaudhary, M.A. and A. Hamid (2001), 'Resource Mobilisation and Tax Elasticities in Pakistan', *Pakistan Economic and Social Review*, 39:1, pp. 25–48.
Chaudhry, M.G., G.M. Chaudhry and M.A. Qasim (1996), 'Growth of Output and Productivity in Pakistan's Agriculture: Trends, Sources and Policy Implications', *The Pakistan Development Review*, 35:4, pp. 527–36.
Chaudhry, M.J. (1990), 'The Adoption of Tubewell Technology in Pakistan', *The Pakistan Development Review*, 29:3+4, pp. 291–303.
Chaudhry, S.A. (1970), 'Private Foreign Investment in Pakistan', *The Pakistan Development Review*, 10:1, pp. 100–11.
Cheema, A.A. (1978) 'Producivity Trends in the Manufacturing Industries' *The Pakistan Development Review*, 17:1, pp. 44–65.
Chenery H., (1960), 'Patterns of industrial growth', *American Economic Review*, 50:4, pp. 624–54.
Chenery, H.B. and L. Taylor (1968), 'Development Patterns Among Countries and Over Time', *Review of Economics and Statistics*, 50:4, pp. 391–416.
Chibber, V. (2003), *Locked in Place: State-building and Late Industrialisation in India*, Princeton, Princeton University Press.
Child, F.C. (1968), 'Reform of a Trade and Payments Control System: The Case of Pakistan', *Economic Development and Cultural Change*, 16:4, pp. 539–58.
Child, F.C. and H. Kaneda (1975), 'Links to the Green Revolution: A Study of Small-Scale, Agriculturally Related Investment in the Pakistan Punjab', *Economic Development and Cultural Change*, 23:2, pp. 249–75.
Chishti, S. and M.A. Hasan (1992), 'Foreign Aid, Defence Expenditure and Public Investment in Pakistan', *The Pakistan Development Review*, 31:4, pp. 895–908.
Chow, G. (1960), 'Tests of Equality between Sets of Coefficients in Two Linear Regressions', *Econometrica*, 28:3, pp. 591–605.
Chuang, Y. and C. Lin (1999), 'Foreign Direct Investment, R&D and Spillover Efficiency: Evidence from Taiwan's Manufacturing Firms', *Journal of Development Studies*, 35:4, pp. 117–37.
Clark, G. and S. Wolcott (2001), 'One Polity, Many Countries, Economic Growth in India, 1873–2000', paper for the Analytical Narratives of Growth Project, Kennedy School of Government, Harvard University.
Clarke, S. (1994), *Marx's Theory of Crises*, London, St Martin's Press.
Collier, P. (2007), *The Bottom Billion: Why the Poorest Countries Are Failing and What Can Be Done About It*, Oxford, Oxford University Press.
Cramer, C. (1998), *Inequality, Development and Political Correctnes*, SOAS, University of London, Mimeo.
Dasgupta, D., P. Maiti, R. Mukherjee, S. Sarkar and S. Chakrabarti, (2000), 'Growth and Interstate Disparities in India', *Economic and Political Weekly*, 1st July, pp. 2413–22.
Deininger, K. and L. Squire (1996), 'A New Data Set Measuring Inequality', *World Bank Economic Review*, 10:3, pp. 565–91.
Delderbos, R., G. Capannelli and K. Fukao (2001), 'Backward Vertical Linkages of Foreign Manufacturing Affiliates: Evidence from Japanese Multinationals', *World Development*, 29:1, pp. 189–208.
De Long, J.B. and L.H. Summers (1991), 'Equipment Investment and Economic Growth', *Quarterly Journal of Economics*, 106, pp. 445–502.

De Long, J.B. and L.H. Summers (1992), 'Equipment Investment and Economic Growth: How Strong is the Nexus?', *Brookings Papers on Economic Activity* 2, pp. 157–211.

De Long, J.B. and L.H. Summers (1993), 'How Strongly do Developing Economies Benefit from Equipment Investment?', *Journal of Monetary Economics*, 32, pp. 395–415.

Dholakia, R.H. (1994), 'Spatial Dimension of Acceleration of Economic Growth in India', *Economic and Political Weekly*, 27th August 1994, pp. 2303–9.

Din, M., E. Ghani and T. Mahmood (2007), 'Technical Efficiency of Pakistan's Manufacturing Sector: A Stochastic Frontier and Data Envelope Analysis', *The Pakistan Development Review*, 46:1, pp. 1–18.

Din, M., E. Ghani and O. Siddique (2003), 'Openness and Economic Growth in Pakistan', *Pakistan Development Review*, 42:4, pp. 795–807.

Dixit, A.K. (1992), 'Investment and Hysteresis', *Journal of Economic Perspectives*, 6:1, pp. 107–32.

Dixit, A.K. and R.S. Pindyck (1994), *Investment Under Uncertainty*, Princeton, Princeton University Press.

Easterly, W. (2001a), *The Elusive Quest for Growth: Economists' Misadventures in the Tropics*, Cambridge, MIT Press.

Easterly, W. (2001b), 'The Political Economy of Growth Without Development: A Case Study of Pakistan', paper for the Analytical Narratives of Growth Project, Kennedy School of Government, Harvard University.

Easterly, W. (2001c), 'Can Institutions Resolve Ethnic Conflict', *Economic Development and Cultural Change*, 49, pp. 687–706.

Easterly, W. (2001d), 'The Lost Decades: Developing Countries' Stagnation in Spite of Policy Reform 1980–98', *Journal of Economic Growth*, 6:2, pp. 135–57.

Easterly, W. and R. Levine (1997), 'Africa's Growth Tragedy: Policies and Ethnic Divisions', *Quarterly Journal of Economics*, 112, pp. 1203–50.

Easterly, W. and R. Levine (2001), 'It's Not Factor Accumulation: Stylised Facts and Growth Models', *World Bank Economic Review*, 15:2, pp. 177–219.

Easterly, W. and R. Levine (2003), 'Tropics, Germs and Crops: How Endowments Influence Economic Development', *Journal of Monetary Economics*, 50:1, pp. 3–39.

Easterly, W. and S. Rebelo (1993), 'Fiscal Policy and Economic Growth: an Empirical Investigation', *Journal of Monetary Economics*, 32, pp. 417–58.

Easterly, W., M. Kremer, L. Pritchett and L.H. Summers (1993), 'Good Policy or Good Luck? Country Growth Performance and Temporary Shocks', NBER, Working Paper No. 4474.

Eastwood, R. and R. Kohli (1999), 'Directed Credit and Investment in Small-Scale Industry in India: Evidence from Firm-Level Data 1965–78', *Journal of Development Studies*, 35:4, pp. 42–63.

Eltis, W. (2000), *The Classical Theory of Economic Growth*, Basingstoke, Palgrave.

Englebert, P. (2000), 'Solving the Mystery of the Africa Dummy', *World Development*, 28:10, pp. 1821–35.

Evans, P. (1995), *Embedded Autonomy: States and Industrial Transformation*, Princeton, Princeton University Press.

Farid, A. and J. Ashraf (1995), 'Volatility at Karachi Stock Exchange', *The Pakistan Development Review*, 34:4, pp. 651–7.

Farooq, G.M. (1973), 'Economic Growth and Changes in the Industrial Structure of Income and Labour Force in Pakistan', *Economic Development and Cultural Change*, 21:2, pp. 293–308.

Fatima, M. and Q.M. Ahmed (2001), 'Political Economy of Fiscal Reforms in the 1990s', *The Pakistan Development Review*, 40:4, pp. 503–18.

Fine, B. (1998), 'Endogenous Growth Theory: A Critical Assessment', Working Paper No. 80, SOAS, Department of Economics, University of London.

Fine, B. and C. Stoneman (1996), 'Introduction: State and Development', *Journal of Southern African Studies*, 22:1, pp. 5–26.

Fischer, S. (1993), 'The Role of Macroeconomic Factors in Growth', NBER, Working Paper No. 4565, National Bureau of Economic Research, pp. 45–65.

Fosu, A.K. (1992), 'Political Instability and Economic Growth: Evidence from Sub-Saharan Africa', *Economic Development and Cultural Change*, 40:4, pp. 829–4.

Franco-Rodriguez, S., O. Morressey and M. McGillvray (1998), 'Aid and the Public Sector in Pakistan: Evidence with Endogenous Aid', *World Development*, 26:7, pp. 1241–50.

Frankel, J.A. and D. Romer (1999), 'Does Trade Cause Growth?', *American Economic Review*, 89:3, pp. 379–99.

Gallup, J.L and J.D.Sachs (1999), 'Geography and Economic Development', Working Paper No. 1, Centre for International Development at Harvard University.

Gallup, J.L. and J.D. Sachs (2000), 'The Economic Burden of Malaria', Working Paper No. 52, Centre for International Development at Harvard University.

George, A.L. and A. Bennett (2005), *Case Studies and Theory Development in the Social Sciences*, Cambridge, MIT Press.

Gerring, J. (2007), *Case Study Research: Principles and Practices*, Cambridge, Cambridge University Press.

Gerschenkron, A. (1962), *Economic Backwardness in Historical Backwardness*, Cambridge, Harvard University Press.

Ghafoor, A. and J. Weiss (2001), 'Performance of the Public Electric Power Industry: Evidence from Pakistan', *The Pakistan Development Review*, 40:2, pp. 115–33.

Ghani, E. and M-ud Din (2006), 'The Impact of Public Investment on Economic Growth in Pakistan', *The Pakistan Development Review*, 45:1, pp. 87–98.

Gillani, S.F. (1986), 'Elasticity and Buoyancy of Federal Taxes in Pakistan', *The Pakistan Development Review*, 25:2, pp. 163–74.

Goldin, C. and L. Katz (1997), 'Why the United States Led in Education: Lessons from Secondary School Expansion, 1910–1940', NBER, Working Paper No. 6144.

Goldin, C. and L. Katz (1999), 'The Shaping of Education: The Formative Years of the United States', *Journal of Economic Perspectives*, 13:1, pp. 37–62.

Gordon, J. and P. Gupta (2003), 'Portfolio Flows Into India: Do Domestic Fundamentals Matter?', IMF Working Paper, WP/03/20, January.

Gordon, J. and P. Gupta (2004), 'Understanding India's Service Revolution', IMF Working Paper WP/04/171, Washington.

Gorg, H. and D. Greenaway (2004), 'Much Ado About Nothing? Do Domestic Firms Really Benefit from Foreign Direct Investment', *The World Bank Research Observer*, 19:2, pp. 171–97.

Government of Pakistan (2008), *Economic Survey 2007–08*, Finance Division, Islamabad.

Government of Pakistan (2009), *Economic Survey 2008–09*, Finance Division, Islamabad.

Government of Pakistan (2010), *Economic Survey 2009–10*, Finance Division, Islamabad.

Grabowski, R. (1994), 'The Successful Developmental State: Where Does it Come From?', *World Development*, 22:3, pp. 413–22.

Griffin, K.B. (1965), 'Financing Development Plans in Pakistan', *The Pakistan Development Review*, 5:4, pp. 601–30.

Griffin, K. and A.R. Khan (1972a), 'Industry and Trade', in Griffin, K. and A.R. Khan (Eds) (1972), *Growth and Inequality in Pakistan*, London, Macmillan.

Griffin, K. and A.R. Rahman (1972b), 'A Note on the Dependence on Foreign Assistance', in Griffin, K. and A.R. Khan (Eds) (1972), *Growth and Inequality in Pakistan*, London, Macmillan.

Guisinger, S. and N.L. Hicks (1978), 'Long-term Trends in Income Distribution in Pakistan', *World Development*, 6, pp. 1271–80.

Guisinger, S. and M. Irfan (1974), 'Real Wages of Industrial Workers in Pakistan: 1954 to 1970', *The Pakistan Development Review*, 13:4, pp. 363–88.

Guisinger, S.E. and S. Kazi (1978), 'The Rental Cost of Capital for the Manufacturing Sector – 1959/60 to 1970/71', *The Pakistan Development Review*, 17:4, pp. 385–407.

Hall, R.E. and C.I. Jones (1999), 'Why Do Some Countries Produce So Much More Output per Worker than Others?', *Quarterly Journal of Economics*, 114, pp. 83–116.

Hameed, A. and H. Ashraf (2006), 'Stock Market Volatility and Weak-form Efficiency: Evidence from an Emerging Market', *The Pakistan Development Review*, 45:5, pp. 1029–40.

Hansen, B. (1992), 'Testing for Parameter Instability in Linear Models', *Journal of Policy Modelling*, 14:4, pp. 517–33.

Hansen, B. (1997), 'Approximate Asymptotic p-values for Structural Change Tests', *Journal of Business and Economic Statistics*, January, 15:1, pp. 60–7.

Hansen, T.B. and C. Jaffrelot (Eds) (1998), *The BJP and the Compulsions of Politics in India*, New Delhi, Oxford University Press.

Haq, K. and M. Baqai (1967), 'Savings and Financial Flows in the Corporate Sector, 1959–63', *The Pakistan Development Review*, 7:3, pp. 283–316.

Hardy, D.C. and E.B. di Patti (2001), 'Bank Reform and Bank Efficiency in Pakistan', IMF Working Paper, WP/01/138.

Harilal, K.N. and J.J. Joseph (2003), 'Stagnation and Revival of Kerala Economy: An Open Economy Perspective', *Economic and Political Weekly*, June 7th, pp. 2286–94.

Harriss, J. (1987), 'The State in Retreat? Why Has India Experienced Such Half Hearted "Liberalisation" in the 1980s?', *Institute of Development Studies Bulletin*, 18:4, pp. 31–8.

Harriss, J. (2000), 'How Much Difference Does Politics Make? Regime Differences Across Indian States and Rural Poverty Reduction', DESTIN, Working Paper 01, LSE Development Studies Institute.

Harriss-White, B. (1996), 'Liberalisation and Corruption: Resolving the Paradox (A Discussion Bsed on South Indian Material)', *IDS Bulletin*, 27:2, pp. 31–39.

Harriss-White, B. (2003), *India Working: Essays on Society and Economy*, Cambridge, Cambridge University Press.

Harriss-White, B. and G. White (1996), 'Corruption, Liberalisation and Democracy: Editorial Introduction'. *IDS Bulletin*, 27:2, pp. 1–5.

Hasen, P. (1998), *Pakistan's Economy at the Crossroads: Past Policies and Present Imperatives*, Karachi, Oxford University Press.

Hashmi, B. (1983), 'Dragon Seed: Military in the State', in Gardezi, H. and J. Rashid (Eds) (1983), *Pakistan: The Roots of Dictatorship: The Political Economy of a Praetorian State*, London, Zed Press.

Hasnain, Z. (2008), 'The Politics of Service Delivery in Pakistan: Political Parties and the Incentives for Patronage, 1988–99', *The Pakistan Development Review*, 47:2, pp. 129–51.

Hatekar, N. and A. Dongre (2005), 'Structural Breaks in India's Growth: Revisiting the Debate with a Longer Perspective', *Economic and Political Weekly*, April 2nd, pp. 1432–5.

Hausman, R. and D. Rodrik (2003), 'Economic Development as Self-Discovery', *Journal of Development Economics*, 72, pp. 603–33.

Hausmann, R., L. Pritchett and D. Rodrik (2004), *Growth Accelerations*, JFK School of Govt, Harvard University, Mimeo.

Hecox, W.E. (1970), 'The Export Performance Licensing Scheme', *The Pakistan Development Review*, 10:1, pp. 24–49.

Hirschman, A.O. (1958), *The Strategy of Economic Development*, New Haven, Yale University Press.

Hobday, M. (1995), 'East Asian Latecomer Firms: Learning the Technology of Electronics', *World Development*, 23:7, pp. 1171–93.

Hoeffler, A. (2002), 'The Augmented Solow Model and the African Growth Debate', *Oxford Bulletin of Economics & Statistics*, 64:2 pp. 135–58.

Huber, E., D. Rueschemeyer and J.D. Stephens (1993), 'The Impact of Economic Development on Democracy', *Journal of Economic Perspectives*, 7:3, pp. 71–85.

Huff, W.G. (1999), 'Turning the Corner in Singapore's Developmental State', *Asian Survey*, 39:2, pp. 214–42.

Huff, W.G, G. Dewit and C. Oughton (2001), 'Credibility and Reputation Building in the Developmental State: A Model With East Asian Applications', *World Development*, 29:4, pp. 711–24.

Hunt, D. (1989), *Economic Theories of Development: An Analysis of Competing Paradigms*, London, Harvester Wheatsheaf.

Huntingdon, S.P. (1968), *Political Order in Changing Societies*, New Haven, Yale University Press.

Husain, A.M. (1996), 'Private Saving and its Determinants: The Case of Pakistan', *The Pakistan Development Review*, 35:1, pp. 49–70.

Husain, F. and T. Mahmood (2001), 'The Stock Market and the Economy in Pakistan', *The Pakistan Development Review*, 40:2, pp. 107–14.

Husain, I. (1999), *Pakistan: The Economy of an Elitist State*, Karachi, Oxford University Press.

Husain, I. (2003), *Economic Management in Pakistan, 1999–2002*, Karachi, Oxford University Press.

Hyder, K. (2001), 'Crowding Out Hypothesis in a Vector Error Correction Framework: A Case Study of Pakistan', *The Pakistan Development Review*, 40:4, pp. 633–50.

Iimi, A. (2003), 'Efficiency in the Pakistani Banking Industry: Empirical Evidence after Structural Reform in the Late 1990s', *The Pakistan Development Review*, 42:1, pp. 41–57.

Ikram, K. (1973), 'Social Versus Private Profitability in Pakistan's Export of Manufactures', *The Pakistan Development Review*, 12:2, pp. 156–67.

IMF (2002), *Pakistan: Selected Issues and Statistical Appendix*, Washington, IMF.

IMF (2004), *Pakistan: Selected Issues and Statistical Appendix*, Washington, IMF.

Iqbal, Z. (1993), 'Institutional Variations in Saving in Pakistan', *The Pakistan Development Review*, 32:4, pp. 1293–1311.

Iqbal, Z. (1994), 'Macroeconomic Effects of Adjustment Lending in Pakistan', *The Pakistan Development Review*, 33:4, pp. 1011–31.

Iqbal, Z. (1997), 'Foreign Aid and the Public Sector: A Model of Fiscal Behaviour in Pakistan', *The Pakistan Development Review*, 36:2, pp. 115–29.

Iqbal, Z. and G.M. Zahid (1998), 'Macroeconomic Determinants of Economic Growth in Pakistan', *The Pakistan Development Review*, 37:2, pp. 125–48.

Irfan, M. and M.A. Ahmed (1985), 'Real Wages in Pakistan: Structure and Trends, 1970–84', *The Pakistan Development Review*, 23:3+4, pp. 423–37.

Islam, A.I.A. (1961), 'Pakistan's Terms of Trade', *The Pakistan Development Review*, 1:2, pp. 55–66.

Islam, A.I.A. (1970), 'An Estimation of the Extent of Overvaluation of the Domestic Currency in Pakistan at the Official Exchange Rate, 1948/49 – 1964/65', *The Pakistan Development Review*, 10:1, pp. 50–67.

Islam, N. (1967), 'Comparative Costs, Factor Proportions and Industrial Efficiency in Pakistan', *The Pakistan Development Review*, 7:2, pp. 213–46.

Islam, N. (1972), 'Foreign Assistance and Economic Development: The Case of Pakistan', *Economic Journal*, 82:325, pp. 502–30.

Islam, N. (1995), 'Growth Empirics: A Panel Data Approach', *Quarterly Journal of Economics*, 110, pp. 1127–70.

Jaffrelot, E. (2002), *A History of Pakistan and its Origins*, London, Anthem Press.

Jaffry, S., Y. Ghulam and J. Cox (2006), 'Impact of Regulatory Reforms on Labour Efficiency in the Indian and Pakistani Commercial Banks', *The Pakistan Development Review*, 45:4, pp. 1085–1102.

Jalal, A. (1990), *The State of Martial Rule: The Origins of Pakistan's Political Economy of Defence*, Cambridge, Cambridge University Press.

Jalal, A. (1995), *Democracy and Authoritarianism in South Asia: A Comparative and Historical Perspective*, Cambridge, Cambridge University Press.

James, W.E. and S. Naya (1990), 'Trade and Industrialisation Policies for an Accelerated Development in Pakistan', *The Pakistan Development Review*, 29:3, pp. 201–22.

Jeromi, P.D. (2005), 'Economic Reforms in Kerala', *Economic and Political Weekly*, 23rd July, pp. 3267–77.

Jomo, K.S. and E.T. Gomez (2000), 'Malaysian Development Dilemma', in Khan, M.H. and K.S. Jomo (Eds) (2000), *Rents, Rent-Seeking and Economic Development: Theory and Evidence in Asia*, Cambridge, Cambridge University Press.

Jones, C.I. (1994), 'Economic Growth and the Relative Price of Capital', *Journal of Monetary Economics*, 34, pp. 359–82.

Jones, C.I. (1995a), 'Time Series Tests of Endogenous Growth Models', *Quarterly Journal of Economics*, 110:2, pp. 495–525.

Jones, C.I. (1995b), 'R&D-based Models of Economic Growth', *Journal of Political Economy*, 103:4, pp. 759-84.

Jones, P.E. (2003), *The Pakistan People's Party: Rise to Power*, Karachi, Oxford University Press.

Kaplan, E. and D. Rodrik (2001), *Did Malaysian Capital Controls Work?*, Harvard University, Kennedy School of Government, Mimeo.

Kaplinsky, R. (1999), 'If You Want to Get Somewhere, You Must Run at Least Twice as Fast as That!: The Roots of the East Asian Crisis', *IDS Bulletin*, 30:1, pp. 1–30.

Kaur, P. (2007), 'Growth Acceleration in India', *Economic and Political Weekly*, 14th April, pp. 1380–6.

Kazi, S. (1987), 'Intersectoral Terms of Trade for Pakistan's Economy: 1970/71 to 1981/82', *The Pakistan Development Review*, 26:1, pp. 81–105.

Kazmi, A.A. (1993), 'National Savings Rates of India and Pakistan: A Macroeconomic Analysis', *The Pakistan Development Review*, 32:4, pp. 1313–24.

Keefer, P.E., A. Narayan and T. Vishwanath (2003), *The Political Economy of Decentralisation in Pakistan*, Mimeo.

Keen, S. (2001), *Debunking Economics: The Naked Emperor of the Social Sciences*, Annandale, Pluto Press.

Kemal, A.R. (1974), 'The Contribution of Pakistan's Large-Scale Manufacturing Industries Towards Gross National Product at World Prices', *The Pakistan Development Review*, 13:1, pp. 1–12.

Kemal, A.R. (1976), 'Sectoral Growth Rates and Efficiency of Factor Use in Large-Scale Manufacturing Sector In West Pakistan', *Pakistan Development Review*, 15:4, pp. 349–81.

Kemal, A.R. (1979), 'Infant Industry Argument, Protection and Manufacturing Industries of Pakistan', *The Pakistan Development Review*, 18:1, pp. 1–19.

Kemal, A.R. (1981), 'Substitution Elasticities in the Large-Scale Manufacturing Industries of Pakistan', *The Pakistan Development Review*, 20:1, pp. 1–36.

Kemal, A.R. (1982), 'Substitution Elasticities in the Large-Scale Manufacturing Industries of Pakistan – A Rejoinder', *The Pakistan Development Review*, 21:2, pp. 159–68.

Kemal, A.R. (1997), 'Pakistan's Industrial Experience and Future Directions', *The Pakistan Development Review*, 36:4, pp. 929–44.

Kemal, A.R. (1999), 'Patterns and Growth of Pakistan's Industrial Sector' in Khan, A.R. (Ed.) (1999), *Fifty Years of Pakistan's Economy: Traditional Topics and Contemporary Concerns*, Karachi, Oxford University Press.

Kemal, A.R. and T. Alauddin (1974), 'Capacity Utilisation in Manufacturing Industries of Pakistan', *Pakistan Development Review*, 13:3, pp. 231–44.

Kemal, A.R. and Z. Alvie (1975), 'Effect of 1972 Devaluation on Pakistan's Balance of Trade', *The Pakistan Development Review*, 14:1, pp. 1–22.

Kemal, A.R., M. ud Din and U. Qadir (2006), 'Economic Growth in Pakistan', in Parikh, K.S. (Ed.) (2006), *Explaining Growth in South Asia*, New Delhi, Oxford University Press.

Kenny, C. (1999), 'Why Aren't Countries Rich? Weak States and Bad Neighbours', *Journal of Development Studies*, 35:5, pp. 26–47.

Kenny, C. and D. Williams (2001), 'What Do We Know About Economic Growth? Or, Why Don't We Know Very Much?', *World Development*, 29:1, pp. 1–22.

Khan, A. (2002), 'Pakistan's Sindhi Ethnic Nationalism: Migration, Marginalisation and the Threat of "Indianisation"', *Asian Survey*, 42:2, pp. 213–29.

Khan, A.H. (1988), 'Macroeconomic Policy and Private Investment in Pakistan', *The Pakistan Development Review*, 27:3, pp. 277–91.

Khan, A.H. and L. Hasan (1998), 'Financial Liberalisation, Savings and Economic Development in Pakistan', *Economic Development and Cultural Change*, 46:3, pp. 581–97.

Khan, A.H., L. Hasan and A. Malik (1992), 'Dependency Ratio, Foreign Capital Inflows and the Rate of Savings in Pakistan', The *Pakistan Development Review*, 31:4, pp. 843–56.

Khan, A.R. (1967), 'What Has Been Happening to Real Wages in Pakistan', *The Pakistan Development Review*, 7:3, pp. 317–47.

Khan, A.R. (1968), 'Some Notes on "Planning Experience in Pakistan"', *The Pakistan Development Review*, 8:3, pp. 419–30.

Khan, A.R. (1970), 'Capital Intensity and the Efficiency of Factor Use: A Comparative Study of the Observed Capital-Labour Ratios of Pakistani Industries', *The Pakistan Development Review*, 10:2, pp. 232–63.

Khan, M.A. and A. Qayyum (2007), 'Trade Liberalisation, Financial Development and Economic Growth', Working Paper No. 19, Pakistan Institute of Development Economics.

Khan, M.A., A. Qayyum and S.A. Sheikh (2005), 'Financial Development and Economic Growth', *The Pakistan Development Review*, 44:4, pp. 819–37.

Khan, M.H. (1991), 'Resource Mobilisation from Agriculture in Pakistan', *The Pakistan Development Review*, 30:4, pp. 457–83.

Khan, M.H. (1999), 'Agricultural Development and Changes in the Land Tenure and Land Revenue Systems in Pakistan', in Khan, S.R. (Ed.) (1999), *50 Years of Pakistan's Economy: Traditional Topics and Contemporary Concerns*, Karachi, Oxford University Press.

Khan, M.H. (2000a), 'Rent-Seeking as Process', in Khan, M.H. and K.S. Jomo (Eds) (2000), *Rents, Rent-Seeking and Economic Development: Theory and Evidence in Asia*, Cambridge, Cambridge University Press.

Khan, M.H. (2000b), 'The Political Economy of Industrial Policy in Pakistan, 1947 – 1971', Working Paper No. 98, SOAS, Department of Economics, University of London.

Khan, M.H. (2000c), 'Rents, Efficiency and Growth', in Khan, M.H. and K.S. Jomo (Eds) (2000), *Rents, Rent-Seeking and Economic Development: Theory and Evidence in Asia*, Cambridge, Cambridge University Press.

Khan, M.S. (2005), 'Human Capital and Economic Growth in Pakistan', *The Pakistan Development Review*, 44:4, pp. 455–78.

Khan, M.Z. (1973), 'The Responsiveness of Tax Yield to Increases in National Income', *The Pakistan Development Review*, 12:4, pp. 416–32.

Khan, N.Z. (1998), 'Textile Sector of Pakistan: The Challenge Beyond 2004', *The Pakistan Development Review*, 37:4, pp. 595–619.

Khan, N.Z. and E. Rahmin (1993), 'Foreign Aid, Domestic Savings and Economic Growth (Pakistan: 1960 to 1998)', *The Pakistan Development Review*, 32:4, pp. 1157–67.

Khan, S.M. (1993), 'Domestic Resource Mobilisation: A Structural Approach', *The Pakistan Development Review*, 32:4, pp. 1067–78.

Khan, S.R. (1997), 'Has Aid Helped in Pakistan?', *The Pakistan Development Review*, 36:4, pp. 947–57.

Khan, S.R. (2004), *Pakistan Under Musharraf 1999–2002: Economic Reform and Political Change*, Lahore, Vanguard Books.

Khan, S.U.K. (2005), 'Macro Determinants of Total Factor Productivity in Pakistan', *SBP Research Bulletin*, 2:2, pp. 383–401.

Khilji, N.M. and E. Zampelli (1991), 'The Effect of US Assistance on Public and Private Expenditures in Pakistan: 1960–88', *The Pakistan Development Review*, 30:4, pp. 1169–84.

King, R.G. and R. Levine (1993), 'Finance and Growth: Why Schumpeter Might Be Right', *Quarterly Journal of Economics*, 108, pp. 717–37.

King, R.G. and S. Rebelo (1990), 'Public Policy and Economic Growth: Developing Neo-classical Implications', *Journal of Political Economy*, 98, pp. S126–50.

Kite, G. and M. McCartney (forthcoming), 'From Boom to Bust and Back Again? Economic Growth in Pakistan 1951 to 2009'.

Knowles, S. and A. Garces-Ozanne (2003), 'Government Intervention and Economic Performance in East Asia', *Economic Development and Cultural Change*, 51:2, pp. 451–77.

Kochhar, K., U. Kumar, R. Rajan, A. Subramanian and I. Tokatlidis (2006), 'India's Pattern of Development: What Happened, What Followed?' IMF Working Paper, WP/06/22, Washington.

Kohli, A. (1987), *The State and Poverty in India: The Politics of Economic Reform*, Cambridge, Cambridge University Press.

Kohli, A. (1990), *Democracy and Discontent: India's growing Crisis of Governability*, Cambridge, Cambridge University Press.

Kohli, A. (1994), 'Where Do High Growth Political Economies Come From? The Japanese Lineage of Korea's "Developmental State"', *World Development*, 22:9, pp. 1269–93.

Kohli, R. (2001), 'Capital Flows and their Macroeconomic Effect in India' IMF Working Paper No. 192, November.

Kok-Fay, C. and K.S. Jomo (2000), 'Financial Rents in Malaysia', in Khan, M.H. and K.S. Jomo (Eds) (2000), *Rents, Rent-Seeking and Economic Development: Theory and Evidence in Asia*, Cambridge, Cambridge University Press.

Kokko, A. and M. Blomstrom (1995), 'Policies to Encourage Inflows of Technology Through Foreign Multinationals', *World Development*, 23:3, pp. 459-68.

Kothari, R. (1964), 'The Congress System in India', *Asian Survey*, 4:12, pp. 1161–73.

Krieckhaus, J. (2002), 'Reconceptualising the Developmental State: Public Savings and Economic Growth', *World Development*, 30:10, pp. 1697–1712.

Krugman, P. (1999), *The Return of Depression Economics*, New York, W.W.Norton.

Kurian, N.J. (2000), 'Widening Regional Disparities in India: Some Indicators', *Economic and Political Weekly*, 12th February, pp. 539–50.

Kurosaki, T. (1999), 'Agriculture in India and Pakistan, 1900–95: Productivity and Crop Mix', *Economic and Political Weekly*, 25th December, pp. A160–8.

Kuznets, P.W. (1988), 'An East Asian Model of Economic Development: Japan, Taiwan and South Korea', *Economic Development and Cultural Change*, 36, pp. S11–43.

Lall, S. (1992), 'Technological Capabilities and Industrialisation', *World Development*, 20:2, pp. 165–86.

Lall, S. (1995), 'Structural Adjustment and African Industry', *World Development*, 23:12, pp. 2019–31.

Lall, S. (1999), 'India's Manufacturing Exports: Comparative Structure and Prospects', *World Development*, 27:10, pp. 1769–86.

Lall, S. (2000), 'The Technological Structure and Performance of Developing Country Manufactured Exports, 1985–98', *Oxford Development Studies*, 28:3, pp. 337–69.

Lall, S.V. (1999), 'The Role of Public Infrastructure Investments in Regional Development', *Economic and Political Weekly*, 20th March, pp. 717–25.

LaPorta, R., F. Lopez de Silanes, A. Schleifer and R. Vishny (1998), 'The Quality of Government', NBER, Working Paper No. 6727.

Lee, J-W. (1995), 'Capital Goods Imports and Long-run Growth', *Journal of Development Economics*, 48, pp. 91–110.

Leftwich, A. (1995), 'Bringing Politics Back In: Towards a Model of the Developmental State', *Journal of Development Studies*, 31:3, pp. 400–27.

Leftwich, A. (2000), *States of Development: On the Primacy of Politics in Development*, Polity Press, Cambridge.

Levine, R. (1997), 'Financial Development and Economic Growth', *Journal of Economic Literature*, 35:2, pp. 688–726.

Levine, R. and D. Renelt (1992), 'A Sensitivity Analysis of Cross-Country Growth Regressions', *American Economic Review*, 82:4, pp. 942–63.

Lewis, S.R. (1964), 'Aspects of Fiscal Policy and Resource Mobilisation in Pakistan', *The Pakistan Development Review*, 4:2, pp. 261–82.

Lewis, S.R. (1965), 'Domestic Resources and Fiscal Policy in Pakistan's Second and Third Plans', *Pakistan Development Review*, 5:3, pp. 461–95.

Lewis, S.R. (1968), 'Effects of Trade Policy on Domestic Relative Prices in Pakistan, 1951–64', *The American Economic Review*, 58:1, pp. 60–78.

Lewis, S.R. (1969), *Economic Policy and Industrial Growth in Pakistan*, London, George Allen and Unwin Limited.

Lewis, S.R. (1970), *Pakistan: Industrialisation and Trade Policies*, London, Oxford University Press.

Lewis, S.R. and S.E. Guisinger (1968), 'Measuring Protection in a Developing Country: The Case of Paksitan', *The Journal of Political Economy*, 76:6, pp. 1170–98.

Lewis, S.R. and S.M. Hussain (1966), 'Relative Price Changes and Industrialisation in Pakistan: 1951–1964', *The Pakistan Development Review*, 6:3, pp. 408–31.

Lewis, S.R. and M.I. Khan (1964), 'Estimates of Noncorporate Private Saving in Pakistan: 1949–1962', *Pakistan Development Review*, 4:3, pp. 1–50.

Lewis, S.R. and R. Soligo (1965), 'Growth and Structural Change in Pakistan Manufacturing Industry, 1954–64', *Pakistan Development Review*, 5:1, pp. 94–139.

Leys, C (1965), 'What is the Problem About Corruption?', *Journal of Modern African Studies*, 3:2, pp. 51–66.

Lipset, S.M. (1959), 'Some Social Requisites of Democracy: Economic Development and Political Legitimacy', *American Political Science Review*, 52:1, pp. 69–105.

Little, I., T. Scitovsky and M. Scott (1970), *Industry and Trade in Some Developing Countries: A Comparative Study*, London, Oxford University Press.

Loriaux, M. (1999), 'The French Developmental State as Myth and Moral Ambition', in Woo-Cumings, M. (Ed.), *The Developmental State*, New York, Cornell University Press.

Lorie, H. and Z. Iqbal (2005), 'Pakistan's Macroeconomic Adjustment and Resumption of Growth, 1999–2004', IMF Working Paper, WP/05/139, Washington.

Lucas, R.E. (1988), 'On the Mechanics of Economic Development', *Journal of Monetary Economics*, 22, pp. 3–42.

Lutz, M. (1994), 'The Effects of Volatility in the Terms of Trade on Output Growth: New Evidence', *World Development*, 22:12, pp. 1959–75.

Maddison, A. (1971), *Class Structure and Economic Growth: India and Pakistan Since the Moghuls*, New York, W.W.Norton.

Maddison, A. (2001), *The World Economy: a Millennial Perspective*, Paris, OECD.

Mahmood, A. (2004), 'Export Competitiveness and Comparative Advantage of Pakistan's Non-agricultural Production Sectors: Trends and Analysis', *The Pakistan Development Review*, 43:4, pp. 541–61.

Mahmood, A. and N. Akhtar (1996), 'The Export Growth of Pakistan: A Decomposition Analysis', *The Pakistan Development Review*, 35:4, pp. 693–702.

Mahmood, A. and M. Azhar (2001), 'On Overinvoicing of Exports in Pakistan', *The Pakistan Development Review*, 40:3, pp. 173–85.

Mahmood, M.A. and S.A. Sahibzada (1987), 'The Performance of Public Sector Enterprises: 1981–86', *The Pakistan Development Review*, 26:4, pp. 793–803.

Mahmood, Z. and M.A. Qasim (1992), 'Foreign Trade Regime and Savings in Pakistan', *The Pakistan Development Review*, 31:4, pp. 883–93.

Mahmood, Z. and R. Siddiqui (2000), 'State of Technology and Productivity in Pakistan's Manufacturing Industries: Some Strategic Directions to Build Technological Competence', *The Pakistan Development Review*, 39:1, pp. 1–21.

Malik, I.H. (1996), 'The State and Civil Society in Pakistan: From Crisis to Crisis', *Asian Survey*, 36:7, pp. 673–90.

Malik, M.H. and A.A. Cheema (1986), 'The Role of Small Scale Industry in Pakistan's Economy and Government Incentives', *The Pakistan Development Review*, 25:4, pp. 789–807.

Malik, S., M. Hassan and S. Hussain (2006), 'Fiscal Decentralisation and Economic Growth in Pakistan', *The Pakistan Development Review*, 45:4, pp. 845–54.

Malik, S.J. and S. Nazli (1999), 'Population, Employment and the State of Human Resources', in Khan, S.R. (Ed.) (1999), *'50 Years of Pakistan's Economy: Traditional Topics and Contemporary Concerns'*, Karachi, Oxford University Press.

Maniruzzaman, T. (1971), 'Crisis in Political Development and the Collapse of the Ayub Regime in Pakistan', *The Journal of Developing Areas*, 5:2, pp. 221–38.

Mankiw, N.G., D. Romer and D.N. Weil (1992), 'A Contribution to Economic Growth', *Quarterly Journal of Economics*, 107, pp. 407–37.

Mas-Colell, A., M.D. Whinston and J.R. Green (1995), *Microeconomic Theory*, Oxford, Oxford University Press.

Mauro, P. (1995), 'Corruption and Economic Growth', *Quarterly Journal of Economics*, 110, pp. 681–712.

McCartney, M. (2009a), *India – The Political Economy of Growth, Stagnation and the State, 1951–2007*, London, Routledge.

McCartney, M. (2009b), *Political Economy, Growth and Liberalisation in India, 1991–2008*, London, Routledge.

Menon, V. (2003), *From Movement to Government: The Congress in the United Provinces, 1937–42*, New Delhi, Sage.

Miguel, E. (2000), 'School Funding and Ethnic Diversity in Kenya', Centre for Labour Economics, Working Paper No. 29, University of California, Berkeley.

Mkandawire, T. (2001), 'Thinking about Developmental States in Africa' *Cambridge Journal of Economics*, 25, pp. 2989–3313.

Moore, B. (1967), *Social Origins of Dictatorship and Democracy: Lord and Peasant in the Making of the Modern World*, Harmondsworth, Penguin.

Mosley, P. (2000), 'Globalisation, Economic Policy and Convergence', *World Economy*, 23:5, pp. 613–34.

Mukarram, F. (2001), 'Elasticity and Buoyancy of Major Taxes in Pakistan', *Pakistan Economic and Social Review*, 39:1, pp. 75–86.

Mulligan, C.B., R. Gil and X. Sala-i-Martin (2004), 'Do Democracies Have Different Public Policies than Non-democracies?', *Journal of Economic Perspectives*, 18:1, pp. 51–74.

Nabi, I. (1984), 'Issues in the Economics of Industrialisation in Developing Countries: A Case Study from Pakistan's Light Engineering Section', *The Pakistan Development Review*, 23:2+3, pp. 311–29.

Nabi, I. (1999), 'The Competitiveness of Pakistani Exports', in Khan, S.R. (Ed.) (1999), *'50 Years of Pakistan's Economy: Traditional Topics and Contemporary Concerns'*, Karachi, Oxford University Press.

Nadvi, K. (1999a), 'The Cutting Edge: Collective Efficiency and International Competitiveness in Pakistan', *Oxford Development Studies*, 27:1, pp. 81–107.

Nadvi, K. (1999b), 'Collective Efficiency and Collective Failure: The Response of the Sialkot Surgical Instrument Cluster to Global Quality Pressure', *World Development*, 27:9, pp. 1605–26.

Nagaraj, R. (1990), 'Growth Rate of India's GDP, 1950–51 to 1987–88: Examination of Alternative Hypotheses', *Economic and Political Weekly*, 30th June, pp. 1396–1403.

Naqvi, S.N.H. (1964), 'Import Licensing in Pakistan', The *Pakistan Development Review*, 4:1, pp. 51–68.

Naqvi, S.N.H. (1966), 'The Allocative Biases of Pakistan's Commercial Policy: 1953 to 1963', *Pakistan Development Review*, 6:4, pp. 465–99.

Naqvi, S.N.H. (2002), 'Crowding Out or Crowding in? Modelling the Relationship between Public and Private Fixed Capital Formation Using Co-integration Analysis: The Case of Pakistan', *The Pakistan Development Review*, 41:3, pp. 255–75.

Naqvi, S.N.H. and A.R. Kemal (1991), *Protectionism and Efficiency in Manufacturing: A Case Study of Pakistan*, San Francisco, ICS Press.

Naseem, S.M. (2002), 'The Crisis of Growth and Economic Management in Pakistan', in Naseem, S.M. and K. Nadvi (Eds) (2002), *The Post-Colonial State and Social Transformation in India and Pakistan*, Karachi, Oxford University Press.

Nasir, S. and M. Khalid (2004), 'Saving Investment Behaviour in Pakistan: An Empirical Investigation', *The Pakistan Development Review*, 43:4, pp. 665–82.

Nasr, S.V.R. (1992), 'Democracy and the Crisis of Governability in Pakistan', *Asian Survey*, 32:6, pp. 521–37.

Naughton, B. (2007), *The Chinese Economy: Transitions and Growth*, Cambridge, MIT Press.

Nawab, S., H. Naqvi and K. Sarmad (1984), *Pakistan's Economy Through the Seventies*, Islamabad, Pakistan Institute of Development Economics.

Nayab, D. (2006), 'Demographic Dividend or Demographic Threat in Pakistan', *PIDE Working Papers* No. 10, Islamabad.

Nayyar, D. (2006), 'Economic Growth in Independent India: Lumbering Elephant or Running Tiger', *Economic and Political Weekly*, 15th April, pp. 1451–8.

Nehru, J. (1946), *The Discovery of India*, New Delhi, Oxford University Press.

Nolan, P. (1995), *China's Rise, Russia's Decline: Politics, Economics and Planning in the Transition from Stalinism*, London, Macmillan Press.

Noman, A. (1975), 'Pakistan and the Socialist Countries: Trade and Aid', *World Development*, 3:5, pp. 315–28.

Noman, A. (1991), 'Industrial Development and Efficiency in Pakistan: A Revisionist View', *The Pakistan Development Review*, 30:4, pp. 849–61.

Noman, O. (1988), *The Political Economy of Pakistan, 1947–85*, London, KPI.

Norbye, O.D.K. (1978), 'Are "Consistent Time Series Data Relating to Pakistan's Large-Scale Manufacturing Industries" Inconsistent: A Comment', *The Pakistan Development Review*, 17:1, pp. 99–108.

North, D.C. (1990), *Institutions, Institutional Change and Economic Performance*, Cambridge, Cambridge University Press.

Ojo, O. and T. Oshikoya (1995), 'Determinants of Long-term Growth: Some African Results', *Journal of African Economies*, 4:2, pp. 163–91.

Olson, M. (1982), *The Rise and Decline of Nations: Economic Growth, Stagflation, and Social Rigidities*, New Haven, Yale University Press.

Olson, M. (1993), 'Dictatorship, Democracy and Development', *American Political Science Review*, 87:3, pp. 567–76.

Olson, M. (2000), *Power and Prosperity: Outgrowing Communist and Capitalist Dictatorships*, New York, Basic Books.

Pal, M.L. (1964), 'The Determinants of the Domestic Prices of Imports', *The Pakistan Development Review*, 4:4, pp. 597–622.

Pal, M.L. (1965), 'Domestic Prices of Imports in Pakistan: Extension of Empirical Findings', *The Pakistan Development Review*, 5:4, pp. 547–85.

Pantibala, M. and B. Petersen (2002), 'Role of Transnational Corporations in the Evolution of a High-Tech Industry: The Case of India's Software Industry', *World Development*, 30:9, pp. 1561–77.

Papanek, G.F. (1964), 'Industrial Production and Investment in Pakistan', *Pakistan Development Review*, 4:3, pp. 462–90.

Papanek, G.F. (1966), 'Tariff Protection, Import Substitution and Investment Efficiency: A Comment', *The Pakistan Development Review*, 6:1, pp. 105–9.

Papanek, G.F. (1967), *Pakistan's Development: Social Goals and Private Incentives* Cambridge, Harvard University Press.

Papanek, H. (1972), 'Pakistan's Big Businessmen: Muslim Separatism, Entrepreneurship, and Partial Modernisation', *Economic Development and Cultural Change*, 21:1, pp. 1–32.

Papanek, G.F (1991), 'Market or Government: Lessons from a Comparative Analysis of the Experience of Pakistan and India', *The Pakistan Development Review*, 30:4, pp. 601–46.

Parikh, A., F. Ali and M.K. Shah (1995), 'Measurement of Economic Efficiency in Pakistani Agriculture', *American Journal of Agricultural Economics*, 77:3, pp. 675–85.

Pasha, H.A. and M. Fatima (1999), 'Fifty Years of Public Finance in Pakistan: A Trend Analysis', in Khan, S.R. (Ed.) (1999), *50 Years of Pakistan's Economy: Traditional Topics and Contemporary Concerns*, Karachi, Oxford University Press.

Pasha, H.A., A. Ghaus-Pasha and N. Aamir (2002), 'Hidden Subsidies', *The Pakistan Development Review*, 41:4, pp. 629–40.

Persson, T. and G. Tabellini (1991), 'Is Inequality Harmful for Growth: Theory and Evidence', Centre for Economic Policy Research (London), Discussion Paper No.581.

Pingle, V. (1999), *Rethinking the Developmental State: India's Industry in Comparative Perspective*, New Delhi, Oxford University Press.

Pio, A. (1994), 'New Growth Theory and Old Development Problems: How Recent Developments in Endogenous Growth Theory Apply to Developing Countries', *Development Policy Review*, 12, pp. 277–300.

Power, J.H. (1963), 'Industrialisation in Pakistan: A Case of Frustrated Take-off?', *The Pakistan Development Review*, 3:2, pp. 191–207.

Pritchett, L. (1997), 'Divergence, Big Time', *Journal of Economic Perspectives*, 11:3, Summer, pp. 3–17.

Pritchett, L. (1999), *Where has all the Education Gone?* December, World Bank, Mimeo.

Pritchett, L. (2000), 'Understanding Patterns of Economic Growth: Searching for Hills Among Plateaus, Mountains and Plains', *World Bank Economic Review*, 14:2, pp. 221–50.

Przworski, A., M.E. Alvarez, J.A. Cheibub and F. Limongi (2000), *Democracy and Development: Political Institutions and Well-Being in the World, 1950–1990*, Cambridge, Cambridge University Press.

Purfield, C. (2006), *'Mind the Gap – Is Economic Growth in India Leaving Some States Behind?'*, IMF Working Paper, WP/06/103, Washington, DC.

Quandt, R. (1960), 'Tests of the Hypothesis that a Linear Regression Obeys Two Separate Regimes', *Journal of the American Statistical Association*, 55, pp. 324–30.

Qureshi, A.K., M. Din, E. Ghani and K. Abbas (1997), 'Domestic Resource Mobilisation for Development in Pakistan', *The Pakistan Development Review*, 36:4, pp. 891–912.

Qureshi, M.L. and F. Bilquees (1977), 'A Note on Changes in Real Wages of Government Servants 1959/60 to 1975/76', *The Pakistan Development Review*, 16:3, pp. 325–44.

Qureshi, S. (1980), 'Islam and Development: The Zia Regime in Pakistan', *World Development*, 8, pp. 563–75.

Qureshi, S.K. (1985), 'Domestic Terms of Trade and Public Policy for Agriculture in Pakistan', *The Pakistan Development Review*, 14:3–4, pp. 363–83.

Qureshi, Z.A. (1981), 'Household Saving in Pakistan: Some Findings from Time-Series Data', *The Pakistan Development Review*, 20:4, pp. 375–97.

Radhu, G.M. (1964), 'The Rate Structure of Indirect Taxes in Pakistan', *Pakistan Development Review*, 4:3, pp. 527–51.

Radhu, G.M. (1973), 'Transfer of Technical Know-How Through Multinational Corporations in Pakistan', *The Pakistan Development Review*, 12:4, pp. 361–74.

Rahman, T. (1997), 'Language and Ethnicity in Pakistan', *Asian Survey*, 37:9, pp. 833–9.

Rao, M.G., R.T. Shand and K.P. Kalirajan (1999), 'Convergence of Incomes Across Indian States: A Divergence View', *Economic and Political Weekly*, 27th March, pp. 769–78.

Rashid, J. (1983), 'Pakistan in the Debt Trap', in Gardezi, H. and J. Rashid (Eds) (1983), *Pakistan: The Roots of Dictatorship: The Political Economy of a Praetorian State*, London, Zed Press.

Rashid, J. and H.N. Gardezi (1983), 'Independent Pakistan: Its Political Economy', in Gardezi, H. and J. Rashid (Eds) (1983), *Pakistan: The Roots of Dictatorship: The Political Economy of a Praetorian State*, London, Zed Press.

Rauf, S. (1994), 'Structure of Large-scale Manufacturing Industries of Pakistan (1950 to 1988)', *The Pakistan Development Review*, 33:4, pp. 1373–84.

Raza, R. (1997), *Zulfikar Al Bhutto and Pakistan 1967–1977*, Karachi, Oxford University Press.

Rebelo, S. (1991), 'Long-Run Policy Analysis and Long-Run Growth', *Journal of Political Economy*, 99, pp. 500–21.

Rhee, Y.W. (1990), 'The Catalyst Model of Development: Lessons from Bangladesh's Success with Garment Exports', *World Development*, 18:2, pp. 333–46.

Rizvi, A.F.A. (2001), 'Post-liberalisation Efficiency and Productivity of the Banking Sector in Pakistan', *The Pakistan Development Review*, 40:4, pp. 605–32.

Rodrik, D. (1989), 'Credibility of Trade Reform – a Policy Maker's Guide', *World Economy*, 12:1, pp. 1–16.

Rodrik, D. (1991), 'Policy Uncertainty and Private Investment in Developing Countries', *Journal of Development Economics*, 36:2, pp. 229–42.

Rodrik, D. (1998), 'Why do More Open Economies Have Bigger Governments?', *Journal of Political Economy*, 106:5, pp. 997–1032.

Rodrik, D. (1999a), 'Where Did All the Growth Go? External Shocks, Social Conflict, and Growth Collapses', *Journal of Economic Growth*, 4:4, pp. 385–412.

Rodrik, D. (1999b), *'Institutions for High Quality Growth: What they are and How to Acquire Them'*, Harvard University, draft paper prepared for the IMF Conference on Second-Generation Reforms, Washington, DC, 8–9th Nov 1999.

Rodrik, D. (2000a), *Development Strategies for the Next Century*, Japan External Trade Organisation, 26–27th January.

Rodrik, D. (2000b), 'Participatory Politics, Social Cooperation and Economic Stability', *American Economic Review*, 90:2, pp. 135–40.

Rodrik, D. (2003a), *Growth Strategies*, Kennedy School of Government, Harvard University, Mimeo.

Rodrik, D. (2003b), 'Introduction', in Rodrik, D. (Ed.) (2003), *In Search of Prosperity: Analytic Narratives on Economic Growth*, Princeton, Princeton University Press.

Rodrik, D. (2005), *Why We Learn Nothing from Regressing Economic Growth on Policies*, Harvard University, Mimeo.

Rodrik, D., A. Subramanian, F. Trebbi (2002), 'Institutions Rule: The Primacy of Institutions over Geography and Integration in Economic Development', Working Paper No. 97, Centre for International Development at Harvard University.

Romer, P.M. (1986), 'Increasing Returns and Long-Run Growth', *Journal of Political Economy*, 94:5, pp. 1002–37.

Romer, P.M. (1990), 'Endogenous Technological Change', *Journal of Political Economy*, 98:5, pp. S71–102.

Romijn, H. (1997), 'Acquisition of Technological Capacity in Development: A Quantitative Case Study of Pakistan's Capital Goods Sector', *World Development*, 25:3, pp. 359–77.

Rowthorn, B. (1977), *Capitalism, Conflict and Inflation*, London, Lawrence and Wishart.

Rudolph, L.I. and S.H. Rudolph (1987), *In Pursuit of Lakshmi: The Political Economy of the Indian State*, Chicago, Chicago University Press.

Rueschemeyer, D., E.H. Stephens and J.D. Stephens (1992), *Capitalist Development and Democracy*, Chicago, University of Chicago Press.

Sabir, M. and Q.M. Ahmed (2003), *Macroeconomic Reforms and Total Factor Productivity Growth in Pakistan: An Empirical Analysis*, paper presented at the 56th International Atlantic Conference, Quebec City, Canada, 16–19th October.

Sachs, J.D., N. Bajpai and A. Ananthi (2002), 'Understanding Regional Economic Growth in India', Working Paper No. 88, Centre for International Development at Harvard University, March.

Bibliography

Sachs, J.D. and A.M. Warner (1995), 'Economic Reform and the Process of Global Integration', *Brookings Papers on Economic Activity*, 1, pp. 1–95

Sachs, J.D. and A.M. Warner (1997), 'Fundamental Sources of Long-Run Growth', *American Economic Review*, 87:2, pp. 184–8.

Saggi, K. (2002), 'Trade, Foreign Direct Investment, and International TEchnolody Transfer: A Survey', *World Bank Research Observer*, 17:2, pp. 171–235.

Sahibzada, S.S. and M.A. Mahmood (1991), 'Efficiency Analysis of Projects in the Pakistan Economy', *The Pakistan Development Review*, 30:4, pp. 983–93.

Sala-i-Martin, X. (1997), 'I Just Ran Two Million Regressions', NBER, Working Paper No.6252.

Sala-i-Martin, X. (2001), 'Comment on "Growth Empirics and Reality" by W.A. Brock and S.N. Durlauf', *World Bank Economic Review*, 15:2, pp. 277–82.

Salam, A. (1981), 'Farm Tractorisation, Fertiliser Use and Productivity of Mexican Wheat in Pakistan', *The Pakistan Development Review*, 20:3, pp. 323–45.

Sambanis, N. (2003), 'Using Case Studies to Expand the Theory of Civil War', *CPR Working Papers*, No. 5, Washington.

Sarmad, K. (1984), 'The Profitability of Public Enterprises in Pakistan', *The Pakistan Development Review*, 23:2&3, pp. 147–63.

Sarmad, K. (1992), 'External Shocks and Domestic Adjustment in Pakistan 1970–90', *The Pakistan Development Review*, 31:4, pp. 857–69.

Sarmad, K. (1993), 'Private Capital Outflow from Pakistan', *The Pakistan Development Review*, 32:4, pp. 619–27.

Sayeed, A. (2002), 'State-Society Conjunctures and Disjunctures: Pakistan's Manufacturing Performance', in Naseem, S.M. and K. Nadvi (Eds) (2002), *The Post-Colonial State and Social Transformation in India and Pakistan*, Karachi, Oxford University Press.

Sen, A. (1982), 'How is India Doing?', *New York Review of Books*, 29:20.

Sen, A. (1999), *Development as Freedom*, Oxford, Oxford University Press.

Shabbir, T. and A. Mahmood (1992), 'The Effects of Foreign Private Investment on Economic Growth in Pakistan', *The Pakistan Development Review*, 31:4, pp. 831–41.

Shafqat, S. (1996), 'Pakistan Under Benazir Bhutto', *Asian Survey*, 36:7, pp. 655–72.

Shah, Z. and Q.M. Ahmed (2003), 'The Determinants of Foreign Direct Investment in Pakistan: An Empirical Investigation', *The Pakistan Development Review*, 42:4, pp. 697–714.

Shaheed, Z.A. (1983), 'Role of Government in the Development of the Labour Movement', in Gardezi, H. and J. Rashid (Eds) (1983), *Pakistan: The Roots of Dictatorship: The Political Economy of a Praetorian State*, London, Zed Press.

Shand, R. and S. Bhide (2000), 'Source of Economic Growth: Regional Dimensions of Reforms', *Economic and Political Weekly*, 14th October, pp. 3747–57.

Sharwani, K. (1976), 'Some New Evidence on Concentration and Profitability in Pakistan's Large Scale Manufacturing Industries', *The Pakistan Development Review*, 15:3, pp. 272–89.

Shirazi, N.S. and T.A.A. Manap (2004), 'Exports and Economic Growth Nexus: the Case of Pakistan', *The Pakistan Development Review*, 43:4, pp. 563–81.

Shleifer, A. and R.W. Vishny (1996), 'Corruption', *Quarterly Journal of Economics*, 108:3, pp. 599–617.

Siddiqa, A. (2007), *Military Inc: Inside Pakistan's Military Economy*, London, Pluto Press.

Siddiqui, R. and R. Siddiqui (1993), 'Household Saving Behaviour in Pakistan', *The Pakistan Development Review*, 32:4, pp. 1281–92.

Sindzigre, A (2007), 'Financing the Developmental State: Tax and Revenue Issues', *Development Policy Review*, 25:5, pp. 615–32.

Sinha, A. and S. Tejani (2004), 'Trend Break in India's GDP Growth Rate: Some Comments', *Economic and Political Weekly*, 25th December, pp. 5634–9.

Slemrod, J. (1995), 'What Do Cross-Country Studies Teach about Government Involvement, Prosperity, and Economic Growth?', *Brookings Papers on Economic Activity*, 2, pp. 373–431.

Sokoloff, K.L. and S.L. Engerman (2000), 'History Lessons: Institutions, Factor Endowments and Paths of Development in the New World', *The Journal of Economic Perspectives*, 14:3, pp. 217–32.

Soligo, R. and J.J. Stern (1965), 'Tariff Protection, Import Substitution and Investment Efficiency', *Pakistan Development Review*, 5:2, pp. 249–70.

Soligo, R. and J.J. Stern (1966), 'Some Comments on the Export Bonus, Export Promotion and Investment Criteria', *The Pakistan Development Review*, 6:1, pp. 38–56.

Solow, R.M. (1957), 'Technical Change and the Production Function', *Review of Economics and Statistics*, 39:3, p312–20.

Solow, R.M. (2001), 'Comment on "Growth Empirics and Reality" by W.A. Brock and S.N. Durlauf', *World Bank Economic Review*, 15:2, pp. 283–8.

Srinivasan, T.N. (2005), 'Productivity and Economic Growth in South Asia', *The Pakistan Development Review*, 44:4, pp. 479–503.

Stiglitz, J.E. and A. Weiss (1981), 'Credit Rationing in Markets with Imperfect Information', *American Economic Review*, 71:3, pp. 393–410.

Subrahmanyam, S. (1999), 'Convergence of Incomes Across States', *Economic and Political Weekly*, 20th November, pp. 3327–8.

Swaminathan, M. (1990), 'Village Level Implementation of IRDP: Comparison of West Bengal and Tamil Nadu', *Economic and Political Weekly*, 31st March, pp. A-17–27.

Syed, A.H. (1977), 'Pakistan in 1976: Business as Usual', *Asian Survey*, 17:2, pp. 181–90.

Tahir, R. (1995), 'Defence Spending and Economic Growth: Re-examining the Issue of Causality for Pakistan and India', *The Pakistan Development Review*, 34:4, pp. 1109–17.

Talbot, I. (1998), *Pakistan: A Modern History'* London, C. Hurst and Co.

Talha, N. (2000), *Economic Factors in the Making of Pakistan, 1921–1947*, Karachi, Oxford University Press.

Temple, J. (1998), 'Initial Conditions, Social Capital and Growth in Africa', *Journal of African Economies*, 7:3, pp. 309–47.

Temple, J. (1999), 'The New Growth Evidence', *Journal of Economic Literature*, 37, pp. 112–56.

Thomas, P.S. (1966), 'Import Licensing and Import Liberalisation in Pakistan', *Pakistan Development Review*, 6:4, pp. 500–46.

Tsakok, I. (1982), 'The Export of Manpower from Pakistan to the Middle East, 1975–85', *World Development*, 10:4, pp. 319–25.

Ul Haque, N. (1999), 'Reform Efforts in Pakistan: Limited Success and Possibilities for the Future', in Khan, S.R. (Ed.) (1999), *50 Years of Pakistan's Economy: Traditional Topics and Contemporary Concerns*, Karachi, Oxford University Press.

Varshney, A. (1984), 'The Political Economy of Slow Industrial Growth in India', *Economic and Political Weekly*, 1st September, pp. 1511–17.

Vartiainen, J. (1999), 'The Economics of Successful State Intervention in Industrial Transformation', in Woo-Cumings, M. (Ed.), *The Developmental State,* New York, Cornell University Press.

Virmani, A. (2004), 'India's Economic Growth From Socialist Rate of Growth to Bharatiya Rate of Growth', ICRIER Working Paper No. 122, New Delhi.

Virmani, A. (2005), 'India's Economic Growth History: Fluctuations, Trends, Break Points and Phases', ICRIER Occasional Paper, January, New Delhi.

Vogelsang, T. (1997), 'Wald-Type Tests for Detecting Shifts in the Trend Function of a Dynamic Time Series', *Economic Theory*, 211:13, pp. 818-49.

Wacziarg, R. (2002), 'Review of Easterly's The Elusive Quest for Growth', *Journal of Economic Literature*, 40, pp. 907–18.

Wade, R. (1990), *Governing the Market: Economic Theory and the Role of Government in East Asian Industrialisation*, Princeton, Princeton University Press.

Wade, R. (1998), 'The Gathering World Slump and the Battle over Capital Controls', *New Left Review*, September-October, CHECK.

Wade, R. (1999), 'Gestalt Shift: From "Miracle" to "Cronyism" in the Asian Crisis', *IDS Bulletin*, 30:1, pp. 134–50.

Wade, R. and F. Veneroso (1998), 'The Asian Crisis: The High Debt Model Versus the Wall Street Treasury-IMF Complex', *New Left Review*, March–April, pp. 3–23.

Wallack, J.S. (2003), 'Structural Breaks in Indian Macroeconomic Data', *Economic and Political Weekly*, 11th October, pp. 4312–15.

Waseem, M. (1992), 'Pakistan's Lingering Crisis of Dyarchy', *Asian Survey*, 32:7, pp. 617–34.

Weinbaum, M.G. (1996), 'Civic Culture and Democracy in Pakistan', *Asian Survey*, 36:7, pp. 639–54.

Weiner, M. (1971), 'The 1971 Elections: India's Changing Party System', in Weiner, M. (Ed.) (1989), *The Indian Paradox: Essays in Indian Politics*, New Delhi, Sage Publications.

Weyland, K. (1998), 'From Leviathan to Gulliver? The Decline of the Developmental State in Brazil', *Governance*, 11:1, pp. 51–75.

White, L.J. (1974), *Industrial Concentration and Economic Power in Pakistan*, Princeton, Princeton University Press.

Winston, G.C. (1970), 'Overinvoicing and Industrial Efficiency', in Griffin, K. and A.R. Rahman (1972), *Growth and Inequality in Pakistan*, London, Macmillan.

Winston, G.C. (1971), 'Capital Utilisation in Economic Development', *The Economic Journal*, 81:321, pp. 36–60.

Wizarat, A. (1981), 'Technological Change in Pakistan's Agriculture: 1953–54 to 1978–79', *The Pakistan Development Review*, 20:4, pp. 427–45.

Wizarat, S. (2002), *The Rise and Fall of Industrial Productivity in Pakistan*, Karachi, Oxford University Press.

Wolpert, S. (1993), *Zulfi Bhutto of Pakistan: His Life and Times*, New York, Oxford University Press.

Wolpert, S. (1996), *Nehru: A Tryst with Destiny*, New York, Oxford University Press.

Woo-Cumings, M. (1999), 'Chalmers Johnson and the Politics of Nationalism and Development', in Woo-Cumings, M. (Ed.) (1999), *The Developmental State in Historical Perspective*, Ithaca: Cornell University Press.

World Bank (1993), *The East Asian Miracle: Economic Growth and Public Policy*, Oxford, Oxford University Press.

World Bank (1994), *Adjustment in Africa: Reforms, Results and the Road Ahead*, New York, Oxford University Press.

Yasmeen, S. (1994), 'Democracy in Pakistan: The Third Dismissal', *Asian Survey*, 34:6, pp. 572–88.

Yin, R.K (2003), *Case Study Research: Design and Methods*, London, Sage Publications.

Zahid, A.N., M. Akbar and S.A. Jaffry (1992), 'Technical Change, Efficiency, and Capital Labour Substitution in Pakistan's Large-Scale Manufacturing Sector', *The Pakistan Development Review*, 31:2, pp. 165–88.

Zaidi, S.A. (1999), 'Is Poverty Now a Permanent Phenomenon in Pakistan?', *Economic and Political Weekly*, 9th October, pp. 2943–51.

Zaidi, S.A. (2005), *Issues in Pakistan's Economy*, Second Edition, Karachi, Oxford University Press.

Zaidi, M.A. and K. De Vos (1994), 'Trend Analysis of Relative Poverty in Pakistan, 1984–85 to 1987–88', *The Pakistan Development Review*, 33:4, pp. 915–34.

Index

Abu Dhabi 146
Afghanistan 145–46, 164, 169, 178, 188, 209–10
Africa 13–15, 18, 24–25, 36, 58, 69, 207
Agricultural Development Bank of Pakistan (ADBP) 129, 144
aid 21, 32, 50, 82–83, 85, 94, 101, 106–8, 128, 145–48, 178–79, 196, 209–10
Awami National Party (ANP) 169, 206
Argentina 13, 124
Asian Development Bank 146, 179
Austria 50, 73, 146
Awami League 94, 134

Baluchistan 93, 120, 147, 163, 166–67, 169
Bangladesh 64, 67–68, 145–46, 146, 163, 165, 186
Basic Democrats 8, 29, 101, 126, 133, 134
Belgium 214
black market 23, 212
Botswana 13, 50
Brazil 13, 50, 58–59, 124–25, 154
Bhutto, Benazir 169, 183, 204
Bhutto, Zulfikar Ali 9, 27, 35, 53, 136–39, 145–47, 149, 153–55, 159–68, 171–72, 189–90, 208–9, 211

Central Treaty Organisation (CENTO) 82, 94, 146
Chile 13, 213
China 13, 26, 30, 35, 82, 108–9, 125, 145–46, 181
civil service 7, 9, 77, 92–94, 127, 130, 131, 136, 142, 162–66
classical 38, 56
clientelism 54–55, 167
colonialism 5, 11, 30, 34, 72–73, 207, 212
Communist Parties 5
Communist Party (Russia) 5

Communist Party (West Bengal) 76
Communist Party (Pakistan) 97
comparative advantage 9, 50, 65–66, 90–91, 115, 154, 186, 213
concentration (industrial) 131–32, 150, 152, 215
conflict 1, 3–5, 7–10, 27–32, 49, 52, 56, 59, 61, 67–72, 74–77, 92–93, 95–96, 98–100, 108, 126, 130, 135–37, 145, 162–63, 165, 167–70, 173, 187, 189–90, 192–93, 203–4, 206–11, 213
Congo 13
constitution(s) 8–9, 74, 93–95, 99, 101, 126–27, 134–36, 162, 164, 167, 169, 188, 205
Convention Muslim League (CML) 134, 165–66
corruption 5, 17, 54, 63, 75, 164, 180, 188–89, 194
Cote D'Ivoire 13, 30
credibility 17–18, 54, 195
cross-country growth regressions 1, 2, 5–6, 11, 15–18, 20–29, 31–32
cross-state growth regressions 19
Czechoslovakia 82, 109

debt 1, 10, 24, 50, 58, 62–63, 70, 107, 142–43, 146–47, 150, 176, 177–79, 182, 192–97, 203, 209, 215
democracy 5, 9, 10, 15, 27, 31, 35, 53, 60, 71–72, 76, 135–37, 162–66, 169, 171, 174, 176, 178, 187–89, 205, 210–11, 213.
Denmark 146
Development Finance Instituion (DFI) 182, 198–99
developmental state(s) 2, 9, 12, 44, 50, 53–55, 58, 62, 72, 95, 137, 148, 162, 204, 207–8, 211, 214
domestic demand 8, 42, 45–46, 77–78, 88, 93, 100–101, 115–16, 148, 183, 200

dictatorship 22, 35, 70–72, 74, 106, 142, 162, 204, 210
Dubai 146

East Asia 13, 18, 49, 54, 58, 64, 75, 213
education 14–16, 18–19, 22–24, 27, 51–52, 64, 69, 71, 81, 98, 122, 130, 159, 166, 168, 171, 176, 189–91, 201, 205, 212
Effective Rate of Protection (ERP) 83–84, 150, 180
Egypt 13, 125, 154
employment 4, 30, 42, 44, 46, 54, 57, 63, 68, 76, 89, 98, 101, 120, 133, 147, 157, 161, 191, 202, 210
ethnicity 11, 23–25, 68–70, 73, 75, 95, 130, 165, 169–70, 190, 213
Europe 14, 59, 82, 156, 189
exchange rate 7–8, 17–18, 77, 79, 84, 89, 101–3, 110, 116, 138, 177, 208, 214
export(s) 4, 8, 10, 15–16, 30, 41–46, 50, 54, 65–67, 70, 77–82, 84–85, 87, 89–90, 93, 100–105, 107, 110–13, 115–19, 121, 123, 126, 128, 132, 13–40, 146–49, 153–57, 160, 173–74, 176, 178–79. 183–86, 192–93, 196–97, 199–200, 202, 209, 214–16
Export Bonus System (EBS) 101–2, 116, 138, 214
Export Preference Licensing Scheme 117
externalities 14, 64, 66, 213

Finland 50
fiscal policy 2, 11, 14–16, 22, 24, 28, 105, 109, 111, 139–40, 156, 177, 181–83, 193, 198, 205
Federal Security Force (FSF) 165
Ford Foundation 82–83, 107
Foreign Currency Account (FCA) 178–79
Foreign Direct Investment (FDI) 10, 25, 62–65, 113–14, 153, 173, 175, 179, 181, 196, 203
France 17, 19, 50, 72, 214
Free List 101, 106, 132

Gabon 13
geography 5, 11, 17, 20–22, 26, 30, 80, 212–13
Germany 17, 19, 156, 184–85, 214
Ghana 13
global financial crisis, 2008–11 10, 190, 203
Green Revolution 8, 24, 43, 53, 100–101, 105, 115, 117, 126, 129, 133–34
growth: agriculture 6, 9, 18, 20, 33–34, 36, 41–48, 50, 53, 77–78, 89, 91–93, 95, 100–101, 117, 125, 129, 133, 136–37, 144, 146, 152, 155, 157–58, 160, 162, 168, 174, 193, 201; capital-intensive 44, 59, 77, 89, 93, 100, 115, 119–22, 124, 136, 149, 154–55, 157–58, 160; case study approach 6, 11, 25–28, 32–33, 207; comparative 19, 34–36; episodes of growth 5–11, 13–15, 27–28, 30, 32–37, 40–41, 43, 47–48, 53, 77–78, 92, 100–101, 126, 173, 192, 194, 201, 203, 207–10, 212; deeper/fundamental sources 5, 20–21, 27; dynamics 6, 11, 23, 26, 49, 55; endogenous 6, 11, 14, 21–22, 26; extensive growth 29; GDP 2, 6, 9, 12–14, 16–20, 23, 28, 33–48, 51, 57. 59, 63, 70, 78–81, 87, 101, 103–6, 108–9, 112–14, 117, 119–20, 125, 132, 137, 139–44, 147–49, 153–54, 157, 159, 162, 173, 183, 186–87, 192–03, 208, 211–13; GNP 41, 80–83, 87, 104–5, 107, 112–13, 131, 137, 147–48; high-road 3, 5, 66; historical patterns 12, 23, 35; industrial 6, 14, 33, 41–42. 44. 46, 74, 78, 82–83, 85, 88, 91, 95, 100–101, 116–18, 126–27, 131, 133–34, 137, 148, 156, 165, 168, 173, 184, 186, 199, 201, 213; intensive 29; labour-intensive 8–9, 66, 100, 115, 119–20, 136, 149, 154–56, 158, 180, 186; long-term 5, 11, 12, 14–15, 22–23, 26, 30, 32, 34, 53, 71; low-road 3, 50, 66; manufacturing 17, 35, 41–48, 50, 61, 66, 78, 85, 88–90, 101, 113, 115–17, 119–20, 122, 124, 131, 137, 148, 153, 155–58, 161–62, 174, 183–86, 193, 201–2, 213, 215; medium-term 1, 5, 7, 30, 207; New Growth Theory 51; phases 34; services 33, 35, 44–47, 48, 160, 174, 193, 199, 201; Solow model, 5, 12, 14, 212; steady-state 12, 14, 23–24; structural breaks 5–6, 1–13, 15, 22–23, 30, 34–35, 38; sustainable 7–8, 10, 12–14, 23, 26, 28, 34, 53, 66, 77–78, 93, 100–101, 131, 136–37, 173, 192, 198, 203, 208–9, 211; universalism 6, 11, 12, 21, 24–25, 32

Harvard Advisory Service 82, 107
human capital 18, 20–22, 51, 122, 126, 158–60, 186, 212
Hungary 73, 82
hysteresis 6, 11, 21, 23, 26, 28

ideology 3, 5, 7–8, 10, 31, 49, 53, 56, 68, 70, 72, 74–77, 92, 99, 101, 126, 134–35, 137, 162, 166, 170–71, 173, 187, 190–91, 206, 211, 213
Islami Jamhoori Ittihad (IJI) 164, 169, 187–88
IMF 10, 19, 82, 174, 177–78, 188, 192, 196, 202–3
Import Substitution 7–8, 41–43, 45–47, 54–55, 65, 77–78, 88, 90–91, 93–94, 100, 105, 115–17, 123, 126, 153, 157, 183,

Index 239

India 5, 7, 19–21, 23–24, 33–36, 39, 51–52, 54–55, 60, 64, 68, 71–72, 74, 76, 81–83, 91–93, 95–98, 101, 105–6, 108, 124–25, 131, 140, 145, 185–86, 209, 213–15
Indonesia 13, 146, 154, 213
Industrial Development Bank of Pakistan (IDBP) 108, 114–15, 184
industrial policy 55, 63–64, 66, 88, 112, 174
inequality 3, 15, 20, 23, 25, 30–31, 69, 74, 132
inflation 17–19, 21, 23, 63, 69, 149, 155, 166, 193, 213
infrastructure 19, 21, 23–25, 51, 54, 59, 64, 71, 87, 114, 163, 174, 196, 199
innovation 2, 29, 50, 55, 60–61, 66–67
institutions 1, 3–5, 7–10, 14, 18–21, 24, 26–32, 49, 52, 55–58, 60, 64, 67–75, 77, 81, 87, 92–93, 95–97, 99–101, 105, 107, 114, 123, 126–27, 130, 134–37, 139, 143–44, 149, 152–53, 162–65, 168, 170–73, 177, 179, 182, 187, 189–93, 195, 199, 203–6, 208, 210–11, 213
investment 2–4, 7–9, 14–23, 27, 29–30, 32, 43, 51–56, 58–60, 62–64, 67–68, 70, 77, 79, 81, 83–89, 91–92, 101, 103, 106–9, 111–13, 115–16, 119, 123, 126, 128–30, 136, 139, 144, 148, 153, 157, 159, 161, 174, 180–83, 185, 193, 197–01, 203, 209–10; crowding in 51, 114, 154, 183; equipment 16–17, 111; portfolio 62–63, 178–81; private 15, 50–51, 54, 61, 87–88, 112, 114–15, 139, 149, 152, 154, 159, 178, 182–83, 195, 198, 208; public 9–10, 32, 51–54, 77, 79, 87–88, 114, 118, 130, 139, 144, 149, 152–54, 173, 175, 182–3, 185, 192–93, 198–99, 207–9, 213
Iran 146
Iraq 5, 146, 178
Inter-Services Intelligence (ISI) 164

Jamait-Ulema-e-Islami (JUI) 166, 206
Jamaat-i-Islami (JI) 169
Japan 17, 19, 50, 59, 61, 65, 72–73, 119, 178, 185, 212, 214
Jinnah, Mohammed Ali 82, 95–96, 134, 165
Junejo Muslim League 169

Karachi Electricity Supply Company (KESC) 112, 123–24, 151, 161–62, 198
Karachi Stock Exchange (KSE) 111, 130–1, 150, 161, 180, 185, 196, 198, 202
Kenya 13, 69
Keynes(ian) 5, 16, 23

Khan, Ayub 8, 27, 29, 35, 53, 75, 93–95, 101, 103, 106–8, 110, 115, 126–27, 130–35, 165, 168, 171, 189, 205, 209–10, 214–15
Khan, Liaquat Ali 82, 96
Korean War 28, 82, 87, 94
Kuwait 146, 178

language 52, 68, 92, 97–99, 163, 168
Latin America 13–14, 61
learning 2–4, 7–10, 18, 29–31, 49–52, 54–56, 58, 60–61, 64–67, 70, 91–92, 100–101, 115, 122–24, 126, 136, 155, 158, 173, 183, 208
learning-by-doing 50–51, 66, 91, 122–23
liberalisation 4–5, 9, 20, 22, 27, 53, 60, 62, 65, 72, 78, 101–2, 137–39, 142, 163, 174, 176, 180, 182–84, 195, 207–8, 212
Libya 146
literacy 4, 18, 24, 51, 68, 74, 122, 159, 171, 186, 189, 201, 210

malaria 11, 20, 30
Malaysia 13, 62–63, 73, 154, 213
Mauritius 13, 50
Mexico 63, 74–75, 124–25, 133
middle classes 53, 75, 131, 134, 165, 190
Middle East 13–14, 138, 145, 147, 149
military 5, 7, 9–10, 27–28, 35, 52–53, 70, 75, 77, 81–82, 92–96, 105, 110, 127–28, 130, 131–32, 135–37, 141–42, 147, 162–65, 171, 173, 186, 178, 187–89, 192–94, 203–5, 208–11, 213–14, 216
Movement for the Restoration of Democracy (MRD) 171
Musharraf, Pervez 27, 35, 295–96, 204–6, 210
Muttahida Quami Movement (MQM) 31, 164, 168–70, 188, 190–91, 206

Namibia 13
National Awami Party (NAP) 145, 154, 166–67
National Saving Scheme (NSS) 177, 199
neo-classical 1, 2, 4, 29–30, 56–57, 61, 65–67, 70, 207–8, 213
Netherlands 214
Nigeria 13
North Korea 75
North West Frontier Province (NWFP) 93, 95, 141, 157, 163, 167, 176, 190, 206

OECD 12, 17, 19
oil 23–24, 82, 113–14, 138, 147, 154, 196–97
Oman 147

Pakistan Industrial Credit and Investment Corporation (PICIC) 87, 108, 114–15, 199

Pakistan Industrial Development Corporation (PIDC) 88, 115, 132
Pakistan Industrial Finance Corporation (PIFCO) 87
Pakistan People's Party (PPP) 9, 31, 133–34, 136, 141, 150, 162–69, 171, 176, 187–90, 205, 208
patron-client 51, 54, 96, 189
patronage 4, 30, 56, 68, 72–74, 97, 99, 130, 164–65, 168, 189–90, 210
Poland 82, 109
political economy 1, 3–4, 7, 22, 29–30, 49–53, 57, 80, 163, 210
population 14, 17–18, 23–25, 41, 43, 51, 72, 78, 93, 95, 98, 101, 131, 133, 141, 147, 154, 160, 168, 170, 176, 201, 212, 214
primary (school) enrolment 14
productivity (TFP) 4, 7, 8–10, 13–14, 16, 18–21, 29–30, 33–34, 36, 49, 51, 53, 56, 61, 65–66, 68, 70, 77, 85, 88, 90–92, 100, 115, 123–26, 128–29, 136, 153, 159–62, 173, 183–87, 189, 192, 199, 201, 210, 214–15
property rights 2–3, 5, 15, 17, 20–21, 57, 70–71, 73, 138, 167, 171, 213
profits 2–3, 7–10, 28–30, 50–52, 55–57, 59, 61, 62, 65–67, 69–70, 77, 79–80, 83–85, 87–89, 94, 100, 103, 105, 109–13, 115, 118–19, 122, 126, 136, 139, 149–52, 161, 166, 173, 175, 180–81, 184, 192–93, 197–98, 203–4, 208, 214
public goods 51, 55, 69, 73, 189, 190
Punjab (Pakistan) 93, 97–99, 114, 121, 130–31, 133–34, 149, 163, 165–66, 168–69, 188–91, 204, 215

Qayyaum/Qaiym Muslim League 95, 166

Rahman, Sheikh Mujib Al 130, 135
railway(s) 24, 83, 87, 110, 128, 132, 154, 181, 185, 198
remittances 32, 113, 138, 147–48, 174, 178–81, 193, 197, 203, 209–10, 215
rents 4–5, 30, 50, 54, 58, 60, 66–67, 73, 104, 123
rent seeking 3–5, 31, 72–73
Research and Development (R&D) 14–15, 19, 51, 64, 202
risk 2, 16–17, 29–30, 57–60, 67, 104, 196
Russia 5, 26, 73

Saudi Arabia 146–47, 156, 197
savings 7–10, 16, 57–58, 70, 77, 79–80, 100, 103–4, 108–9, 136, 139, 140, 144, 148, 153, 173, 175–76, 178–80, 182, 192–94, 201, 203, 209–10, 214–16; corporate 105, 109, 143, 175; financial 87, 177; foreign 81–82, 106, 108, 144, 146, 178, 196; household 29, 58, 60, 105–6, 143–44, 175, 214; private 9, 58, 60, 81, 103, 105–6, 108, 114, 136, 139, 143, 175, 177–78, 182, 195; public 9, 50, 58, 79–81, 105–6, 108, 136, 139–40, 177, 195, 203, 213
secondary (school) enrolment 14
Sharif, Nawaz 169, 188, 204–5
Sindh 92, 95, 99, 131, 141, 163, 166–69, 171, 176, 189, 190–91, 205
Singapore 13, 50, 62, 156
state owned/public enterprises 9, 50, 52, 59, 62, 112, 123, 136, 139, 149–50, 155, 161, 174, 181, 197–98, 208
South Asia 18, 98, 171, 190
South East Asia 59, 62
South East Asian Treaty Organisation (SEATO) 82, 145
stock market 10, 63, 106, 119, 131, 143–44, 157, 173, 175, 179–80, 182, 185, 193, 196, 202
South Korea 12–13, 34, 50, 54, 59, 61–65, 72, 124, 140, 213
Sri Lanka 69, 75, 186
State Bank of Pakistan (SBP) 81, 106, 113, 176, 178–79, 181, 188, 195, 203
structural change 2, 38, 42, 44, 46–48, 101, 134, 155, 186
subsidy 2–3, 5, 28–29, 50–52, 54–55, 57–61, 65, 67, 84, 89, 94, 105, 109, 111, 117, 119, 138–39, 142, 149–50, 176, 178, 182, 213, 216
surplus 1–3, 7–10, 28–29, 49, 52, 55–59, 61, 64, 68, 77, 79, 83–85, 88, 100, 103, 109, 115, 120, 136, 139, 144, 154–55, 158, 173, 175, 178, 183, 192–93, 197, 199, 203, 210

Taiwan 13, 34, 50, 54, 59, 61–62, 65, 213
tax 3–4, 7–9, 15–16, 29, 52, 57–58, 60, 70, 72–73, 77, 79–81, 84, 100, 103–4, 109–10, 119, 122, 133, 136, 139–42, 150, 161, 175–76, 177, 182–83, 194, 203, 213; agricultural 104, 141, 188; corporate 8, 72, 80, 85, 87, 100, 103–5, 109–10, 131–32, 140, 198, 208; elasticity 141–42, 175–76; evasion 64, 140; excise duties 80, 104, 140–42, 152, 175, 214; exemptions 6, 142, 176, 194; holidays 80, 87, 104–5, 109, 111, 139–40, 142; incentives 2, 28, 59, 139; indirect 84, 90, 104, 141, 175; land 105, 141; personal income tax 72, 80, 104, 109,

139–42, 175–76, 179, 194; presumptive 140; sales tax 80, 132, 140, 142, 152, 275, 194, 202; tariffs 23, 65, 79, 83–84, 89–90, 94, 102, 105, 111, 122, 128, 138–9, 174, 202, 215; trade taxation 65, 77, 80, 105, 110–11, 119, 140–42, 155, 175–76, 202, 214; wealth Tax 80, 104–5, 140–41, 176, 179
technology 2, 7–8, 14, 18, 20, 27, 29, 43, 49–52, 54, 56, 60–61, 63–66, 77, 93, 113, 117–18, 120–21, 129–30, 185–86
terms of trade 11, 50, 56, 62, 70, 78–79, 85–86, 103, 109–10, 118, 137–38, 149, 209, 212
textiles 41–44, 46, 64, 67, 78–79, 83–85, 88–91, 94, 110–12, 115–21, 123–25, 128–29, 132, 134, 150, 152, 154, 156–58, 160, 184–86, 196, 198, 202, 215
Thailand 63, 124, 156, 213
transaction costs 3, 31, 57, 60, 73–74, 96
Tunisia 75

Uganda 13
unions (trade) 8, 61, 69. 95, 97–98, 100, 103, 126, 128–29, 133–34, 163, 208
United Kingdom (UK) 17, 34, 185, 214

uncertainty 2, 17–18, 20, 25, 30, 50, 67, 205, 213
upgrading 3, 7–10, 29, 49, 56, 65–66, 101, 124, 126, 136, 155–56, 158, 173, 183–84, 192, 199, 202, 208
USA 1, 5, 12, 17, 19, 34, 53, 69, 82–83, 94, 107–9, 119, 125, 145–46, 156, 178, 184–85, 196–97, 203, 109, 214
USSR/Soviets 82, 108–9, 145–46, 178, 209

Vietnam 75

wages 18, 50, 56, 60–61, 63, 69, 85, 92, 110, 120, 128–29, 142, 149, 166, 185–86, 214
Water and Power Development Authority (WAPDA) 112, 118, 123–24, 129, 152, 161–62, 192, 198
WTO 174

Yugoslavia 82, 109

Zarai Taraqiate Bank Limited (ZTBL) 144
Zia, Ul Haq 9, 27, 35, 53, 137–38, 141, 146–47, 149, 153, 162–66, 169–72, 189–90, 205, 208–9, 211